# Offering Flowers, Feeding Skulls

# Offering Flowers, Feeding Skulls

*Popular Goddess Worship in West Bengal*

JUNE McDANIEL

2004

OXFORD
UNIVERSITY PRESS

Oxford New York
Auckland Bangkok Buenos Aires Cape Town Chennai
Dar es Salaam Delhi Hong Kong Istanbul Karachi Kolkata
Kuala Lumpur Madrid Melbourne Mexico City Mumbai Nairobi
São Paulo Shanghai Taipei Tokyo Toronto



Published by Oxford University Press, Inc.
198 Madison Avenue, New York, New York 10016

www.oup.com



Library of Congress Cataloging-in-Publication Data
McDaniel, June.
Offering flowers, feeding skulls : popular goddess worship in West
Bengal / June McDaniel.
p. cm.
Includes bibliographical references.
ISBN 0-19-516790-2; ISBN 0-19-516791-0 (pbk.)
1. Kali (Hindu deity)—Cult—India—West Bengal.
2. Shaktism—India—West Bengal. 3. West Bengal (India)—
Religious life and customs. I. Title.
BL1225.K33 W36 2003
294.5'514'095414—dc21 2003009828

9 8 7 6 5 4 3 2 1

Printed in the United States of America
on acid-free paper

# Acknowledgments

Thanks go to the Fulbright Program and its representatives, whose Senior Scholar Research Fellowship made it possible for me to do this research in West Bengal, and to the College of Charleston, who granted me a year's leave for field research. Thanks also to USIS in India, who were very helpful, especially in New Delhi and Calcutta. Two of my best informants were anthropologists, Satyakam Sengupta and Pashupati Mahato. Both spent weeks and months in long discussion with me about Bengali folk religion, and they were wonderful sources of information and gossip. I'm glad that I had the opportunity to know them. Thanks also go to Narendranath Bhattacharyya and Debabrata Sen Sharma for their detailed information on Bengali and other forms of tantra, and to Probhal Sen, Asha and Bijoy Mukherjee, Ranjit and Kumkum Bhattacharya, Tushar Niyogi, George Matthew, Surajit and Purnima Sinha, Amit and Mandira Sen, D. D. Mukherjee and Swami Lokeshwarananda, and Ashok Mukherji.

Thanks go also to Jayashri Ma, Gauri Ma, Archanapuri Ma, Tapan Goswami, Amiya Kumar and Mrs. Sinha, M. Chattopadhyaya, A. K. Chakraborty, Parvati Soren, Bacchu Ghosh, the Andul Kali-kirtan Samiti, and the priests, local healers, sadhus, tantrikas, holy women, artists, patuas, story-tellers, merchants, waiters, gardeners, farmers, taxi drivers, doctors, engineers, housewives, grant administrators, and Shakta devotees of all sorts, who kindly gave me their opinions about everything imaginable. Thanks also to the British Library, for access to some very old books, and to Jill Yarnall, for her story.

Special thanks to my husband, Jim, photographer and support system extraordinaire, and Constantina Rhodes Bailly, for inspiring discussions. Also special thanks to Cynthia Humes, who went through this manuscript in its original, thousand page form, and gave useful suggestions for cutting it down to virtually half its length—this is true academic fortitude.

Some passages in this book are revisions of articles that I have previously published. The introductory section of folk Shaktism in chapter 1 was published in a similar fashion in my book *Making Virtuous Daughters and Wives: An Introduction to Women's Brata Rituals in Bengali Folk Religion* (Albany: State University of New York Press, 2003), pp. 1–11. The biography of Tapan Goswami in chapter 2 may also be found in similar fashion in "Interviews with a Tantric Kali Priest: Feeding Skulls in the Town of Sacrifice" in *Tantra in Practice*, edited by David Gordon White (Princeton: Princeton University Press, 2000), pp. 72–80.

# Contents

# Notes on Transliteration

There is something ironic about a book on Indian popular religion that is inaccessible to a popular audience because of the use of Bengali and Sanskrit diacritical marks, whose symbolism is only understood by specialists. Therefore, in this book I have minimized the use of diacriticals. They appear only in direct quotations, and bibliographic information—and in a list of terms, where full diacritics are given.

Transliteration is always a difficult issue, especially in books that are strongly regional and use a large number of foreign terms. Most of the terms used in this book are Bengali, and there are two major issues involved. One is diacritical marks. Should the standard Sanskrit spelling and diacriticals be used, which will please the classical Sanskrit scholars but may alienate the non-Indologist readers? Or should terms be spelled phonetically, which will allow non-Indologists greater access to the material, but may alienate Sanskritist readers? The second question is the use of the Sanskrit v, which is the Bengali b (and the Hindi w) and the general question of whether to Sanskritize the Bengali or write it in the colloquial style that is actually used.

This book will try to compromise on these issues. In the text, Sanskrit and Bengali terms will be spelled phonetically and without diacriticals. The letters ś and ị will be written sh, and both c and ch will be written ch. The letter ṛ is transliterated ri. Bengali and Sanskrit terms will appear in the list of terms, which will not include place names or the names of historical or living individuals. Thus the text will be easier for non-Indologists to read, but diacritical information will be accessible. The documentation will include full diacritical marks for titles, but individuals' names will be spelled phonetically or as the author spells it in English.

The question of whether to use Bengali, Sanskritized Bengali, or Sanskrit terms in the texts is more difficult. I decided that terms that I heard continually in the Bengali form I would leave that way (using *brata* instead of *vrata*, for instance), but terms used more rarely I would leave in the Sanskrit (thus, Sarasvati rather than Sarasbati, or the more phonetic Shawrahshawti). Book titles will work the same way: terms like *bangala* for Bengali will be used rather than *vangala*, but more familiar Sanskrit terms will be retained.

I hope that, by this system, the book will be accessible both to specialists and to interested nonspecialists.

# Offering Flowers, Feeding Skulls

# Introduction

In the spring of 1998, India detonated five underground bombs at Pokhran, in northwestern India. Some Indian newspapers declared Pokhran to be a *shakti pitha*, a place sacred to the goddess Shakti. Western observers wondered whether this was some sort of religious justification for India's nuclear testing.

The term *shakti* has a variety of meanings in India. According to the *Saṃsad Bengali-English Dictionary*, it means power, strength, might, force, capability, energy, and potency (and it was a name for an ancient missile). Shakti also means the female principle taking part in creation, or the female deity.[1]

The goddess Shakti is the essence of divine power, whose presence is believed to be manifest in certain places on earth. As the story goes, when the goddess in her incarnation as Sati committed suicide (due to her father's insults to her husband, Shiva), Shiva was maddened with grief and danced with her body in his arms. The gods wished to stop his mad and destructive dance, so they chopped her body into pieces. These pieces fell in different places in India, and each place became sanctified ground. These are the *shakti piṭhas* or *sati piṭhas*, and today these places are recognized as shrines, which are visited by religious pilgrims. The goddess is believed to reveal her power of creation and destruction in such places—and what place could reveal power more clearly than a place where nuclear weapons have been detonated?

India is an important area of study for goddess worship. Whereas many feminist theologians and mythologists struggle to reconstruct ancient goddess traditions from the artifacts found in such ancient cultures as Celtic Ireland and Periclean Greece, India has been worshiping goddesses continuously for thousands of years, and continues to do so today. If we accept the thousands of stone statues of women found at such ancient Indus Valley sites as Harappa, Mohenjo-Daro, and Lothal (these centers are usually dated from 2500 BCE to 1500 BCE) as goddess statues, as do many scholars, then goddess worship has been going on in India for at least four thousand years.

Geographically, Shaktism or goddess worship in India has primarily been of two types—the south Indian worship of the goddess Shri or Lakshmi and the worship of the goddess Kali. These types have different values and rituals and emphasize different goddesses (or different forms of the same goddess, depending on the theology). The first type, located primarily in southern India, sees the goddess as the embodiment of good fortune, fertility, and wealth, and it respects the brahmanical tradition (the orthodox Hindu tradition, which emphasizes caste and purity). It tends to follow the classical or *shastriya* approach, with knowledge of and respect for scriptures. Shri is a goddess of blessing and auspiciousness.

The second type is found mostly in northern and eastern India, especially in West Bengal, Assam, Bihar, and Orissa. The focus of this Kali lineage is upon the goddess as the source of wisdom and liberation. It has a complex relationship with the brahmanical tradition, which many of its practitioners understand to be overly conservative; brahmanical tradition rejects, they say, the experiential aspects of religion in favor of scholarship and social status. Practitioners whom I have interviewed often claimed to be nonscriptural or *ashastriya*, finding books to be only a beginning of deeper knowledge of the divine. Kali, Tara, and sometimes Durga are the main forms of the goddess in this tradition, and there are ten different forms of Kali that are worshiped (the ten Mahavidyas or great wisdom figures). There is also worship of both local and pan-Indian goddesses, who are described in stories written in Bengali and in Sanskrit sacred texts. All of them may be understood as aspects of Shakti, the feminine power of creation and transformation.

There are many origin stories of the goddesses. According to the *Vayu Purana*, a medieval Hindu text, the god Shiva was of twofold nature (male and female). Shakti or his female nature also had two aspects: one half was *sita* or black, and the other half was *asita* or white. The black or fierce nature included such goddesses as Kali, Durga, Chandi, Chamunda, Bhadrakali, and Bhairavi, whereas the white or peaceful nature included Uma, Gauri, Parvati, Maheshvari, Lalita, and Annapurna. The fierce forms became important as part of the Kali tradition, and the Devi in fierce form is seen in such medieval texts as the *Markandeya*, *Skanda*, *Devi*, *Garuda*, and *Shiva* puranas, as well as such tantric encyclopedias as the *Tantrasara*. The worship of Durga in her fierce form of Mahishamardini (the conqueror of the buffalo demon) was also widespread.

In her peaceful form the goddess is wife, mother, and daughter, loving and supportive of her husband. Whereas the fierce forms tend to portray the goddess as independent, often creating and destroying worlds and lives on her own initiative, the mild forms present a nurturing and sympathetic goddess, not acting alone but rather in a family situation. As Parvati, the goddess practiced asceticism to gain Shiva as a husband (and thus brought out for the world's benefit the immense energy he had gained through his meditation). The Vaishnava tradition also has peaceful goddesses, such as Lakshmi (the wife or consort of Vishnu), Shri, Vaishnavi, and Radha. Lakshmi is associated with fertility, royal authority and power, wealth, and good fortune. Some traditions give her an opposite force, Alakshmi or bad luck, who must be chased away before Lakshmi and her blessings will enter the home.

Theologically, understandings of the identity and origin of the goddess differ. Some Shakta traditions say that all goddesses are manifestations of the same great goddess, Adi Shakti or Parama Shakti, while others say that the many goddesses are separate and unique, or sometimes that they are manifestations of one or more gods. There is Shakta monism, in which all phenomena are the parts of the goddess, whose deepest nature is *brahman* or universal consciousness. There is Shakta monotheism, in which all other deities are aspects of a single goddess, who has created the universe. There is Shakta dualism, in which the divine couple Shiva and Shakti are the primordial deities, and Shakti is the more important figure, the mother of the universe. There is Shakta polytheism, in which many goddesses hold great power, and sometimes compete for power and devotees with other goddesses or with male gods. And there is Shakta henotheism, where many goddesses are recognized as legitimate, but one is most powerful.

Monism, monotheism, dualism, polytheism, henotheism: all of these are legitimate positions in Shaktism, and each is widely held; sometimes more than one position is held at a time. They are theological claims, due to the existence of several approaches to Shaktism. Goddesses fuse and separate; as Pupul Jayakar observes:

> As they traveled along the ancient primitive tracks, the prehistoric routes of migration, the thrusting powers of the goddesses met and mingled and gained common identity. In their journey across the great land mass, as they absorbed into their identity the massive earth *mātṛkās*, virgins yet mothers; the water and vegetal spirits, the *apsarāsas* and *yaksinīs;* the serpent-headed *nāginīs*, the female ghosts, the *bhūtinīs;* the blood-thirsty *ḍākinīs;* the *yoginīs* or the *jogans*, the practicers of magic, the forms of the sacred one underwent continuous transformations. A composite form of the female energies emerged as Mātā or Devī . . . When she entered the *purāṇic* pan-

> theon the virgin Earth Mother become Durgā and, changing with provenance and tribe, her names and anthropomorphic forms are legion.[2]

Shaktism is a vast maze of belief systems and practices; how shall we begin to understand it?

## The Types of Shaktism

In my last book, a study of ecstatic experience and its religious interpretations in West Bengal,[3] one chapter explored such experiences in the context of Shaktism or goddess worship. In that chapter, I spoke of the strands or types of Shakta belief and practice that have interacted to form the tradition known as Bengali Shaktism. This book is an expansion on that study, a deeper exploration of the types of Shaktism.

The three types of Shaktism described in that book include the folk/tribal strand, involving possession, healing, and animism; the tantric/yogic strand, involving meditation and visualization; and the devotional or bhakti strand, involving love of a particular form of the goddess and her worship. They are often found in combined form, like strands of a rope braided together. In this book, these categories are expanded and explored in detail, revealing some of the tensions that exist within and between these strands: the folk/tribal strand with its regionalism and competition between local forms of the goddess; the tantric/yogic strand with its oppositions between classical Vedanta philosophy and goddesses who represent infinite consciousness, and its magical and forbidden side, with goddesses who grant supernatural powers; and the devotional strand, with its tensions between goddesses understood as living deities and goddesses who are symbols of universal principles. These types and their tensions will be elaborated in later chapters of this book.

In looking at the structure of Indian religion, one of the most important distinctions that has been made is the distinction between Great and Little Traditions. Originated by Robert Redfield and followed by Milton Singer, M. N. Srinivas, and other anthropologists of India, it divides Indian religious traditions into the "Little" or nontextual, regional folk religion, and the "Great" or pan-Indian literate Sanskritic form of religion. This formulation has been both supported and criticized by scholars in the field. The Great Tradition has been described and formulated in a number of ways; Singer's early list is fairly typical:

1. A body of sacred scriptures and texts in which the Great Tradition is embodied and expressed;
2. A class of literati who have the authority to read and interpret the sacred scriptures;

3. Leading personalities, such as Nehru and Gandhi, who convey their vision of the Great Tradition to the masses of the people;
4. A "sacred geography" of holy places—rivers, holy places of saints, temples, and shrine centers—defining a set of "sacred centers" that provide the forum, media, and vehicle for expressing the Great Tradition;
5. A "sacred calendar" of rites and ceremonies marking the important occasions of the individual life cycle and of the seasons[4]

This is generally opposed to the Little Tradition of village India, which is portrayed as a nonliterate tradition of the "unreflective many" rather than the "reflective few," and variously called "primitive," "unevolved," and "superstitious."

There have been many critiques of this opposition—most emphasizing the fact that Hindu tradition is a continuum rather than a polarity. We may simply note that, for Singer's list, the Indian Little Tradition has its own narrative texts (though they tend to be handed down by oral tradition rather than written), its own interpreters and strong personalities (especially leaders who have received dream commands from deities), a sacred geography in which deities dwell, and cyclical holidays and festivals. All of the categories listed by Singer for the Great Tradition are also present in the Little Tradition, and the opposition between these two is thus problematic.

However, this opposition of traditions is a useful beginning. In this book, I suggest that a better model for the study of Bengali Shaktism is a triune one rather than a polarity. It consists of folk, tantric, and devotional types or strands. Although we clearly see a folk dimension in Shakta tradition, the presence of a Sanskritized Great Tradition is much less clear. We see a Sanskrit aspect of Shakta tantra in classical tantra (especially in the use of Sanskrit mantras), and a Sanskrit aspect of Shakta devotionalism (in various Sanskrit hymns and pan-Indian puranic stories). But there is no single Bengali *shakti marga*, no Great Tradition of Sanskrit literature and commentary respected and followed by all Shakta groups. Instead, we have at least three traditions, which mix together and show a wide variety of beliefs and practices.

In fact, concepts of these traditions have changed over time. Today, the "little tradition" is not only folk religion, it is resurgent tribalism—with low-caste and outcaste groups demanding human rights, government benefits, and land ownership rather than working for landowners. As for the "great tradition" today, it is no longer Sanskritization—it is Westernization. Gurus gain status by going to California and having Western disciples, temples gain status when they attract Western tourists and donations. The cachet of having world respect is more appealing even for many traditional groups than simply quoting respected texts in Sanskrit. The tension between little and great traditions today is a tension between the particular and the universal, the villages of "golden

Bengal" and the great world outside. It acts as a background for the categories to be explored in this book.

### *Folk/Tribal Shaktism*

The first and probably oldest type or strand of Shaktism is the sort still found in rural areas of India, which here will be called folk or tribal Shaktism. It involves the worship of both tribal goddesses (often in the form of the *budi*, the old woman or ancestress) and local Hindu goddesses who have revealed themselves to villagers (often in rocks or other natural objects). There is no sharp line between tribal and Hindu goddesses, and both tribal people and villagers often worship both types. These goddesses are amoral and often dangerous, and require propitiation by worshipers. But once they are shown proper respect, they become benevolent, and willing to help their worshipers. Sometimes such goddesses begin as unhappy women who have died by suicide or murder, and their later worship atones for their previous bad treatment and renders them harmless.

There are religious specialists in Bengali folk Shaktism, nonbrahmin priests and priestesses, as well as trance mediums, who learn how to contact the goddess and become a channel for her personality. In tribal areas, the specialist may be a person trained in invoking deities and in magical healing: the *ojha* or *gunin*. More informally, traditions of worship and contact with the goddess may be taught by the older women of the community, especially through *bratas* (vows and ascetic practices primarily performed by women and girls). In more urban areas, the "*bhar*-lady" is a professional medium who becomes possessed (usually by Kali). The goals of folk Shaktism tend to be the healing of disease or discord in the group, fertility (for plants, animals, or people), protection from danger, and the ability to prophesy and to exorcize spirits and ancestors.

The folk/tribal strand could also be called the shamanic strand, as its ritual specialists (especially the *ojha* and *gunin*) function in many similar ways to the practitioners described in the literature on shamanism. There is a variety of different definitions of shamanism, however, which emphasize different shamanic experiences and abilities. The most famous understanding of shamanism probably comes from the writings of Mircea Eliade. Eliade's "shamanic complex" included initiation (with illness, solitude, an ordeal of fear, apparitions, and death and rebirth experience); magical flight and descent into the underworld; communication with spirit and guardian deities; abilities of spiritual healing, and the guiding of souls.[5]

The ritual specialists of Bengali folk Shaktism fit several of these abilities and experiences. They are initiated in solitude, in the burning ground or forest at midnight, and have visions of both ghosts and goddesses. They gain power over spirits, sometimes using a bone from a corpse or some other magical object. They have control over trance states, in which they communicate with ancestral spirits and deities, and have magical powers, including healing, control of the weather and fertility. In these ways, they follow Eliade's shamanic complex. However, they generally do not undergo illness, death, and rebirth (though this does sometimes happen, and is associated with periods of both madness and bad luck from curses or astrological influences). They do not always fly into heavens or hells, or act as psychopomp and guide the souls of the dead (though there is often a confrontation with a deity associated with death). In these ways, they would not fit Eliade's qualifications of a shaman.

In Bengali folk Shaktism, the goddess may be worshiped in several forms. For example, she may be the tribal Kali, dark and powerful; the hunters' goddess, Chandi; Manasa, the snake goddess, or Shitala, the smallpox goddess. She may also be worshiped as a variety of village goddesses (*gramadevatas*) or powerful supernatural women (*yoginis*). These last forms have an ambiguous nature, sometimes dangerous and threatening, sometimes protective. A goddess may appear in the form of an old woman, whose knowledge is reflected in her years, as well as the forms of mother and warrior. As Mother, she grants fertility and happiness; as Warrior, she grants protection from death and threat; as Old Woman, she teaches tribal traditions and gives revelations.

The folk tradition is primarily an oral tradition, handed down from village elders or priests, or from guru to disciple. This is partly because many of the village people who choose to become priests and healers are illiterate, and partly because a direct transmission of power and experience of the goddess is a decisive part of the instruction. Encounter with the goddess may occur in dream or vision, and on rare occasions results from reading books. Traditions of goddess worship are handed down in family and village groups. They may incorporate some elements of more brahmanical Hinduism (such as Sanskrit mantras or brahmin priests).

There are also similarities with folk tantra: we may note that both tribal shaman-healers (*ojhas*) and Shakta tantrikas have initiations at the burning ground, hoping for a gift of power from the goddess.

### *Tantric/Yogic Shaktism*

The second form or strand of Bengali Shaktism is that of tantric or yogic Shaktism. Its origins are much debated, but there are tantric elements from writings of the sixth century CE, and texts called tantras by their authors were written by the ninth century CE. In the Shakta tantric strand, the goddess is reached by certain forms of meditation and visualization, and by tantric ritual worship (making use of tantric mantras, hand positions, and imagery). Yogic practice is often involved, especially kundalini yoga. There are two major subtypes of this strand in West Bengal, which we shall call folk or popular tantra, and classical or scholastic tantra.

In folk or popular tantra, the emphasis is upon ritual practice, direct experience, and pragmatic results. The goddess gives supernatural abilities (*siddhi*) and power (shakti), and she appears to the practitioner in the forest or burning ground. She may also be ritually located in various parts of the human body by the practice of *nyasa*, in which deities are visualized in parts of the body. She may appear as a seductive and beautiful woman, or a warrior of frightening demeanor, and she may grant boons to the folk tantrika in exchange for worship. The folk tantrika (male or female) invokes the goddess, and may temporarily merge with her or her consort, Shiva, or be ritually possessed by them. Traditionally, the folk tantrika sits at the burning ground performing tantric worship, purifying his body and visualizing the goddess. He may empower amulets, offer animal sacrifices, and interact with the souls of the dead. He is usually isolated, occasionally keeping in touch with his own guru, or meeting with others in a tantric circle of ritual participants (chakra). There is generally little consistent community, unless he takes on the role of priest. Folk tantra is largely an oral tradition, in which the term "tantra" refers primarily to a practice or *sadhana*. There is little emphasis on reading texts, and many folk tantrikas are illiterate. When texts are used, the ritual instructions are not interpreted in a symbolic manner; they tend to be taken literally, and the rituals are physically acted out. However, due to the lack of text and tradition, much of popular tantra seems to be based on a sort of trial-and-error approach.

In classical or scholastic tantra, the goddess is symbolic of liberation (*moksha*), and is understood to be a personification of infinite consciousness (*brahman*). She is able to grant the classical tantrika the gift of omniscience (*brahmajnana*) or liberation in response to his spiritual insight and knowledge. Her forms, whether beautiful or terrifying, are understood to be illusory, a part of her *maya*. They are used to test the tantrika's worthiness and knowledge. The classical tantrika (they are generally male) is usually a scholar (*pandit*), a brahmin with some priestly training and a wide knowledge of Sanskrit religious texts. He might be an academic, a teacher of Samkhya philosophy in a study circle, or a guru teaching yoga, but his tantric side is usually not publicized. Classical tantra has a strong literary focus, and the term *tantra* refers primarily to a set of texts. Informants frequently called tantric practice the active or ritual aspect of Vedanta philosophy, and the texts are usually understood metaphorically.

The division into types is important in Shakta tantra, for the secondary literature on tantra includes frequent arguments. It debates whether tantra is "really" a degenerate collection of obscene rituals that are acted out by ignorant practitioners, or a rational, abstract, philosophical system that makes use of metaphor and symbol, and whose practitioners would never dream of acting out the rituals or interpreting the texts literally. Understanding folk and classical tantra as types or categories of tantra allows for their study without engaging in endless arguments about legitimacy, authenticity, and superiority.

### *Shakta Bhakti*

The third and most widespread strand of Shaktism in modern West Bengal is that of Shakta devotion, or bhakti. In medieval times, Shaktism was largely an esoteric religion practiced by small groups of tantric yogis, until the puranic texts popularized the powers and adventures of the goddess, and later poetry portrayed her as beautiful and loving. The eighteenth-century poet Ramprasad Sen showed her as a loving mother and a beautiful young girl, and devotional worship grew around these images. Devotees worship the goddess with great intensity, as Kali Ma (who is sometimes frightening on the outside, but inwardly loving and compassionate), Tara Ma (who gives knowledge and liberation), and many others. Shakta bhakti also emphasizes that intense love of the deity is more valuable than simple obedience, thus showing the influence of Vaishnava ideas (where the passionate relationship between Krishna and Radha is also the ideal relationship between the god and the devotee). These older ideas still influence modern Shakta devotionalism.

There are four subtypes of Shakta bhakti described in this book. The first is folk Shakta bhakti. This type of bhakti is strongly influenced by the folk Shaktism, and has goddesses who demand devotion and followers. When she is obeyed and given devotion, especially in the form of ritual worship and offerings, the goddess will grant happiness, wealth, victory in law cases, and good fortune generally to her chosen male or female devotees. As in folk Shaktism, however, if she is thwarted in her goals she may curse the devotees and take revenge upon them. Whereas in folk Shaktism the goddess's primary focus is the welfare of the group (especially the tribal group), in folk Shakta bhakti, her emphasis is upon a particular individual, and there is often a long and exclusive relationship between the demanding goddess and her chosen worshiper.

The second subtype is emotional Shakta bhakti.[6] In this type, the goddess has a variety of roles—mother, child, friend, virgin. She expects passionate love and dependence from her devotees, who are most often described as her children. The most intense love is not romantic love but rather parent/child love. Some devotees begin with the emotion of fear toward her terrible forms, but they end up loving her when they see the sweetness within her. The devotee loves extravagantly; he (or she) swings between elation and depression, loving the world because the goddess is present there or hating it because she has not appeared. The ideal attitude is total dependence, with love evoking divine vision (darshan), in which goddess and devotee meet and recognize each other. There are many miracle stories passed down showing the goddess's love toward her chosen devotees. She grants salvation and entrance into her heaven to those who love her, and she appreciates their poetry and songs. Worship may be on a small scale, with household altars and family ceremonies, or it may be on a larger community scale, with large shrines, jeweled statues, and sacred food piled high on silver trays, at festivals such as Durga Puja and Kali Puja. Devotees tell the stories of the goddesses and read from the puranas, or meet to sing *Kali-kirtan*, hymns to Kali.

The third subtype of Shakta bhakti is political Shakta bhakti or Shakta nationalism. In this type, the goddess represents the land—she is Mother India, Bharat Mata, or Bharat Devi. She is like the folk goddess who represents the village but on a larger scale. She calls upon her children to rescue her when the land is in trouble, and they do so by protest, war, revolution, or other political actions. Since the mid-nineteenth century, the goddess has become a symbol of Indian nationalism, the Divine Mother who is herself the land of India. This was seen especially vividly in Bankimchandra Chatterji's novel *Anandamath*, based upon the sannyasi rebellion of the eighteenth century. From this novel came the *Bandemataram* (Bow to the Mother) anthem, in which the country is identified with the goddess. It was sung by those opposing the partition of India, and by those in favor of self-rule in India. The goddess evokes patriotism, which is in this case a form of devotion. Mother India is understood to be both a poetic image and a real entity. This subtype has been less popular since Indian independence, but has been resurrected by the nationalist parties in India.

The fourth subtype of Shakta bhakti is Shakta universalism or Shakta Vedanta. This view became widespread among Indian Shaktas with the popularity of Ramakrishna Paramahamsa and Vivekananda in the late nineteenth century, and it is still an important perspective among Shaktas outside of India, especially in the United States. In this approach, emotional bhakti is linked with classical tantra, and we have the combination of the goddess as a loving mother who is also infinite consciousness. It combines aspects of devotional Shakta bhakti with elements of Vedanta philosophy and the Brahmo Samaj protests against the limitations of caste and status. It tends to reject tantra as an inappropriate path, which is too close to folk religion and superstition. The goddess is understood to be symbolic of deeper states of consciousness, and though the mother is the chosen symbol for this mystical state (and she is often understood to be equivalent to *brahman* or the ocean of consciousness), other deities and symbols may also represent it. Thus it may be called "nonsectarian Shaktism." If all is truly one, there is no need for the limitations of caste rules and traditional rituals. This goddess is not a jealous goddess—the altar of a Shakta universalist may have the symbols of many deities, both Eastern and Western. In the twentieth-century literature of Shakta Vedanta, the goddess is more frequently described as a philosophical concept than as a metaphysical form or personality.

Shakta universalism has been strongly influenced by Ramakrishna Paramahamsa of Dakshineshwar. Ramakrishna was priest of a Kali temple, and worshiped the goddess throughout his life, but he also claimed to have attained spiritual realization through other paths, such as Vaishnavism, Islam, and Christianity. Modern popular Shaktism echoes this universalist sentiment, saying that the ultimate aim of all religions is the same. Though Ramakrishna stated that all religions of the world were valid paths to the divine reality, and all forms of the deity equally valid, he preferred Kali; though all forms of religious rituals were valid, he preferred worship of the goddess. According to his biographies, Kali told him to be in the state of *bhavamukha*, in both the spiritual world and physical world at once. He understood the Mother to be both form and formlessness, and as such he could be called both a monist and a dualist. This approach has been followed by later Shakta universalists.

Table 1 show how each strand generally views some important aspects of Shakta religion, which will be examined in more detail in later chapters. It must be noted that these are ideal types of Shakta belief and practice. This means that although we can find pure examples of these styles of Shaktism, the cultural tendency is to mix and match, and most of these will be seen in combination with other types of Shaktism, as well as other forms of Hinduism and even other forms of religion. As we shall note, it is extremely difficult to define who is a Shakta.

TABLE 1. Three Strands' Views of Important Aspects of Shakta Religion

| | Folk/Tribal | Tantric/Yogic | Bhakti |
|---|---|---|---|
| Path | propitiation | meditation | devotion |
| Goddess image | mother, old woman, protector | consort, warrior | child, mother, country |
| Goddess's locale | nature (rocks, crops, statues) | burning ground, human body | statue, heaven, human heart |
| Goddess's gifts | life, health, fertility | knowledge, power | heaven, salvation, love |
| Ritual specialist | *ojhā*, *gunin*, *deyashi*, medium, bhar-lady | tantric sadhu, *siddha*, guru, pandit | bhakti guru, pujari |
| Rituals | healing, *bratas*, asceticism | tantric worship kundalini yoga | puja, *kirtan* |
| Practitioner roles | servant, healer | hero, sage, ascetic | child, parent, servant |
| Practitioner emotion | submission, fear, gratitude | detachment, courage | dependence, love, passion |
| Religious experience | possession, dream command | liberation, vision | darshan, selfless love, dream command |
| Supernatural figures | ancestors, ghosts | yakshinis, yoginis | servants of the goddess |
| Community | family and village | guru and disciples, chakra | worship groups, temple, ashram |
| Follows dharma | rarely | sometimes | generally |

## Who Is a Shakta? Problems from the Turn of the Century to the Present

Although we can give a general definition of Shaktism, there has been much difficulty in determining who is a Shakta. This means that calculating the Shakta population is very difficult. One could not do better than to take a look at the definition of Shaktism in the 1928 *Encyclopedia of Religion and Ethics* to get a clear look at one of the problems—a tradition of prejudice by Western scholars:

> This licentious type of Hinduism appears still more clearly in the form of Saktism, the worship of the active female principle (*prakṛti*) as manifested in one or the other of the forms of the consort of Śiva—Kālī, Devī, Pārvatī, and many others. The general character of this, the most debased side of Hinduism, is fairly well known; but comparatively little study has been devoted to it by European scholars, and the secrecy under which its rites are celebrated ensures that its mysteries are revealed to none but the initiated . . . On the one hand, it has been supplied with a philosophical justification, being a popularized version of the Śāṅkhya principle of the union of the soul of the universe (*puruṣa*) with the primordial essence (*prakṛiti*). . . . On the other hand, Śaktism has a second and less reputable side, and this is more present to the majority of its adherents than any philosophical speculations and reminiscences of Vedic doctrines . . . In Bengal, again, the worship of Durgā is accompanied by wearisome puerilities and gross idolatry. The cult of Kālī-Devī is also associated with the horrors of Thagi.[7]

The facts presented here are generally accurate, but distorted by the value system of the writer. The forms of Shaktism described here fit well the distinction between classical and folk tantra, but there is so much condemnation in the writer that it is difficult to see such a definition as objective (the tradition is disreputable, debased, licentious, gross, full of horrors, and so on). It is rather like trying to understand the theologies of the heretical Christians of the patristic period by looking at the writings of their orthodox opponents: it is not impossible, but it is a challenge.

We see the bias against nature-oriented, "primitive" Shaktism as opposed to philosophical, civilized, "advanced" Shaktism. The problem is not unique to Western observers, for we see this perspective frequently in Indian writers. Writing in 1916, the historian Ramaprasad Chanda describes this contrast:

> From this sketch of the traits of the goddess it is possible to distinguish two different strata—one primitive and the other advanced.

> The primitive form of Durga is the result of syncretism of a mountain-goddess worshiped by the dwellers of the Himalaya and the Vindhyas, a goddess worshiped by the nomadic Abhira shepherds, the vegetation spirit conceived as a female, and a war-goddess. As her votaries advanced in civilisation the primitive war-goddess was transformed into the personification of the all-destroying time (Kali), the vegetation spirit into the primordial energy (Adya Sakti) and the saviouress from *samsara* (cycle of rebirths), and gradually brought into line with the Brahmanic mythology and philosophy.[8]

Victorian observers valued philosophy, ethics, and abstract notions of divine monotheism, and we see a similar sort of value system in many educated Indian observers of popular religion. Any aspect of Indian religion associated with the Vedas and Upanishadic philosophy tends to be understood as respectable and valuable, whereas any aspect associated with nature and fertility is understood to be unevolved and crude. Monotheistic salvation and philosophical speculation are understood to be essentially superior to nature religion, which is merely superstition. Because it has been so frequently either dismissed or maligned, it has been difficult to get a clear idea of the beliefs and practices of folk Shaktism.

Another problem is that there is no Bengali or Sanskrit word for sect or denomination, though sometimes the word *samaj* (society or community) is used. In the West, there is usually exclusive worship of one deity, and that is further broken down into sect or denomination, but in India many deities may be worshiped at once. Many Shaktas with whom I have spoken have said that the goddess Kali is sociable, and likes to be worshiped with her friends, the other gods and goddesses. Is one a Shakta if he or she worships another god? What about if the person worships a collection of gods and goddesses?

In interviews with practicing Shaktas, I asked how one could tell who is a Shakta.[9] I heard these answers as the major responses:

1. One who calls him or herself a Shakta
2. One who has Kali or Durga as his or her personal deity (*iṣhṭādevata* or *iṣhṭādevī*)
3. One who has any goddess as his or her personal deity
4. One who describes his or her family as Shakta
5. One whose family priest (kula guru) is Shakta
6. One who has taken Shakta initiation (*dikṣha*), with a Shakta mantra
7. One who has private, personal faith in a goddess, or goes to visit Shakta *pīṭhas*
8. One who celebrates Durga and Kali puja, especially in the family house
9. One who has had a special call from a goddess

10. One who has had a vision (darshan) of a goddess, while awake or in a dream

Dictionaries and encyclopedias also have a variety of definitions: both the *Baṅgala bhasar abhidhān* and the *Saral bangala abhidhan* wrote, "a Shakta is one who has been initiated by a shakti mantra; a worshiper of Shakti; a tantrika."[10] The *Vyavaharika Sabdakosa* wrote that a Shakta is "a worshiper of Shakti; a tantrika, a member of a Shiva or Shakti lineage (*sampradaya*)."[11] The *Bangiya sabdakosa* wrote, "A Shakta is one who is related to Shakti, or related to the goddess Shakti, or a worshiper of the major goddesses (Durga, Kali, Jagaddhatri, etc)."[12] The *Sabdabodha abhidhan* wrote that "A Shakta is a worshiper of Shakti, or a member of a special tantric lineage."[13] Note that most of these definitions equate Shaktism with tantra or membership in a tantric lineage; this is a great problem for both Shakta bhakti and Shakta universalism.

The *Bharatvarsiya upasak-sampradaya* gives a definition of Shakta that is quite different, and its definition of Shaktism includes both tantra and brahmanical ritual worship or puja:

> Those who are worshipers of Shakti or Shiva's wife are called Shaktas. The tantric literature is full of rules regarding this lineage. The style of worship is different from that of the Vedas. What is special about tantric worship is that the worshiper must first build an image of the goddess, then bring "life" into it by chanting mantras, and welcome her descent as a living and physically visible goddess. The worshiper must offer water, offerings, objects for bathing, perfume, clothing, and other items. Some people who are eligible worship with liquor and meat. The Shakti lineage worships Shakti, Kali, Tara, Shiva-shakti, or other deities. However, the personal deity may not be the same for all, depending on the lineage of guru and disciple. Some worship Kali, or Tara, or Jagaddhatri, or others.[14]

Finding a consistent definition is one problem in understanding Shaktism, whereas defining its membership is another. Determining membership is extremely difficult in the case of Bengali Shaktism. The government census takers no longer ask questions about religion, and those who try are often met with suspicion by the populace. West Bengal is currently a Communist state, and people often hesitate to speak too strongly about religious affiliation. In earlier days, when religion was considered to be a legitimate question, there were usually only two choices: Hindu or Muslim. The many forms of Hinduism were not defined or categorized.

It is also difficult to determine who is a Shakta because people often do not define themselves in this way. A person may be considered a Shakta if he or she worships only Kali as Shakti, but not if he worships the goddesses Durga or Jagaddhatri. Some Shaktas worship a family deity statue in a house altar, some go only to the big goddess festivals, and some go to the goddess festivals as well as those of other deities.

Determining the tradition of the initiating guru is not always an answer, for often people do not know the lineage of their gurus, or the gurus worship many deities. Many people cannot find gurus they like, and never get initiated. Some people are secret Shaktas, unwilling to admit their faith because it is not as well accepted as Vaishnavism or Shaivism; they take Shakta tantric initiation and do tantric spiritual practice (*sadhana*), but keep a Vaishnava Narayana stone on the house altar for guests to see and they pretend to be Vaishnava. Some people have Shakta tantric family priests (*kula gurus*), but claim to be personally agnostic or atheist. Some people have a goddess as their personal deity (*ishtadevata*), but may keep other deity images in the house for public worship. Several tantrikas interviewed made the claim that all Vaishnavas are secretly Shaktas.

Early-twentieth-century writers made attempts to determine Shakta affiliation and to make estimates of the Shakta population. As Joseph Wilkins observes in his 1901 *Modern Hinduism*, "It has been estimated that of the Hindus in Bengal about three-fourths are devoted to the worship of Śakti; i.e. the power or energy of God as represented in many female forms. Of the remaining quarter, three parts are Vaishnavas, and the remainder mostly Śaivas. Each deity has his consort, to whom the worship of the people is often more freely given that to her husband . . . as without the female the male is unproductive, she is regarded as the real force in nature, hence the almost exclusive adoration that is paid to the female deities by so many."[15]

There seems to have been a consistent Shakta presence around the turn of the century in Bengal; writing in 1907, John Campbell Oman also estimates that three-fourths of Bengalis are Shaktas.[16] However, modern estimates vary wildly. According to one researcher interviewed on Bengali folk art and culture, "In one sense, all Bengalis are Shaktas . . . but if we were to estimate how many people were ardent worshipers of the goddess Kali, and worshiped no other deity, I would estimate about ten per cent of the West Bengal population."[17] On the other hand, a professor of history and Bengali Shakta expert claimed that almost 90 percent of West Bengal is to some degree Shakta.[18] This gives us a Shakta population ranging from approximately eight million to almost eighty million. Clearly, the estimates can range widely.

There are many relevant questions about membership. Can one be a Shakta without initiation? Can one be Shakta with a Vaishnava family background? Can one be a Shakta without faith in the goddess? Can the Muslims who work to construct the *pandals* for Durga Puja and worship her be called Shakta? How about the many Muslim Thugs of the nineteenth century who worshiped Kali?

Some urban gurus and high-caste practitioners with whom I have spoken have tried to narrow the definitions of who is a Shakta. "False" Shaktas are people who are uneducated, who have not read the texts and do not know the major commentators of the Shakta tantric tradition. "True" Shaktas are educated, literate, and understand the goddess to be merely a manifestation of *brahman* or ultimate consciousness, as manifest through the Samkhya category of active matter (*prakriti*). Shaktas who worship their village goddesses are merely superstitious, and not really Shaktas. Their rituals, such as animal sacrifice and ascetic practices, are primitive if not abominations. Low-caste Shaktas think that their goddess image is alive and conscious, and that their goddess is an individual who cares for them and makes demands rather than a philosophical principle. We see a drawing of boundary lines, an emphasis upon differences, a distinguishing between the educated insider "true Shakta" and the superstitious outsider "false Shakta."

From this brahmanical perspective, often found among many Western-educated Shaktas, the boundaries of true Shaktism extend to the educated elite and their followers, but can include any people with philosophical knowledge and a universalist perspective. There is a subtle political claim here, basically that the rational and educated elites of all countries and faiths are closer to each other than members of the folk tradition and the elite classical traditions of the same country, even if they worship the same deity.

For other practitioners, Shaktism is defined in opposite terms. Philosophers studying dead ideas are not real Shaktas. Only people who have faith in the goddess, who sense her presence or have her vision, are Shaktas. Shaktism is bhakti devotionalism, and the true Shaktas are those who love the goddess, and are chosen by her. Lack of love is the boundary, especially as seen in people who are untrue to that other important goddess, Bharat Mata or the homeland of India. It is people influenced by foreign philosophies who lose their love and substitute rationality and claims of political oppression for respect for their own families and traditions. People who speak foreign languages and think in foreign categories are not really Shakta, or even Hindu. They have lost their lineages. This approach has become important with the rise of Hindu nationalism. There is another underlying political claim here: one cannot be a Shakta and subordinate the goddess India, for nationality unites people more strongly than similarity of belief system.

There are many local definitions. Caretakers of Shakta temples and shrines define Shaktism in terms of temple ritual: who comes to the temples, who pays for goddess worship, who gives offerings at the shrines? Shakta gurus define Shaktism in terms of lineage: to which guru lineage (*sampradaya*) do people belong, are their mantras empowered, are they doing their rituals (*kriyas*), and are they following proper behavior? Shakta healers define Shaktism in terms of abilities and results: does the goddess listen to the person's requests and prayers, does she come in dreams and call the person to follow her instructions? Householder Shaktas define Shaktism in terms of devotional behavior and family relationship: how much time does the person find to perform the rituals, how much food is given, how many silk saris and ornaments are offered to the statue, how many relatives are invited to the ceremonies? There are professional definitions, regional definitions, even eccentric individual definitions.

Because Shakta practitioners interviewed have given all of these definitions, the definition that I use in this book will incorporate as many of these understandings as possible. Thus, a Shakta is a person who worships, loves, seeks power from, becomes possessed by, or seeks union with any regional or pan-Indian goddess, and he or she is not disqualified by caste, worship of other deities, initiations, or level of education.

Shaktism is a very old tradition of goddess worship in India, a tradition with both written and oral literature. Its festivals and worship ceremonies are artistic and beautiful, and Bengali Shaktism is a good case study of a particularly rich form of Shaktism. It is an intermediate, bite-size religion, midway between the broad study of Hinduism throughout India and the close study of religion in a single temple or village.

## Some Background on Bengali Religion and Literature

For readers who are not Indologists, I include some brief background on locale, history, literature, and religious traditions of the area under study.

West Bengal is a state in northeastern India, widely recognized as a center for philosophy, poetry, and intellectual pursuits. It is bounded on the east by Bangladesh and Assam, on the south by the Bay of Bengal, on the west by Bihar and Orissa, and on the north by Nepal, Sikkim, and Bhutan. It became West Bengal to separate it from East Bengal, also known as East Pakistan (which became the country of Bangladesh in 1971). Before Indian independence from British domination in 1947, the boundaries of Bengal had shifted over the centuries, and at various times included parts of the neighboring states of Orissa, Assam, and Bihar.

The Bengal area has been variously called Banga, Bongol, Bangala, Bengalla, and Suba Bangla, and its regions also had separate names. The term Banga referred to the southeastern area, and Rarh or Radha to the southwestern area. Gaur originally referred to middle Bengal (first Murshidabad and Birbhum, and then Malda and Burdwan), and later spread southward. Northern Bengal was called Pudangala or Pundranagara.[19]

The Bengali language is an Indo Aryan-language, a relative of Sanskrit. It developed from the ninth century CE on, when Bengal became a distinct region under the Pala Dynasty. According to Shashibhusan Dasgupta, both Bengali language and religion arose with the development of smaller sectarian groups that tended to protest against the larger and more orthodox religious systems of India.[20] As of 1999, Bengali was the seventh most widely spoken language in the world, with approximately 211 million speakers.[21]

Most scholars begin Bengali religious literature with the *charyapadas*, the esoteric poetry of early Bengali Tantric Buddhists (and some Shaivite yogis) discovered in this century in some manuscripts that had been stored in Nepal. They are written in Old Bengali, a form of the language that existed from 950 CE to 1350 CE, according to Sukumar Sen.[22] These writings are full of symbolism, and many are thought to represent yogic practices that were also seen in the Shaiva and Shakta tantra of the time, as well as among the Naths and Sahajiya Vaishnavas. These groups were separate from both the brahmanical tradition of the time and from the Islam of the Muslim conquerors, who came to dominate Bengal politically, and whose influence is still visible in syncretistic groups such as the Bauls (who use both Hindu and Muslim imagery in their poems and songs).

Bengal was relatively isolated from the growing Hindu tradition, but by the end of the Gupta era (6th century CE), brahmin culture had come to Bengal, and brahmins were given land grants for housing and temples—before that, it was often called the "land of foreigners" in Hindu texts from other regions. However, the brahmanical system had only a few centuries to become organized in Bengal. The Muslim invasion at the beginning of the thirteenth century overthrew the major centers of Buddhist and brahmanical learning and culture in the Bengal area, especially the great monastic centers such as Nalanda and Vikramashila. Scholars fled the destruction of temples and monasteries. The thirteenth and fourteenth centuries had little literary production—Sen calls this period "a perfect blank" for literary and cultural history,[23] in which the Muslim armies destroyed both the complacency of the rulers and prestige of the brahmanical priesthood.

Although the Sanskrit pandits were silenced, alternative traditions developed, with myths and stories that gathered around new deities. The Vaishnava movement had been growing in Bengal, influenced by puranas from other areas of India (especially the *Bhagavata Purana*, thought by many scholars to have been written in south India). Vaishnavism became a full-fledged devotional movement in Bengal with the love poetry written by Chandidasa, Govindadasa, and Vidyapati. Perhaps the most famous love poem of the Bengali Vaishnava tradition is Jayadeva's *Gita Govinda*, a love song between the god Krishna and his beloved Radha.

Around this time, the language form developed into Middle Bengali. The major figure of the rising Bengali Vaishnava tradition was Chaitanya, the sixteenth-century religious leader who was understood by Bengali Vaishnavas to be a joint avatar of the deities Radha and Krishna, incarnate together in one body. Chaitanya was an ecstatic who emphasized the importance of divine love, and his approach was codified into a theology by his companions and followers, the six *goswamis* of Vrindavana. Whereas earlier Vaishnavism emphasized stories of Krishna and the cowherd girls (*gopis*), and to some extent the worship of the god Rama, in later Bengali Vaishnavism the figure of Chaitanya became a center of meditation and worship, and worship of Rama began to lessen. The school of Bengali or Gaudiya Vaishnavism developed a large literature over time, and came in some ways to resemble a brahmanical tradition, with an emphasis on the use of Sanskrit, textual knowledge, a tradition of commentary, and a hereditary lineage of gurus.

During the time of the emergence of Vaishnavism in Bengal, both Shiva and Shakti were popular, and there were long lists of deities in the *mangal-kavyas* or sectarian religious poems of the time. Imagery of the god Shiva changed over time. In the earlier period (tenth to fourteenth centuries CE), Shiva was described as an all-powerful deity with supreme knowledge. In later popular literature, however, he became a Bengali farmer with a troublesome family, a nagging wife, and dissatisfied children. There are no devotional hymns to Shiva extant from medieval Bengali literature (although there are many from south India and other areas of India). Our information about him comes largely from references to him in the Shakta *mangal-kavyas*, especially those dedicated to the goddesses Chandi and Manasa.[24]

The *mangal-kavyas* were poems glorifying particular deities, and in the Shakta literature of the fourteenth to the seventeenth centuries they were very important. They were read in public, and often chanted through the night during festivals. The two most important goddesses were Chandi (also called Kali or Kalika in these texts) and Manasa, the goddess of snakes. There were also *mangal-kavyas* to other goddesses, such as Shashthi (goddess of child welfare), Lakshmi (goddess of wealth and fortune), Shitala (goddess of disease, especially smallpox), and Ganga (goddess of the Ganges River), but there is much less literature available in Bengali on these latter goddesses. There are also occasional *mangal-kavyas* to gods, such as Dharma and Dakshin Ray (god of the Sunderbans jungle).

These *mangal-kavyas* arguing for the superiority of particular deities were the primary forms of popular Shakta literature, but at the end of the eighteenth century we see the growth of devotional poems to Kali, called *shyama-sangit* or songs to the dark goddess. This tradition was begun by Ramprasad Sen, and later echoed by many other writers in Bengal.

In the seventeenth century, Bengal was still dominated by the Muslims, and ruled by Muslim governors and officers from Delhi and Agra. There were wealthy landholders and feudal chiefs, and the beginnings of a patronage system for writers and artists, which expanded in the eighteenth century. At that point, Bengal was growing more independent of Delhi, and local rulers and landholders (zamindars) had court poets and dramatists.

Because Persian was the offical language of the Muslim Mughal court, that language came to be the most important one for upwardly mobile professionals to learn. Little attention was paid to Sanskrit, even by scholars and doctors. Colloquial Bengali versions of priests' handbooks, books of logic and philosophy, and hymns and songs to deities were popular (and these are still used by Shakta priests today). The Muslim court patronized literature, especially romances and adventures. Plays were popular, as well as stories of royal figures.

By the nineteenth century, the British had become the dominant figures in Bengal, replacing the Muslim rulers. They brought the printing press, which spread Western ideas and revolutionized Bengali literature. Now all sorts of writing were widely available—dramas, novels, poetry, textbooks, encyclopedias. Western ideas became fashionable, and with the consolidation of British power in Bengal, English became an important language. In the area of religion, the writings of Raja Ram Mohan Roy on the Brahmo Samaj became well known (as well as those of Debendranath Tagore and Keshub Chandra Sen), and the religious novels of Bankim Chandra Chatterji were popular. Rabindranath Tagore wrote poetry and novels uniting the religious and the aesthetic, which he said could not be separated.

By the twentieth century, political and social writing came to be important literature in West Bengal, especially with the influence of communist versions of history and literature. Even popular poetry had Marxist metaphors. But since the fall of the Soviet Union, the writers and politicians of West Bengal have been seeking a new identity. Different factions support a religious Hindu state, a renewal of the current secular democracy with religious freedom, a new kind of communism that is atheist but with a market economy, or some other political structure combining the best of East and West.

It may also be noted that West Bengal has an unusual caste structure. Whereas traditional Hinduism has four castes, Bengal has traditionally had two major castes: brahmin and shudra, the highest priestly caste and the lowest servant caste. Since the time of the Muslim invasion of India, the kshatriya caste of rulers and warriors, and the vaishya caste of landowners, agriculturalists, and artisans, have declined. There have been several theories about this—some writers say that because the Muslim presence in Bengal was so dominant these ruling and landowning functions were taken over by the Muslim rulers and zamindars and there was no room for the Hindus of these castes. Whatever the reason, as Sen Gupta observes, "the two intermediate varnas have disappeared."[25]

In the centuries of foreign domination, Shaktism has remained an underground current. Though it has occasionally had royal patronage, it has mostly been noninstitutional, with little dependence on temples, as is seen in south India. It is very much a part of village life, but only dominates occasionally in the cities, especially during the great fall worship or puja festivals.

Oddly enough, most practicing Shaktas that I have interviewed had little interest in history. Biographies and oral stories of Shakta saints and practitioners routinely ignore wars, famines, invasions, and plagues, and take little notice of either the Muslim or British presence. Most Shaktas interviewed were not involved with the political parties of West Bengal, with their problems of caste and nationalism and affirmative action. It is amazing that many Shaktas, who worship shakti or power, somehow manage to ignore the concerns about power and politics that fascinate the denizens of Bengali tea stalls.

## Methodology

Shaktism in India has been studied academically in a variety of ways. Five major approaches have been broad historical surveys, studies of Shaktism in specific locales and situations, detailed studies of specific goddesses, translations and analyses of Shakta texts, and studies of Shakta tantra and its literature.

The first approach, broad historical surveys, tend to look at Shaktism as a developing tradition, beginning with the archaeological findings at Harappa and Mohenjo-Daro, continuing through Vedic goddesses, using archaeological and literary references. Most work using this approach is done by Indian writers; some examples include: Narendranath Bhattacharyya's *History of the Sakta Religion* and *Indian Mother Goddess*, Sukumar Sen's *The Great Goddesses in Indic Tradition*; and Vijaya Lakshmi Chaudhuri's *The Development of Mother Goddess Worship*.[26] Pupul Jayakar's *The Earth Mother* uses art history and crafts to study the development of Shaktism in a similar fashion. Ernest A. Payne's 1933 book *The Saktas* is not quite as organized historically, but it is a particularly useful early source for the history of Shaktism in West Bengal.[27]

The second approach, the studies of Shaktism in specific locales and situations, usually involves the use of social science methodology: psychology of religion, anthropology of religion, sociology of religion, and sometimes history of religions. Rather than looking at broad sweeps of history, this approach emphasizes detailed studies of persons, places, and events. Some studies using this approach show Shakta religious experience (such as Kathleen Erndl's *Victory to the Mother*) and the effects of Shakta religion upon social interaction (such as William Sax's *Mountain Goddess*[28]). Some are biographical, focusing upon specific religious figures who are Shakta practitioners, such as Jeffrey Kripal's study of the saint Ramakrishna Paramahamsa, *Kālī's Child*; others are psychological, exploring the influence of early childhood on Shakta belief, such as Stanley Kurtz's *All the Mothers Are One*.[29] This style makes use of fieldwork, interview, and biography, and focuses on the present rather than the past.

The third approach, the studies of specific goddesses, usually involves literary analysis as well as analysis of their myths and iconography. Goddesses are studied as topics in themselves, rather than for their influences upon specific regions or situations. Three useful sources on Indian goddesses are David

Kinsley's *Hindu Goddesses*, John Hawley and Donna Wulff's *Devī: Goddesses of India*, and Tracy Pintchman's *Seeking Mahādevī*.[30] Indian writers often go into greater detail on individual goddesses, with entire books devoted to varieties of a single goddess; two good examples for West Bengal are Subrata Kumar Mukhopadhaya's *Cult of the Goddess Sitala in Bengal* and Pradyot Kumar Maity's *Historical Studies in the Cult of the Goddess Manasā*.[31] There are books of this type that focus on many of India's major goddesses.

The fourth approach, translations and analyses of Shakta texts, follows the traditional Indological focus on sacred text. It often emphasizes the cultural influence of specific books and writers. There are several Shakta texts that have been historically and theologically important. These include the *Devi Bhagavata Purana*, studied by C. Mackenzie Brown in *The Triumph of the Goddess*; and the *Devi Mahatmya* studied by Thomas Coburn in *Encountering the Goddess* and *Devī-Māhātmya*.[32] There are translations and analyses of Shakta poetry, such as Rachel Fell McDermott's *Mother of My Heart, Daughter of My Dreams*, and Leonard Nathan and Clinton Seely's *Grace and Mercy in Her Wild Hair*.[33] Other writers analyze Shakta themes in literature; these include Tracy Pintchman's *The Rise of the Goddess in Hindu Tradition*, Usha Dev's *The Concept of Śakti in the Purānas*, and Pushpendra Kumar's *Śakti and Her Episodes*.[34]

Finally, there have also been many books on tantra as a subtype of Shaktism. Shaktism has often been associated with, and sometimes equated with, tantric belief and practice. One way to gain insight into Shaktism as a religious tradition is to understand its tantric aspects. There are useful studies of tantric literature, such as Teun Goudriaan and Sanjukta Gupta's *Hindu Tantric and Śakta Literature*; tantric goddesses, such as David Kinsley's *Tantric Visions of the Divine Feminine*; and tantric history and development, such as Narendranath Bhattacharyya's *History of the Tantric Religion*.[35] There are writers on specific perspectives in Shakta tantra, such as Sir John Woodroffe (*Shakti and Shakta* and *Principles of Tantra*) on the classical or brahmanical form of Shakta tantra, and Douglas Brooks, *The Secret of the Three Cities*, on south Indian Shri Vidya tantra.[36] There are also books on other types of Bengali tantra that can relate to Shaktism, such as the Vaishnava Sahajiyas (Edward C. Dimock's *The Place of the Hidden Moon*) and the Kartabhajas (Hugh Urban's *The Economics of Ecstasy*).[37] There are no books to my knowledge that focus solely upon folk tantra: it is found primarily in the tantric texts themselves, and in anthropological and folklore studies. Relatively few tantras have been translated; most writings on tantra are secondary sources. There is also writing on the more questionable and syncretistic "Western tantra" (which will be briefly described in chapter 5 of this book).

This book primarily follows the second approach: Shaktism in a specific locale, West Bengal, during the modern period (late nineteenth through twentieth centuries). It examines the varieties of popular Bengali Shaktism. Its interest is in the dynamics of modern popular Hinduism, and more specifically in its various understandings of and approaches to Bengali goddesses. It seeks to discover how Shaktism works as both a social and imaginative reality, by considering the various experiences and perceptions of its practitioners. It involves a recognition of multiple types and conceptions of Shaktism, for there is no one set of beliefs or practices that can be said to incorporate all of Bengali Shaktism.

The main vehicles for access to the understanding of Shaktism in this book are stories, songs, poems, biographical narratives, interviews, legends, articles, historical documents, and participation in and observation of Shakta rituals. The perspective is to some extent interdisciplinary. My training as a scholar has been in the history and phenomenology of religions, and I have found the technique of organizing data into a typology, associated with traditional approach of history of religions and writers like Joachim Wach and Mircea Eliade, to be extremely useful as a way to understand the subtle interactions within Shaktism as a whole. This book is based on a typology of Bengali Shaktism.

I hope to focus here on the lived religious experience of Shaktism. Because this book seeks to focus upon the experiences of popular Shaktism, interviews have been important: of artists and writers, farmers and healers, temple priests and holy women, wandering tantric sadhus and waiters and merchants and rickshaw drivers, as well as professional anthropologists, sociologists, folklorists, and religionists.

I went to West Bengal for fieldwork from 1983 to 1984, with an American Institute for Indian Studies grant for the year, and from 1993 to 1994, with a Fulbright grant for the year. On the earlier trip, I studied ecstatic religious experience in West Bengal, and was impressed by the many Shakta tantrikas and devotees that I met at that time. They struck me as vital and enthusiastic, with shining eyes and dramatic flair, acting out their interactions with the goddess with mime, song, and exaggerated facial expressions. Ten years later the Shakta tantrika informants I had known had disappeared. Tantrikas had often undergone persecution in India, but I found that a new set of persecutions had started, which were described to me in low voices by the tantrikas that I could find, scattered throughout West Bengal disguised as Vaishnavas and Bauls, secular teachers and engineers and doctors. This made finding informants much more difficult.

Although I started out using questionnaires, I found that open-ended interviews worked much better. When informants could speak freely, they tended to tell detailed stories about their own experiences with various goddesses and those of their friends, their dreams and visions, their beliefs and their fears.

The next few chapters will examine the strands of modern Bengali Shaktism in greater depth, noting the literature and oral traditions associated with them. In deference to current concerns in the field of anthropology of religion, I shall include some data written in the first person singular, to show the presence of the author in the ethnography.

# I

# Folk Shaktism

## *Life with the Goddess*

### Concepts of Goddess among the Adivasis and in Folk Hinduism

We see among the Indian tribals (Adivasis, those who first lived on the land) a wide variety of notions about the nature of goddesses. They are not "high goddesses," as we see in the pan-Indian brahmanical forms of Hinduism, but rather they are regional deities, intimately associated with the members of the tribe. Some would not be characterized as goddesses by many people, for those supernatural entities that are given offerings and worship include ghosts, ancestresses, water and plant essences, guardian spirits, and disease controllers. We see some overlap of tribal deities in the village gods or *gramadevatas* of village Hinduism, who may be field spirits or angry ghosts of women who died violent deaths. There is not a sharp differentiation between the goddesses of the Adivasis and the goddesses of folk Hinduism. Rather than a polarity we see a continuum, for both traditions worship many goddesses in common. There are four themes that may be noted in the worship of folk and tribal deities:

*Regionalism.* These deities are associated with specific places, temples, fields, and streams. The Kali of one village is not the same as the next village's Kali. One Chandi gives good hunting, another Chandi cures disease. Goddesses are not pan-Indian; they are specific to a person's tribal or caste group, extended family, neighborhood, or village.

*Pragmatism.* These deities are rarely worshiped in a spirit of pure and abstract devotion. Worship is for a specific end: fertility, good harvest, good weather, cures for diseases. If goddesses are not worshiped, it is well known that they may get irritable, especially when they get hungry.

*Human personality.* Deities are like human beings, including both their negative and positive sides. They may be impatient, ill tempered, impulsive, lustful, greedy, and angry, as well as merciful and benevolent to their worshipers. Sometimes they are jealous gods, who get angry if they are neglected or if their devotees show more attention to other deities.

*Variation of form.* Deities can be shape-shifters, appearing as natural objects at one time and as human beings at another. One's aunt may be human, or she may be a goddess in disguise. Supernatural power appears in various figures: nature spirits, ghosts, ancestors, regional deities. Gods and goddesses are not limited to disincarnate entities ritually incarnated in statues or appearing spontaneously in particular places. Some deities were once people, or are transformed people.

Adivasi goddesses tend to be aniconic—the goddess might manifest in a stone, in a lake, an unusual tree, or a pile of earth or cowdung. This contrasts with the brahmanical Hindu tendency to craft the goddess into statues and images that are recognizably human, and that are offered incense and flowers and sweets. Adivasi goddesses are generally believed to appear of their own accord in natural objects and places rather than responding to ritual calls. Goddesses may desire worship, but they are ultimately independent of human wishes and follow their own inclinations.

Adivasi goddesses may be upwardly mobile, originally dwelling in a rock in a field, having that rock moved by devotees to a sacred grove, and then to an altar in its own hut. With Hindu influence the rock may be moved into a small temple, then a larger temple, and then the goddess may get a statue who is a personification. In some rural temples, goddess statues can be seen in classic Hindu form—but at the goddess's feet is the stone from which she arose, and where some aspect of her remains. In other temples, the goddess who showed herself in the great banyan tree is still worshiped at the base of the tree—but also in the temple with a proper statue. The rock is often a stone slab painted with vermilion and surrounded by offerings. Such rocks are frequently found as a result of a revelatory dream, or by the request of the goddess, who appears in the form of an old woman. It is important to respond to such calls, as a family may be punished with disease and death if the goddess calls but is ignored. However, the family may be rewarded with wealth and happiness for treating the goddess well, especially feeding and worshiping her.

Many rural goddess temples in West Bengal have been built because of a call from the goddess. A stone, bas-relief, or statue is found in which the goddess is understood by her devotees to dwell, and it is moved to the base of a tree for outside worship, then to a small thatched enclosure (*than*), then to a small building with plaster or cement walls, and then to a full-fledged temple. There are goddesses (and gods) in all of these environments in West Bengal, and the movement from the water to the land is usually understood to be a sort of increase in status for the goddess. This is because a goddess with a temple has more devotees than an unknown goddess beneath a pond, whom nobody worships.

There is a common origin story for the stone in which the goddess dwells. A person (usually male) will be asleep at night, and receive a divine call or command in a dream (the Bengali term for this dream command is *svapnadesha*). It is from a goddess, who is generally dissatisfied with her current situation. She is in a lake, pond, or river, or sometimes underground, and she is tired of staying there. She wants to be in a place where she will get more attention, more offerings from devotees, and have more influence on the world. Frequently she complains of being hungry, and not having eaten in several hundred years. Deities without offerings are understood to be starving; as the snake-goddess Manasa tells Behula in one of the *Manasamangal* poems, "These twelve years, my child, I have been without food. I have spent these twelve years eating the wind."[1]

Although the goddess's power may be found in temples, burning grounds, and other sacred places, very frequently it is found in black, rounded stones. Stories along this theme are heard all through rural West Bengal: a person dreams at night of a call from the goddess, who is located in a rock at the bottom of a pond, river, or lake. She wishes to get out of the water, and come onto dry land and be worshiped. The person finds the petrified goddess the next morning, sets her up in a shrine, and offers her ritual worship. She is then satisfied, and shows her appreciation by giving miraculous healings and bringing luck. This set of events is so well known that there is a "rock scam" described by several urban informants. The goal is wealth, for in India, sanctity can be wealth-producing. People offer money to deities hoping for a large return on this relatively small investment, and the person who takes the money is usually the owner or priest of the deity. He is the one who controls access to her.

According to informant descriptions, a person (or persons) conspires to become the caretaker/ owner of a deity in a rock, as a hopefully lucrative career. The person buries a rock with special markings (often a rough figure of a multiarmed Kali or Chandi incised into the stone) near a body of water. After a few weeks or months, he announces to the village a dream that calls him to dig up a rock in that very place. It was revealed to him in the dream that there is a goddess underground who wishes to be recognized and worshiped. He goes over with a few villagers who later can act as witnesses, digs the rock up, and brings it home. If a confederate from his own or a nearby village can be cured of some chronic health problem (of which he has been visibly complaining for the past few weeks), the caretaker of the deity becomes gainfully employed "in the god business." There is no further validation needed, because deities are elusive and do not appreciate being tested. Doubters need to be careful—what if the goddess really is in the rock, and one is speaking against her? It is a bad idea to make a goddess angry. The goddess in the rock has automatic status. Additionally, temples can become major businesses in towns where there is a scarcity of resources. To doubt a neighbor's vision may also prevent the growth of a major business opportunity, and do a disservice to the community.

Most traditional informants said that this simulation must be rare, for the goddess is known to have a quick temper, and gets angry at people who try to use her. Thus, even if the village liar were to have a dream call, it would be likely to be believed, for chancing the goddess's anger is dangerous and the man would have to be mad to do it. Doubting the goddess's call might make her angry, so people should hesitate to be skeptical. Now that Western ideas have penetrated into the most rural of areas, however, we do see a growing skepticism and even denial of the truth of the dream commands. Nevertheless, many people still go to the temples, deciding to be on the safe side.

When asked how the goddess got into the rock in the first place, people generally responded with blank stares. They said, "How are we supposed to know how goddesses do that sort of thing?" Informants willing to deal with this question generally had two speculations; either she was in the rock since the beginning of time, or she entered the rock later on. Those of the eternal school had the goddess in the rock forever, sleeping or dreaming or semicomatose, until one day she awakens and decides that she doesn't like the environment. Either she broadcasts a general call at that point to be taken out and worshiped (and whoever is suitably receptive hears her and comes to rescue her), or she waits for decades or centuries until just the right person comes along (her criteria for the right person are known only to herself). For the more particular goddesses, this may mean years in a quite undignified position. Some rocks are used as laundry stones, where washermen and women come to beat dirty clothes against rocks, some are trod on by low-caste and outcaste people, and some are thrown by children and kicked by animals. The goddess stoically bears years of pounding by the laundryman's cleaning of saris and *kurta* shirts, however, waiting for her rescuer and her new status as village goddess.

Sometimes goddesses, or even human women, are said to be incarnate in rocks as a result of a curse. An early example of this is the *Ramayana* story of the sage Gautama's wife, Ahalya. Indra, king of the gods, lusted after Ahalya, and slept with her after taking on the illusory form of her husband. Despite the fact that she thought she was with her husband, Gautama was nevertheless quite angry, and cursed her to be transformed into a rock until she would be liberated by the god Rama during his incarnation on earth. In the *Adhyatma Ramayana*, a version of the *Ramayana* found in West Bengal, Gautama cursed Indra, and told his wife that she would suffer as a rock until the god Rama incarnates on earth and touches her with his foot.[2]

Some informants mentioned a myth of a primordial dismemberment of the goddess at the beginning of the world, a cross between the Purusha Sukta story in the *Rig Veda* and the myth of Sati. The earth was made from the body of the goddess, and some of her body parts were more conscious than others (these became the sacred rocks). Other informants said that the consciousness of the goddess Prakriti (the goddess of matter) is scattered throughout all the world, though more visible in some places than in others.

Those who believed that the goddess's entrance into the rock was a later event had a variety of theories as to why this might have occured. Some informants speculated that perhaps the rock was originally a statue, enlivened by a brahmin priest through the ritual of *prana-pratishtha* (when a deity is called down by mantra to dwell in a statue), but the statue was worn away over time, with the goddess somehow trapped inside. Others said that there were many invasions throughout Indian history, and the deities fled the invaders just as the town or village inhabitants did, somehow ending up in a rock or tree, or buried by devotees in Mother Earth. Sometimes she was taken away from a temple in a war zone or area of famine by a fleeing priest; or her caretaker followed her instructions to move her elsewhere and died while bringing her to the desired locale, and the presence of her statue was unknown or forgotten by others. On occasion, the statue might be buried and a false or "decoy" statue set up to fool the invaders. But if the invasion lasts for a long time, people may not remember what happened and take the decoy to be the true deity, and the original statue is left forgotten.

Sometimes a statue was taken by the priest, and sometimes it left on its own, floating through the air or animating its stone legs to run. The statue's running away was not viewed as cowardice on the statue's part but rather as its faithfulness to its priest, caretaker, or village population—it did not want to be dishonored, or even worshiped, by foreigners. Sometimes the statue or rock could be convinced to return if the invaders promised to worship it and give large amounts of offerings, but usually it refused to return and roamed the forests and jungles until it found a suitable lake in which to rest. However, it is difficult for statues to move, and often they cannot do so and must suffer silently.

The stone seems to have gotten into the lake or ground in a variety of ways. Sometimes the stone is considered to be spontaneously alive (*svayambhu*), and the goddess has chosen to dwell there for her own reasons. She has been sleeping there for centuries, and she has suddenly awakened (or she has been waiting for the right person to finally call). Sometimes the statue is deliberately kept hidden in the water, especially to escape "torture by Muslim rulers."[3] A statue that is understood to be conscious would not enjoy having its nose or limbs knocked off, which often happened during Muslim attacks. This is locally understood by informants as deity torture. When the dream command comes to the sleeping person, the goddess has generally decided that it is time to move.

The person who has the dream, according to the origin stories, usually goes out and finds the rock or statue, and arranges for its worship.[4] Sometimes people ignore the dream, and then it recurs over and over until the person finally agrees to rescue the goddess. If the person is stubborn and will not get her, the goddess may curse him with all sorts of disasters until he feels compelled to get her rock or statue. After the rock is recognized as a goddess and given offerings, the dreams stop, and the person can either be the special caretaker of the goddess or leave her to a priest. It is rare that she chooses to return to the lake or river, but it does occasionally happen.[5]

Goddess stones are occasionally said to change size. For instance, at Makardah village in Howrah, the stone of the goddess Makar Chandi was said to have become smaller over time. According to the story, the stone was once large enough to require the priest to climb a ladder to perform the daily worship. But when a priest came to resent the size of the stone and the extra work that was entailed for its worship, the goddess was upset, and sank into the earth and disappeared. The priest was then sorry for his resentment of the oversized goddess, and begged her to return. She did so, but only in her current, diminished form.[6]

Stones and statues of gods and goddesses are often called *thakurs*, or lords, by many village people. *Amar thakur*, my lord, does not generally refer to a deity in heaven but rather to a deity on earth: the stone or statue in the house worship room (*thakur ghar*). Thakurs have both upward and downward mobility. A rock or other object may be determined to be the dwelling place of a deity, placed in a house to be worshiped, and gain the respect of the family. If that family is blessed with luck, especially cures of disease, the family deity may start to be worshiped by the village. For instance, the Manasa stone of Tantipara was originally the household deity of Nityananda Dhibar, and it gradually became known as the village deity.[7] The Uluichandi stone in the family house of one informant became popular as a living deity. It then was named as the village deity, and the informant's grandfather became its priest.[8]

As a village deity, the goddess stone may have its own temple and a full-time priest, who can accept offerings from the villagers and ritually offer them to her. People from other villages may come over with offerings. It can acquire a reputation as a deity that is alive and active, and its temple can become a place of pilgrimage. Sometimes it may be taken in procession to other villages, which keep an empty seat for its visit. In the town of Shibpur, there is joint worship of Kali by all villagers. Whenever a marriage party comes into the village, the couple must first bow down to the goddess, or trouble may occur.

Once a couple did not bow to Kali, and as soon as they passed her shrine, the handles of the wedding palanquin broke, which was very inauspicious for the wedding.[9]

In the case of goddess stones, if the temple is built where the stone was found, it may get the reputation of being a hidden *sati piṭtha*, or place blessed by some body part of the goddess Sati. Or it may be a new Shakta site, not a historical one, blessed by the goddess's choice to dwell there. In the nineteenth and twentieth centuries, new *pithas* have been publicized in West Bengal; probably the most famous of the newer ones are Tarapitha and Adyapitha.

There is also downward mobility among *thakurs*. When a stone or statue has not been doing its job, and the town or family has been unlucky, the statue may be understood as weak. If there are real disasters, however, the statue may also be understood to be strong but angry, and needing propitiation. If the statue is determined to be weak, or its worshipers leave and nobody else wishes to take on the responsibility of caring for it, it loses status. It may be consigned to the Ganges River or some other body of water, or it may be put into a temple of some other deity as an additional god or goddess, also cared for by the priest. Some temples become a sort of "old-age home" for *thakurs*, with unwanted gods donated along with money for their upkeep. There are sections for old goddess stones, *lingas*, Narayana stones, and even small statues and photographs, in some temples.

However, the topic of getting rid of unwanted *thakurs* seems to be an embarrassing one for informants, perhaps comparable to getting rid of unwanted relatives. People are uncomfortable at leaving their grandfather's goddess in the spare room or sending her off to live on a temple's charity (such shame may show a bhakti or devotional element in this folk worship). In some cases, a deserted temple with a living deity may have the equivalent of "home health care"—a group or society may decide to hire a brahmin to visit the temple each day, to feed and care for the deity. This is because the ground on which the temple sits is sacred ground, and it has been revealed that the deity wishes to stay in its own temple, on its own ground. In Adivasi society, old deities are frequently lost through forced migration (especially during the building of roads and dams), when the traditional home lands must be left, and the rocks and ground sacred to the deities must also be left behind.

In recent years, there has been more of an attempt to incorporate Adivasi and folk religion into the study of Indian religion (which historically has tended to focus upon literary, brahmanical Hinduism). For instance, in his *Banglar laukika debata* (Bengali folk deities), Gopendra Krishna Basu describes three types of folk ritual worship. The first type is forest ritual, which is simple and led by a *gunin* (tribal healer/shaman) or headman, in which there are offerings and prayers to a local deity in a natural setting. The second type is fringe ritual, which has a complex annual ceremony, with simpler sacrifices at other times. A village headman or local brahmin may perform the worship, and the deity has a shrine that is decorated. There is frequently animal sacrifice. The third type is village worship, which is more complex, with a brahmin to perform expensive annual worship and daily worship at the shrine. There is also special worship of goddesses on Tuesdays and Saturdays, and often vows (*manat*) to thank the deity if a request is answered.[10]

Tushar Niyogi, in his *Aspects of Folk Cults in South Bengal*, examines the growth of ritual environments from the base of a tree without a worshiper to the local folk shrines called *thans* (small temporary buildings, usually with thatched roofs), supported by devotees, to permanent buildings with priests.[11] Sometimes deities share a shrine, so that one might see Shitala and Panchananda standing together. Niyogi also notes that the local deity (*laukika devatā*) assimilates the attributes of puranic deities, and gains status by more brahmanical Hindu associations. At popular ritual sites, deities are offered special incentives (*manat*) if they will cure illnesses (especially rickets in babies and menstrual disorders), help women give birth to healthy children, and bestow victory in court cases. Some of the *manat* vows involve a certain degree of asceticism, such as *hatya deya* (lying down before the image of the deity and undergoing self-torture before its very eyes, to motivate it to act) and *dandi khata* (crawling to the altar or shrine from, say, a distant lake).[12] *Manat* is found at many levels of ritual environment, for it is believed to be an especially effective way of gaining a deity's attention.

In the tradition of folk Shaktism, we see many Adivasi and Hindu folk goddesses who are called Budi Ma or Buri Ma. In modern Bengali, *budi* means "old woman," but the Adivasi or tribal meaning of the term is "ancestress," the woman who is old because she originated the group. She is not merely old but ancient, and revered for her age and power. Some of these older goddesses are associated with trees (such as Vana Durga or Durga of the forests, and Budi Ma or Rupasi who dwells in the sheora tree). Nanimadhab Chaudhuri calls the Old Lady's worship "the cult of a tribal clan deity," and mentions as examples Buri Thakurani, Burhia Mata, and Burhi Mai.[13] Hathi-Dhara-Buri, the Old Lady who catches elephants with her hands, is said to have cleared the Midnapore jungle for her tribal followers by killing and chasing away the wild elephants (though now she has come to be brahmanized, and is also worshiped by Hindus). Sometimes the Old Lady is worshiped along with her consort, the Old Man, in the cult of Bura-Buri. This worship occurs especially in West Bengal, Bihar, and Assam. Chaudhuri notes three aspects as important in the worship of the Burdi: the absence of any statue of the deity (she is worshiped as present in nature rather than in a particular form), the presence of outdoor shrines (*than*), and the *deyashi* or nonbrahmanical priest who leads her worship.[14] The Old Lady may be worshiped in a tree, in groups of plants with offerings of hibiscus flowers and vermilion, or in a rock or rocks in the shrine. She may also be worshiped in the *burir jat* ritual, in which dancers hold decorated bamboo poles and perform animal sacrifice, and there are dances involving ascetic practices (iron rods are passed through various parts of the body, and lighted torches are attached to them).

Sometimes there are yearly festivals to the Budi. An interesting example was described to me by an anthropologist from Purulia. The village of Tentulhuti held a yearly festival to their goddess Jatra Budi, the ancestress of the tribe. It occurs on New Year's Day, which falls in mid-January (the tribal calendar is a slightly different from that followed by the brahmanical Hindu majority). As we see in many villages, New Year's Day is celebrated by the custom of having people in all occupations put on a new set of clothes and perform their work consciously as a religious ritual, blessing the work as a sacred action for the year. Even farmers will plow in new clothes, blessing the work and the land. The ritual of animal sacrifice involved a moral imperative of unselfishness:

> At the Jatra Budi festival, the tribal priest (*laya*) is not a brahmin, and he performs worship at the foot of a sal tree. "Budi" means ancestress, and Jatra Budi was worshiped at the tree, with offerings of pan, bangles, sweets, ghee and rice, rice saplings, thick sugar (*gur*) and grass. The area was cleaned with cowdung, and two piles of cowdung were placed there. A crowd gathered, and many people came with white cocks on ropes, and they tied about forty to the tree. There was also a lamb tied to the tree. Then the cocks were released into the air, and about one hundred boys in loincloths jumped into the air to catch the cocks. They tore the birds apart, many grabbing at the same birds. Whoever got the head was the winner, and they later tore the lamb apart.
>
> I asked why this was done, and an old woman said, "How else can you get people to share when they go to hunt? If you try to take all of the prey yourself, the others of the group will not allow you to do this. If you have killed a boar, other members of the hunting group will prevent you from being greedy and selfish. You should share with others, and you should only keep what you can hold in your hands."[15]

Goddesses in the form of old women are rarely seen in brahmanical Hinduism—the major goddesses tend to be portrayed as young and beautiful. But sometimes various forms of the Old Lady are adopted into Hinduism. In this case her name changes (she becomes Vriddheshvari, the Aged Goddess), and the priest is usually a brahmin. A good description of this transformation was given by a zamindar: "The cult prevails also among the higher castes among whom the Burī is known as Vṛddhésvarī. A Brahman officiates as priest. In the Brahmanical form of worship the goddess is meditated on as follows: 'Goddess fair-complexioned, adorned with all kinds of ornaments, dressed in yellow garments, two-eyed, two-armed, beautiful and smiling, who always grants boons to her votaries.' She is invoked as the nurse of the universe (*Jagatāṃ dhātrī*) and consort of Rudra (*Rudrakāntā*). Goats and pigeons are sacrificed to her."[16] We may note here that the aniconic Adivasi goddess becomes a fair-skinned great goddess or Devi, the old goddess becomes young, and the nature goddess is transformed into a distant deity of wealth and power, consort of a Hindu god.

We see a similar phenomenon in the village of Asansol in Burdwan, with another Old Lady, Ghaghrabudi. It is said by the people of the village that Ghaghrabudi dwelt within large pieces of stone under a tree on the bank of the river long before the village was built. She was found due to a flood in 1956, which uprooted the old tree and revealed the egg-shaped stones that were her home. According to the story, she had been the deity worshiped by a tribal community living in the forests, but as the tribal people moved out and brahmanical Hindu groups moved in, Ghaghrabudi decided to get worship from the Hindus. She appeared as an old woman wearing a sort of skirt (*ghaghra*) before a depressed, suicidal brahmin named Kangal Chakravarti. She told him not to commit suicide but instead to worship her in the form of the stones. He did so, worshiping her with the visualization of the goddess Chandika. As she was accepted by the Hindu community, her name was changed from Ghaghrabudi (the Old Woman or Ancestress in a skirt) to Ghaghrachandi (the tribal and folk goddess Chandi in a skirt) to Ghaghradevi (the Hindu goddess in a skirt).[17] She was thus transformed from the tribal ancestor (Budi) to the folk or village goddess (chandi) and then to the brahmanical Hindu goddess (Devi).

Although the figures of older goddesses and ancestresses are found fairly frequently in Adivasi religion, they are rare in brahmanical Hinduism. This may be a result of the different conceptions of power in tribal religion and in brahmanical Hinduism. The Old Woman of the Adivasis has the knowledge that she has gained through age, and like the creatures of nature, she shows both increase of knowledge and increase of years. The Hindu goddess may enter nature, but her home is elsewhere, and she takes on the form that represents her power: the face of a sixteen-year-old girl and the breasts of a nursing mother. She thus combines the powers of eternal youth, beauty, and immortality with the symbols of nurturing and motherhood. Her power is not in her wisdom gained in years of survival, but is a part of her essence. The major Bengali Hindu goddesses—Kali, Durga, Tara, Lakshmi, Sarasvati—are generally shown as young and attractive. Even Kali, whose images in other regions of India are emaciated and ugly, is frequently shown as beautiful and voluptuous in West Bengal. It is the youth of the Hindu goddess that shows her power, as it is the age of the Adivasi goddess that shows her wisdom. An example of a goddess seen in both Adivasi and Hindu folk religion is Chandi.

Chandi is a goddess who was partially adopted into the Hindu pantheon. Sometimes she is the patron deity of tribals (especially in texts such as the *Chandi Mangal Kavya*, in which she is worshiped by a hunter and his wife), and sometimes she is a village housewife. The name Chandi may refer to a specific tribal goddess, such as Chandi Bonga or Marang Chandi, who has a special affinity for hunters and is usually represented by a rounded black rock. It may also refer to the *hurung chandiko*, the six spirits who bestow luck, either as one spirit in different forms or different related spirits).[18] Sometimes hunters would carry her rock for luck in the field, though more often it would rest beneath a sacred tree, or in a small hut.

Village Hindus and tribal people often worship the same goddess in different forms and with different attitudes. As one Adivasi informant explained, "The Hindus worship Chandi too, but they worship different forms than we do. Sal Chandi is a forest deity, and Shanka Chandi is a river goddess, Jaherera Chandi lives in the sacred grove (*jaher than*). Rangahari Chandi protects us, protects the village as a group. Ambavati Chandi is the mother goddess for adolescent girls, for she is the goddess of menstruation and the earth. Our Ambuvaci is different from the Hindu ritual, which is mostly fasting. Our women enjoy the festival, they swing [on swings], and they do no work that day. Mashani Chandi is our guardian and the goddess of death, and she takes the soul to rebirth in a new body, or to a heaven or hell."[19] Tribal worship at Ambuvaci is celebration, whereas Hindu worship at Ambuvaci involves renunciation.

As a Hindu goddess, Chandi is represented by a dark rounded rock or a piece of the remains of a bas relief, often daubed with vermilion. Sometimes the area of her face may have silver eyes or a mouth drawn on, and be kept on a wooden throne. She is often accompanied by clay and terracotta horses and elephants, a pitcher or "god-pot," and a post for animal sacrifice. Whereas in the Adivasi style she is worshiped by the village headman (*deyashi*) or his wife (*deyashini*), in the Hindu style she is worshiped by a brahmin priest. Both may involve processions with music and song. As she is further Hinduized, she may acquire a human body, carved out of clay or wood. For instance, the Chandi at Barisha shows Hindu tantric influence: she is carved in human form, and sits on a seat of skulls (*pancamunda asana*) painted brown, pink, green, yellow and blue. She has four arms, a garland of skulls, a crown and ornaments, and a red sari.[20]

Some rituals combine both styles, and the goddess may be worshiped by both a nonbrahmin priest (often the headman) and a brahmin priest. An example is seen in the village of Khairadih near Bakreshwar. Mangal Chandi is usually kept in a mud temple there and worshiped by a nonbrahmin priest of the weaver caste, but on her annual festival the nonbrahmin priest pays the expenses, and a brahmin priest from another village is called to officiate. The shrine is cleaned and whitewashed for the occasion, and clay models of religious figures are exhibited. The goddess Manasa from Tantipara village is also brought for a visit. Mangal Chandi is placed by the brahmin priest on a wooden throne to circumambulate the village, and carried by members of the headman's family. The women of the headman's family lead the crowd, carrying the sacred pitcher, blowing conch shells and making the trilling sounds of ululation. The procession goes out to a sacred pipal tree, to perform the *gach-bera* ritual, encircling the tree with thread. The procession then returns, and the deity is put back in her shrine.[21] Then the brahmin priest sits down to worship Mangal Chandi, while the headman observes from a distance. The brahmin performs a fire sacrifice (*yajna*) and chants mantras in Sanskrit.[22] The goddess has not communicated whether she prefers a tribal or Hindu style of worship.

Some rituals that involve both brahmin priest and tribal nonbrahmin priest retain ascetic practices rarely found in mainstream Hinduism. In the annual festival of Chandi at Dhibar, Chandi is accompanied by *dakini* and yogini rocks (rocks in which these demigoddesses dwell), and terracotta horses. The tribal priest and devotees fast, and a wooden seat with iron spikes is brought to the shrine, and later carried through several villages. The devotees fast for days, and march in processions through the villages during the heat of the month of Jaistha (May/June). They later hold thorny shrubs in their hands, beating each other with the thornbushes and later rolling around on beds of thorns. There are further processions and praises of the goddess, and Shiva is later worshiped as Lord of the Underworld. There is also worship of Panchananda, Kali, and Buda Shiva (Shiva as an old man). Toward the end of the ritual, Chandi is returned to her shrine, and the brahmin priest performs ritual worship. Later there is animal sacrifice, mostly of goats and rams.[23]

Chandi as a folk goddess may be associated with good fortune or with disaster. She has many auspicious forms: Mangal Chandi, who is generally worshiped in a pitcher without an image, and brings good fortune; Jai Mangal Chandi, who gives children; Harish Mangal Chandi, who brings joy to the household; Sankat Mangal Chandi, who frees people from dangerous situations; Uday Mangal Chandi, who brings marriage, riches, and children; Natai Chandi, who is worshiped with joy, and recovers lost treasures or relatives, and Rana Chandi, who brings victory in war.[24] However, she may also be a disease goddess, especially as Olai Chandi, the goddess of cholera. She has also been associated with plague, eye trouble, and cattle diseases. The goddesses reflect the pragmatic concerns of folk Shaktism, overcoming the fear involved in war, disease, and danger, and bringing happiness and security.

Chandi may be invoked for both love magic and exorcism. Among the Savara people, a tribal group known for their skill at snake charming, Chandi is called by the shaman (*ojha*) for the ritual of *dhulopara*, the magical use of dust. The man who desires a woman gets the dust from her footsteps and brings it to the *ojha*, who chants an incantation three times. The man then scatters the dust onto the woman, and she finds herself attracted to him. The *ojha* chants:

Dust, dust, dust, queen of dust
O beloved one, listen to my words.
I have taken the dust of the path with three fingers
Very carefully, and with Mahamaya's blessings.
I will take this dust in my fingers
And I will scatter it on you
When you are at the market, or elsewhere.
It will bind you to me, you will be mine forever.
By whose will? By the will of the goddess Kamakhya of Kanur.
By whose will? The goddess Chandi, the Hadi's daughter.
This dust will work quickly.[25]

Chandi and Kali are both used as exorcism goddesses by the Savaras. The *ojha* finds out who is possessing a person by looking into the water in a clay pitcher; it becomes a mirror where images of the supernatural are seen. After he sees the image, he performs a chant, listing the various possible entities who could be causing the trouble, and he exorcises the possessing entity in the names of Kali and Chandi.[26]

Chandi is an example of a folk goddess still ritually worshiped by both tribal people and village Hindus. But while we can understand certain aspects of folk Shaktism through ritual, it is also useful to examine female figures in Bengali folklore.

## Folklore Heroines and Tough Goddesses: Some Folk Shakta Role Models

If we look at traditional Bengali religious and folk literature, we may note that there are many strong female figures. Some are human women (though they may be incarnations of goddesses) who show the meaning of shakti as the ability to accomplish desired goals, often in the face of adversity. These women are not stereotypically passive and obedient, obeying traditional rules. Instead they act upon their desires, often ignoring social disapproval. Their ends are usually ones acceptable to society—finding or saving a husband or child—but their means violate traditional women's behavior or dharma. Thus we see the odd situation of "good" women violating dharma in order to accomplish goals sanctioned by dharma.

Kalika/Uma of the *Kalika Purana* goes out to gain Shiva as a husband by becoming a yogini, despite family and social disapproval. Behula of the *Manasamangal* stories travels on a river with her husband's corpse to win back his life, and Malanchamala of the *Thakurdadar Jhuli* stories wins back her infant husband's life by resisting the death demons after she and the dead infant were thrown into the funeral pyre. As the more traditional figure of Savitri was able to challenge and outwit Yama, lord of death, these women are willing to sacrifice normal lives and roles to act independently in order to gain their goals. In such examples, we see various ways in which folk Shaktism emphasizes the power of heroic women, both supernatural and human.

### *Kalika*

The story of Kalika (also called Uma) of the *Kalika Purana* acts as a major religious justification in West Bengal for female ascetics, who often claim to be following her example. She performed meditation and austerity for 18,000 years (or perhaps what seemed like 18,000 years) in order to gain Shiva as a husband. He was an ascetic and yogi, so it was a challenge for a woman to attract him. She left a royal home to perform austerities, and willingly endured pain to gain yogic strength of mind and purification of desire.

There are several puranic versions of Kalika's becoming an ascetic, but the most popular Bengali version of this story is probably the version in the *Kalika Purana*, which will be described here. Though the story is from a purana, a classical source, it shows both traditional and folk elements, and it is often told by local storytellers who emphasize the human elements of Kalika's life.

Kalika was the daughter of Menaka and Himalaya, lord of the mountains. She was a beautiful young girl, and a reincarnation of Sati, Shiva's wife in a previous life. In that earlier life, Shiva and Sati had a very close and erotic relationship. The *Kalika Purana* goes into great detail of their pleasure day and night, Shiva's collecting wild flowers to make Sati garlands and braiding and combing her hair, painting her feet with red lac dye, and becoming invisible so that he could surprise her with embraces.[27] He thought of her constantly, and they made love in forest groves and in mountain caves. His loving glances and romantic words entered her heart, as a yogi enters the state of self-knowledge.[28]

Sati's father Daksha had a sacrifice to which Shiva and Sati were not invited, however, and Sati decided to attend anyway. When her father insulted Shiva there, Sati decided that this conflict within the family was unbearable, and that she would commit suicide. She decided that Shiva would be her husband in her next birth. Sati sat straight in yogic posture, and with eyes reddened in anger she closed the nine doors (or orifices) of her body. She made a sound (*sphota*) that sent her spirit out through the top of her head (which is often called the body's tenth door). This caused her death, and the assembled gods and guests mourned her passing. When Shiva heard of this, he went mad and destroyed the sacrifice.

Sati was reborn as Kalika, daughter of Menaka and Himalaya. She grew up as a beautiful and happy child. The sage Narada was sent by Indra, king of the gods, and came to visit Kalika. He told her that she must not accept anybody but Shiva as her husband, and that she must meditate on him with devotion for a long time. She must chant the mantra *Om namah Shivayah* and practice austerity, and visualize Shiva's image. If she did this for long enough, Shiva would come down to her.[29]

Kalika told her mother Menaka of her intention to marry Shiva and perform austerities. Menaka told her not to perform austerities, that she was not a sage and too delicate for such practices, and that even her worst enemies would not wish her to be exiled from her home. She told her mother not to stop her, that she would leave that very day, and if her parents would not allow her to go then she would go secretly in disguise. Her mother suggested worshiping in the house, and told her that unmarried women should not live in the forest. Kalika ignored her mother, and came to be called Uma (or "O girl, do not go") because her mother forbade her from going to the forest. She told her father (through her friends) that she was going to the forest, and he was unhappy, but he reluctantly accepted her decision.[30]

She went to a place where Shiva had meditated in the past, and was initially full of sorrow. However, she overcame her emotions, and began to meditate. She meditated upon Shiva while sitting in the midst of five fires (four fires around her on the ground, plus the sun). She wore tree bark for clothing, and ate only fruit, and later only leaves fallen from trees. She spent the summer in the midst of the fires, and the winter in cold water. Eventually she ate nothing at all, and stood on one foot chanting *Om namah Sivayah*. She became emaciated, with matted hair, and stayed in meditation for 18,000 years. Eventually, Shiva came down, and after testing her devotion, took her as his wife.[31]

Thus, her meditation was successful, and her disobedience to tradition was rewarded. In this case, though she was a princess, her behavior was justified by her previous lives. Though Kalika was a human renunciant, her goal was a divine husband, and she used her spiritual powers to attract him and got him to marry her. Whereas the classical yogic tradition emphasizes the goal of liberation, the folk tradition of yoga often has stories of yogic power used pragmatically to gain mates, servants, or supernatural abilities. And whereas the puranas are texts accepted by brahmanical Hinduism, this is a story with the values of folk Shaktism.

### *Behula*

Behula was a heroine of the *Manasamangal* stories, which tell the difficulties of the snake goddess Manasa in gaining devotees and respect by the other gods (Manasa's story is related in more detail in the section on folk Shakta bhakti). Like Savitri, Behula wins back her dead husband's life, though from the goddess Manasa rather than the god Yama. Whereas Savitri gains her husband's life through cleverness, Behula wins it by courage. In the Bengali Shakta tradition, she is the ideal devotee, and there are many songs about her.

According to the version of the story by Bipradas, Behula was caught in the machinations of the goddess Manasa, who wanted two of Indra's heavenly dancers to incarnate on earth (this was part of a complex plot by Manasa to gain worship from the stubborn merchant Chando). Manasa first went to Indra and requested them, but Indra refused. Manasa then caused the male dancer, Aniruddha, to make a mistake in his dancing. This made Indra angry, and he cursed Aniruddha to be born as a mortal. Aniruddha's wife Usha cried and begged for him to be spared, and eventually chose to go with him to earth. Aniruddha was born as the human Lakhindar, son of the merchant Chando, while Usha was born as Behula, daughter of the merchant Sahe.

Chando was much persected by Manasa, but eventually returned to his house at Champaknagar when his son Lakhindar was old enough to be married. As it had been predicted that Lakhindar would die on his wedding night, most local parents did not want their daughters to marry him. However, Chando found out about the merchant Sahe in a distant town, who had a daughter of the right age, named Behula. Chando arranged the marriage through his family priest, and Sahe agreed to the marriage. When Chando went to Sahe's house to celebrate the betrothal, he asked for iron pills (or beans) to take as medicine. Sahe's wife could not cook them, but Behula was able to cook them, and thus please her future father-in-law.[32]

As it had been predicted that Lakhindar would die on his wedding night, Chando built a sealed room for them. However, Manasa came and threatened the architect, so that he left a tiny hole. The wedding day was stormy, and Behula worshiped Manasa, who appeared in her flying chariot accompanied by snakes. On the first night, Behula caught the four snakes sent by Manasa to bite her husband. On the second night, Lakhindar wanted to make love (a violation of proper marriage tradition), and Behula refused. They both fell asleep, and a snake was able to enter and bite him. Lakhindar woke Behula with his scream of pain, and she cut off the tip of the snake's tail as it escaped, and she kept it. The family mourned, and Chando's wife blamed it on Chando, who had angered Manasa by his refusal to worship her.

Behula would not leave her new husband's corpse. She refused to accept widowhood, and said that she would float with her husband's corpse down the river until she met the goddess Manasa, whom she would beg for her husband's life. She decided to float down the river Gungari on a raft made of the trunks of banana trees.[33]

Chando tried to dissuade her from this rash and dangerous act, and told her that she would be welcome in his family (sometimes widows are not welcome in the families of their dead husbands). She would not listen to him, however. Chando finally ordered the raft to be made, and Behula sat on it behind the corpse. The raft was launched and carried off by the current.

She stayed on the raft with the corpse, despite the dangers of the river and the fact that the corpse was decaying. She was threatened by many people on her journey: a lustful man who stopped the raft and wanted her, an old and ugly man who turned out to be a relative of Chando, a group of gamblers (she bribed them with gold to leave her), and a crippled hunchback. She was threatened by animals—a crow who tried to eat the corpse's flesh (this was Manasa in disguise), then vultures and a tiger. She was also attacked by robbers in the guise of holy men, but she defied them. She was protected by Manasa, who struck them blind. Eventually she landed at Chaumukha, where she saw a laundrywoman with her child. The laundrywoman killed her son before starting her washing, and brought him back to life when she was finished. Behula told the laundrywoman her story, and the woman, whose name was Neto, told her to go on to the court of Indra.

Behula followed Neto's advice, and went to Indra's court. There she danced for the gods, who were impressed with her skill, and then she told them her story. They sympathised with her, and called Manasa to court. Manasa initially denied her role in killing Lakhindar, but admitted it after Behula showed the group the snake's tail that she had cut off. Manasa agreed to bring Lakhindar back to life if Behula could get her father-in-law Chando to worship Manasa. Behula was sure that she could do this, and Manasa brought Behula's husband back to life. Again, this time accompanied by Lakhindar on the drum, she danced for the gods. As a result of this second dance, she got back the lives of Chando's other sons whom Manasa had killed.

On their way back to Champaknagar, Behula asked Manasa to recover Chando's lost treasure, and Manasa agreed. Behula was welcomed back with great joy, for due to her devotion she had gained the lives of her husband and his six brothers, and she had brought back a great treasure of gold from Chando's sunken ships.[34] She then persuaded Chando to grudgingly worship Manasa.

Although a normal Bengali housewife would not dance publically for strange men, or travel alone on a boat with an impure corpse, Behula was rewarded for doing this, and it was acceptable for her husband and family. In other versions of the story, Lakhindar does not approve of her dancing in public (even though it brought him back to life), and Behula's chastity is tested upon her return to Lakhindar's family (and she came through the testing successfully, like Sita in the *Ramayana*).[35] Here we have a story in which the strong woman rescues the helpless man, with such folk elements as miraculous cooking (of iron beans), a chariot of flying snakes, and resurrection of the dead by a goddess. We may also note that in pragmatic folk Shaktism the desired ends justify the forbidden means.

### *Malanchamala*

A more complex tale is the story of Malanchamala, who brings not only her own husband back from the dead but an entire murdered city as well. The story is from the *Thakurdadar Jhuli* collection by Dakshinaranjan Majumdar. As Dineshchandra Sen comments on this story, "it presents the old ideal of womanhood in the most striking manner, and is typical of the great virtues of the fair sex as conceived by the Hindu nation."[36] Malanchamala's virtues are traditional, but her behavior and abilities combine folk Shaktism with tantric ritual.

As the story goes, a childless king finally had a son, but the Fates (Dhara, Tara, and Bidhata) decreed that the infant would die when it was only twelve days old. The leader of the gods came down to the palace, and said that the infant son would survive if he were married to a girl who had her twelfth birthday on that day. Messengers were sent throughout the land to find a girl born on that day, but the only one they could find was the poor but beautiful Malanchamala, the daughter of the police chief (*kotwal*). The king did not wish to marry his princely son to a commoner, but he had no choice. He went to get the girl (who had meanwhile found a diamond left for her by the gods). Her parents did not want her to marry an infant and become a widow, but they were forced to agree.

The marriage was quickly performed, but the baby died. In a rage, the king killed the *kotwal*, and cut off Malanchamala's hands and blinded her. She was dressed in rags from the burning ground, and her head was shaved; the king declared her to be a witch. She was thrown into the baby prince's funeral pyre, and her nose and ears were cut off.

Malanchamala sat in the funeral fire with the baby on her lap, and demons came, demanding the baby's body and making the wood of the funeral pyre dance. She was threatened by ghosts and spirits, but she stayed courageous. She stayed for months within the pyre, in the midst of darkness, and a forest grew up around her. Yama's brothers came for the body, but she defied them. She called the gods to witness that she was a chaste and devoted wife, and her intensity frightened away the night. As the day dawned, the ghosts disappeared, and the child began to move. She willed herself to see the baby, and her sight returned, she sought milk for it, and her hands grew back. Her nose, ears, and hair grew back as well.

When the night disappeared, the forest had become a sandy desert. She went out to find milk for the baby, while she fasted herself. She cared for him until she could no longer find milk, and had to travel to keep him alive. A tiger volunteered to be their guardian, and his tigress nursed the child. Malanchamala named the child Chandramanik. She went out and found him fruit and flowers, and they stayed with the tigers until the child was five years old. At that point, she decided that the child needed a tutor, and human society. The tigress and her mate were grief-stricken.

Malanchamala and Chandramanik wandered into a barren area of thorny plants and snakes. When she sat down there, the trees and plants burst into flower. The flower-woman who lived there was impressed at this, and gave them a place to stay. Malanchamala lived nearby, but separately from the child, for seven years—she did not want him to take her for his mother. She could live off the money from the diamond that she had found long before, and she sent him to school with the princes of that city.

The child had many challenges at school from the princes, who resented his good looks and intelligence, but Malanchamala saved him from all threats. Her gifts to him came from her virtues from past lives. Chandramanik grew up, and at age twelve he married the princess of that kingdom. He did not know that Malanchamala was his wife.

She sent a letter to Chandramanik's father, saying that his son was alive and married, and that he should visit the kingdom to see him. She then went to drown herself in her father's pond, for her husband was now happy, and her responsibilities were over. All that was left to her was death.

However, Chandramanik was imprisoned by his new father-in-law, and when his own father came with his men, there was a great battle, and the king too was imprisoned. Malanchamala heard this, and came in to her husband invisibly, along with her tiger friends. She broke his quadruple chains with her teeth (losing her teeth in the process). Chandramanik did not notice her, and went out to the tigers. They got their tiger companions, and attacked the kingdom, killing its ruler and soldiers. The old king was liberated from the jail, and marched off with Chandramanik and his princess-wife. When he met Malanchamala, he refused to speak to her, though he knew that she had saved both him and his son many times. The tigers volunteered to eat him, but she would not let them do so.

She returned to her original kingdom, again planning to drown herself. She saw Chandramanik with his princess, and prayed for their happiness. Again, she did not commit suicide, and instead left the city. After she left, the city was subject to a whole series of disasters. Finally, the king was out unhappily wandering, and he asked for water from a woman at a dry lake. She gave it to him, and he blessed her, saying that she should be happy in her father-in-law's home. It was Malanchamala, who sang out that these were the first sweet words that she had heard from his lips. He bowed to her three times, and invited her back to the palace. She refused, and he was sorry for his past behavior. She agreed to come in a few days.

She returned to the destroyed kingdom in which her husband had been imprisoned, and on the night of the full moon she lit eight butter lamps with shreds from her clothes. She sat in the great empty hall in yogic meditation for three days and nights. At that point, all of the city's dead inhabitants came back to life. She took all of them back with her, including the slain soldiers from her father-in-law's kingdom. As she entered her father-in-law's kingdom, both humans and flowers celebrated—for the true bride was coming home. She brought her dead relatives back to life, and the gods came to welcome her. She was welcomed with royal drums. The poor people ate butter-and-milk desserts, and the king made her father a noble. Chandramanik made the princess his chief queen, and the people recognized her virtues, and called her the goddess of the palace. All people, birds, beasts, and even insects were happy.[37]

Here Malanchamala is a human woman with supernatural powers. She has no religious training, but her powers come from her role as a chaste wife (*sati*), and from her religious practice in previous lives. She can stay alive in the midst of a fire at the burning ground wearing rags from corpses, and bring a dead child back to life; by yogic meditation she can bring an entire dead kingdom and population back to life. She can defy the messengers of Yama, lord of death; control wild animals; and affect the fertility of the land. She also shows supernatural unselfishness: she could rejoice in her husband's happiness with another wife, and forgive the many people who had harmed her. She lived a celibate life, for not until the end of the story did her husband realize that she was his wife. Much of her life was spent in yogic renunciation and poverty. Although her story is a folk tale—of the true wife whose virtues win out in the end—there are many tantric and yogic elements involved, especially in the conquest of ghosts at the burning ground, in her gaining supernatural powers through meditation, and in her control over the forces of life and death.

In all of these cases, we have independent women who do not follow their prescribed roles, but instead violate the typical woman's responsibilities (*stridharma*) for a greater good. Their closeness to nature and accomplishment in the present life is typical of the folk tradition. All of them show aspects of Shakti in human form, overcoming human problems and death itself.

## Folk Shaktism: Possession, Asceticism, and the Goddess in Nature

Folk Shaktism often involves possession and asceticism as major ways of getting in touch with the goddess. Ritualized possession is more controllable than dream-commands and visions, which generally occur rarely and erratically. It also allows for an alternative priesthood, of holy women and nonbrahmin men who are chosen by the goddess and can act as her instruments. Because folk Shaktism is not organized around temples or other institutions, its religious professionals need evidence of the validity of their calls. Possession (and its associated miraculous abilities like enduring burning and pain) provide the evidence.

Although possession may be understood as either a positive or negative phenomena, it is usually viewed as positive in the Bengali religious context. We see several forms and understandings of possession in rural West Bengal:

1. Voluntary group possession
2. Voluntary individual possession by a ritual specialist

3. Voluntary individual possession for the fulfillment of vows
4. Involuntary possession, as a divine call
5. Involuntary possession, as pathology
6. Simulated possession

1) Group possession is important in Adivasi religion, in which the goddess (often the tribal ancestress) will possess a number of people at the yearly festivals and dances. Such possession is a shared phenomenon, in which many people at once many be possessed, or the goddess may jump from person to person. In such cases, the dancing often becomes stylized, the head is thrown back, and the gestures are extravagant and expressive. Among the tribal Oraons, the Old Lady of the Grove jumps from one dancer to another, uniting them in their shared experience. Group possession is not usually marked by supernatural events such as spiritual healing or prediction of the future, but rather by a heightened sense of group unity and importance. There is also separation by gender, as groups of men and women usually dance separately, and the deity usually possesses one group of dancers at a time.

We also see group possession in folk Hinduism, in such public festivals as the Charak Gajan. In rural areas, the Charak Gajan involves a set of ascetic rituals, but it was more like entertainment in urban Calcutta. I observed a street parade of ecstatic dancers in 1983, costumed as various gods and sages. The group was circumambulating the Kalighat temple after they had fasted for ten days, only drinking water before sunrise and after sunset. Many of the marchers had matted hair and held large tridents and wore garlands of flowers. They danced and fell on the ground, rolling and leaping and waving their arms, speaking incoherently or in deep voices. They danced to drumbeats and shouted chants, waving fans and making hand gestures. When a child in the crowd fell to the ground with convulsions, a man in the costume of the goddess Kali chanted mantras over him, and did a wild dance. The child's symptoms subsided, and onlookers in the crowd explained to me that the man had been specially possessed by Kali to heal the child.[38] The other dancers were possessed in a more general way, and some were understood by observers to have a special relationship with the deities whose costumes and attributes they wore. There were both men and women apparently possessed in this group. Such possession was considered to be a gift, and a blessing from the deity.

2) For some women (rarely men in West Bengal), possession becomes a career track. Some women become specialists, getting possessed once a week and having a group of devotees and an audience who pay by donation. Such specialists are usually contacted for healing stubborn diseases and for predicting the outcomes of relationships, job possibilities, and lawsuits. It is understood to be a difficult career to enter, for the presence of a goddess in one's mind and heart is not easily accepted psychologically, and there is often a series of trances, breakdowns, periods of madness, and mood swings in the person's

life.[39] People who do seek to experience possession states may use vermilion from a statue of Kali, or pieces of bone and ash from the burning ground, to gain the requisite power and attract the goddess. However, it is believed by Shaktas that such states cannot be generated by human will; they are a gift of the goddess. There is usually a set pattern for possession: the person receives a prophetic call from a god or goddess, who wants to be worshiped, and if the person will not worship, the god or goddess possesses the reluctant devotee. The person is attacked psychologically by the deity until he or she gives in and is willing to form a relationship with the deity. Unless the person is chosen by the deity, this is not a possible career.

Once a relationship has been forged with the deity, possession can be controlled, subject to negotiation between the person and the deity (usually a goddess). It may be once or twice a week, or once a month, if proper worship is offered on other days. The major possessing deities in Bengali folk Hinduism are Shiva and Kali. The god Shiva usually possesses men, especially in situations of physical strain (after long dancing and drumming, during hook-swinging or other ascetic practices, or after fasting at the burning ground). The goddess Kali usually possesses women, especially in situations of emotional suffering and family conflict. She may appear in both ritual and nonritual contexts, and I encountered many more women possessed by Kali than men possessed by Shiva.

In some cases a person is understood to be possessed by more than one deity. One holy woman that I interviewed outside of Calcutta had two possessing personalities. When she spoke as Kali, she spoke in a female voice, and when she spoke as Shiva, it was in a deep male voice. In her case, the possession was associated with healing disease and with materialization of objects. She was initially called by the goddess, and possessed against her will, but she came to accept the states and chose to be possessed voluntarily. In order to evoke trance, she would sit down to meditate, visualizing a blue light. When the light turned yellow and disappeared, her normal consciousness disappeared, and the deities would take over. However, sometimes trance came spontaneously, expecially when she was confronted with a person in need of healing. She took no credit for materializations, saying that the deities acted, and she did nothing.

However, in interviews her disciples spoke of a number of miraculous acts that would occur during trance. They said that she would materialize medicine, amulets, and sacred food (*prasad*)—often food that had been offered to the goddess in a different town. She would also speak in tongues (especially in Sanskrit, a sacred and mysterious language in the folk tradition, which might be the Indian equivalent of the Pentecostal "language of the angels"); have mantras appear on her body (in both Bengali and Devanagari script), even on her nails; and the air around her would smell of flowers and incense. She would dance in trance state, red *sindur* powder would fall from her hands, and her matted hair would drip honey. She was often immune to pain in these states, and several disciples said that they saw light around her.[40]

Such possession is generally described by the persons involved as pleasurable, or like a dream state. There is often no memory of events, or only a hazy memory; as one holy woman said, "Don't ask me what happens what I get possessed, I never know—ask my disciples, they keep track of such things." Another woman who often became possessed spoke of the goddess as a "quiet darkness" that descended upon her, removing all pain. Her ordinary personality fell asleep, or watched what went on from a distance.[41]

These states are generally respected by the traditional community, and if the woman is married, she may become the wage earner of the family. Although some husbands object to their wives working in this way, others say that it is the goddess's will, and that it is necessary for the wife to do this. They then live off the wife's earnings.

3) People may became possessed for brief periods of time in order to fulfill vows. This is seen especially in vows involving austerities, such as hook-swinging. In this practice, both men and women swing from hooks inserted into the back or chest, and often are spun until the hooks are ripped from their bodies. People who had performed this ritual claimed not to feel pain, for they were possessed by Kali at the time, and she took away their pain (men were also possessed by Shiva during this ritual). Possession might also help to limit pain as people fulfill vows of offering blood, and carrying hot coals in the hands or in a pot on the head.

The practice of hook-swinging has been banned, though it is occasionally practiced today in rural areas, where the police are not informed or somehow manage to come too late to stop it. A wooden platform with a large central pillar is set up, and hooks are hung from a cross-beam. People who have dedicated themselves to swing as a vow to the god or goddess have the hooks set into their backs or chests, and they are swung around until the revolving beam stops or the hooks are pulled out of their bodies by force of the spinning. Several people interviewed who have performed this ritual said that it was not really painful, because they were possessed so quickly that they felt nothing. The deities protect their devotees from the pain of their devotions, even though that pain is often the payment for the deity's past benevolence. The ritual of carrying three burning pots of coal is still practiced, and I have seen several dancers holding them at the Durga Puja processions at Belur Math, near Calcutta. Vows may be taken in thanks for past gifts, or in hopes of future boons.

4) Possession may come involuntarily, as a result of goddess's call. Some holy women have involuntary possession trance as the prelude to a lifelong relationship with the goddess, and it may come to women as part of a prophetic call, telling them to leave their normal lives and go out to become wandering devotees. Although the call usually comes in dreams and visions, sometimes it comes by trance. In the initial call, the goddess may speak through the mouth

of a young girl or a married woman, telling her family that it is the goddess's will that the woman should leave her family and become a holy woman. I heard many accounts of women being called in this way, though very few for men—they tended more frequently to make a conscious decision to become yogis or sannyasis.

One articulate holy woman that I interviewed spoke of the self as a two-part entity; it consists of the "lower" personal self or ego, the *jiva*, and the "higher" divine self, the *atma*. When the goddess comes down, she puts the *jiva* to sleep, and her personality takes over for the *jiva* and speaks with the other people. This is ordinary possession (*bhar* or *bhor*), in which the individual self is eclipsed, and the deity's personality is superimposed.[42] This is why there is generally no memory of the events—the individual self is understood to have been elsewhere, possibly asleep or unconscious.

Consistently with the Hindu folk tradition, possession tends to have practical ends—healing, predicting the future, and asking deities for favors. It is usually found in rural environments, and is often associated with lower-caste people and especially with women. Such possession tends to come spontaneously, without any yogic training on the part of the women, so it is often dismissed by the Hindu yogic and devotional elite. Some high-caste observers note that the goddess could have done better, and chosen somebody with a better-disciplined mind and more spiritual training. *Bhar* is believed by them to be using possession in a mercenary way, toward practical ends, rather than showing pure love or devotion to the goddess.

One form of spontaneous possession is found more frequently in practitioners of tantra and bhakti yoga. This is colloquially called *bhava*, short for *devabhava* (a general term for divine state or state of unity with a deity) or *bhavavesha* (the state of being overwhelmed or possessed by *bhava*). *Bhava* combines possession and devotional love, allowing the possessed person to retain consciousness in the midst of the goddess's power and presence. It shows intense love of a deity, and a person's humility and willingness to submit to the goddess.

Informants who had experienced this state described it as a penetration of the *atma* rather than the *jiva*, the divine self rather than the human one. The goddess's presence or power enters the divine self, filling it with light and bliss during the time of the possession, bringing greater strength, concentration, and energy than the personal has normally. The ordinary personality stays in place, as does the person's memory, but the divine self is filled with the goddess's presence. Thus the person's ordinary language, ideas, and memory are present, but the motivation, energy, and underlying will belong to the goddess.

This state is often temporary, but I spoke with two holy women (in different areas of West Bengal) who had been in this state of altered *atma* for a long time. Both of these women had undergone ascetic training, one as a tantrika, and the other as a sannyasini or female renunciant, and had strong powers of concentration. They called this state *ekatmika bhava*, or unified *atma*, in which the person's *atma* becomes united with the deity's personality and essence. In one case, the holy woman had her *atma* fused with the goddess Kali, and in the other it was fused with the spirit of her guru (a devotee of Kali), who had died many years before. In both cases, this was understood to be a permanent fusion of souls, brought about by meditation and the will of the goddess or guru. Despite the notion of one shared *atma*, there was a strong component of devotional love in both women. The shared essence seemed to generate strong love in the individual personality, and a continual focus upon the deity or guru as the object of that love. Though both women were well educated and familiar with the categories of mind from Samkhya philosophy, they spoke of their own experience in the language of Vedanta: as a transformation of *jiva* and *atma*.[43] Though this state resembles possession trance in many ways, it might be better described as a form of mystical union through love, for the individual soul remains present and fully conscious. This *bhava* is a highly respected state.

5) We also see forms of possession understood as pathology. Such possession is usually involuntary, and the possessed person is not happy about the fits, lost time, and compulsion involved in these states. In rural areas, the causes for such states may be understood in traditional ways: an ill-tempered ghost, angry ancestor, or planetary spirit (*graha*) has descended upon the person, usually a woman, and often one who was possessed while in a state of impurity, such as after contact with a corpse. This spirit or ancestor has come to make demands, usually for attention and ritual worship, and will not leave until these demands are fulfilled. Such situations often call for an exorcist; tribal healers such as the *ojha* and *gunin* often perform this role. He would usually first try to please the spirit, finding out if it wanted plant or animal offerings, whether it was angry because it had been murdered or mistreated, and if it might be violent. However, the exorcist might also tie the woman down and torture her, to chase away the hostile spirit inside her. Such practices might include mantras, putting red pepper juice on her body or in her eyes, putting burning smoke in her eyes, putting chicken bones up her nose, hitting her with shoes, and other ways of making the spirit feel unwanted. One holy woman interviewed described her exorcism in great detail—her family thought she was possessed, and tried these traditional remedies.[44]

Although these actions are believed to make the spirit uncomfortable, it is the mantras of the exorcist that are believed to do the actual work of expelling the spirit. Such torture is justified because it is believed that only the spirit's feelings are affected, and that the woman herself feels no pain. According to several informants who had been exorcised, however, this belief is not accurate, and such exorcisms can be quite painful.

The psychiatrist L. P. Varma and his coauthors describe the clinical features of possession syndrome: the woman (they found that most of the possessed patients were women) senses that the goddess is coming, she sleeps on the floor and fasts or eats very little, she unties her hair and moves her head erratically. She becomes careless about her appearance and her dress, and makes odd movements. He eyes are bright, and she becomes restless and overactive; she shouts, curses, and blesses people around her. When she speaks as the god or goddess, people prostrate themselves before her, and she can treat elders as children. Sometimes the goddess may disturb sleep with nightmares, or possess the person while he or she is drowsy.[45] Psychiatry is largely an urban discipline, however, and in the rural areas we see a mixture of remedies, including folk amulets and spells to get rid of spirits, Ayurvedic and homeopathic cures, and Western "medical stores" with their strange medicines (often taken at random and without a prescription).

There are situations in which a person appears to be possessed, but may actually fit better into the Indian medical category of insanity, with an imbalance of Ayurvedic humors. Some informants told of new brides who claimed to be possessed but really had a humoral imbalance from the shock of their changed environments. In traditional situations, the young bride is taken from her parents' house before puberty and placed in the household of a groom found by parents and matchmakers, often a groom she has never met. Between often unwelcoming in-laws and an alien environment, many young girls have ended up claiming that a revered ancestor has taken them over, demanding better treatment or protesting the marriage. It is the sort of possession whose veracity is frequently doubted (such skepticism is also sometimes seen in claims of possession by the elderly). However, most people in traditional households hesitate to dismiss claims of possession, as they hesitate to dismiss dream commands; one simply never knows what a deity or ancestor may decide to do. More skeptical Bengali observers with Western training and little sympathy for folk religion often dismiss possession trance entirely, saying that the people involved are either hysterical, schizophrenic, or simulating trance states in order to gain attention or a job as a trance medium.

6) There is also the phenomenon of false possession, not as pathology but rather as strategy. In this case, the person hopes to benefit from a simulated trance, either to gain money and status by a mediator role, or to influence events by saying that a deity wants certain things to occur. Many informants spoke of such deception, but there was no clear way to distinguish between true and false trance. A false trance could be a genuinely believed trance by the possessed person, or trance as an anxiety-reaction, or a deliberately simulated trance. As observers sometimes say, "Only Shiva knows the true sadhu" (or, religious experience is difficult to gauge if you are not a god).

Possession is becoming less frequent as a practice in urban West Bengal, though it is still practiced in rural areas. Traditional rituals are dying out, and they are only seen on holidays or in distant villages. In more urban settings, skepticism has discouraged trance states as religious rituals. The Rationalists and other modern movements have encouraged doubt, and there are sometimes verbal (and physical) attacks on people while they are in states of possession.

Another aspect of folk Shaktism that is dying out is ascetic practice. Although ascetic practices used to be widespread, they have lost much of their prominence. Some people vow to perform ascetic practices and specific ritual actions to honor the goddess, in return for a specific favor. Such vows are called *manat* or *manasika*. Some of the major forms of ascetic practice promised include blood sacrifice (one's own, or sometimes that of an animal), fasting and vigils, and performance of *bratas* or mild calendrical ascetic practices, primarily by women. Common *manat* vows include going a ritual distance by falling flat on the ground the whole way (*daṇḍavat*), pilgrimage, circumambulating a temple, and carrying hot coals and smoking incense. In former days, people would make vows to do hook-swinging, branding, and other painful forms of ascetic practice, but such practices are largely illegal today. These practices were thought to elicit the goddess's mercy, and she would come down to soothe the devotee's pain, often by possessing his or her body. Sometimes people would go to dream temples to wait for a vision of the goddess—though the most famous dream temple in West Bengal, the Tarakeshwar temple, is dedicated to the god Shiva. In these cases, people stay at the temple and fast for days, praying and doing prostrations, until the god or goddess grants a dream that gives a boon or answers a question, or comes to possess the person.

The blood from animals is a frequent ritual offering, but blood from oneself, usually from the chest, is also believed to show the goddess one's reverence and dedication. Older folk stories emphasize total self-sacrifice, to the point of cutting off one's head or entering the fire, but more modern stories emphasize substitutes, such as using animal blood or a few drops of human blood, to gain the same effect. Sometimes the goddess is offered blood at ritual times, such as on Durga Puja, in her role as Durga/Kali/Chandika. It is rarely seen today, but was important in the nineteenth century. Pramanatha Bose describes the offering to Chandi to gain health in his 1894 book; as he writes, "There is scarcely a respectable house in all Bengal, the mistress of which has not at one time or the other, shed her blood, under the notion of satisfying the goddess by the operation."[46] The blood is taken from the chest with a knife, put on a bel leaf, and offered to a goddess, usually Kali.

Human blood, and human pain, have supernatural power. Some temples specialize in asceticism. At the temple of Dakshinakali at Moyda in the 24 Parganas District, there is a temple where Kali grants boons to those who perform ascetic vows. It is a sort of center for lay asceticism, begun when a stone form of Kali was found. According to a merchant interviewed:

> Everybody knows this story. The whole area here was forest, and when the land was reclaimed, many things were discovered. This

> place was identified because cows used to come over and stand in one place. People were curious about why eight or ten cows would stand in one place, and it was noticed that their milk came down there [he used an English term, "automatic milking"]. When one cowherd saw that his cows gave no milk, he asked questions and followed one cow. He saw that the cow let down milk over a stone slab. This stone was identified by him as a form of Kali. Then the priest dreamed that Dakshina Kali came and directed him to the stone. It (or she) said, "I am a stone form of Kali" (*patramurti*). He found the stone, and made a thatched room for it to shade it from the sun on the property of S. Chaudhuri.
>
> Kali is generous with her blessings. If you ask for a boon (such as curing disease or infertility) it can be fulfilled, if you perform austerities for Kali. Some people do *dandavat*, falling straight forward like a stick, circling the temple five times after a bath in the Kali pond. [One woman at the temple was performing this ritual as we spoke to thank Kali for the birth of a son; she threw herself over and over to the ground; she wore a sari with no blouse and she was covered with mud.][47]

Another ascetic practice is *dhunapore*. Practitioners take earthen pots and put burning charcoal in them, and the fire is kept lit with a bel branch. The person must hold one pot in each hand, and have one pot on his or her head, and powdered incense is thrown in to cause thick smoke. These must be held until the coals go out, and some people dance to the goddess while holding them. The ritual is usually conducted by a priest, who chants mantras. Then the pots are put into the river with prayers to Ma Kali.[48]

In the Hindu yogic and brahmanical traditions, asceticism brings power, knowledge, and purification. In the folk Shakta tradition, however, one of the major functions of asceticism is to pacify the angry goddess. Goddesses are easily angered, and prone to revenge if not propitiated. If you are already suffering, then she need not punish you—and her imagination for torture is doubtless much more creative than that of the average person. The minor pain of ascetic practices is much less than the agony of the goddess's wrath. Better the pain one knows and controls than the pain one cannot control or even imagine.

## Experiences of Folk Shaktas: Parvati Soren and Prahlad Brahmacari

One way to gain insight into folk Shaktism is to look at the lives of practitioners. Here we have two very different folk Shaktas: a tribal priestess and healer respected by the local village Hindus for her closeness to Hindu goddesses, and a male worshiper of the Old Lady or tribal form of the goddess Kali, who was an untrained priest, a devotee, and a yogic practitioner.

### *Parvati Soren*

Parvati Soren is a Santal tribal woman, who lives in a village outside of Shantiniketan in Birbhum. She is about forty years old, though she appears younger, with dark skin and a bright smile. She worships Manasa, a Hindu goddess, as well as Kali, Durga, Shiva, Krishna, and Dharma Thakur, in several thatched huts that serve as temples. The clay horses that are offerings to the god Dharma Thakur rest next to black Shiva stones covered with vermilion in one hut. She keeps a large, ornate statue of Manasa in another hut, which holds grey snakes and stands behind a large jar of vermilion (*sindur*). She proudly states that stones and statues are more established and alive than gods made only of mud, and she respects that life by giving fruit and flower offerings. She is nontraditional in that respect, as most Santalis prefer to worship the traditional Santal *bongas* or deities. However, Parvati had a special destiny. Her story is included because she received a sort of prophetic call, which resulted in her conversion from Santal tribal religion to Hindu folk Shaktism.

As a child, she saw snakes in visions and dreams, and when she traveled to other villages, snakes would lead her places. She often spoke with them, and relatives and neighbors heard her speaking to the snakes. However, they did not assume that she was mad, as often happens in such situations. The snake visions began when she was seven or eight years old, and were especially vivid whenever she had fevers.

It may be noted that Hindu religious visions may be considered as a form of upward religious mobility for Santals. Acting in the fashion of the Hindus (the high-profile majority group in India) denotes higher status than acting like a Santal (tribals generally do not consider themselves to be Hindu, and are not considered to be so by caste Hindus). Thus, a call from a Hindu deity may put a tribal person into a liminal and in some ways privileged position.

The issue of status also arises in the area of possession by deities. Other residents of Parvati's village discussed how she was often possessed, and was a female tribal healer (*ojha*). However, Parvati denied this, saying that she was only a devotee (*bhakta*) of the goddess. Possession (*bhar*) is considered to be a low-status act, whereas devotion carries high status. To avoid any conflict on sensitive issues, I did not confront her with the statements of her neighbors, but wrote her life story as she told it, here uniting stories told over several different interviews. Parvati shows elements of folk Shaktism in her shamanic-style call by means of illness, her supernatural ability at healing, and her worship and dreams of the goddess in animal form. The goddess's jealousy and the fact that she forbids worship of the Santal tribal deities (as shown by the goddess causing her illness if she disobeys or is unfaithful to her) shows an influence of folk Shakta bhakti, as well. Her story follows.

> I grew up in this village, and I married when I was eighteen years old. I did not worship Manasa when I was young. But after I got married, I got a fever and I was very ill. I could not leave my bed from the month of Chaitra to the month of Asar [four months]. I was so sick that I couldn't eat, even rice or water, because my body was in great pain.
>
> When I was in a delirious state, I would speak continually, often to the goddess Manasa. She would come to visit me, and I could see her. I could see other goddesses and gods too, especially Kali. I would worship them while I was unconscious. Sometimes when I would look out from my bed, I would see sacred stones appear. When I would get up to put cow dung on the floor, stones would appear there.[49] I asked Manasa and Kali where these stones were coming from, but they did not tell me. Urdesi [a local elder] told me that gods were staying within me, and that I should serve them. I saw Manasa most frequently, and eventually I began to worship her. My health improved, but my hair began to become matted, and looked like honeycombs hanging down.
>
> When I was sick, sometimes I would see a snake come out of its hole, and I think that perhaps the snake brought the stones. I was suffering intensely then, and my hair was all matted, and I was like a mad person. Manasa began to say, if you don't worship me, you will never get well. So I had to obey, and I began to pamper the stones. When I worshiped the stones, my fever began to subside. Now I perform pujas to Manasa, and sometimes people come to me for medicine, which I give them.
>
> Why do I worship Manasa and not the Santal gods? Manasa came to me, only the gods know why. The goddess played a game with me. She made my hair get matted and knotted, so that it was huge and heavy, like honeycombs. But I finally cut off some of them, because they were so hot. Manasa got angry at me for cutting off the matted hair and she brought back my fever. Now I am afraid to cut my hair any more.
>
> When I was a child, I used to see visions of Manasa, but then she was in the form of a snake. I saw her in visions, when my eyes were closed, and also in broad daylight. She would visit me in my dreams at night.
>
> The snake would speak to me, and say, "Worship me!" Manasa wanted me to worship her, even back then. She would speak to me

just as we are speaking now, with the same loudness. Neighbors could hear us speaking, and they would ask me who I was talking to. I would tell them that I was talking to the incense sticks. This was when I was seven or eight years old. I still see and hear the snake when I get fevers.

I am not a tribal healer/sorceress (*ojha*). I only worship gods and goddesses. People call me *deshi* (rural) and *thakur bhakta* (devotee of god), but not *ojha*. I cannot say anything about possession, it is not a thing to be spoken about. I only worship with bel leaves and flowers.

Manasa helps me to cure people, and I give them roots which make them better. I ask Manasa what to do. I say to her, "You have made me worship you—now tell me what to do." Then Manasa will appear to me, and tell me which roots to use. She tells me the names of the roots, and then I go and find them and give them to the people. I give them in her name, but I don't chant any mantras over them. If a brahmin priest had worshiped and given medicine, he would chant mantras, but for us there are no mantras. Sometimes I will say the names of various gods—Manasa, Krishna, Narayan, Kali, Durga, Dharma Deva. I do not mention the names of Santal gods, for worshiping them was forbidden by Manasa. She does not like me to worship other gods besides herself.

Sometimes I see Durga and Kali also, but I don't accept them. I tell them in the vision (darshan) that I cannot worship them. I tell them that maintaining Manasa is expensive enough for me. I say, "How can I provide for your puja with the little money that I have?" They get angry, but I say, "How can I meet the expense?" What money I had was used up when I was first very ill. I had many gold ornaments then, but now they are all gone.

Durga and Kali were angry at me for not worshiping them, and they didn't believe me, but what could I do? Sometimes they give me fevers. They argue with me at night, but I always tell them that I don't have the money. Recently I have started asking them for the money, but I will have to struggle before I see any reward. I tell them, give me something and I would accept you all, but they didn't listen.

At Manasa Puja, we sacrifice goats, ducks, and *magur* fish [a kind of fish that has no scales]. Manasa appears either in her original form [as a human being] or in snake form. I have been worshiping her for three or four years, and I do puja on Tuesday and Saturday. The day before puja I fast, and I only drink lime water. The next day I take food after the puja is over, mainly chapattis made of

> wheat flour. Manasa likes fruit offerings best, especially bananas. During the big festival in the month of Asar, everybody gives sacrifices to her, and people come and sing kirtan hymns and tell stories.
>
> Now people come here for medicines and blessings. Women come here who cannot get pregnant, or who cannot give birth to live babies, or who have menstrual problems. Men come for wealth, or to cure constipation. Yesterday several people came, but no one has come yet today.
>
> My son was born with matted hair, showing that he too was wanted by Manasa. So now he also worships her. He began at about the age of fifteen years. He will continue to worship Manasa after me.[50]

Though she has been a devotee of Manasa for about twenty years informally, she has only been a professional healer/priestess for the past four years. As a human being, she does not have the authority to demand things from the deities, but she cajoles them in an attempt to get them to fulfill her desires. She enjoys doing ritual worship and healing, though they involve fasting for several days. She is developing a reputation as a healer in the low-caste Hindu community outside of Shantiniketan, and several informants (both tribal and Hindu) in the area called her the most devoted woman that they knew, though she is illiterate, and had little education. She combines elements of folk Shaktism with bhakti toward the goddess.

### *Prahlad Chandra Brahmachari*

Prahlad Chandra Brahmachari was a devotee of the goddess Kali who was inspired by dreams and subject to trance states and visions throughout his life. He spent his later years as an informal Kali priest in Ramnathpur, West Bengal, holding large goddess celebrations that came to attract thousands of visitors. He never learned about Shaktism from a guru, nor was he trained as a priest. He was illiterate and uneducated, but was instructed by the goddess in dreams. He is included here as a modern combination of a village priest and Shakta devotee who incorporated such elements of folk Shaktism as worship of the Old Woman (Budi Ma), supernatural healing and knowledge through trance states, and prediction of the future. He combined folk Shaktism with emotional Shakta bhakti and yogic meditation. I met him long ago, when some of his devotees had brought him to Brooklyn, New York. The data here comes mostly from his devotees (several of them spoke Bengali—he spoke no English, and at that time, I spoke no Bengali myself).

Prahlad was born into a poor brahmin family in Orissa, somewhere betweem 1900 and 1910 (the date is uncertain). He was one of five brothers, none of whom ever attended school. His father would spend time in meditation, and smoke *ganja* and sing to Rama. The family lived on land that could grow rice only for four or five months during the year, and the rest of the year was a time of semistarvation for the family. Occasionally his father might act as a priest, and receive a small amount of money. Prahlad remembers his mother as always hungry, and without good clothing. The children had rickets and malnutrition, subsisting during the lean months on one meal a day of bread made from grass roots. Prahlad one day stole some green mangos from a neighbor's tree, and brought them to his mother as food for the family. When his father found out later, he was furious, and started hitting the child with an axe. Prahlad ran away bleeding, covering the wounds with grass.[51]

He ran off into the woods, and traveled at random until he passed out from weakness. He awoke to see a sannyasi before him, smiling and compassionate. The sannyasi gave him some chapattis to eat, and touched his wounds with a log of wood. After that touch, the pain disappeared. Prahlad kept that log with him throughout his life. Then the sannyasi searched for a kind of leaf with a tough stem, and grabbed Prahlad's tongue and wrote lines on it with the leaf. He etched the lines so hard that Prahlad's tongue bled, and his "senses were lost," as Prahlad went into a state of trance.

He regained consciousness at sunrise, and the sannyasi was gone. He could only see the remnants of a ritual fire (*dhuni*) and some coins. He considered his survival of his father's beating to be a new chance at life. He rode the train in rags to Howrah station, and lived in Calcutta on the banks of the Ganges for several years, sleeping on burlap sacks. He survived in a variety of ways, first by begging, and then by acting as a wandering Kali devotee with a picture of the goddess hung around his neck. He would visit shopkeepers and bless them with the goddess's image, and they would give him a few pice (less than a penny).

Sometimes he would work as a servant, a dishwasher, or a sweeper, ignoring the caste of the people for whom he worked. He was unhappy at these jobs, but at night he received instructions on yoga in his dreams from the goddess Kali. During the day, he would contemplate these dreams and fall into trance states. This made him a poor worker, and he was often condemned by his employers. However, he did save some money, and decided to visit his parents after a gap of several years. His youngest brother had died, and his father took the money to renovate the deity's room. Prahlad continued to have visits from the goddess in his dreams, and she gave him instructions in meditation and hatha yoga. She told him to leave the household again, and he did so.

He returned to Calcutta, and first took a job as a servant, and then became a wandering priest. The goddess continued her yogic dream instructions, and he perfected his yogic positons, (*asanas*), staying in one position for the whole night. Accompanying these practices were states of bliss. He had kept the sannyasi's log of wood, and the goddess told him in a dream command to chew it. He would scrape off small pieces of the log to chew, and he started having visions. He could hear verses from the sacred books of India, and see pages writtten in gold letters (though he had not learned to read). When a person stood before him, Prahlad could "read his heart," and know the person's innermost secrets. He gained an ability to tell the future, and took up a new career as an astrologer. Whereas people had looked down on him previously for being ignorant, now they would call him anxiously to tell their futures, and his predictions were often accurate.[52]

He practiced yogic exercises revealed by the goddess, seeing himself as a tool in the goddess's hands. He continued chewing splinters from the log, and he lost track of time, with "tidal waves" of Sanskrit coming out of his mouth without forethought, in the form of hymns from the Vedas and puranas. He would see visions of light before him, and lose track of his surroundings.

At the age of twenty-four years he attended a funeral ceremony (*shraddha*) in Hooghly district, where his abilities to predict the future made him a valued guest. His hosts insisted that he continue his visit at their house. He did a large number of predictions, and many people with diseases and legal problems came to speak with him. He underwent mood swings and would often enter into depressions, but he felt that he was following Kali's will. He acted briefly as priest in a small Kali temple nearby, but upset the villagers there by offering the goddess cooked food.[53] They came en masse to the man with whom Prahlad was staying, and Prahlad was forced out of the house.

He wandered out and eventually sat beneath a large tamarind tree, in an open space with bushes and thorns. The goddess came to him in a vision, and told him that he should not spend his life with householders but should create his own space. She said that he would have the barren land on which he sat. The next day, the owner of that land gave him permission to build a small ashram there, and he determined to settle there in Ramnathpur, West Bengal. He spent the next four years in meditation, often at a nearby burning ghat. He found it frightening, but went there because it was the Mother's command.

When he had extra money, he mailed it to his parents, and they sent back a demand: Prahlad must marry. His father had chosen a girl, and told his son to marry her. Prahlad returned to Orissa to argue with them, but they were unwilling to listen to him. He went into a single yogic position and trance state for four days and nights, and returned to normal consciousness with indifference toward his potential bride and his family. He explained again his unwillingness to marry, and his view of all women as only embodiments of the Divine Mother. He then left the house silently, and disappeared into the woods. He took a private vow of renunciation, and put on the clothes of a sannyasi.

He returned to Ramnathpur, and again started doing yogic practice at night. During the day, he would lead worship ceremonies for the villagers and foretell the future. Every new moon, he worshiped the goddess at the burning ghat. On one new moon in February, the villagers insisted upon following

Prahlad to witness his puja to Ratanty Kali. About fifteen people came, bearing lights and long sticks. Prahlad took a sharp knife and cut his arm, to offer his blood at the Mother's feet. The wind whistled, and a storm came up, blowing out the lights and frightening the villagers so that they ran away. Outside the burning ghat the weather was quiet, and the villagers then returned. They found the altar blown over, and Prahlad unconscious and lying in a pit. They sprinkled his face with Ganges water to awaken him. During the storm he had had a vision of the goddess as infinite light, and he had been absorbed into the Mother's spirit.[54]

About three years after his sudden exit from the wedding, another message came from his parents: Prahlad must return, because his father was dying. He went to his parents' house, and he gained his father's blessings. Among other requests, his father told him that he must not neglect the worship of the family deity Rama, even if Kali was his special goddess. After his father's death, Prahlad was grief-stricken, and roamed through south India as a beggar for a month. He then returned to Ramnathpur.

When he came back to the village, two men asked for initiation from him as their guru. He also became the guru for their families. He then initiated the wife of a sadhu, and then many other people. When he entered a house, the villagers would offer him fruits and sweets, and wash his feet.

However, the villagers would go through periods of doubt, and once they condemned Prahlad as a false sadhu, saying that they would only believe him if he could stay in his room without food or water for seven days. He went into the dark room, and knelt down before the statue of Kali, who filled the room with light. She came in visionary form and took Prahlad onto her lap, and he felt that their souls merged for seven days. The villagers watched carefully, and he did not eat, drink, or leave the room during that week, until the trance ended at the appropriate time. It was his last trial by the villagers at Ramnathpur.

He had a variety of places where he would meditate. Often he would spend time in contemplation within a hollowed-out tree. He also had a meditation hut on a raised area between some rice and betel fields. Buried under the floor of this hut were five skulls, and he would sit over these skulls. The room also had a trident and an *omkar* (Sanskrit letter OM) painted on the wall. Later there were pictures of deities, and stick figures on the wall, and a large altar with a picture of a blue Kali. He warned others that this room had great power, and that it would be dangerous for others to live there. Apparently one person stayed in this hut while Prahlad was on a pilgrimage, and this visitor died after a few days there of snakebite. It is still said that the goddess Kali speaks to people who enter the hut.

Prahlad called himself a kite in the hands of Kali, which she keeps whirling. She is infinite light, showing herself as a candle, or as the soothing morning sun, or the violent and scorching sun at noon. He followed her will in practicing yoga and meditation at Ramnathpur ashram for over fifty years. In folk Shakta and tantric style, he would offer Kali blood on new-moon night, when he would slit his wrists, and his disciples would hear him moan and gasp. He was often asked for boons by his disciples, especially for healing disease, for children (especially sons), and for predictions of the future; here they appreciated his practical folk Shaktism. He had a coconut marked with vermilion powder and a long tongue, a form of Kali whom he called Old Mother or Ancestress (Budi Ma). He performed rituals to Old Mother each day, and he chanted mantras and did his *homa* fire offering. When visitors would ask him to do things for them, he would ask Old Mother's opinion. He would put a flower on top of the coconut, and if it remained there, he would agree to the request. If it fell, he would not accede to the request.

Prahlad gained disciples outside of West Bengal in his later life, including ones from the United States. In India he had a core group of about forty disciples, though he initiated large numbers of people; he looked for various physical signs, such as a sharply pointed tongue, which was the sign of a Kali devotee. Some Western disciples came to India and brought him to Brooklyn on several occasions. He would fall into trance states frequently there, becoming the child Krishna, the goddess Kali, the flirtatious Radha, and the warrior Arjuna (among other roles), and he would perform *homa* fires and pujas. He was careful about having people touch his feet; he said that if they had bad karma, it made his feet burn. He knew no English, and refused to touch money, living the life of a renunciant Kali priest as well as he could. Though he would also worship Krishna, Rama, and Narayana (in the form of a stone), Kali was his most important goddess.

He spoke to his Bengali devotees about prayer:

> You must always pray to the Mother. It is Mother who takes you on her lap. She is Mahamaya, the great Kundalini Shakti. You have to wake Her first, and pray to Her first. That is why our worship of the Mother must come first. Because who is he who is my Father? Only the Mother knows. She will take me to him in her arms. . . . Mother is the provider; without the mother, there is no father. When the Mother takes me in her lap, she will merge me with *brahman*. Mother knows my father's name, and my caste, and she knows the path to infinity. Without Mother, one cannot find that impossible path.[55]

The goddess is reflected in human women, and also in statues:

> You must first pray to the outer mother, only then can you gain the Mother within. It is like seeing your face in mirror. You must see the outer image, so that you can know what you look like. . . . Ma is in many places. Once when I was defecating, I was digging with a

> stick, and a small statue appeared. The goddess within it spoke to me, and she said, "I am Anandamayi." I took it back and cleaned it very well, and it shone like gold. Some robbers saw it and thought it was real gold, and they took it away. I began to cry, and the Mother came and said to me, "Let the statue go. Have no fear. They have only taken my outer form. The statue which is established inside you is still there, the robbers have not been able to take it."[56]

According to his disciples and to people who knew him, he had a variety of psychic powers, especially the abilities to induce visions and to communicate at a distance. As one American informant observed, "When Baba [Prahlad] was doing his *homa* fire, I saw a vision of the goddess, Ma Kali. She was dancing in a river of blood, like a waterfall, but she was beautiful and laughing. She had blue skin and six arms, with weapons and other things in her hands. She laughed with bliss."[57]

His devotees spoke of his having a "cosmic telephone." He would put his finger on the ground, as if pressing a button, and say that he was in touch with someone at a distance.

He was said to be particularly adept at entering the dreams of his devotees. As an American informant said,

> I once had a dream of Baba before I met him, in which I was playing a guitar and singing kirtan. He appeared in a loincloth, dancing with one arm up in the air, his legs moving rapidly, stomping to the rhythm of the song. Suddenly, the scene changed, and he was staring at me, six inches from my face, his eyes focused intently on me. A strange power radiated from his eyes. I felt myself expand inwardly, and my heart was full of a bliss that spread through my body. Later I learned that one of his devotees had given him a picture of me. When I met him months later, as soon as I walked into the room his translator told me that Baba wanted to know if I remembered him, that he had visited me. He did not say this to any of the other thirty people in the room. I think he had used the picture as a means of contacting me.[58]

His American devotees were worried about his active practices:

> Once during *kirtan* of the Hare Krishna mantra, I remember that Baba became more and more agitated. During the chanting, he suddenly jumped to his feet and started dancing faster and faster, jumping and shouting. He looked as if he were losing control of his body. His oldest devotee became worried that he would have a heart attack [he was in his seventies], that his health would not sustain such activity. She jumped up and tried to quiet him, putting her arms around him and lowering him to a sitting position. She asked peo-

> ple not to encourage such-kirtan. She said that he had done such active kirtan often, in his younger days, and used it as a means of entering an altered state.[59]

One disciple, who said that she had seen Baba in a dream over a year before she met him, spoke of her love and dedication to her guru. She said that he knew things about her at a distance; he had warned her not to cover her altar at home with a cloth (she had done so before going to see him, but had not told him about it), and not to perform the *homa* fire ritual outside the ashram (which she had done). She said that when she felt his spiritual presence, it energized her body, and made her feel "out of this world," seeing a deep purple-blue light and feeling love for all living things. This occured when he would go into a special state of blessing, with one hand on her head, and one hand in the air, reaching toward the Mother.

Prahlad Chandra Brahmachari visited the West several times, gained small groups of disciples, and died in 1982. He was thrilled at sinks and bathroom showers, considering them to be a great blessing. He would act out the roles and identities of various Hindu gods and goddesses in the house in Brooklyn, apparently in possession trance. A group of disciples continues to meet and celebrate his birthday each year.

## Closing Notes

Folk and tribal Shaktism include a wide variety of goddesses, who are usually understood to be separate individuals with different likes and dislikes. Some goddesses specialize in birth and death, some in agriculture and fertility.

In West Bengal, there is a different set of major goddesses from those we see in other areas of India. For instance, Lakshmi is not the dominant goddess that she is in south India—her annual worship is on a relatively small scale. She is present in villages and worshiped in the form of rice, coins, and cowdung (sometimes she is also worshiped in tulsi plants, but more often Tulsi is a rival to her). Her iconic images are rare, mostly seen in small stores (and worshiped for wealth). Sarasvati is worshiped in books, desks, pens, inkstands, and musical instruments, but statues of her are also rare (except during her yearly puja). She tends to be worshiped by musicians and artists, and by students before tests, but she is not a dominant goddess. Parvati is rarely mentioned, unless as another name for Uma or Kali. In two years of fieldwork, I don't believe I ever heard informants refer to Sita, and there was only one mention of Draupadi (as an example of the sexual insatiability of women from northwestern India, a woman who required five husbands to satisfy her).

In the folk tradition, major pan-Indian goddesses like Kali and Durga are treated as local protective goddesses, supporting "their" village in opposition to the Kalis and Durgas of other villages. Their rocks or statues are powerful and competitive, demanding attention and threatening retribution. They work through amulets, curses, and miracles, rather than supporting political groups and causes (such as Durga's role as Bharat Mata).

Until the entrance of Western medicine and the widespread "medical stores," disease goddesses were important figures in folk Shaktism, especially Shitala the smallpox goddess, Olai Chandi the cholera goddess (who is worshiped by Bengali Muslims as Ola Bibi), and Shashthi, protector of children, especially from tetanus. Since the decline of smallpox as a threat, Sitala has been less worshiped. However, in the past ten years she has taken on a new specialization and become the AIDS goddess. She has had folk poetry (*mangalkavyas*) written to her in medieval times; today, the *patua* artist-singers write and illustrate new stories about her. One *patua* interviewed had a whole scroll illustrating the adventures of Shitala as the AIDS goddess, traveling to different countries and spreading the disease. She rode on her donkey (though she was clothed—her older statues portray her as naked) and she was shown both causing and curing AIDS. The victims were symbolized by weight loss—they were shown as thin and sticklike, being weighed on a scale, very light in one pan against the weight in the other pan. People who did not worship Shitala died miserably, while those who had faith were saved, and gained weight again. AIDS was brought by Shitala because people were neglecting her worship, and this was her divine revenge upon irreligious and secular people.[60]

Shashthi is the guardian of children, especially babies and newborn children. She was kept in the house in the form of a cow skull, bamboo churning stick, or millstone during times of danger for children. The greatest danger was childbirth, when many infants caught tetanus from the rusty sickle used to cut the umbilical cord. Although education about the dangers of this practice have reduced it, there are still many dangers to infants in West Bengal, and Shashthi is still worshiped in the villages.

There are many local nature goddesses and female ghosts worshiped in village West Bengal. Folk goddesses often took the role of guardians, and their statues were installed at village boundaries to avert disease and bad luck. They represent particular areas (such as Narayani of the Sunderbans, and Dhelai Chandi of Midnapore and Hooghly), and are tied to locales in nature. Whereas folk goddesses give blessings, ghosts give curses, and they are worshiped and propitiated to avoid bad luck. The ghosts (*bhutas* and *pretas*) who are most feared are those who died by violence, for they become angry and vengeful. Women who die during pregnancy or childbirth are also very dangerous, for they come back trying to lure children into the world of death to be with them. Frustrations that remain in the individual at the time of death are believed to continue into the afterlife. Worship gives these ghosts the love and respect that they missed during life, and helps to keep them well behaved.

Whereas ghosts who revisit the earth are consistently portrayed as angry or depressed, goddesses may be happy or sad. Folk goddesses may represent a wide area, or live within specific natural forms—in the rocks, the river, the mountain, the tree. Some informants have said that this is closer to the Vedic religion of ancient India, for they too did not have deities living in statues. The goddess dwelling in natural forms might be understood as divine immanence if seen in a more positive light, or animism or fetishism if seen in a more negative one. For Shaktas of the folk/tribal strand, the natural order is blessed by the goddess's presence, and certain places are made sacred by her presence.

Though brahmanical Hindu goddesses tend to be transcendent and impersonal, folk goddesses tend to be present in the natural world, and often involved in village problems. They support protest of unjust situations, and the willingness of followers to sacrifice for specific goals. They are part of daily life, in both its positive and negative aspects. Folk goddesses and supernatural women are not bound by the traditional dharmic morality of more brahmanical Hinduism.

In modern and urban West Bengal, the folk aspect of Shakta religion has declined. There is little public practice of asceticism in cities, though one does hear in villages of the wandering troupes called "karma eaters" who go to weddings and births and deliberately cause themselves pain (thus taking on the bad karma of the newlyweds or newborn children), and the illegal but occasionally practiced hook-swinging. Possession is also relegated to villages and small neighborhoods—and sons who are doctors and engineers are embarrassed by their mothers and grandmothers who visit women possessed by Kali. Worship of nature deities is less popular in urban areas than Vedanta philosophy and science, and hard to maintain when villagers have moved away from sacred ground for the sake of jobs and wealth.

Yet folk religion continues to be an important influence on Bengali Shaktism, and one area where we can see its influence is Shakta tantra.

# 2

# Tantric and Yogic Shaktism

## *Knowledge of the Goddess's Ways*

### Tantrikas Are Everywhere and Nowhere: The Modern Situation

I must repeat that, as a race, Bengalis are basically followers of tantra. As a fish lives in water yet does not contemplate the importance of water, so Bengalis, though living in a world of tantra, have not only forgotten its existence but also cannot understand its value.[1]

The practice of Shakta tantra has become highly politicized over the past few decades in West Bengal, and there has been a great change in the population of Shakta tantrikas. In the 1980s I was able to find many tantric practitioners, whereas in the 1990s I found very few. Practitioners that I had known had disappeared, and nobody knew where they had gone. Between the pressures of Communism (which declared the tantrikas to be economic parasites, superstitious charlatans, and malingerers), and the pressures of spreading Westernization (which caused them to be viewed as ignorant and socially useless), tantrikas were having a very hard time surviving. Informants told me of antisuperstition clubs in the elementary and high schools, which organized students to go out and harass tantrikas in their villages. Students were organized into groups to attack the tantrikas and prevent them from meditation and ritual practice. There were also political clubs, and an elementary school principal interviewed went into great detail about the actions of adult club organizers. He stated that Communist clubs began in the elementary schools, and younger children learned to harass sadhus by name-calling and throwing rocks.[2]

In the cities, party memberships (and thus many jobs) were often denied to people who showed sympathy with the religious traditions. Yet this harassment was hidden, described at length by tantrikas (especially tantric sadhus) in many cities and rural areas, but quite unknown to almost all nontantrikas interviewed.

Some Shaktas were also Communists, members of the CPIM. They could justify their Communist beliefs by saying that Communism was only an economic system, not a religious one, and the spheres were mutually exclusive. Others could say that Westernization and Communism had nothing to do with tantra, or that they would add to tantric knowledge. However, these were uneasy rationalizations. In general, shakta tantrikas were very difficult to find.

Yet informant after informant stated outright that tantrikas were everywhere: artists, musicians, anthropologists, religionists, shopkeepers, waiters, taxi drivers. Everybody knew they were everywhere, but nobody knew precisely where. Since India was such a religious country, according to some informants the most religious country in the world, it was obvious that tantric practitioners must be everywhere. Just because one couldn't find tantric sadhus didn't mean they weren't there. It just meant that the tantrikas were secretive, and wouldn't identify themselves. Indeed, according to several informants, the fact that people said that they weren't tantrikas proved that they were tantrikas, since everybody knows that a real tantrika wouldn't admit his or her identity. Any true tantrika would deny that he was a tantrika, so many of those denying any knowledge of tantra were certainly tantrikas themselves. Tantrikas also were believed to know everything, but they wouldn't tell you anything that they know, unless you deserve to know it, which you probably don't.

West Bengal was called by informants the Bengali Shakta heartland, but I found that Shakta tantrikas there were few and far between. I could tell things were different on the second trip when I only saw one sadhu in ochre robes in Calcutta after I had been living there for six months. And he was himself not quite traditional: he was barefoot and in rags, but carrying a plastic shoulder bag with an embossed, full color picture of Mickey Mouse on it. I traveled through rural areas of Birbhum, on rusted and overheated buses through groups of huts clustered around lakes, to find a respected tantrika of whom I had heard. I was told that he would be difficult to reach, as he had just moved to California.

The tantrikas that I met swore me to secrecy, asking me not to reveal that they were tantrikas, fearing local publicity that could bring out harassment. One woman was an elementary school teacher. She was part of a Shakta lineage, with tantric training, but feared losing her job if her religious practices were known. Another tantrika made his living by combining astrology, palmistry, and a variety of divination methods. He defined himself publicly, however, as a biographer of saints and sages (though he did humbly admit in conversation to being all-knowing). Another tantrika was the priest of a Kali temple, who feared that he would be bothered by his neighbors if they knew that he was a tantrika. Other tantrikas sold astrological gems, jewelry, or objects for worship.

Stalking the wild tantrika is a time-consuming affair, where each person involved is speculating upon the hidden roles and practices of the others. The tantric sadhu may be everywhere and nowhere, but the researcher must follow in his or her footsteps. The researcher must be everywhere to seek out practitioners, in cities, villages, skull seats, burning grounds, and as friends of friends of friends. But the researcher must also be nowhere, for Western assumptions can mask insight into the informant's perspective, and responding to even a sympathetic Westerner forces the informant into the role of a defender of his religion, elaborating myths and emphasizing his own status.

While it seemed that in the 1990s most serious Shakta tantric renunciants had died or left West Bengal (according to informants), there were still householder Shaktas who worshiped the goddess as part of ordinary life. They rarely had much esoteric education, however. Their tantric rituals were usually learned from their family guru (kula-guru), or from the red paperback tantric texts published by Nababharat Press. There were mass-produced posters of deities for worship, and mass-produced cassette tapes of hymns, *kirtans*, and mantras. Shakta tantric worship would often take place at night, after a long day of selling vegetables, pulling a rickshaw, or working at a bank. For some practitioners, the only distinction between tantric and brahmanical devotional worship was which mantras were used. Cassette tapes seem to have fit fairly comfortably into the space left empty by the lack of a guru; I attended tantric circles that gathered to listen to tapes of their dead gurus. Tantra was, and is, a tradition in decline in West Bengal, yet the majority of people with whom I spoke there did not appear to notice. They were still convinced that tantrikas were everywhere, their presence proved by their absence.

## What Is Bengali Shakta Tantra?

There have been many definitions of tantra in the religious literatures of India and other countries with tantric traditions. Some definitions focus on history, some on doctrines, some on goals, some on practice. For some, tantra is primarily a type of text, for others it is primarily a form of ritual practice. Some definitions follow the "out of India" model, emphasizing the importance of an Indian lineage for practices in Tibet and Japan; others focus on one particular aspect or on family resemblances between tantric traditions in various countries.[3]

There is a variety of marks and "warning signs" of tantra, though no individual definition or set of qualities seems to satisfy everybody. According to the *Varahi Tantra*, there are seven major issues that a tantric text or agama must include: the creation and destruction of the universe, the devotional worship of deities, spiritual practice (*sadhana*), ritual worship (*purashcharana*), the six magical powers (*shatkarma*), and yoga that involves visualization (*dhyana yoga*).[4] Other subjects often included in tantric texts are the origin of the gods and goddesses, various classifications of beings and worlds, the spiritual structures of the human body, human obligations or dharma according to different stages of life, the creation of statues, the uses of mantra, meditative imagery (yantra) and symbolic hand positions (mudra), the design of shrines, vows, and various forms of meditative practice.

More popular definitions tend to focus on tantra as a practice that unites discipline (yoga) and pleasure (*bhoga*), and these two terms are widely found in the tantric texts. Some affirm tantra as an intellectual discipline suited for scholars and high-caste people educated in the Indian sacred texts and in Sanskrit, while others find tantra to be a set of magical rituals practiced by low-caste people who want an excuse to gain magical power and practice illegitimate sex. Some people find in tantra a transformation of the individual's mind and self, while others find it a technique to change the world through the use of supernatural powers. Tantric ritual is generally understood by practitioners to bring the ability to heal or harm members of the community, and support or undermine organizations and governments (though Bengali tantra has never had official government sponsorship, as we see in some forms of tantra in China). As Satindranath Chattopadhyaya states in his *Tantrer katha*, "Hindu tantra is a melting pot for all [religious] ideas. It is like a pilgrimage center for all types of traditions. Vedic, Vaishnava, Shaiva and Shakta—everybody has a place in this dharma. Even the Buddhist stream can enter. Thus it becomes attractive to many."[5]

For the purposes of this book, we shall have a simple definition of tantra: the use of *sadhana* to gain the knowledge of *brahman* (*brahmajnana*), shakti, and *siddhi*. In other words, tantra is the use of ritual practice (meditation with mantra, mudra, yantra) to gain religious wisdom and access to the goddess, and also to gain supernatural power or perfection. This definition tends to privilege Bengali folk tantra, which I found to be the major type of tantra practiced, with its emphasis on experience. Whereas scholars often define tantra primarily as a text or set of texts, hidden by layers of secrecy and cryptic commentaries, practicing tantrikas tend to identify tantra as a practice, a *sadhana*, which is performed rather than analyzed. The most frequent goals stated by tantric practitioners in interviews were *shakti labh kara* (to gain Shakti or divine power), *siddhi labh kara* (gaining supernatural power), and the attainment of *brahmajnana*, the state of infinite consciousness or omniscience.

Virtually every tantrika interviewed defined tantra as a *sadhana*. When I asked about texts, they tended to answer, "Yes, there are texts that help in our practice, which are called tantras." However, the use of such texts seemed to be secondary, and for some tantrikas excluded by their lack of literacy. Bengali

Shakta tantra is marked by the use of death imagery, seeking the goddess at the cremation ground, having her symbolism bound up by the use of skulls and ash from funeral pyres, and the goddess's dance upon her prone husband, Shiva, who appears as a corpse. Although Shakta tantra in other areas of India may emphasize sexual ritual as a spiritual path, Bengali Shakta tantra emphasizes death, power, transcendence, and supernatural knowledge, gained by the tantrika who overcomes his fear and fights the ghosts of the burning ground to overcome his human limitations and become a spiritual hero.

The goal of *brahmajnana* is important for those types of Shakta tantra which understand their origin to be the Vedas and the Upanishads. For this group, which may be called classical tantra, tantric practice is understood to be the ritual application of Vedic philosophy. The goddess is symbolic of deeper states of consciousness. Classical tantra emphasizes philosophical debate and interpretation of text, cosmology, teleology, and studying the ultimate nature of the goddess and the universe. Its practitioners must have a good education in Hindu religious literature, and long study of Sanskrit texts. Although the literature of classical tantra may also involve transgressive rituals of death and sexuality, such rituals are usually understood to be only symbolic, one visualizes the activity rather than performs it, as each action is symbolic of a mystical event or quality. If the ritual is actually performed, it is only acted out in a ritual context for a brief period of time, and after that the participants return to a traditional dharmic life in which the caste and purity rules remain in effect.

The goal of attaining Shakti, who is understood as a living goddess, is seen in those forms of classical tantra strongly influenced by the Bengali Shakta devotional tradition. The tantrika of this type is also a devotee or bhakta, who loves the goddess with all of his or her heart. The practititioner uses tantric ritual to attract the goddess, to win her love and respect, and to motivate her to give blessings and a place on her lap after death (thus taking the role of her child).

In contrast to classical tantra, which seeks ultimate knowledge through the goddess, gaining supernatural power (called *siddhi* or shakti) is an important goal of the form of tantra that I call folk tantra or popular tantra. Folk tantra is more widely distributed, and more widely condemned by high-caste observers. It emphasizes direct experience of the goddess (as well as of ghosts, ancestors, yoginis, and other beings), and ways to gain supernatural powers, health, wealth, and fertility. Its rituals often involve death, and occasionally involve nontraditional sexuality; such rituals tend to be understood literally in folk tantra. Its practitioners may have little formal education; many are illiterate, and have learned about tantra by oral tradition or dream initiation. This approach follows Robert Levy's description of tantra's rebellious aspects: it shows the "individualistic, anti-Brahmanical, anti-caste aspects of Tantrism."[6] In folk tantra, the goddess is a real being, to struggle with and to love, a personal deity who chooses individuals and is willing to do favors for them.

A common term of respect for a folk tantrika is *siddha*, a practitioner who has attained a particular spiritual goal. A common term of respect for a classical tantrika is *pandit*, a scholar with a broad knowledge of his field. Sometimes these roles may be complementary, but often they are in conflict. This is because these two types of tantra have different values and goals, which we shall examine.

## Folk Tantra: Handbooks, Amulets, and Yoginis

There are many informal definitions of tantra in West Bengal, and many of them revolve around tantra's bad reputation: a tantrika is a person who hypnotizes people, who drinks alcohol and takes various drugs, who sleeps with girls who are underage and low-caste. The "tantra-mantra" man is a black magician, spending time with evil spirits and demons. However, this is tantra as observed from the outsider perspective, the popular fantasy of people who do not want tantrikas in their homes and are not interested in what they do or why they do it. As we look at the dark underbelly of tantra, we may note that what is being despised is basically folk religion: practices that cure disease or induce it, that bring rain or drought, or fertility or infertility. Folk tantrikas are believed to speak with ancestors and ghosts, deal with the forces of good and bad luck, avert earthquakes and invasions, and seek control over an unpredictable world. They are often thought to be addicted to alcohol and drugs. As one Kali priest stated, "I have sat upon the five skulls, and called down the goddess and spirits, I have practised *tantra sadhana*. But I am not a tantrika. A tantrika is a person who drinks wine, and who takes much hashish and opium. I do not drink and take drugs, therefore I am not a tantrika."[7]

Folk (or *laukika* or *deshi*) tantra is popular religion. The practitioner is said to use forbidden rituals and secret mantras to gain wealth, social status, abilities at public speaking and hypnosis, the admiration of women (supernatural and otherwise), and the use of various nonphysical entities as servants. This type of tantra generates the sensationalized image of tantrikas in West Bengal, who are widely regarded as unwashed eccentrics who spend time at the burning grounds, eat human flesh, seduce girls (lately young blond Westerners rather than low-caste village girls), and smoke hashish. Such people (usually men) are feared rather than respected, and are understood to be dangerous and possibly insane in the popular view. And indeed, after spending time away from society, there are some tantrikas who do violate Indian social etiquette in some rather extreme ways. Folk tantra is a path that may eventually lead to mystical union with the goddess, but it focuses in the present upon supernatural powers (*siddhis*) and nontraditional behavior. It largely follows oral tradition, and its relatively few texts are usually written in the vernacular languages.

Folk tantra is the best-known sort of tantra in popular culture, and its practitioners are better known than its texts. As Satindramohan Chattopadhyaya states in *Tantrer katha*, "Tantra is a type of literature, which inspires people to worship various gods and goddesses, or achieve supernatural power. [But] the image of tantra in Bengali society has come to be associated with the sannyasi at the burning ground, the practice of forbidden acts (*panchamakara*) and the magical actions which control others (*shatkarma*)."[8]

One Bengali academic informant trained in the West described his youth in a small village in Birbhum. His uncle, whom he referred to as Uncle Tantrika, was the dreaded occasional visitor to his family household (a village joint family). Uncle Tantrika was his mother's elder brother, who had left home at an early age to travel and perform ritual. He was often unwashed, with wild eyes. Uncle Tantrika would rarely speak, preferring to growl, and at night he would go out in the woods and scream horribly, making inhuman noises and frightening the household and village. Nobody knew why he was screaming, and nobody wanted to ask. Sometimes he would sit alone, mumbling and making gestures. He would disappear as suddenly as he came. It was a great relief to the household when he would end his visits.[9]

Folk or popular tantra is in some ways an easier topic for field research than classical or scholastic tantra, because everybody has an opinion about it. Most of these opinions are negative, of course, placing the tantrika in the role of the "bogeyman" who might steal children away if they are bad, and who is an outsider in every sense. I did meet informants whose parents had threatened them when they acted badly, saying that the tantrikas would come and eat them. Still, tantrikas are understood to have secret knowledge, to be able to predict the future and find lost objects, and discover who is harming a person and whether a marriage will be successful. They are mediators between the human world and the world of gods and goddesses (especially Kali, Tara, and Shiva), as well as the world of ghosts and spirits, who could manipulate karma and influence luck, cure snakebite and incurable diseases, but who could also curse those with whom they were angry. A person would resort to a tantrika only if it were truly necessary; unfortunately for many, it was often necessary.

Shakta tantric sadhus tend to be loners; most of those whom I have interviewed kept to themselves, did not know people in nearby villages, and could not suggest anybody else who they thought might have had religious experiences or might be doing serious practice. I do not believe that they were trying to mislead me or deliberately hide fellow Shaktas. I think that they simply never spoke to each other. This is partly because their practices are secret, and their mantras would lose power if they were discussed in casual conversation; and partly because tantric group worship of the goddess is rare, and usually seen only in Shakta temples with Vaishnava influence.

Some tantrikas whom I have encountered were deliberately eccentric, carrying human skulls and red tridents, narrating and acting out life-and-death adventures with the goddess, smoking endless numbers of small cigarettes and lounging around cremation grounds. The goddess shrines (*shakti pithas*) have no official organization that would bind them together, and often priests at one shrine will insult the priests and hangers-on at other ones; priests at virtually all shrines criticized the shrine at Tarapitha, which has gained some notoriety based on accusations of illicit drugs and sexuality. There is often little focus on gurus. Even Shaktas who have been initiated by gurus often do not know of the guru's history, or whereabouts, or whether the guru has ever initiated others. And despite the instructions to follow a guru in almost every tantric text, most of the Shakta tantrikas interviewed had no guru. They claim to have been initiated directly by Kali in a dream, or they had visions of the goddess that counted as initiation, a sort of "prophetic call" that drew them into the field. Sometimes they picked up tantric handbooks to look at, and started performing the rituals on their own. Some had tantric relatives, and their knowledge of tantra was "in the blood." Others stated that Shakti as universal energy is obviously there in the body already, so there is no need of formality or ritual contact with a guru. One only needs to realize a truth that is clearly present.

Folk tantra differs from traditional religious practice in India in its attitude toward authority, and especially toward the religious books (shastras) that control and define Hindu religiosity. Many folk tantrikas call themselves *ashastriya*, nonshastric or opposed to the traditional sacred books of Hinduism. They do not accept the usual bases of truth in Hindu philosophy, preferring experience to tradition or authority, and they deny the need for intellectual knowledge. Some texts make reference to this approach; as the famous nineteenth-century shakta tantrika Shivachandra Vidyarnava Bhattacharya wrote, tantra and text (shastra) are opposed:

> Relying on the strength of its own arms, Tantra does not recognize the efficacy of anything, call it reasoning or evidence, judgment or inference. All Śāstras, in making ordinances in conformity with Tantra, have guarded their individual honour. For as it would matter little to the sea if all the waves were to become cross and to turn their currents away from it, so it would matter little to the Tantra even if all other Śāstras were to go against it.
>
> You may rush towards a lion with marshalled herds of furious elephants, but at the moment the resounding roar is heard of the maned King of Beasts, subduing even the loudest voices, then everyone will fly, one knows not whither. Similarly, place all Śāstras on one side and Tantra on the other, and then you will see that the directly perceptible war cry of [the] Mantras, resounding like the solemn booming of thunderclouds, will make them senseless, and disperse and drive them away to places of which there is no knowing.[10]

In other words, tantras and brahmanical books are opposed to each other—and when the tantras speak, the traditional Hindu texts are frightened and run away in fear.

In folk tantra, the statements about tantra being open to everybody, even women and low-caste people, are taken quite seriously. Anybody who wants to practice and who can find a guru or a ritual handbook is acceptable. The tantric deities are much like folk deities in that they are neither good nor evil, high-caste nor low, spiritual nor material—they are simply powerful. As such, they can be coerced into helping any practitioner by the successful use of meditation and ritual.

The sensationalized image of the tantrika who smokes hashish and drinks alcohol and violates social norms is widespread. This is because the brahmanical, Veda-based, classical style of shakta tantra, in Bengal often called the Kali-kula or tradition of Kali worship, has almost died out as a practice. It has been under siege by communist ideology and Western science, both of which have redefined the nature of knowledge. Informants who used to know Kali-kula practitioners say that these teachers have died and taken their knowledge with them, both because they were persecuted and because no good students had come to them to carry on the tradition. But folk tantrikas still survive, advertising their abilities at astrology and the creation of astrological rings (certain jewels attract the energies of various planets), palmistry, alternative healing, spells for accomplishing various goals, and dealing with family problems. Some have storefronts, with lines of unhappy-looking customers waiting.

One group of tantrikas with a folk dimension which has recently organized itself in a more classical style is the Bangiya Tantrik Samaj (Bengali Tantric Society) of Calcutta, which describes itself in its handbook as a forum for research and development in the field of tantra. Such an institutionalizing of tantric practice is unusual. Tantra is described by this group as a form of science (more specifically, a "divine science") whose authenticity can be proved by experimental methods. It is their stated intent to encourage tantric research, generate tantric consultants, create places to maintain elderly and ill yogis and tantrikas, grant degrees and honorary titles, organize research libraries with "authentic books," and distinguish true tantric practices from false ones. They also intend to create committees, cultural programs, films, trusts, yogic and tantric ashrams, centers for tantric practice, organizations for parapsychological research, and yogic hospitals and colleges. Their president (who identifies himself as a *tantrikacharya* and astrologer) emphasizes the importance of astrology and other forms of divination. In their requirements for membership, there is no inquiry about Vedic knowledge or background, though both general education and eagerness to learn are taken into account.[11] Thus far, they have begun a one-year correspondence course in tantra.

Folk or popular tantra has generated a good deal of hostility from scholars, both Eastern and Western. Western scholars at the turn of the century who first encountered tantra tended to idealize ethical Christianity, and Indian religions were acceptable insofar as they resembled it. If a religion did not focus upon a deity who represented the good, and have an ethical code based on love, the religion was dismissed as primitive. It was easy to dismiss folk tantra, for it accepted the goals of pleasure and power as part of the spiritual path, and did not have a clearly marked ethical code. It tended toward a literal interpretation of text and ritual, and did not insist on attaining ultimate spiritual knowledge as the religious goal. The tolerance for what the Victorians viewed as immoral actions, and goals that they saw as selfish rather than self-sacrificing, caused a flurry of horrified descriptions of tantra as composed of "vile, bestial, primitive superstitions."

Yet Indian writers on the whole were no more sympathetic—and some of those least sympathetic to folk tantrikas were classical tantrikas. Especially among those Indians influenced by Western education, there was a glorification of Veda and Vedanta, of India's great philosophical heritage, which was thought to resemble Western philosophy and Christianity in many ways. Along with this came a rejection of village religion, the worship of idols and use of animal sacrifices, which were considered to be superstitious beliefs of the illiterate. Vedantins and members of the Brahmo Samaj both sought to free Hinduism of its false encrustations of primitive belief and ritual, to reveal its true, pure, ideal center. True tantra was like true Vedanta, full of accretions believed by the ignorant, but also full of the wisdom of *brahman* if these ignorant practitioners and their beliefs could be exorcised from the true religion. Tantra had to be separated out from tribal religion and "primitive superstition," and defined instead as philosophy.

Many tantric writers proceeded to do just this, the most famous of whom is Sir John Woodroffe, who wrote under the name of Arthur Avalon. This approach, however, leaves out a large amount of tantric ritual, especially rituals that show tribal and folk roots. The goal of supernatural powers is also condemned, along with such folk goals as a good marriage and luck in life.

Despite the efforts of the classicists, it can be difficult to make an absolute separation between tantric and folk practice, for there are rituals in tantra *sadhana* that are very similar to folk and tribal practices. These rituals are not generally visible in the popular village festivals and daily ceremonies, but rather in the training of the tribal religious specialists, the *ojha* or *gunin*. As an example, we may look at the rituals of the tribal healer in a particular Bhumij village, Bhumij Dhan Sol, in West Bengal.

In this village, the *gunin* or tribal shaman-magician is taught by apprenticeship to be a healer, using mantras and herbs. He is a master of ghosts, spirits, and deities, and he can make amulets to counteract evil influences. He is initiated into mantras by his teacher, an experienced *gunin*, who gives him a practical demonstration of their power by invoking gods and spirits. The apprentice must then practice the mantras and visualizations given by his teacher, preferably at a burning ground or alone in the woods. His final test should occur on a Tuesday or a Saturday, during which he must enter the burning ground, sit on a pyre, and chant mantras to appease and enlist the help of spirits. If he is full of power, the bamboo poles used for holding down and moving burning corpses will stand up at attention. If he is frightened or nervous, he will die. The brave *gunin* will dominate the spirits by the use of an empowered human bone (especially the upper arm bone). The apprentice sits on the pyre, and offers parched grain to ghosts. He draws down a spirit, gets an agreement that it will assist him, and digs up the ground and cuts away bone from what remains of the corpse. This bone controls the spirits, and lets the *gunin* know when a person is possessed. He may also learn some forms of divination, by blowing air, water, dust, salt, mustard seeds, and other substances, and reading the future based on the patterns these substances take.[12] He then becomes the master of these spirits.

Such rituals are not generally part of classical or scholastic tantra, but they are widely seen in folk tantra. In this tribal ritual, we see the sitting and meditating at the burning ground, the conquest of spirits, initiation by mantras from a guru, the use of bones, and prediction of the future. We also see the drama of the burning ground, the young initiate risking madness and death for the sake of his ritual practice, the use of parched grain to pacify spirits, and rituals on Tuesday and Saturday, which are days sacred to Kali, the most powerful tantric goddess. The initiation of a Bhumij *gunin* is a tribal ritual with many tantric elements.

This description of Bengali initiation is recent, but there are similar descriptions by observers writing over fifty years ago. In his article, in 1949, W. J. Culshaw discusses the training of *ojha*s among the Santal tribal people. He describes the *ojha* course as continuing from May to October, during which time the disciples come to the house of the teacher each evening until they are initiated. Some wear special outfits, such as women's dress. The Santal *ojha* draws blood from his arm, chest, or thigh, and uses it for magical purposes. He mixes it with sun-dried rice, and scatters it on the ground to propitiate the gods or *bongas*. Once they have been propitiated, the *ojha* gains control over them.[13] In this case, we see the use of blood and the conquest of spirits, both aspects of folk tantra.

Sometimes the rituals of folk tantra are written down in handbooks. Folk tantrikas may use certain tantras as instruction manuals (such as the *Kali Tantra* and the *Mundamala Tantra*), and there are low-priced popular handbooks (often called *gutikas* or *paddhatis*) sold at Kalighat temple and other sacred sites that give instructions in ritual and magical skills. Occasionally tantrikas may have older palm-leaf manuscripts, and use these as ritual texts (in rural areas, where books are rare, such manuscripts are sometimes ritually worshiped—I saw a couple offering lights to one). However, folk tantra is often an oral tradition, where wandering tantrikas support themselves by finding some disciples willing to learn a few skills, and they may have some short-term apprenticeships. Such tantrikas may also have skills as *ojhas* and *gunins*, healers who travel through rural villages with no paved roads or electricity, and who heal snakebite and disease through ritual actions and calling on the goddess's power.

The tantras that are used by folk tantrikas tend to be those which focus upon the goals of folk religion: health, wealth, fertility, and supernatural powers. Sometimes these texts are in the form of locally available ritual handbooks, such as the *Dakini Tantra*. These handbooks are rarely examined by scholars or accepted as legitimate tantras. Folk tantrikas may also use officially recognized tantric texts that have a large magical component.

The *Dakini Tantra* is a small handbook available at several of the Bengali Shakta sacred sites (*shakta pithas*) and at Shakta temples such as the Kalighat Temple. It is a good example of a folk tantra. It is the sort of book used by local tantric healers who had an initiation but not much else from their gurus (or who never had any initiation, or who had dream initiations). It is written in Bengali, though it includes many Sanskrit mantras among its chants, and it is about 180 pages long. The cover, printed in color, shows a tantrika in meditation. His matted hair is partly twisted into a bun atop his head, and he wears rudraksha beads around his neck, upper arms, and wrists, as well as a necklace of bone. His loincloth is a tiger skin, and he sits at the foot of a tree upon what appears to be a leopard skin. He sits behind five human skulls, and there are other skulls and bones near his fire. Behind him is a blue Kali with four arms, a necklace of heads, a belt of hands, and a golden crown with jewels. She looks at him affectionately, almost patting him on the head. It appears that she was drawn to him by his meditation, and her compassionate look toward him may indicate that she is willing to grant him a boon. The book is printed entirely in red letters, and begins with a salute to the gods and sages, and a meditation upon the goddess Jayadurga.

The book is written by Tantrik Acharya Shri Bhairava Shastri, Siddha Bhairava (or Respected Tantric Practitioner, Ascetic and Pandit wise in scriptural knowledge, who has also gained supernatural powers). He is subtitled as the author of many tantric writings.[14] On the whole, tantrikas are not remarkable for their modesty.

The first chapter gives general instructions upon a variety of useful skills: attracting other people, enchanting them, dealing with bad luck, making people sleepy, turning black hair white (and vice versa). The second chapter is on medical magic, specifically dealing with mantras to cure snakebite. It is a very long chapter, and includes mantras to heal snake bites, scorpion bites, rat bites, dog bites, spider bites, tiger and bear bites, accidental ingestion of datura and other poisonous plants, and a host of all-purpose remedies. There are specific mantras for specific types of snakes.

The third chapter deals with ghosts, spirits and witches (*bhutas*, *pretas*, and *dakinis*), and gives mantras with which to see and control them. There are chants for exorcism, telling the spirits to return to the burning ground, and uses of spices to chase them away. There are chants to get rid of the "witches' glance" (the evil eye or *dainir drishti*), and cure spirit possession in children. A variety of deities are invoked against the spirits, including the goddesses Chandi, Chamunda, and Kamakhya Ma (the goddess of Kamakhya in Assam), and the gods Narasimha, Ramachandra, and Mahadeva. The Narasimha mantras invoke the avatar of Vishnu (though the book does not mention the stanza from Jayadeva that is most widely used by Vaishnavas and others to conquer fear). Several of the exorcism chants have a rhythmic invocation of deities; after the spirit is ordered to leave, the exorcist says, "At whose order? At Chandi's order. At whose order? At Kamakhya Ma's order." The fact that it is the invoked deity who orders the spirit out is emphasized.

The fourth chapter describes cures and mantras for fevers, cholera, bleeding, spasms, and other ailments. Some also suggest herbal remedies or foods to eat. The fifth chapter gives mantras to bring luck and keep away evil. They keep away spirits and generate courage, bring power and perfection (*siddhi*), and protect onself and one's household.

The sixth chapter, entitled "Tantric Ritual Practice" (*tantrik sadhana*), gives meditations, visualizations, and offerings to deities that are more complex than those in previous chapters. It includes invocations to nature goddesses (yakshinis) associated with specific gifts (happiness, wealth, sensuality, sons, victory, political power). It also invokes yoginis, such as Surasundari, Kameshvari, and Padmini. The yoginis are understood as supernatural women rather than human female practitioners. These and other goddesses are given a variety of offerings, including animal sacrifice, and addressed with tantric mantras. These mantras are to be chanted one thousand or more times to gain the blessings of the goddesses. There are also practices to gain *vak siddhi*, so that whatever the practitioner says comes true, and book *siddhi* (in which a yakshini comes down in response to ten thousand mantras, and allows the practitioner to spontaneously and easily master all forms of knowledge).[15]

Other practices also involve semigoddesses. In the dancing-girl meditation,[16] the tantrika's mantras bring down a celestial dancing girl to appear in the form of the tantric practitioner's wife. She gives him gold every morning to cover his expenses, and blesses his life. There are also mantras for shapeshifting, and the tantrika may change his form into that of a dog, horse, cat, or other creature. There are such esoteric practices as *preta sadhana* (how to get a ghost under your command) and *chetika sadhana*, which is basically how to get a maid, preferably one of supernatural background (*bhuta*, yaksini, or *nagkanya*). Introductory magical spells of the notorious "black magic" (*shatkarma*) rituals are also included. The seventh chapter, on a more positive note, gives information on creating peace and health, protecting for harm, warding off trouble from one's home, bringing happiness and romance, and generating wealth and rice.

The next four chapters detail the *shatkarma* rituals. Traditionally, the *krishna shatkarma* or black magic rituals teach the tantrika how to control both other people and the physical world. *Marana* teaches how to destroy an unwanted person or object, *ucchatana* shows how to generate passion in others, *vasikarana* teaches control of others through telepathy or hypnosis. *Stambhana* allows for control of earthquakes and storms, as well as making people powerless, and *vidveshana* creates hatred between people. The last type, however, is *svastayana*, which gives blessings to individuals and families, and peace, wealth, and happiness. It also lets the person overcome difficult astrological situations, and gives freedom from danger and disease.

The eighth chapter focuses on varieties of hypnosis (*vasikarana*), and the ninth chapter gives more detailed instructions for creating paralysis or immobility in persons and events. The tenth chapter gives instructions on bringing and ending disease, madness, and fights, and the eleventh and twelfth chapters focus on various forms of destructive behavior (drying up milk and destroying oil and grain, as well as getting rid of lice and unwanted hair).

The thirteenth chapter covers binding and loosening in general, and the fourteenth chapter is a sort of appendix, giving instructions in a variety of areas: the corpse ritual (*shava-sadhana*, in which yoginis and *dakini*s are invoked), sacrificial offerings, controlling kings, attracting men and women, and other such topics.

We can see the range of topics covered in the *Dakini Tantra*, ranging from hypnosis and healing to invocation of deities and gaining supernatural powers. There are almost no references to other texts, and few brahmanical Hindu practices (except for mantra, which is quite prominent) are described. It is typical of the handbooks available for aspiring folk tantrikas, with very little theology and a great emphasis on ritual.

One widespread practice of folk tantra involves the making of amulets. Many wandering folk tantrikas have amulet making (sometimes along with fortune-telling) as their major way of making a living. These amulets serve a variety of functions: they bring luck, cure disease, attract or avert planetary influences, bring the blessings of deities, and help the wearer to attain his or her desires. These may be sold premade by wandering tantrikas and sadhus, or put together locally especially for the client. The amulet is usually made of metal (especially copper), and engraved with lines or figures. It may have the names of deities (especially Kali, Shiva, or Ganesha) or have symbolic footprints of gods. Some have mantras engraved, or pictures of human figures. Most are like lockets, and open up to show a space in which some writing or healing object may be placed. Various plant roots are most commonly used, though flowers and leaves may be found. Iron is a traditional protection against evil spirits, and sometimes iron nails or pieces of old tools may be used. Food or other items offered to gods may also be used, and renunciants and yogis may donate pieces of their nails, hair, or loincloth, or wood from their ritual fires. There may be dust from shrines or ash from corpses, or various bits of dead animals.

Sometimes the amulet is created as a result of a dream, and there are many stories of such dream amulets. In one case, a Calcutta student was sent home on a medical leave because of a hernia, and told his parents of a dream in which the family goddess Kali appeared to him and told him what would cure him. He pulled up a plant growing near the Kali temple and hung it around his neck. He was fully cured by it.[17] In another case, a woman suffering from hysteria dreamed of a root that would cure her, and had her husband dig it up. She placed the root in an amulet on her left arm and was cured.[18]

The amulet is usually worn on the upper part of the body, around the neck or on the arm. It is often first put on at a special time (full moon, new moon, after a bath), before the image of a god or goddess whose aid is invoked. The person must follow detailed purity rules, for the amulet's power will leave after contact with impure objects and situations. Unless the contents of the amulet are revealed in a dream, they are normally kept secret.

Such amulets and mantras may give the wearer great powers. According to the *Kalika Purana* (chapter 56), the supernatural powers given by the Mahamaya *kavacha* (an amulet dedicated to the goddess Mahamaya) include the ability to repel diseases, be protected in battle, be safe from sorrow and from wild animals and traitors, live one hundred years, be immune from danger by fire and water, control other species (such as ghosts and demons), and have no obstacles to success. Amulets may give the goals of classical tantra: the person may become virtuous and a scholar, a poetic genius who can compose thousands of verses, and he or she can gain union with the goddess. Amulets may also allow a person to have success in the eight traditional ordeals or *ashtapariksha*: the ordeal of finding a hidden ring; the ordeal of walking seven times over a hot fire while covered with cotton; the ordeal of being thrown into water bound hand and foot (and being able to escape); the ordeal of remaining suspended in the air without any support; the ordeal of taking a ring out of a jar full of boiling ghee; the ordeal or taking the jewel from the hood of a snake; the ordeal of holding red-hot iron; and the ordeal of becoming light as a piece of gold while being weighed.[19]

Some amulets show more Sanskritic influence, and involve long ritual invocations on the part of the person who is making the amulet. Upendrakumar Das, in his *Bharatiya Shakti-sadhana*, cites a long prayer from the *Rudrayamala* used in the making of an amulet; such prayers may be chanted when the metal amulet box is filled, and may also be written on a piece of bark or paper and placed inside the box. It is reproduced here (in slightly condensed form):

Maheshvari in the form of Brahma, please save my head
Maheshvari in the form of a *bija* (mantra), save my forehead
Maheshvari in modest form, save my face
Tarini Shakti, save my heart
Goddess who gives the fruits of salvation, save my body
Goddess who banishes fear, save my cheeks
Lambodari, female Ganesha, save my shoulders
Bearer of the tiger skin, save me from everything
Harapriya, beloved of Shiva, save my genitals
Goddess who protects from evil spirits, save my knees . . .
Goddess with power over bows and arrows, save me in difficulty
Goddess of snakes help me in everything
Goddess with the severed head, save me in forests
Snake goddess, help me if I fall into hell . . .
[the text then comments]
Whether in a pure or impure state, anybody can chant [the mantras of] this amulet. He [who wears it] becomes wise in all forms of religious literature, can hypnotize all people, is victorious in war, gets sons and wealth in life. His enemies become his slaves, he is loved by all, and can control the time of his death.[20]

This prayer invokes a whole series of major and minor goddesses. The worship of minor goddesses (including yoginis and female spirits) is important, for folk tantra tends to emphasize regional goddesses rather than the classical all-powerful ones.

Yoginis have been important figures at certain periods in tantric history, and are still important goddesses in folk tantra. Sometimes yoginis are understood to be the supernatural attendants of more powerful goddesses, and sometimes they are independent goddesses, who can give favors to those who worship them. The term *yogini* may also refer to human female practitioners of yoga, to female tantrikas of the *kaula marga* tantric tradition who act as consorts in chakra rituals, and to dangerous sorceresses who were believed to turn men into animals (often by tying a thread around the victim's neck) and bring the dead back to life. Yoginis were also thought to fly through the air, and meet at burning grounds to form a circle (*yoginichakra*) to offer sacrifices to Shiva Bhairava. They were said to be able to transform themselves into birds in order to cross rivers.

According to Vidya Dehejia, although yoginis may have begun as regional goddesses, tantrism gave them new forms and importance as goddesses who could give magical powers to their worshipers.[21] In both folk religion and tantra, yoginis are depicted as beautiful women with large breasts and hips and narrow waists, with heavy jewelry and flower garlands. Sometimes they are shown with animal heads, such as the yogini sculptures from Lokhari, which show yoginis with rabbit, snake, lion, and buffalo heads. The *Kaulajnana-nirnaya* describes yoginis wandering the earth in the forms of the dove, vulture, swan, owl, crane, peacock, jackal, goat, cat, tiger, elephant, snake, and other forms.[22] The *Skanda Purana* gives a list of sixty-four yoginis, of which nearly half have bird or animal heads.[23] At other times, they are given human bodies but have animal vehicles or mounts that they ride, and these are often carved at their feet in statuary. Yoginis are said to live in the sky, on earth, in water, and in space, and have been appointed by Shiva to protect the tantric kula tradition. Like Pargana Bonga in the midst of the circle of Santal witches, Shiva Bhairava is at the center of the circle of the yoginis, and he is called the beloved of the women.

In many tantric texts, yoginis are protectors of those following the Kaula path, who bless those who support the Kaula tantrikas, and curse and destroy those who oppose them.[24] Yoginis are often anti-Brahmanical, and they punish those who make caste distinctions within the *kula chakra*.[25] They motivate practice when they punish those who are able to perform rituals (people who are initiated) but do not practice them.[26] Yoginis are also protectors of women, and they are angered if a tantrika insults a woman. Chanting the names of the yoginis is said to heal all diseases, remove all obstacles, cure children's diseases, remove labor pain, and give victory in the royal court and in legal battles.[27]

The tantric practitioner may do ritual worship specifically to the yoginis, especially using the Karnapishachi mantra. Yogini *sadhana* is usually performed in springtime, in distant and sacred areas. The yogini appears in three roles (*bhavas*): as protector, as princess, as giver of boons. All of these are able to fulfill the goals of folk tantra. In the protective *matribhava*, the yogini appears as a mother who looks after her son. In the *bhaginibhava* she is a princess or niece, who can give the gifts of royal power and knowledge. In the *bharjabhava*, she is the regional goddess Bharjar, who gives food and wealth. The major yoginis to whom the tantric sadhu prays are Surasundari, Manohara, Kameshvari, Ratisundari, Kanakavati, Padmini, and Natani.[28] Surasundari is said to be the most important of the yoginis, and Kubera is said to have become the lord of wealth by worshiping her. Her face is like the full moon, round and fair; she is voluptuous and wears many beautiful forms of dress. If a dedicated tantrika meditates upon her for a month and gives her special worship on the last day of the month, she will then appear before the tantrika at midnight.[29] The *Tantrasara* gives instructions for visualizing the eight major yoginis; all are attractive, though some have fierce faces and dark complexions.[30]

Sometimes the roles of the yoginis are simply called mother, sister, and wife moods. If the yogini is worshiped as a mother, she gives wealth and kingship. If she is worshiped as a sister, she takes care of the tantrika like a brother and gives gifts that including divine maidens (future consorts for him).

If she is worshiped as a wife, she gives him knowledge of past, present, and future, and she gives him the power to travel throughout the three worlds. In this role or *bhava*, he must stay only with her and avoid involvement with other women.[31] If he is unfaithful to her, she may leave him or take revenge upon him.

There is some overlap in the worship of yoginis and yakshinis. In his article on esoteric consort worship, Bholanath Bhattacharya equates yoginis with yakshinis, though yakshinis are usually nature spirits whereas yoginis are supernatural women. Bhattacharya describes of the practice of yakshini worship among the esoteric practitioners that he has met. The yakshinis Surasundari, Pishachi, Subhaga, and Bhutini were invoked with mantras for wealth and worldly blessings, whereas Ratisundari, Kameshvari, Ratipriya, and Padmini were evoked with mantras, visualizations, and images. Some of the yakshinis are believed believed to be very jealous, and should not be invoked by married practitioners. Ratisundari, Padmini, Subhaga, and Kameshvari demand total devotion, and the yakshini is said in some cases to become the supernatural wife of the practitioner. She will take care of him in this world and also in the next one—as long as he is faithful to her.[32] According to folk tradition, people who have attained perfection in meditating on yakshinis (*yakshini siddhi*) can see the yakshinis like shadowy images, moving on walls or in the room, like a black shadow. The shadow will shake or move quickly as a warning in times of danger, and when no longer wanted it will fade away and the shadow-form will disappear.

The Kaula *Uddisa Tantra* has a chapter entitled "Yakshini sadhana" which states that yakshinis may be approached as sister, mother, daughter, or wife. Yakshinis are shape-shifters, and can approach the practitioner in various forms. To worship the Yakshini as wife, a couch should be strewn with flowers for her.[33] In another Kaula text, the *Yogini Sadhana Prayoga*, the yogini may be worshiped as mother, sister, or wife; as wife, she can make the practitioner a great king. These texts are apparently derived from the *Bhutadamara Tantra*, whose chapter on "Yogini sadhana" gives the major yoginis as Surasundari, Kanakavati, Ratipriya, Padmini, Kanakeshvari, Mahanati, Sarvamanohari, and Anuragini.[34]

Often these yoginis are worshiped in trees sacred to tantric tradition, called kula trees. There are varying lists as to which trees are kula trees, but they usually include the wood-apple, mango, rudraksha, tamarind, asvattha, and nim trees. As the *Shaktanandatarangini* states, "The *kula yoginis* always dwell in all these kula trees. No one should sleep under the kula trees nor injure them."[35] The *Kularnava Tantra* states that people should never eat food from the leaves of the kula trees, and that they should be worshiped, for the kula yoginis live in them. People should never sleep under them or disturb them or hurt them, and always salute them.[36]

Yoginis may act as protectors or destroyers. The missionary William Ward described worship of the yoginis in order to destroy enemies: "This worship is addressed to the yoginēēs, or other inferior deities, before a female image made of cow-dung, or a pan of water, on a Tuesday or Saturday, at the darkest hour of the night. Many incantations are repeated, and some bloody sacrifices offered. The worshiper expects, that by the power of these incantations his enemy will be seized with some dreadful disease, and will thus perish by the unseen hand of the yoginēēs."[37]

This shows the darker side of the yoginis, in which they are equated to the *dakinis*. In Hindu lore the *dakinis* are witches, rather than the spiritual guides and sky-walkers of Tibetan Buddhism. One example, the description of Queen Kuvalayavati in the *Kathasaritsagara*, shows a queen who became a *dakini* in her childhood. It is a very tribal description, and could have come directly from a Santal storyteller. The king returns home unexpectedly, and finds his wife naked in the midst of a bloody circle, with her hair standing on end, chanting mantras. She admits that she is a *dakini*, and gained her power to fly in the air by eating human flesh. She was initiated as a girl into the group (which she chose to do because she wanted supernatural powers, especially the ability to fly) by the chief *dakini*, Kalaratri (or Black Night). As she describes the ritual:

> She made me take off my clothes and perform, standing in a circle (mandala) a horrible ceremony in honour of Śiva in his terrific form, and after she had sprinkled me with water, she gave me various spells known to her, and human flesh to eat that had been offered in sacrifice to the gods; so, after I had eaten man's flesh and had received the various spells, I immediately flew up, naked as I was, into the heaven with my friends (*dakinichakra*) and after I had amused myself, I descended from the heaven by command of my teacher, and I, the princess, went to my own apartments. Thus, even in my girlhood I became one of the society of witches (*dakinichakra*), and in our meetings we devoured the bodies of many men.[38]

As witches, yoginis and *dakinis* can control life and death, killing those who anger them and animating skeletons for their own purposes. They are said to meet in circles after flying in the air, to offer human sacrifices and eat human flesh, to perform destructive magical actions—much like the traditions of witches in the West.

There are other Bengali understandings of the term *yogini*; these include the ritual partner in the tantric chakra, goddesses who dwell in the chakras of the body in kundalini yoga, attendants of various Great Goddesses, goddesses who astrologically represent the powers of the planets, female ascetics and healers, and women possessed by goddesses. Narendranath Bhattacharya suggests that they were originally priestesses possessed by the goddess, who were later raised to the status of deities.[39] There are also yogini rituals that come from the time of the tantric Kapalikas. Some Kapalikas sought to unite with the yoginis. The practitioner would offer them blood from his body, call them down to take the offering, and then be accepted into their band as a leader and ascend into the sky with them. Later on, the yoginis came to be understood as deities or personifications of the senses, sharing the sensory intensity of the practitioner's experiences. If his mind is clouded by this sharing, he becomes their slave, but if he transcends through the senses to his realization of his deeper identity as Bhairava, the yoginis are attracted to him and fuse with him in his ultimate identity as lord of the kula.[40]

There are many different lists of yoginis in the tantric literature: some have groups of sixty-four yoginis, some have eight or sixteen, some have three or four yoginis. In the iconography, they tend to have multiple heads and many types of weapons. H. C. Das speculates that some lists were linked with the ten Mahavidya or great wisdom goddesses, while others incorporated local goddesses into the ranks of the yoginis.[41]

According to Vidya Dehejia, it is likely that Bengal has historically been a center of yogini worship, as it has been a center of tantric practice, and several major texts that speak of yoginis (the *Mahabhagavata Purana*, the *Brihad-dharma Purana*, the *Agni Purana*, the *Kalika Purana*) were probably written in the Bengal area. However, the yoginis started disappearing by the sixteenth century, the time of Krishnananda's *Tantrasara*.[42] Although yoginis have disappeared from brahmanical Hindu worship, they survive in folk Shakta tantra.

Yoginis give power, and this is a repeating theme in folk tantra. We see this theme of power in both informant reports and the local handbooks and instruction manuals. This theme appears in different ways.

First, the reports and manuals may describe the virtue of *siddhis* or supernatural powers, and the justifications for their use. Although classical tantra (in both Hindu and Buddhist traditions) ignores these as wastes of time and energy, and as moral temptations, folk tantra highly values such powers. They are justified as accelerating spiritual evolution by giving knowledge of other worlds and their inhabitants, and by fulfilling desires in this life so that the person does not have to be reborn to fulfil any nagging frustrations. Some of the most popular powers are eloquence, spontaneous knowledge, rapid travel to far-away places, mind reading, and gaining the affection of supernatural women. *Siddhis* also include the classical yogic abilities: becoming as small as an atom, making the body light or heavy, touching any object at a distance, irresistable will, the ability to direct natural forces and elements, unrestrained freedom, and the ability to materialize desired objects. Some texts include folk tantric Buddhist powers as well, such as gaining the power to see hidden treasure, invisibility, the ability to disappear rapidly, the power to turn metals into gold, gaining immortality, the power to travel anywhere on earth and in the air, the power to visit the hell worlds at any time, and the use of an enchanted sword that wins all battles.[43] Traditionally, there are five sources for supernatural powers or *siddhis*.

1. *Birth related.* These are present from birth or appear during childhood, and these powers come from actions in previous lives. The person may have been a yogi during that time, or may have done some good deeds for which he or she is being rewarded. These powers may also come from astrological influences.
2. *Mantric.* These are powers which result from skill at the use of mantra, and include associated techniques of breath control and hatha yoga. When mantras are activated correctly, they can generate a variety of apparently miraculous phenomena.
3. *Penance related.* Performance of austerities may generate the accumulation of spiritual power (*tapas*), and are generally combined with concentration and withdrawal from the world. This allows the practitioner to develop supernormal powers. The person may fast, stay awake for long periods of time, experience severe heat or cold, mortify the body in various ways, and perform complex yogic asanas. Some groups have specialized in these practices, especially the folk tantric sects of Nagas, Avadhutas, Aghoris, and Kapalikas.
4. *Drug and herb related.* Practitioners have used a variety of substances to gain supernatural powers, including plants, metals, precious stones, poisons, and such hallucinogens as hashish and marijuana. These have been purified and combined into drinks, elixirs, and pellets, especially by members of the Nath, Siddha, Rasa and Unani schools.
5. *Sadhana related.* These powers come as a result of intense meditation, at certain auspicious times (especially midday, midnight, and the eighth and fourteenth days of the dark fortnight of the lunar month), in certain environments.[44]

Other abilities are also possible in the folk tradition. The person can communicate with animals, read thoughts, transform the body into any shape, have knowledge of past lives, change people into beasts or trees or stones, become invisible, gain one or many bodies, pass through walls and mountains, dive into the earth like water, walk on water, and control both persons and worlds. The tantric yogi could also make the Hindu gods act as his servants. The *Sadhanamala* lists an alternative eight siddhis: the gift of a sword that always wins in battle; eye makeup that allows a person to see buried treasure, an ointment for the soles of the feet that allows a person to travel unnoticed, the power to become invisible, to turn base metals into gold, to gain immortality, to fly, to travel anywhere swiftly on earth, and to live underground.[45]

A second ability claimed by folk tantrikas is power over mortality. Tantric practitioners claim to approach immortality by exceedingly long life spans or conscious reincarnation. There has been a limited Nath (alchemical) influence in Bengali Shakta, so that some small groups work with mercury and attempt to gain infinite life in this way, but it is rare. Much more widespread is the claim that one's guru is centuries old and lives in the Himalayas, only rarely coming to visit specially chosen disciples. Or that the guru looks young because his body is young (though his mind is thousands of years old). He or she can also consciously exchange bodies (this claim is justified by saying that many historical adepts could do this, from Vikramaditya to Shankaracharya). Either the practitioner exchanges bodies permanently at death, consciously leaving his body when the life force wanes and finding a new body, or he does it temporarily during his life. This may be in order to gain knowledge, or as a game, or to better teach disciples. There are popular stories of tantric practitioners who are thousands of years old.

Related to this power over their own mortality, folk tantrikas also claim to influence the incarnations of others. Some who have mastery over the spirits (*bhuta siddhi*) claim that they can give sons to barren women by influencing the incarnation of the spirits they control. There are many spirits desiring rebirth, and the tantrika can act as a mediator or middleman, linking families who want children with spirits who want a body. In earlier days, selling fertility spells was an important profession for tantrikas.

Another sort of power is influence over the world of the ancestors and the dead. Many sorts of arrangements can be made with ancestors and other spirits. Sometimes they can help the folk tantrika in his or her meditation, and sometimes they can fight off negative entities who might wish to harm the tantrika. In folktales, they can bring treasures and build giant palaces, but we rarely see such claims in modern West Bengal. Spirits are generally more modest, simply offering a transfer of power, the trade of empowered mantras for supernatural power which has accumulated over time. They are often contacted at the burning ground, where they are believed to lurk in a dissatisfied state, and the connection is often established through the use of skulls and bones. As ancestors, they may have a particular closeness to the practitioner. As spirits or low-level deities, some struggle may be involved in conquering them. If the practitioner is weak, he is said to run the risk of going insane from such battles.

Gaining power over or from female deities is also widespread in folk tantra. There are many regional and lower-status goddesses invoked by folk tantrikas. These include more classical demigoddesses, such as the yakshini (nature goddess), *apsaras* (heavenly dancer), *kinnari* (celestial dancer and musician), and yogini. If such a goddess becomes satisfied with the tantrika's meditation, she will appear in female form, and give boons to the tantrika. These may include earthly pleasures for five thousand years, a vacation in a celestial paradise, and then rebirth as a king.

Finally, folk tantrikas also claim the ability to control their own or others' luck by the control of karma that causes bad luck and disease. Sometimes this karma is simply burned away, sometimes it is transferred to another person or to an animal, sometimes it is buried in some unlucky spot or nailed to a tree, and sometimes the bad karma is experienced by the guru. Thus we have stories of disease transfer, and of tantric gurus who fall ill to keep the illness from a cherished disciple.

The values and virtues of folk tantra are quite different from those of the more academic and disciplined style of classical tantra.

## Classical Tantra: The Basics of the Kali-kula

Whereas folk tantra emphasizes applied spiritual and supernatural knowledge, classical or scholastic tantra emphasizes "pure" and unapplied knowledge. Classical shakta tantra, traditionally called the Kali-kula or lineage of Kali, is a complex blend of philosophy and ritual. It uses interpretation of texts and a variety of philosophical systems to attain the goal of knowledge of the universe. As Narendranath Bhattacharyya writes, "The followers of the Kālikula are exclusively monist. They hold the Śakti is the same as brahman in its three aspects of *sat* (reality), *cit* (consciousness) and *ānanda* (bliss), and not its *māyā-vivarta* or transformatory aspect."[46]

Classical tantra of the Shakta variety is interested in the abstract nature of the goddess, the ways in which she creates and destroys, and in the relationships between the physical and spiritual worlds. Shakti, the goddess, is understood to be a form of *brahman*, ultimate reality, and learning about the dynamics of the universe allows one to reach toward that goddess's state of infinite consciousness. Though its Vedic roots are emphasized, the background philosophy is actually a mixture of Samkhya and Advaita Vedanta (it is sometimes called *shaktadvaitavada*, the path of nondual Shakti). This sort of tantra is generally more respected than folk tantra, and requires a broad education in religion and philosophy. It requires the ability to interpret Sanskrit texts, which means that its practitioners must be scholars who can read Sanskrit. This skill is becoming rare in West Bengal, as respect for a religious vocation is dying out and young men look forward to a career in engineering or business rather than to the renunciant life.

According to the theology of classical Shakta tantra, Shakti is the supreme deity, inseparable from her consort Shiva. This approach is Shakta monism, in which Shiva and Shakti are ultimately one, both aspects of the same eternal *brahman*, identical like heat and fire, light and luminosity, sweetness and sugar. It is partly based on Samkhya philosophy, in which the male is the silent and passive observer, and the female is the active participant. It is Shakti who created the universe, and she rules it and cares for it. She is divine energy, as opposed to Shiva who is static and motionless, and she is creator, preserver, and destroyer. She contains all three qualities of the universe (*gunas*), of spirit, energy, and inertia. She is also manifest in the power of all deities, who depend upon her for their abilities to act. There is also Vedanta influence. As the primal manifestation of *brahman*, Mahashakti is the source of all energy and divinity in the universe. Through her, the human soul can realize its ultimate unity with *brahman*. The approach of classical Shakta tantra differs from Advaita Vedanta in its emphasis upon both meditation and ritual action (*kriya*), for Vedanta believes that people may attain realization by meditation alone, whereas the tantric approach emphasizes the importance of practice (*sadhana*), especially the use of mantra. There is a greater tantric emphasis on mantras as revelatory and the means of liberation, and the ritual identification of the worshiper with the deity worshiped during tantric meditation.

Classical or scholastic tantra emphasizes the Vedic origin of tantric beliefs and rituals, and uses relevant Vedic texts in worship, such as the Devi Sukta of the Rig Veda (X.125). This hymn declares:

> 3. I am the Lady, ruler of the worlds, bestower of wealth on my devotees. I have seen the Supreme Self in my nature, Whom all are enjoined to worship. I am the Supreme Deity to Whom oblations should be offered to a sacrificial fire. I reside in the essence of the universe. I make Atman enter into all individual souls. All direct their acts of devotion to Me. . . .
> 6. I created the earth and heaven, and entered into them. I reside in them as their Inner Controller.
> 7. I created the sky as Father, created the waters in the seas as Mother, pervade all worlds as their Inner Supreme Self, and manifest them with my effulgent body.
> 8. I have created all worlds at my will without being urged by any higher Being, and dwell within them. I permeate the earth and heaven, and all created entities with my greatness and dwell in them as eternal and infinite consciousness.[47]

Some writers also argue that the Ratri Sukta of the Rig Veda (X.127) is also a precursor to Shaktism, especially to the worship of Kali. Classical tantrikas also note early Shakta ideas in some Upanishads (such as the *Tripura-tapini Upanishad*, *Bhavrichopanishad*, *Guhyakalupanishad*, and *Devi Upanishad*). Here Shakti is understood to be the creative power of Shiva, mother of the universe, sometimes identical with Prakriti and Maya. These Shakta Upanishads do show tantric influence: many use tantric ritual terms like *yantra*, *bindu*, *bija mantra*, *shakti*, and *chakra*.[48] The goddess is identical with *brahman*, as the Devi Upanishad declares:

> 2. She replied: I am essentially Brahman. From Me [has proceeded] the world comprising Prakṛti and Puruṣa, the void and the Plenum.

> I am [all forms of] bliss and non-bliss. Knowledge and ignorance are Myself. Brahman and non-Brahman are to be known—says the scripture of the Atharvan-s.
> 3. I am the five elements as also what is different from them. I am the entire world. I am the Veda as well as what is different from it. I am the unborn; I am the born. Below and above and around am I.[49]

Classical shakta tantra, which is called the Kali-kula in West Bengal, is a part of the Kaula tantric tradition of India. This tradition is said to be beyond all paths (*atimarga*), a sixth current of revelation beyond the traditional five sources of Shaivite tradition. According to Sanderson, it originated in the rites of yogini cults practiced by householders.[50] Some writers claim that the Kula and Kaula cults are identical, while others state that the Kaula group has Shakti dominant over Shiva. The Kali-kula worships the Great Goddess, who is infinite consciousness, and also the Mahavidya or great wisdom goddesses.

Hindu shakta tantra has often been divided into two types, the southern Shri Kula and the northeastern Kali-kula. As one sectarian practitioner told me:

> In India, there are two schools of Tantra. In the south is the Shri-kula; they worship Lakshmi, seeking wealth. In the north is the Kali-kula, in Bengal, Assam, Bihar, and Orissa. We worship the ten wisdom goddesses (Mahavidyas), especially Kali, Tara, Chinnamasta, and Bagala, and our greatest wealth is *brahman* wisdom. We of the Kali-kula are different from the Shri-kula. We start from night and reach toward the day, while they start from light but then go toward night. The Kali-kula says, "Let the darkness come first! I will fight against darkness—come with your sword, Mother! I am in the fight, Ma, come and help me. Let all the other wisdom goddesses follow—but first, let us fight!" If Ma does not come, we say, "I hold a gun to you, goddess, give me knowledge! You are my mother, you are wealthy, so I am wealthy—give me my birthright! I have been deprived of my wealth, so now I am poor—but I come from my Mother, and I demand my inheritance."[51]

Dating these traditions is very difficult, but the Kali-kula is usually considered to be an older tradition than the Shri-kula, despite the latter's tendency to push its origin back to the Vedas. As Teun Goudriaan and Sanjuka Gupta assert, "The beginnings of Kalikula literature can be traced back further than those of the Srikula."[52]

Both of these traditions describe stories of the incarnations and adventures of the gods, especially Shiva and Shakti. However, in classical shakta tantra, the philosophical approach interprets mythic stories to be symbolic of greater truths, and the ritual gives the practitioner insight into those truths. The goal of tantric practice in classical tantra is the identification of the practitioner with Shiva or Shakti, or with ultimate reality (*brahman*).

Although many classical tantrikas are content to be primarily scholars, others incorporate practice. We may describe some of the practical ritual details of classical Shakta tantra:

*When*: Shakta tantric ritual may occur at any time, though the most important times for worship of the goddesses in West Bengal are the new-moon night, Tuesday and Saturday during the week, and the days of the great celebrations of worship, such as Kali Puja or Durga Puja. There may also be special vows taken by individuals for weekly worship.

*Why*: Tantric ritual may be performed for a variety of reasons. Whereas folk tantra tends to focus on attainment of supernatural power, classical tantra tends to focus on gaining knowledge (especially *brahmajnana* or omniscience), verbal ability, artistic inspiration, and insight into difficult situations. There are also practitioners who seek union with the goddess, either in a temporary ritual setting, or in a permanent mystical merging of identity with her.

*How*: The goddess is worshiped in ritual style, with the use of mantras, visualizations, offerings of flowers and incense, breath control, and hand and body positions. The deity may be invoked to possess the worshipers, or to unite in a deeper way with the worshiper's spirit. The rituals are often complex, and an important type is *purascharana*, the fivefold ritual of chanting mantras, worshiping deities, offering water to the ancestors, doing the *homa* fire ritual, and feeding brahmins. There are distinctions like *vamachara* (the so-called 'left-handed path,' or reverse path practiced at night) and *dakshinachara* (the traditional path of worship in the daytime with symbolic offerings and respect). The *Pranatoshini* distinguishes between "wet" practice (involving the "five m's" or practice of forbidden rites) and "dry" practice, which does not involve such practices.[53]

*Who*: Although folk tantra tends to be open to anyone who can find a ritual handbook or amenable guru, or to people who can have vivid and prophetic dreams, classical tantra tends to emphasize the notion of worthiness or competence (*adhikara*). There are only some people who are worthy to be initiated and to practice tantra, and many tantras have long lists of their qualities. For instance, the *Kularnava Tantra* states that initiates must be pure, obedient, and heroic, they must be devoted, with auspicious features, clean, truthful, modest, and honest, and they must thrill with joy at the remembrance of the guru.[54] Among other negative qualities, they must not be wicked, ugly, vain, impotent, deformed, blind, deaf, dirty, diseased, ill-smelling, lazy, addicted, tending to hide behind walls or pillars, dishonest, tend to exaggerate, unable to keep a secret, or sneaky; they must not practice magic, or be quarrelsome, foolish, unreliable, or boring; he must not speak like a brahmin, or be proud or passionate; they must not keep evil company, or be gluttonous, traitorous, lustful, cowardly, or dissatisfied; they must not be insulting to parents and guru or hate women; nor should they be rejected by the tradition or cursed by a guru.[55]

For those rituals which require a female consort, she must be beautiful, young, serious, a follower of the *kulachara* path, pious, happy, generous, quiet, devoted to god and guru, intelligent, and of good personality and character. A female consort should be avoided who is lazy, old, cruel, angry, frightened, greedy, in love with someone else, diseased, missing some bodily organ, bad-smelling, ugly, stupid, insane, lustful, or a follower of a different religious path.[56]

Practitioners are often divided into three states or *bhavas*: the animal or *pashu* state, the heroic or *vira* state, and the divine or *divya* state. The person in the *pashu bhava* is bound by instincts and attachments, like an animal, and must follow the traditional rules of dharmic life; the person in the *vira bhava* is willing to violate traditional rules and customs, in a ritual setting, to gain freedom from his or her past and its conditioning; the person in *divya bhava* is in a state of freedom, and divinity needs no ritual practice. The person in *vira bhava* may attain a temporary union with the god or goddess, whereas in the *divya bhava* state that union is permanent.

*Where*: Shakta tantric ritual and worship may occur in any locale that is sacred or private. If the ritual is understood as symbolic, no literal or external action needs to be taken, and the visualization can be done in the home. If it is understood literally, it may be performed in burning grounds, at deserted temples, by the bank of a river, under a large bilva tree, at a crossroad, or in mountains or deserts. Sometimes meditation is performed at the confluence of rivers, or in holy forests. The place should be free of barbarians, wild beasts, snakes, and noise, and should not be near the homes of leaders or warriors. The practitioner should sit on a seat of cloth or animal skin.

Occasionally groups assemble in sacred places, often with equal numbers of men and women, for chakras or ritual circles. There is temple worship for the great pujas, the ceremonies of devotional goddess worship, and people may come to temples for individual worship or occasionally for *Kali-kirtan* hymns, but we do not see the same congregational spirit that is seen in some forms of Vaishnavism. Although the religion itself is largely noninstitutional and there are no weekly congregational meetings or official shrine memberships, there is often a sense of affiliation of devotees with a particular temple or sacred place, and many people go on vacations or pilgrimages to visit sacred locales.

Classical tantric ritual has many categories and subcategories of practice. Some major practices include the use of powerful words (mantra), initiation by a guru (diksha), ritual placement of deities within the practitioner's body (*nyasa*), and the use of visual representations (yantra).

A mantra is the sound-form of the god or goddess, and chanting *bija* mantras (tantric seed mantras) is thus a theistic practice, which can make the deity visible. Mantras are inherent in the world, resonating in all beings, from the gods to the tiniest worm. Mantras are within creation like the sprout in the seed, like heat in fire, like sweetness in sugar, like Shakti in Shiva.[57] Chanting mantras allows a person to gain the four goals of life, gain knowledge of the fourteen worlds, attain pleasure and liberation, destroy sin, and install statues that are ritually enlivened. According to the *Sharadatilaka*, mantras are also gendered: those ending in-*hum* and-*phat* are male, those ending in-*tha* are female, and those ending in-*namas* are neuter.[58]

The mantra is understood by Shakta tantrikas to be a sort of living entity. When the chanting of mantras or *mantrajapa* is begun, the mantra has the impurity of birth, and when the chanting is ended, it has the impurity of death; these must be cleansed so that the mantra can work properly. A mantra can be conscious and living, and when such a mantra is chanted, the knots or blockages of the heart and throat snap open, and the person experiences ecstatic symptoms. However, as living entities, mantras may also have personality defects: they may be confused, angry, immature, proud, intoxicated, hostile, hungry, dangerous, cruel, lazy, deformed, and ashamed, among other flaws.[59] There are ritual practices for getting rid of defects in mantras. Success (*siddhi*) in mantras may come from the power given originally by the guru in initiation (when the mantra is first given), or from practice of the mantra in a previous life, as well as from disciplined practice in this life. Mantras must be given by teachers, and mantras should not be chanted that are seen or heard accidentally, or read in a book. This leads to misery, disease, and disaster.[60]

*Diksha*, or initiation, is very important in classical tantra. In the *Kularnava Tantra*, Shiva states that there can be no liberation without initiation.[61] This must be given by a guru who is capable, supports his tradition, knows mantras and sacred texts, and follows the rules of proper ritual behavior. Such a guru is protected by the gods, gains a shared identity with Shiva during life, and gains liberation at his death.[62] Initiation must be given to a worthy disciple, or it is wasted, like mixing cow milk with dog milk.

The guru should test the disciple on knowledge of mantra, hymns, visualization, and ritual. If the disciple is competent, he or she may be initiated. Different types of initiation may bring different speeds along the spiritual path. The initiation ritual may focus on karma or action (which is as slow as an ant climbing a tree), dharma or tradition (which is of middling speed, like a monkey jumping from branch to branch), or *jñana* or wisdom (which is fast, like a bird flying straight to the goal). The disciple may be initiated by sight (as a fish is said to nourish its young), by touch (as a bird nourishes its young by the warmth of its wings), and by thought (as a turtle nourishes its young by thinking of them).[63] Initiation may occur by ritual (with a fire-pit and pitcher), by letters (placed on the body or the tongue), by placement of *kalas* (special mantras for sections of the body), by touch (invoking the deity in the hand), by speech, by the guru's gaze, and by thought transference (the guru sends thoughts into the disciple's mind, and frees him or her from bonds). The guru may be male or female. According to the *Nila Tantra*, the goddess is the supreme guru, while Shiva is the guru who dwells in the highest place. There are also sages who are linked with specific mantras (*deva-gurus*), and *tara*-gurus, which include divine, perfected and human gurus. Women may be gurus, and their names should end in *-amba* (whereas the male guru's name should end in *-ananda*). The most important guru is one who transmits the tantric mantra.[64]

There is outer initiation, which involves ritual action (especially puja and *homa* fire), and also inner initiation, which involves direct transmission of power (and helps in awakening kundalini energy). Both are legitimate. Ideally, the impact of a tantric initiation is strong, and the disciple falls into a state of bliss. Initiation is believed to instantly burn up millions of sins, sever attachments, destroy caste distinctions, and give competence for further ritual practice. The disciple gains a glimpse of a godlike state, and is thus motivated to continue practice.

Some forms of initiation are said to give such intense grace and power that the person gains knowledge of *brahman* instantly, whereas others give visions of Shiva and Shakti and divine light (sometimes accompanied by visions of letters and mantras). Some give mild grace, allowing union with the guru through thought or touch, or the guru himself may become the mantra and enter into the person. Grace may rain down, or the guru may pull the disciple up through the chakras (described in kundalini yoga), past the sahasrara chakra, which allows the disciple to unite with Shiva and Shakti, in the state of *samāvesha* or perfect union.

*Nyasa* is the ritual placement of deities within the body. Usually this is done in the form of *bija* mantras, or mantras that are understood to be smaller forms or microcosms of tantric deities. This sanctifies the body and protects it from instinct and evil impulse. *Matrika-nyasa* is the placement of Shakti mantras, and at times it may induce a form of possession or glossolalia. As Gopinath Kaviraj writes,

> By the practice of matrika-nyas (relinquishing the power of speech to God and to realize that God speaks through our mouth), we are able to unite our individual power of speech with the supreme undivided faculty of speech and to realise the Eternal Shabda-Brahman or the Indivisible Divine Energy. The Mother then gets an opportunity to speak through our mouth without any obstruction and to transform our speech into the words of the Vedas which are the manifest form of Shabda-Brahman and the source of all knowledge. In this state, the seeker feels that the Mother is reciting the Vedas

> through his mouth and is revealing Shabda Brahman—the Divine Knowledge. As a result of matrika-nyas, the Rishis surrendered themselves to God.[65]

While the practice of *nyasa* may allow the goddess to speak, it may also invoke other entities, such as the sages (*rishis*): "Our customary Sarasvati-worship is meant to acquire knowledge of matrika-nyas. By resigning ourselves to Rishis we get animated by their thoughts and are impelled by their vibrations and are thus able to realize our spoken word as the word of the Rishis or the Vedas. Then our body and organ of speech become worthy of being regarded as instruments of the Rishis i.e. of God."[66]

*Nyasa* involves a surrender—of ownership of the body, of control of one's action, of perception. It is generally understood as a practice that lessens the power of the ego, for it allows both mind and body to be under the control of the goddess or god. Once that state is reached, the person can recognize that the articles of worship, and the universe in which they lie, are also essentially divine. It is usually preceded by the ritual of *bhutashuddhi*, the purification of the five elements (*bhutas*) of the body and environment.

Yantra is the instrument or tool that helps fix the practitioner's mind on the deity, and subdues instincts. It may vary in design and model, though there is usually a geometrical pattern that reveals the characteristics of the deity, and a square with four doors that separates the world within the yantra from the outer world. It may be drawn on cloth, leaf, stone, or metal, and is the body or abode of the deity, and a seat in which the god or goddess may dwell. It is normally for only one deity (whereas a mandala may incorporate many deities). There may be deities who surround the yantra, and these are called the veiling deities (*avarana devatas*). As the body of the deity, the yantra itself becomes a divinity. As the *Kamakala-vilasa* states, the wise "know no difference between the goddess (Maheshi) and the yantra."[67]

The practitioner must call the goddess down into his own body, and then install her into the yantra by the practice of *prana-pratistha*, or infusing life into its form, so that it is filled with power and awareness. The yantra is ritually established on a wooden pedestal, purified by worshiping the deities of the area (*pitha puja*) and the lords of the four directions. The negative or evil forces in the area are dispelled, the four quarters of space are bound or fenced. The worshiper's body is purified by the symbolic dissolution of the five elements (*bhutashuddhi*), and each element is dissolved by a mantra. Divine beings or energies are brought into the body by *nyasa*, and the worshiper brings the yantra deity down through the central spiritual channel of the spinal cord (*sushumna*) into his or her own body, and then exhales the deity out. It may go onto a flower, which is then placed in the center of the yantra, or onto the worshiper's fingers, which are then placed onto the yantra.[68]

Yantras are not limited to classical tantra. There are also folk uses of yantras, such as conquering enemies and attracting women. The yantra of Nava-Durga (Durga surrounded by nine shaktis) hung by a thread around the arm or neck prevents disease, whereas a yantra of Lakshmi brings fame and wealth, and keeps away danger and anxiety. Sometimes yantras and mantras are linked, so that a yantra associated with enlightenment is matched to a mantra that brings on a trance state, or yantras that guard a place from harm may be associated with protective mantras.

Yantras are often equated with mandalas. The term *mandala* refers to a colored diagram used for worship, and it is associated with the term for circle (*chakra*). The term *chakra* is used in kundalini yoga for an energy center, and the term is also used for group tantric ritual. The worship is called *chakrapuja*, or worship within a circle. Such group rituals are not necessary for tantric practice, but are sometimes performed. Male tantrikas are accompanied by female consorts who are either their wives, or are ritual "wives for a night." It is generally organized by a leader, and only tantrikas at the *vira* or heroic stage are permitted to join, for they are the ones seeking to overcome their instincts by means of the ritual.

All of these ritual images and practices, and many more, create the spiritual practice of the tantrika who worships and meditates upon the goddess as the source of creation and salvation from rebirth. When practiced following yogic rules of discipline, they are understood to lead to the goal of classical Shakta tantra, which is union with the goddess as ultimate consciousness.

## The Kularnava Tantra: Folk versus Classical Shakta Tantra

The *Kularnava Tantra* is the major text for Shakta tantric practitioners in West Bengal. Even during Sir John Woodroffe's time (the early twentieth century) it was an important text—he calls it "the most frequently cited text in the Tantra literature," and "a leading and perhaps the foremost Tantra of the Kaula School."[69] As Chattopadhyaya says flatly, "The most important text of Shakta tantra is the *Kularnava Tantra*, which bears the inner image of the tantric literature."[70] Many Shakta tantric practitioners in 1983–1984, and also in 1993–1994, told me that in their opinion the *Kularnava Tantra* was the most important Shakta tantric text. Some said it was the only text that they accepted. Interestingly, practicing tantrikas of both the folk and classical styles argued that it supported their own quite different understandings of tantra.

In this discussion I shall work from the Bengali translation of the *Kularnava Tantra* published by Nababharat Publishers, which was the version used by most informants.[71] It is a medieval text from at least the end of the thirteenth century, when it was mentioned in the list of texts written by the scholar Lakshmidhara. Although it is primarily a classical text, it includes critiques of Vedic knowledge and scholarly pride frequently seen in the folk and devotional traditions. It may be noted that Woodroffe made a partial translation of the Kularnava Tantra, rephrasing and censoring many of its anti-Vedic statements. From his translation, one would imagine the text to largely support the Vedic and Sanskritic philosophical tradition.

I include a brief section on this text here to show how arguments for both folk and classical tantra can be found within it, and how a single text can be used to justify both traditions. This ambiguity is important, because such interpretations are the basis for many of the arguments about what is "true" and what is "false" tantra.

Although Shiva does most of the talking in the *Kularnava Tantra*, and the highest state is often called "Shivahood" (*shivatva*), the text is nevertheless understood as Shakta by many practicing tantrikas, for Shiva and Shakti are ultimately the same deity, and their separate forms are only a superficial difference. Both deities are to be worshiped together as a unity.

The text has a few lines that support the notion that it follows and respects the Vedas. As Shiva says in chapter 2:

> 85. The six philosophies are my [Shiva's] six limbs: my two hands, two feet, stomach and head. Therefore whoever differentiates between them mutilates my body.
> 86. Beloved! These six philosophies also make up the six limbs of the Kula. Therefore, you should realize that the Kula texts can also be called Vedic texts.

Chapter 3 also has a line that speaks in favor of the Vedas:

> 113. There is no truth higher than the guru, there is no god greater than Shiva, there is no knowledge greater than the Vedas, there is no philosophy equal to Kaula [philosophy].

These lines appear to support the notion that study of the tantras is equivalent to study of the Vedas. The *Kularnava Tantra* also speaks occasionally about how Vedic practice and knowledge give a person a longer life (1.48). However, the text is clearly not in favor of Vedic scholars and priests. As chapter 1 asserts of them:

> 72. Such men are constantly performing their own caste duties and little else, O Parvati, they do not know the highest truth, and thus they perish.
> 73. Some carefully perform rituals, some roam about fulfilling vows and doing sacrifices, but they are ignorant and they cheat themselves and others.
> 74. They do rituals, but they are satisfied with only the name. They roam about in circles, repeating mantras, performing *homa* (fires) and elaborate sacrifices.

A problem here is that the word *jnana* (knowledge) is used in several different ways. Ostensibly all senses are equal, as chapter 1 observes:

> 109. There are two kinds of knowledge: one comes from the agama texts, and the other comes from insight (*viveka*). Knowledge gained from texts is truth in the form of sound (*shabdabrahman*), and that [gained from] insight is ultimate truth (*parabrahman*).

Now, both of these are *brahman* or ultimate truth, so both should be of equal value. However, as we look at the text, it is clear that they are not. Vedic study and book learning is stated to be inferior to spiritual insight. The shastras are said to delude people, and do not give real knowledge, though many people are fooled by them and spend their time in arguments. Here, in chapter 1, the text skewers brahmin intellectuals:

> 87. O Beloved! Many ignorant people fall into the deep well of the six philosophies, but they are controlled by their instincts and cannot attain the highest knowledge.
> 88. They are drowning in the dreadful ocean of the Vedas and shastras[72], and they are driven in one direction and then another by philosophical discussions and debates, which are like terrible waves and crocodiles.
> 89. [There are] people who have read the Vedas, agamas, and puranas, but who do not know the highest truth. All their knowledge is like the cawing of crows, and nothing more.
> 90. O Goddess, they turn their backs on truth, and read books day and night, always worrying about what they should be learning, saying this is knowledge or that is knowledge.
> 91. They know literary style, syntax, and poetry, and ways to make writing attractive, but they are fools, and they are confused and worried . . .
> 94. They chant the Vedas and fight among themselves, but they do not know the highest truth, as a cooking ladle does not know the taste of the things in it.

Studying the Vedas and sacred texts does not give the seeker what he needs, which is insight and ecstatic consciousness. The first chapter of the *Kularnava Tantra* condemns shallow scholars:

> 97. Discussion of ideas cannot destroy the illusions of the world, as talk of a lamp will not get rid of the darkness.
> 98. A person who studies but does not gain true wisdom is like a blind man looking at his face in a mirror. Only people with experiential wisdom can really understand the shastras.

Theology without direct experience is generally seen by this tantra as a waste of time, for a person can spend a thousand years listening to shastric knowledge, and never understand it or reach its end.[73] In the following stanzas from chapter 1, the term *tattva* is used many times; I shall translate it as "truth":

> 99. [Even] men famous for their wisdom, generosity, and acts of merit quarrel over truth, chasing truths forward, backward, and sideways, talking about this kind of truth and that kind of truth.
> 100. This is truth, that is truth, truth is distant (or extensive)—they speak this way. Since they have no direct experience (*pratyaksha*), and no realization (*upalabdhi*) of truth, how are they going to attain truth by merely talking [about it]? Those who spend their time talking about truth, will remain ignorant and very far from the [real] truth. There is no doubt about this.

Perhaps the best understanding of the Vedas here is by a developmental model. Such texts are important for beginners, but no longer necessary for more advanced seekers (we see this in the famous listing of practitioner styles, in which Veda is the lowest type and *kulachara* the highest). Although the Vedas do not give liberation, they do give other knowledge, as chapter 1 continues:

> 103. As a person who collects rice grains leaves the rice husks behind, so the intelligent person should learn all religious texts, grasp their inner truths, and then leave them all behind.
> 104. Goddess, as a person who has drunk divine nectar is satisfied and needs no other food, so a person who has experienced truth (*tattvajnana*) needs no other [knowledge of] shastras.
> 105. Liberation is not gained by chanting Vedas, studying philosophy, or all of the shastras. O Goddess of the Viras! Only experiential knowledge (*jnana*) gives liberation.

The tantra also satirizes overdependence on ritual. As its author bluntly states of shallow yogis and scholars in the first chapter:

> 79. There are donkeys and other such animals who see house and forest as the same, and who wander around naked and without shame. Does this make them all yogis?
> 80. If people could gain liberation by rubbing themselves with dust and ashes, does this mean that village people who live amid dust and ashes are liberated?
> 81. Forest creatures like deer eat only grass, leaves, and water. O goddess, does this mean that they are yogis [because they are vegetarian]?
> 82. Frogs and fish live until they die in [holy] rivers like the Ganges. Does this mean that they have gained special power (*tapas*)?

> 83. O Goddess! Parrots and mynah birds happily recite stanzas [from holy books] to the people; should they be regarded as great scholars (*pandits*) because of this?

Rather than book-learning in one life, what is required for enlightenment is learning over the course of many lives, as the second chapter asserts:

> 28. As dream visions give a sleeping person knowledge without any other instruction, so spiritual knowledge (*kulajnana*) arises without instruction, due to spiritual practice in past lives, and the soul's development.
> 29. That understanding, determined by a thousand previous lives, only that gives realization, instruction accomplishes nothing.
> 32. Spiritual knowledge is revealed to those people who have been freed from sin by asceticism, chanting mantras, charity, sacrifice, bratas, pilgrimage, and other practices performed in the past.

Although the Vedas and shastras are a useful beginning, they are not necessary:

> 78. Even without knowledge of the Vedas and shastras, one who knows the Kula is omniscient, while a scholar of Vedas, shastras, and agamas, who is ignorant of the Kula, knows nothing.[74]
> 79. (O Goddess!) Only your devotees know the Kula's glory, and others do not, as the chakora-bird knows the taste of moonbeams, but other birds do not.[75]

Chapter 11 explains that although the Vedas are claimed to support the tantric chakra ritual, it must nevertheless remain private:

> 84. O Goddess! The *kula* ritual should always be kept secret, as a woman does not reveal her pregnancy by her lover.
> 85. The Vedas, puranas, and shastras display themselves like prostitutes, but this wisdom is hidden, like a daughter-in-law.

The *Kularnava Tantra* emphasizes the importance of Kula practice, which involves the worship of the goddess by various ritual and devotional means. The term *kula* is a difficult one to translate, for it variously means family, clan, lineage, pedigree, aristocracy, family religion, race, tribe, species, class, collection, herd, flock, and swarm.[76] In this text, the term *kula* refers to the practice of the *kuladharma* lineage, and a person may be called a *kula* or *kula sadhaka*, while the practice is *kula* or *kula sadhana* (such abbreviations are common in Bengali religious traditions, as for instance many kinds of altered states are simply called *bhavas* for short). The term *kula shakti* refers to both the goddess and the woman who joins in the ritual practice. In order to practice properly, one must be devoted to the goddess. Those who join the tradition and do not worship the goddess in these ways will suffer, for they will be tortured by elemental beings.[77] The second chapter explains:

> 68. Those who are scholars of all four Vedas, but do not know the Kula tradition, are inferior to the lowest-caste person (Chandala). However, if a low-caste person knows the Kula tradition, he is superior to a brahmin.
> 69. O Goddess, the person who gains the guru's grace, has lost his evil tendencies through initiation, and who enjoys [the worship of Shakti within the ritual of] *kulapuja*, only he is the true kula [practitioner], nobody else.

The fifth chapter describes the goddess's response to her worship, and the importance of devotion:

> 58. O Goddess! When you are worshiped by men, women, and people of the third gender,[78] in the four castes and the four stages of life, you fulfill their desires.
> 59. Goddess, if people perform your worship, you are a woman like Lakshmi [toward them], and fulfill their worldly and spiritual desires. But if they do not worship you, you are a woman like Alakshmi, and you cause them to suffer.
> 60. An evil, foolish person who acts in this way [does not worship Shakti] and does not perform Kula worship, will go to the hell-worlds, as will his twenty-one previous generations of ancestors.

Can a text that speaks of "throwing away" the shastras like husks of rice, that compares the Vedic texts to prostitutes and its students to fools and crows, really be said to view the Vedas as a "final authority?" If it does not, what is its final authority? Can a text which says that shastras are unnecessary and do not lead to liberation be called shastric?

Clearly the *Kularnava Tantra* has placed a high value on religious experience. Although its Vedicizing commentators tend to emphasize the intellectual goal of tantric study and practice, and use such words for tantra's goal as *vidya* (learning or scholarship), *tattva* (essential nature, truth, philosophical knowledge), and *jnana* (wisdom, understanding, consciousness), we see the text itself using terms like *pratyaksha* (immediate experience), *bhava* (mood, feeling, emotion, ecstatic state, trance), *upalabdhi* (realization), and *ullasa* (blissful joy). True knowledge comes from the various forms of initiation by the guru, in spontaneous knowledge that arises from past lives, and from ecstatic states that occur in ritual contexts. This experiential emphasis is seen among tantrikas who emphasize that tantra is practice (*sadhana*) rather than text (shastra).

We see within the *Kularṇava Tantra* the tensions between two major types of tantric traditions. Both classical tantrikas and folk tantrikas cite it as an authority for their very different perspectives (including folk tantrikas who are illiterate). The text is also both Shaiva and Shakta (the major deity may be understood as Shiva, Shakti, or the couple), dualistic and monistic, in favor of both conscious union and possession by deities. Because it is ambiguous, it can support opposing interpretations, and thus different schools of tantra.

## Tantric Yogas: The Practice of Kundalini Yoga

Much of Shakta tantric ritual involves yogic discipline and practice. The most frequently seen types of yoga are hatha yoga (sometimes as a subtype of raja yoga) and kundalini yoga. Some writers view kundalini yoga as a subtype of *samadhi* yoga, which also includes devotion, meditation on sound, and visualization practices. Sometimes *nath* yoga is incorporated, especially in alchemical practices intended to bring immortality. Practitioners draw various fluids of the body upward, where they are stored and combined in the highest chakra at the top of the head. These eventually bring spiritual energy and purity to the yogi. Yoga and bhakti are also involved in the worship of the tantric *Mahavidyas* or great wisdom goddesses.

Kundalini yoga is widely practiced by both folk and classical Shakta tantrikas, and thus needs to be mentioned. This look at kundalini yoga will be brief, as there is already a wide literature on the topic in English[79]. We shall look at its assumptions about the body, its goals, and its methods.

The term *kundalini* is derived from the Sanskrit term *kundala*, meaning coiled. It refers to the energy (shakti) of the body, which is personified as a goddess, Kundalini Shakti or Kundalini Devi. According to the mythology of kundalini yoga, she rests in a secret place at the base of the spine in the form of a coiled snake. The goal of this tantric yoga is to cause her to rise up the spine, passing through various chakras or energy centers as she does so, in order to meet her consort Shiva in the thousand-petaled lotus, a spiritual center above the brain known as the *sahasrara* chakra. This rising of kundalini to meet Shiva is called the piercing of the chakras (*shat-chakra-bheda*), and their meeting is said to fill the practitioner with bliss. This practice is also sometimes called laya yoga, the practice of fusing, merging, or dissolving the secular self into a greater spiritual being.

Kundalini yoga may be understood in a more theistic or a less theistic fashion. In the more theistic style, Kundalini Devi is a separate deity who dwells within the body, and the practitioner guides her along the spiritual path to Shiva, who is also a separate deity, and they unite in the end. In less theistic style, kundalini is a form of energy that must undergo transformation and merge with Shiva. In both cases, the goal is to awaken a sleeping energy and cause it to rise and be transformed.

A theistic approach is seen in this prayer by Swami Sivananda, in which Kundalini is addressed as a goddess and a spiritual guide:

> O Divine Mother Kundalini . . . Thou art Kali, Durga, Adisakti, Rajarajeswari, Tripurasundari, Maha-lakshmi, Maha-Sarasvati! Thou has put on all these names and forms. Thou has manifested as prana, electricity, force, magnetism, cohesion, gravitation in this universe. This whole universe rests in Thy bosom. Crores of salutations unto Thee. O Mother of this world! Lead me on to open the Sushumna nadi and take Thee along the Chakras to Sahasrara Charkra and to merge myself in Thee and Thy consort, Lord Siva.[80]

As he explains:

> Kundalini Yoga actually belongs to Tantrik Sadhana, which gives a detailed description about this serpent-power and the Chakras. . . . Mother Divine, the active aspect of the Existence-Knowledge-Bliss Absolute, resides in the body of men and women in the form of Kundalini, and the entire Tantrik Sadhana aims at awakening Her, and making Her to unite with the Lord, Sadasiva, in the Sahasrara. Methods adopted to achieve this end in Tantrik Sadhana are Japa [repetition] of the name of the Mother, prayer, and various rituals.[81]

The goddess Kundalini can also help people through her grace, and lead them to liberation. As Swami Vishnu Tirtha asserts:

> When awakened She is experienced by Yogins as a spiritual guide who directs, controls, governs and leads the aspirants on the spiritual path to *moksa* like a living conscious divine help-mate, with Her vigilant hand helping Her favourite all the twenty-four hours in sleep, dream and waking state, and at times takes him up for the *samadhic* communion with Her Lord. . . . Her movements are then felt, Her voice heard, and Her presence experienced. She then becomes a Reality and not simply an object of imagination and conjecture.[82]

The less theistic style tends to focus on the impersonal energies involved in tantric spiritual physiology. This physiology is based around a central channel, the *sushumna,* and its two major spiritual nerves or *nadis*, the *ida* and the *pingala.* The term *nadi* literally means stream, and there are said to be seventy-two thousand *nadis* in the body. The *sushumna* is a vertical channel that corresponds to the spinal cord in the body, and the chakras are found along it. The *ida* and *pingala* run along the left and right of the central channel, intertwining like the snakes of the caduceus of Asclepius (the symbol of physicians). They start at the base of the spine and twine upward, ending at the nostrils. The left *nadi* or ida is associated with the moon; it is said to be cool, feminine, wet, and soothing. The right *nadi* or pingala is associated with the sun; it is red, fiery, dry, and masculine. All of the *nadis* channel vital energy or breath (*prana*) throughout the body. According to the physiology of kundalini yoga, the physical body should be dissolved into this subtle body of channels and lotuses, which is visualized during yogic practice, as are the deities that exist within each chakra.

When Kundalini awakens, she rises up the spine in the form of the "Upward Moving Breath." She penetrates the various levels of consciousness symbolized by the chakras along the spinal cord, increasing in both vital breath (*prana*) and mantric power, until she reaches the highest chakra, and the highest state of pure bliss. This bliss is then said to permeate the lower chakras of the body, energizing and purifying them.

Sometimes the chakras are associated with spiritual worlds, and are understood to be microcosms of the larger universe. We see, on the part of some practitioners, an equation of the seven chakras with the seven worlds (*lokas*): Bhurloka, Bhuvarloka, Svarloka, Maharloka, Janaloka, Tapoloka, and Satyaloka. The earth with its seven continents is the Bhurloka, the sky and its stars are the Bhuvarloka, and the others are beyond human sight. Depending upon the level of ascent through the chakras while on earth, in the afterlife the person can ascend to the corresponding world.[83] Chakras are also associated with ruling deities who are said to reside there (these are often from brahmanical Hinduism, though visualized in tantric style with multiple heads and arms).

Writers and practitioners are quite inconsistent on the chakras; they have varying deities, colors, qualities, locations, and number, and some may also be located outside of the physical body. Kundalini rises up from one chakra to another, sometimes smoothly and sometimes suddenly and erratically. Practitioners may be helped in kundalini meditation by their gurus, who can help in the raising of kundalini by touch, look, or thought. This help is called *vedha diksha*, or the piercing through, because during initiation the guru causes the kundalini to rise. It is more popularly known as the ritual of *shaktipat*, in which the guru transmits spiritual energy.[84] In this ritual, receiving kundalini energy is understood to be a result of the guru's grace.

When the energy of kundalini is aroused, it is said to affect the body in many ways. According to the book *Devatma Shakti*, these ways include bodily shaking, involuntary deep breathing, trembling, having the hair stand on end, laughing, weeping, stammering, involuntary postures, fixation of sight, and waves of bliss. The practitioner may undergo the spontaneous exercises called *kriyavati*, when the hand and body positions and breath exercises of hatha yoga occur involuntarily. The person may hear various sorts of music: bells, drums, the buzzing of bees, the strumming of stringed instruments. There may be vibrations within the spinal cord, a lack of feeling in the body, or intense feelings in the body, at times leading to orgasms or apparent intoxication or convulsions. There may be fearful visions, and the person may feel as if he were dead or paralyzed. The body may fall to the floor and rotate like a grinding stone, or jerk and toss, and the person may squat cross-legged and jump from place to place like a frog, or act as if possessed by animals (making the sounds of jackals, dogs, tigers, or birds). The person may have religious visions and gain supernatural powers, speak in tongues, or believe him or herself to be possessed by other entities. The world may resonate with mantras (especially Om), and the person may feel currents of breath energy or *prana* traveling through his or her body.[85] The person must gain control over these symptoms through yogic discipline.

Kundalini yoga is understood to give a variety of benefits to its practitioners. Besides the bliss from the meeting of Kundalini and Shiva, this yoga can also give insight into a variety of types of supernatural power (*siddhi* and *vibhuti*). It can give the power of great enjoyment (*bhoga-shakti*), the power of knowledge (*jnana-shakti*), the power of action (*kriya-shakti*), and the power of consciousness (*caitanya-shakti*). In the bliss of union of the god and goddess, the practitioner may share in their joy, and gain infinite wisdom. In a more mundane way, it can give both knowledge and awareness of the subtleties of bodily sensation.

The goddess Kundalini is sometimes portrayed in the form of Durga, as a beautiful woman who rides a lion, as a symbol of strength, courage, and virtue. When kundalini energy is aroused in a person, the goddess rides the lion of yoga, and begins to devour the weakness and the attachment to instinct of the yogi. With her weapons she attacks the passions, and she conquers them. The instincts are sacrificed before her, as during Durga Puja goats and buffaloes are sacrificed to the goddess Durga Mahishamardini.

Kundalini is a goddess of yoga, but also of tantra, and the practice of kundalini is widespread among Bengali tantrikas. As tantric goddesses are understood both in devotional or abstract ways, so is Kundalini both a woman and a form of spiritual energy. Although the focus of kundalini practice is ideally religious insight, and thus it is accepted as a path of classical tantra by most informants, there are some practitioners who use it toward supernatural powers or *siddhis*, and thus follow the ideals of folk tantra.

## Women and Shakta Tantra: Some Notes on Gender

Tantric texts describe three major roles for women: as ritual incarnations of the goddess, as ritual consort for sexual *sadhana*, and as female gurus. These are the major roles emphasized by the texts, though other roles are occasionally mentioned. Women's roles in tantric practice are much broader than these three roles, however. We see female tantrikas who are renunciant practitioners, holy women of various types: the woman who has renounced worldly life (sannyasini), the woman who is dedicated to celibacy, service, and obedience to a tradition (*brahmacharini*), the woman who practices yoga, especially kundalini yoga (yogini), the woman who is married but has left her husband to pursue a spiritual life (*grihi sadhika*). A woman may be a devotee of Kali or Tara, and worship the goddess with tantric mantras, or she may get possessed by Kali as a vocation (*bhar*-lady). The female tantrika may also be a wife who practices tantric sexual ritual as a part of her marriage, in obedience to her husband and guru, or a professional ritual partner in tantric sexual practice. She may be a female teacher (*stri-guru*), usually celibate and head of a group of devotees or an ashram. She may also be a widow or celibate wife, whose practice involves ritual tantric worship (puja), or whose practice involves a mixture of devotional love of a goddess (*shakta bhakti*) and tantric ritual.

The roles for women in tantric texts tend to follow an exaggerated style—the images of women are strongly sexual, or idealized, or both. One does not often get the sense of real women used as models for textual ritual. Rather, these women are "perfect" in various ways (beautiful, graceful, happy, quiet, obedient), or they are imaginary women, also beautiful and graceful but dwelling on lotuses wearing silk and jewels, sometimes having a frightening demeanor. Women in tantric texts tend to be described primarily in terms of their ritual actions—the tantrika finds a suitable woman (according to a long list of qualifications), and then performs various rituals with her. The *Kularnava Tantra* states that the woman must be beautiful, young, pious, devoted to her guru and god, always smiling, pleasing, and without jealousy, among other qualities.[86] A kula woman cannot be unattractive or old or sleepy, and she cannot feel desire or argue with her partner—these disqualify her from tantric practice, even if she has been initiated.[87]

The attitude toward women in tantric texts is more positive than in many Hindu ritual texts. Many tantric texts say that women can be tantric gurus, and a practitioner's mother is the best guru possible (this is different from brahmanical Hinduism, in which male gurus are either required or preferred). A woman may be knowledgeable as a tantric consort, whether she is the tantrika's wife or the wife of another man, a courtesan or laundrywoman or dancer or fisherwoman, a woman who sells meat or works with leather. Some tantras encourage the worship of goddesses within living women and girls, for women may incarnate Shakti. Some tantras say that one must never harm a woman or look down upon her, or even hit her with a flower. In the *Kali Tantra*, women are respected, especially the kula-woman (a female tantric practitioner of the *kula marga*):

> 5. [The practitioner] should imagine the whole world as female (*stri-maya*), and he should also think of himself as female.
> 6. A wise person should consider drink, food to be chewed or sucked, all edible things, the household, himself and everything else, as a young woman. When he sees a kula-woman, she should bow [to her] with reverence.

7. If by good fortune he should encounter a kula-woman, he should mentally worship her.
8. He should bow respectfully before a young girl, a teenaged girl, an old woman or a young woman, even if she is nasty, ugly, or bad.
9. Women should never be beaten, insulted, or cheated, and should never be treated badly. If a person does treat a woman badly, he will be unable to attain success [in his practice].
10. Women are deities, women are the life force (*prana*), women are beauty [or the ornaments of life, *alamkara*].[88]

The first tantric role for women is as a ritual incarnation of the goddess, and a suitable woman is found and offered worship. Sometimes a young girl is worshiped (*kumari* puja), and sometimes a mature woman is the object of worship (*stri* puja or *shakti* puja). *Kumari* puja is often performed during the holiday of Durga Puja, and brings great blessings. The *Kubjika Tantra* details the worship of young virgins in the *kumari puja* (primarily for girls ranging in age from five to twelve years, though the Mahachina mode includes worshiping girls ranging from one to sixteen years), and girls from the ages of six to nine years old are especially to be desired, as such worship grants the devotee all wishes. This tantra also includes worshiping both one's own wife and the wives of others as goddesses, repeating mantras 108 times and seeing the woman as the *yantra* in which the goddess dwells.[89] As well as being within the woman, the goddess may be located in food, wine, fish, red cloth, red flowers, and a red sun. The *Guptasadhana Tantra* speaks of the nine types of virgin girls or *navakanya*, including the actress, prostitute, brahmin woman, the shudra woman, the wives of washerman and barber, the daughter of a Kapalika (skull-bearing tantrika), cowherd, or garland maker.[90]

In the *Kulachudamani Tantra*, the goddess describes the worship of eight women, who represent the eight shaktis or Mothers. They are sometimes called the consorts or powers of the Vedic gods (as one may deduce from their names, such as Brahmani, Maheshvari, and Indrani). However, they are usually worshiped independently of the gods, and they are said to grant supernatural powers, good karma, and the removal of obstacles to the desires of the tantrika. The text gives directions, suggesting that the tantrika bring the women to a deserted place, such as a riverbank, a crossroads, a burning ground, or the foot of a bilva tree. He brings the women sanctified water, and looks closely at them.

28. By observing the differences in the appearance, mood and behaviour of the women, they are given the names of the eight *saktis* beginning with Brahmāṇī, etcetera.
29. offering them a seat and welcoming them with a mantra, (he should present) blessed water for drinking, water for the feet, plain water and an offering of milk and honey.

> 30. He should bathe and dress the hair with scents and flowers and after censing the hair, he should offer silken garments [to the *śaktis*].
> 31. Then spreading out a seat in a different place and having led the *śaktis* there, when he has given [them] a pair of sandals [and] adorned [them] with jewels and ornaments,
> 32. He should offer ointments, scents, and garlands. And having invoked the *śakti* of each of them, he should place [the designated *śakti*] on the head of each of the women.[91]

The practitioner gives each woman the name of one of the Mothers, and he chants a brief hymn to each woman. The goddess explains that without these hymns, the tantrika will lose the fruits of his worship. He should also give them betel and sweet seeds, as well as a garland with sandalwood paste and perfume. The goddess also discusses other options.

> 49. If there be some who do not leave the scene [at this time], such as—his own daughter, his younger sister, elder sister, aunt, mother, or she who is co-wife with one's mother,
> 50. an old caste women, or even one without caste- these make the most excellent kulas [here meaning śaktis, or objects of worship]. They are to be worshiped by all the excellent kulas [here, *kula sādhakas* or tantrikas] who have given up their egoism.
> 51. In the absence of all [of the above women], any one [of these *śaktis*] is to be worshiped with all one's strength, be she purified or unpurified, a mother, or one without a husband.
> 52. In the absence of the former, the latter may be worshiped as all women are a part of me.

In the interests of inclusiveness, the goddess adds:

> 52 . . . Oh Bhairava! If there is a man there who knows the kula teachings, he [too] is deserving of worship![92]

The worship of the human woman as the goddess is generally a temporary phenomenon—the goddess does not remain in her body after the ritual is over. The human woman is much like a statue in this ritual, and acts as a temporary home for the goddess who comes to visit. Goddesses may ritually dwell almost anywhere—from trees to corpses. However, because the human female has her own feminine power or shakti, she is an especially appropriate place for a goddess to dwell.

Another role for a woman in the tantric texts is the role of ritual consort. The *Niruttara Tantra* suggests worship of the *veshya* (the term traditionally means prostitute), including those who come from a tantric family, those from a householder family, those who come from *kaula marga* family, those who are independent of family, those who join (the profession) voluntarily, those who are married to *vira sadhakas*, and those who have been united with the deity in a chakra ritual.[93] It seems that the term does not refer specifically to a prostitute, but rather to a woman who roams about freely like a prostitute, and enjoys herself like Kali. She is a female practitioner who has sex accompanied by *mantrajapa*, and meditates upon the union of Shiva Mahakala and Kalika. Although such an image may initially give an impression of a free woman in the modern sense, this is not the case—her freedom is limited. She is not a tantric *veshya* if she becomes involved with a man other than her husband; as the text states, if she worships a Shiva other than her own Bhairava, she will live in the fierce hells until the destruction of the universe. If she gets involved with other male practitioners due to passion, desire for money, or other temptations, she will go to hell. She is then called an animalistic prostitute (*pashu-veshya*). Any man involved with her will suffer disease, sorrow, and loss of money. The proper *veshya* must be chaste and pious, doing rituals with her own partner. When she desires sex during menstruation, she takes on the form of Kalika and grants success.[94] However, she does not have the choice of taking on a new partner.

Sexual practice within a single couple is called *lata sadhana*, the spiritual exercise in which the woman is like a vine (*lata*) growing around the man. *Lata sadhana* is individual practice, with a single couple alone practicing mantras, breath control, and other forms of meditation in a ritual context. The *kula chakra* is a group practice, where men and women sit in a circle in couples, and perform the ritual of the *panchatattva*, taking the five forbidden things, one of which is intercourse. The tantric texts tend to be rather evasive as to the details of *lata sadhana*—these should come from the guru. However, a good deal of ritual worship is involved, as the *Maya Tantra* stipulates:

> 4. Bring a woman while she is menstruating, and at midnight worship your *iṣṭadevata* (personal deity) within her *yoni*.
> 5. After that, the practitioner must chant 336 mantras daily [the text does not specify which mantras], for three days. By means of this, he can gain the fruit of one thousand corpse rituals. There is no doubt about it.
> 6. Here is another type [of ritual], please listen carefully. First, to gain perfction in the four paths, [the practitioner] should chant mantras 108 times. Then he should worship his personal deity in the *yoni* of a woman who is not his own. Then he should worship Mahamaya 108 times, using menstrual blood.[95]
> 7. After that, he should offer a burnt offering, and chant mantras 108 times. He should become devoted to the practice, and be continually absorbed in Mahamaya.
> 8. If he does this daily for sixteen days, he will become rich, power-

> ful, an orator and a poet, and loved by all. There is no doubt about it.[96]

As an example of *chakra sadhana*, the *Kamakhya Tantra* declares:

> 35. [The practitioner] will bring an initiated woman, and establish a ritual circle [*kula chakra*].
> 36. Then the practitioner will joyfully worship the goddess, [especially within] her *yoni*. Then he will sing hymns sweetly and chant mantras continuously, while looking at his partner.
> 37. That person who chants mantras continuously while in this state will be lord of all supernatural powers in the Kali yuga.[97]

Here the tantrika is involved with a woman, but only worship and mantras are mentioned as ritual. The text emphasizes gaining *siddh*is or supernatural powers, the goals of folk tantra. The female perspective on this practice is not mentioned in the text.

The most vivid description of the female role in a more orgiastic style of chakra is probably found in the *Kularnava Tantra*. It is an interesting description, as it violates the notions that kula men and women should not be desirous. However, the passions are here justified because the participants are in an altered state (*ullasa*), and because everything in the chakra is transformed (eating becomes fire sacrifice, sight is meditation, sleeping is worship, and union with one's shakti is liberation). This ritual reversal is guarded by the yoginis, who will punish anybody who condemns the participants:

> 67. Intoxicated by passion, the women take shelter with other men, treating them as their own. Each man also takes a new woman (*śakti*) and treats her as his own, when in the state of advanced ecstatic joy.
> 68. Seized by delusion, the men embrace other men. . . .
> 71. O Shambhavi! The yogis take the food from each other's plates and dance with their drinking pots on their heads. . . .
> 73. The women who are not in their normal senses clap and sing songs whose words are unclear, and they stagger while dancing.
> 74. Yogis who are intoxicated with alcohol fall upon the women, and the intoxicated yoginis fall upon the men, O Kulanayika! They are induced to perform such actions, to fulfill their mutual desires.
> 75. When this state of ecstasy is not accompanied by corrupt thoughts, the bull among yogis reaches the state of godhood (*devatabhāva*).[98]

The effect upon the cow among yogis is not clear, but one assumes that the women would have similar ecstatic experiences, as they are also ritual participants.

A third female role is that of the guru. In some tantras, we see female gurus idealized. The *Guptasadhana Tantra* gives a visualization of the female guru: she is located in the *sahasrara* lotus above the head, and her eyes look like lotus petals. She has high breasts and a slender waist, and she is shining like a ruby. She wears red clothes and jeweled ornaments, and is eternal. She is seated at the left of her husband, and her hands show mudras giving boons and freedom from fear.[99] She is graceful, delicate, and beautiful.

Such an image is quite different from the reality of the physical female tantric gurus, who tend to be older, unmarried, sometimes bald, often toughened from ascetic and outdoor life, strong and without jewelry, and clearly avoiding sexual attractiveness. The last thing they want to be is beautiful and delicate. For these human female gurus, tantra is not a fantasy but rather a struggle.

Among human practitioners, we see these textual roles, but they are lived out in more complex fashion, and women are not limited to such roles. The living female tantrikas whom I have interviewed tended to fall into five categories.

1. *Celibate tantric yoginis.* These women, whose status was the highest among women interviewed, were lifelong celibates. Many were gurus with disciples, and some headed temples, ashrams, or tantric study circles. Some also emphasized the importance of bhakti toward the goddess or guru. Tantra for them was a dedicated practice involving mantras, visualizations, austerities, worship (puja), and ritual actions (*kriya*). The goal of tantra was to gain Sakti, both as the goddess and as power.
2. *Holy women* who had been married (*grihi sadhika*), but left their husbands and families. These women had lower status, but some had disciples. Some would wander, practicing tantric meditation and worship, and live at temples or ashrams. Some holy women would go into states of possession by the goddess Kali, induced by chanting tantric *bija* mantras or singing hymns to the goddess (Devi *bhajans*). Tantra for them was ritual action, worship, and possession, usually in response to a call by the goddess. The goal of tantra was to follow the goddess' will in an ascetic setting.
3. *Tantric wives.* These women performed tantric ritual sex and worship as part of devotional action toward their husbands and gurus. The woman was often initiated by the same guru as her husband, and followed his teachings. Tantra was a form of service, involving obedience and following a women's marital obligations. The goal of tantra was to follow dharma and fulfill social obligations.
4. *Professional consorts.* These women performed ritual sex and worship as a way to make a living, and the consort (as well as any children)

was generally supported by the man who was her ritual partner. Often, the woman moved from one sadhu to another, depending on who would shelter and support her. Tantra here is sexual practice, and a subcategory of prostitution. The goal of tantra was to make money, and possibly get a home and a male protector. (I did not find any of these women for interviews: my informants stolidly refused to introduce me to any of them. They are considered to be of low status, though slightly higher than ordinary prostitutes.)[100]

5. *Celibate wives and widows*, who incorporated tantric practice as an aspect of devotion to the goddess. Tantra was a form of devotion, especially in combination with bhakti yoga. The goal of tantra was to please the goddess while living a householder life.

Most female tantrikas interviewed were not only celibate but insistently so. Several said that tantric meditation involves purity and concentration, and that desire would be a distraction and would cause them to fall. I interviewed three women in depth who were female gurus, initiated into Shakta tantric lineages. Two of them practiced tantric rituals themselves, and the third was of Shakta universalist perspective who knew many practicing women tantrikas. All of these women were highly respected, and all of them were celibate. In fact, the highest-status tantrikas that I met, male or female, were celibate, and none had ever attended a *tantric chakra* of the sensationalized variety.

For Gauri Ma, head of an ashram in Bakreshwar, *tantra sadhana* revealed a person's "inner history," giving the power to "see inside," to watch the inner life of the spirit. The goal is to gain Shakti, to have her dwell in the heart. As she said, "It is Shakti who enlightens you, who brings you to the highest states. Shiva is as useless as a corpse, and that is why he is portrayed as one in the iconography." In kundalini yoga, the male and female aspects of the person are inwardly united, and there is no necessity for any union between them in the physical world. The *panchatattva* or forbidden rituals of tantra are symbolic, with wine representing control of the breath, and ritual sex representing the sort of union seen in yogic meditation. She made a special point of saying that no outward practice is necessary for a strong and disciplined tantrika, and that tantric rituals are symbolic of inner transformations.[101]

For Jayashri Ma, *guru ma* of a group of devotees, *tantra sadhana* is a way of achieving a fused identity with Shakti, which lasts over a lifetime. Jayashri was initiated by her tantric guru while they sat on matched sets of human skulls, and with the mantra came the direct entrance of the goddess Adya Shakti into her heart. The mantras, mudras, trances, and rituals were ways of preparing her body for Shakti's entrance. Union with Adya Shakti is the highest state possible, for she is identical with *brahman*, and mother of the universe. Jayashri Ma is a celibate tantric guru, who no longer needs to perform rituals because the goddess has already taken up residence in her heart.[102]

For Archanapuri Ma, *tantra sadhana* is a practice that has a strong component of devotion. Archanapuri is head of an ashram in Jadavpur, and a celibate member of a Ramakrishna lineage. Her guru was originally Vedantin, but later became a devotee of Shakti in the form of Kali Bhavatarini. He performed tantric meditations and offered blood to Kali Bhavatarini, and he taught Archanapuri Ma many meditative techniques. Her understanding of tantra is heavily infused with devotion, and she finds celibacy necessary for both service and religious love.

This role of female guru or *stri-guru* is allowed in the tantric texts, unlike more brahmanical forms of Hinduism. In the last century, the best-known case of a female tantric guru was probably that of Bhairavi Brahmani or Yogeshvari, a woman tantrika who came to see Ramakrishna Paramahamsa and stayed with him for about three years. She is described in Ramakrishna's biographies as almost forty years old yet still attractive, and she supported Ramakrishna's spiritual status. She had him sit on skull-seats, chant mantras, eat fish and human flesh from a skull, and perform the practices described in the major tantras. She brought him women with whom Ramakrishna could perform some of the rituals, but the biographies are unclear about his practice with them—Ramakrishna claimed to have fallen into trance, and been unaware of performing anything.[103] There is no direct evidence that Yogeshvari at any point lost her celibate status.

Ramakrishna seems to have been quite ambiguous toward these practices, partly accepting her as a guru, and partly rejecting tantric practices generally. His followers were also ambiguous about the Bhairavi. Some found her teaching acceptable, as she was of high caste, and even sexual practices were allowable if a guru were present (rather like having a chaperone). Other disciples found her a bad influence, and were glad when she left.

Tantric holy women who have been married but left their homes due to a religious call have lower status, though their religious dedication and celibacy still gain them respect. The holy woman who has left her husband and gone out on her own, only returning occasionally to visit her children and household, does not have an easy life. Often she has been initiated by the Shakta household priest (kula-guru) and hears a prophetic call from the goddess, who asks her not to oil her hair, not to eat certain foods, and to go on a pilgrimage to one of the goddess's holy sites. She leaves the household, and may survive by begging, telling fortunes, or being possessed by the goddess and gaining donations from observers. She gains status when she starts to attract devotees, and sometimes she may claim a special set of supernatural powers given by the goddess (especially healing or materializing food). She may be possessed by the goddess, as well as by other deities.

Such calls often begin while the girl is very young. Lakshmi Ma was a devotee of Kali and Tara, both traditionally tantric goddesses, and she used to see Kali and play with her when she was a child. After she married, she continued to see Kali, who would complain if she did not get sufficient offerings. She told her family of her visions, and they bound her with ropes and had her undergo an exorcism. It was unsuccessful, though they burned her and later bound her in iron chains. The goddess gave her matted hair (*jata*), which was her call to go out and be a holy woman. The family calmed down when her husband had a dream of Kali, telling him to build an altar for her, and they began to worship there. She later lived separately from her husband, performing rituals at Tarapith and other places. She stated that she planned to perform the *shava-sadhana* corpse ritual, in which the practitioner meditates upon and sits on a corpse at the burning ground, when the time was right for it. She dressed in classic tantric fashion—red clothing, matted hair, heavy strings of rudraksha bends (*malas*), and she often carried a trident.[104]

Another type of tantric holy woman is the tantric wife, and in this case *lata sadhana* is performed within a marriage that is otherwise traditional. For tantric wives, the religious goals tend to be devotion and obedience to husband and guru, following tantric dharma, and desire for union with Shakti. I spoke several years ago with a Sahajiya couple who wanted me to be initiated into their circle, and the perspectives of the man and the woman in the couple were very different. Although Sahajiya is Vaishnava tantra, the focus on Radha shows Shakta influence. The man emphasized adventure and pleasure (male tantrikas could have sex for four hours), and increased attractiveness (for tantra worked as a sort of birth control, allowing women not to get pregnant and turn into wrinkled old hags by the age of twenty-four years, which he said was what happened without it). Tantra was fun, exciting, and a way to escape the routine. He felt that it made Indian men superior to Western men in endurance.

His wife's perspective was quite different. Tantric practice was obedience to guru and god, and a way to help her husband and please him. Tantra was not rebellious but rather following *stri-dharma*, a wife's obligation, for it was the wish of her husband and guru. Tantra was a way to serve them. She was unwilling to give details of her practice unless I was initiated, but she did say that her guru's face was present at all times within her mind during the ritual.

This couple lived in a large joint family that farmed land in rural West Bengal. They would leave the house late at night to practice, after everyone else was asleep, and returned in time to get some sleep before the day's chores began. Nobody in the family knew they were practicing tantrikas. Many householder tantrikas seem to practice this way: either the family does not know of their practice or the family is of tantric lineage and they know, but the neighbors do not.[105]

Such practice among couples is highly secretive, known only to other religious practitioners. The guru Archanapuri Ma knew some women who were in tantric arranged marriages. She described them as married women who were helpers to their husbands, who were religious practitioners. She said that these women were not used and thrown away, as most people believe.

> Tantra is like this: India has always tried to elevate all traits of the human character through religion. The mind is the eternal playground of sensual desire. While Western psychology has accepted this carnal tendency of mankind as his original or root (*mula*) inclination, Hindu religion has tried to transform it through the path of spiritual discipline, to divinize all tendencies of the person. This is the basis of *virachara* practice, and it is very difficult, because some rituals involve taking a woman companion (*bhairavi*). Though these paths appear difficult to us, they are very potent and useful for the deserving aspirants, and have been revealed by liberated people. *Shakti-sadhana* centers around *shakti* or strength, and requires a powerful mind and great concentration.
>
> We must also pay attention to the female tantrika (*bhairavi*). Is her part only mechanical, required only by male aspirants to prove their mental and spiritual strength? Is her life useless once the above purpose is served? No, for there are many female tantrikas who can legitimately be called equal travelers of the spiritual path and equal sharers in its benefits. Some have attained to great religious heights, but most prefer to remain inconspicuous, and people do not know about them.
>
> In some cases both husband and wife take part together in the Bhairavi Chakra, and practice together while leading an active householder's life. I have met a few such female tantrikas who are engaged in spiritual practices, despite the responsibility of bringing up children. They only belong to one chakra, for a female tantrika who participates in a chakra conducted by one male tantrika does not join any other chakra conducted by some other male tantrika. In some chakras, the mental strength of the tantrika is put to severe tests. A young sixteen-year-old girl is brought to the ritual, who has all of the prescribed auspicious signs, and is pure and holy in both her character and her mind. Her company will lead the tantrika across the difficult path to perfection.[106]

Tantric wives are rare, and they tend to identify themselves as basically traditional wives who are following dharma. This is because the sexual rituals and their accompanying yogic practices are performed under the instructions of the guru, and in obedience to a husband who wishes to perform the ritual. Thus, the wife is traditionally obedient to husband and guru. Some practitioners have said that it is better to have the wife as partner, for otherwise the woman may not be respected. As the Sahajiya husband described earlier said, tantric practice is believed to maintain youth in the woman. This is better than childbearing, which ages the woman and brings her close to death. Men get strength and virility, and more energy for meditation and other pursuits, and the woman retains her beauty.[107]

Some female tantric practitioners are professional ritual assistants, who practice tantric sexual ritual with different male Shakta tantrikas. Such a role is a very low-status one, and nobody that I interviewed could tell me anything of such women, or would admit to knowing any. Thus, my information on these women is second-hand, depending on speculations from informants and writings by previous researchers. These women were understood as having a specialty within prostitution, as some women had skills in dominating men. It was rather like an addendum to the courtesan's traditional sixty-four arts, an extra set of skills that professional women could gain. I was told that most of such women were low-caste and wanted to gain extra money for the household, or else they were widows (especially child widows) who had no other way to make a living. Several informants expressed sorrow over their unfortunate state.

This analysis was supported by Bholanath Bhattacharjee, who interviewed forty-eight women who were professional ritual consorts, and gave detailed case histories for four of them.[108] These women were called either *bhairavis* (those involved in Shakta ritual) or *sadhikas* (those involved in Vaishnava rituals). The term *sadhika* is a general term for holy woman or female religious practitioner, while the term *bhairavi* refers to the consort of a *bhairava*, a male Shaivite tantrika. A majority of the women followed this profession as a family occupation—it was almost a caste, as the job was handed down within the family, and was hereditary. A minority were converted to the profession by people whom they met. Almost all were initiated and given new names. The ritual consorts who were most desirable were those who had the marks of the yakshini, or nature goddess.

Their gurus taught the women breathing techniques and mantras to lessen passion, as well as positions and muscular contractions to control the pace of intercourse. These techniques allow the woman to be qualified to practice with either one man for an extended period or with a variety of men over time. For those women following their hereditary role, these practices are understood to be both service, helping the male practitioner to gain awareness of *brahman*, and following their own dharma, which brings spiritual advancement in this life.

Many of these women learned this profession while they were young girls, orphaned or without a father, from much older men. Bhattacharya's article described four case histories. In the first case, an orphaned girl of seventeen years met an elderly man who taught her these practices; she later practiced with at least fifty other male practitioners in Birbhum. When her main *sadhaka* (male ritual partner) performed the practice improperly and she became pregnant, he left her (this type of tantra does not allow ejaculation—if a woman gets pregnant, this shows a problem in the ritual). However, he later came back, saying that if his guru liked practicing with her, he would take her back, and also pay her rent and support their baby. She said that she was forced by poverty to agree to this. The guru appreciated her abilities, and asked her to become his own *bhairavi* and leave the other man (he also was willing to support her and her baby). She stayed with him until his death, and then lived in a sexual relationship with a *bhairava* who came for shelter to her hut. She trained her daughter as a consort, and the daughter learned the sexual rituals from the *bhairava* with whom they were living.

In the second case described by Bhattacharya, a widow was forced by hunger to become a prostitute. She later learned the skills of a *sadhika* from a guru. She found living with the guru preferable to prostitution, as she did not have to entertain many men, though she still called it hard work. Her guru was almost twice her age. In the third case, the woman was born due to an accident in her mother's ritual practice with a *bhairava*. She felt that she was under obligation to follow in her mother's footsteps, and also become a *bhairavi*. She and her own guru initiate couples, and teach them techniques of sexual *ritual* in the same bed (though she seemed more concerned that they practiced "even by day, if necessary.") They are taught various rhythms, and to visualize ocean waves and lions and tigers rather than images like snakes (which bring loss of control). She said that, in case of problems in the practice (usually pregnancy), the woman returns to prostitution.

In the fourth case, the *bhairavi* (her name meant "one given to weeping") was the daughter of a cook who was very poor. The cook asked a *bhairava* who was a relative of the household for which she worked to find a match for the daughter. He was much older than the girl, and he decided to initiate her as his *bhairavi*. At the time of the article, she had lived with him for nine years. The *bhairava* had also slept with the cook, the girl's mother.

These women have come to accept their roles as consorts as their lot in life. Several were forced by poverty and hunger into these roles, and they needed money to care for their children. Often they were bound by considerations of dharma; since their mothers were *sadhikas*, they too must follow that profession, thus, it becomes a caste, and the woman is bound to its obligations. Many of these relationships are semi-incestuous, where the man with whom the mother is sleeping is also sleeping with her daughter. However, because it is placed in a ritual context, the father-figure becomes the guru, and relationship can be understood as a sort of religious apprenticeship.

Although role of the consort is often idealized in the West as a sort of freedom and liberated sexuality (which it may perhaps be in some cases, if the woman has a choice of career), there are clearly problems for women who are forced involuntarily into the role and would themselves prefer a more traditional life. The great problem is pregnancy, which is generally blamed on the woman's lack of meditative ability, despite the clear responsibility of the man.

Quite unlike the ritual consort, we also see the situation of the celibate wife, who uses tantric mantras and visualization to worship one of the goddesses. The celibate wife is in the household, but has already had children and wants no more, or has been celibate since the time of the marriage (as in the famous case of the female guru Anandamayi Ma). The wife becomes a devotee of the goddess, and leads a privately ascetic life. She spends most of her time in the *puja* room before the goddess's image, while the husband acquiesces and stays celibate as best he can. Sometimes the wife may become a worship leader (*pujarini*) for a group of other women, or the leader of a *Kali-kirtan* singing group, or run a major center for worship in her neighborhood. In such cases she gains a reputation as a holy woman, while the husband stays in the background. Many husbands are quite amenable to the wife becoming a celibate yogini in later years. They often believe that they will benefit spiritually by supporting such wives, in the same way that others benefit by supporting a guru who may help them in the afterlife. Such service will allow them to "ride the coattails of their wives" to get to heaven.

We may also see tantric and devotional practice within the home as performed by widows. The householder widow who spends her life in religious ritual and pilgrimage may be respected or disparaged. I have seen Bengali Shakta religious widow matriarchs, who are called *sadhikas* by members of the extended family, who domineer both their households and brahmin priests called in to perform rituals. They literally hold the keys to the household, and to the moneybox as well. However, I have also seen Vaishnava widows ignored and pushed aside, in situations where they are humbled with their heads shaved, and where Vaishnava males and even their own gurus look down on them.[109] There are many views of widows.

The popular notion of a tantrika is not a person performing austerities or a householder worshiping a goddess, but rather a person seeking pleasure—preferable in a group. This is not an accurate picture. At least in West Bengal, most Shakta tantrikas tend to be loners, and they rarely get together for rituals. Most Shakta tantrikas interviewed could not identify other Shakta tantrikas in the vicinity, or even at a distance. Chakras seem to be one of their few reasons to interact (perhaps along with holidays and a few pilgrimages).

On the rare occasions when Shakta tantrikas do have chakras, they are secret and underground, as chakras are illegal in West Bengal. The religious goal of the chakra is not pleasure but rather the vision of the deities or unity with them, by emotional sharing or by possession. The chakra is understood to change identity; as the *Kularnava Tantra* says, "Within the chakra, all men become identical to [or like] Shiva, and all women become identical to Shakti."[110] When they leave the chakra, identity with the deity disappears, and the ordinary identity returns, along with caste limitations and traditional dharmic rules. When chakras are performed for religious reason, temporary possession by a deity is usually the goal of the chakra, induced by the normally forbidden ritual actions that are sacred to Shiva and Shakti.

The chakra is not intended as an arena for wife-swapping (indeed, ideally it is his wife who accompanies the male tantrika) but as an *imitatio dei*, an imitation of divine behavior like the Babylonian rituals of divine kingship or following the Stations of the Cross in Catholicism. Shiva and Shakti spend a lot of time having sex in the myths, if you want to imitate them in order to induce possession by them, you do what they do. Whereas the Stations of the Cross give insight and compassion, the chakra ritual is intended to give fused identity—and it is because of the deities' presence that forbidden behavior becomes acceptable. The participants are not doing anything themselves; the gods are acting. The disadvantage is that one should not be feeling anything personally—if the gods are really in full possession, they are the ones acting through your body, and the individual does not feel individual pleasure any more than the hook-swinger should feel pain from the hooks in his back and shoulders. It is the worshiper's goal to transcend the normal boundaries of society, and by doing so unite with the deities. The ritual is the method of reaching that point. If the worshiper is experiencing sensations as an individual, then the deity is not fully present. The goal is a perfect union with the deity, a ritual foretaste of a state in which the identity is permanently fused.

In recent years, however, a reverse chakra has begun to be practiced, a sort of Black Mass version of the original. It is called the *pashu chakra*, and its intent is pleasure rather than union with the deities. In the tantric tradition, there are three levels of practitioners. The animal or *pashu* person is not ready for tantric rites, as he is still bound by lust, greed, and ignorance, and needs to stay within the traditional bounds of orthodox dharma. The *vira* or hero has gained some detachment from his instincts, and wishes to experience union with the deities. He is the one who takes initiation and instruction, and performs the chakra in proper tantric manner, according to the shastras. The third type is the *divya* person, who has gained the spiritual goal, and no longer needs to practice rituals.

The *pashu chakra* is thus performed by inappropriate people (the animal people) for inappropriate reasons, such as spending time with attractive low-caste women. Rather like a medieval Black Mass, it inverts the religious goal of the ritual. There are rumors of alcoholic delirium, drugs, orgies—the sort of thing that many Westerners associate with the original ritual. I heard many rumors of evil, perverse, degenerate people practicing this chakra in North Calcutta when I was there in 1994 (in fact, I received an invitation to one, which I declined). This corrupt chakra is exactly the sort of chakra mentioned in most of the books written on tantra, both by high-caste (nontantric) Hindu outsiders and by Western missionary outsiders. One wonders if the organizers of the *pashu chakras* have been reading the Hindu theologians or the Western missionaries who wrote in the nineteenth century (emphasizing India's religious corruption and thus its need for Christianity). Of course, they may also have heard of or visited Rajneesh's ashram in Pune (which has practiced its own form of "neotantra" for many years). It becomes a case of fact imitating fiction.

Much literature on tantra has sensationalized the sexual aspects of tantra, making it the one necessary thing. Sexual ritual is clearly not necessary, however, or even common, among tantrikas. Women tantrikas spoke of it as unimportant. Most said it was rarely practiced, and some said that such practices were almost never performed, like the large Vedic sacrifices performed by kings long ago. Some women tantrikas have told me that the individual sexual ritual is really only for men, who have difficulty controlling their instincts, and that it is rarely useful or necessary for woman. Because of the way Indian girls are brought up, it is rare to find any who cannot control their instincts; Indian sons are indulged and petted, while Indian daughters are taught to give the best food and toys to their brothers. Indian women thus learn to sacrifice their desires at an early age. Sexual ritual is basically for people who are weak rather than strong—and weak people do not belong at the burning ground.

For many female tantric gurus, sexual ritual was understood to be peripheral rather than central. It is a practice done for people trying to control their instincts, by people (generally male) who do not have the necessary yogic discipline for real practice and need to take a few extra remedial courses to qualify for advanced practice. The issue is not that the *vira* tantrikas are sinful, but rather that they are weak, and spend their time at the lower end of practice rather than the higher end. Some female tantrikas implied that men were generally weaker than women in this area, and more compulsive about needing sexuality. As Gauri Ma explained, "Most women have no need of sexual ritual (*lata sadhana*). It is for men, who are bound by lust (*kama*), and need to overcome it. Then they take a consort. In women, lust is not so strong. *Tantra sadhana* is meditation (*kriya*) and worship (puja)."[111] No female tantrikas said that *lata sadhana* was evil, or sinful, or scandalous. They did not appear to be hiding their secret, forbidden practices. They simply said it was rare, and unnecessary. Some female tantrikas were outspoken, saying that no man was going to take away the shakti they had gained by hard austerities and long recitation of mantras.

Tantric literature does speak of the union of *yoga* and *bhoga*, or *mukti* and *bhukti*—liberation and enjoyment. However, women tantrikas interviewed have interpreted this to mean that the world is a positive and existing place (as opposed to the Vedantic denial of the world's reality through *maya*). Such statements represent a belief in the unity of natural and supernatural, and a denial of dualism. The term *bhoga* did not mean ritual sex to them, but rather that one can appreciate the beauty of the world and still be spiritual.

When we look at the relationship between the descriptions of tantric women in the texts and in practice, one thing that is striking is that the freedom seen in the textual women is rarely seen in the culture. The most important aspect of tantra for the female tantrikas interviewed was not union with men but rather union with Shakti, which could be attained in a variety of ways, and does not require a male partner.

It is difficult to evaluate tantra as a tradition when the written sources and the living practitioners understand the tradition in different ways. We can support the text over the practitioners, saying that the texts were written by *pandits* and experts, and that the tradition should be understood by its most literate and articulate exponents. Or we can say that the texts are fantasies, written by an elite that had the leisure to play imaginatively with mantras and fantasize kula women as universally beautiful and available, free from the rules of society.

It is hard to gauge the historicity of these texts, as there was little fieldwork reporting before the twentieth century, and even less that covers the area of tantra; the emotional statements of nineteenth-century missionaries and critics on the matter were usually not based on first-hand observation. Were these chakra rituals performed in the past? Or were they merely fantasies of frustrated males that people enjoyed reading, religious justifications for illegitimate sexual behavior? It may be something like the situation of Satanism in medieval Europe, where Catholic clerics seem to have invented the Satanic pact and the Black Mass. Many writers suggest that these rituals came to be practiced long after the literature about them was published and disseminated.

As to the role of women, the texts are ambiguous and often inconsistent. The female tantrika's freedom is emphasized, yet she is bound to one man, and if she chooses another, she will burn in the fierce hells. The situation today seems to be the same—of the few women who belong to a chakra, they may only go with their husbands, and to no other chakra group, and with no other man. It is her husband who decides, for she is his helper. It is *stri-dharma*, not the violation of dharma. And while her power is emphasized, she must still be beautiful and agreeable. According to most tantric texts, if she is not pleasing to her partner, she does not count as a kula woman, no matter what sort of power or virtue she possesses.

For the more independent women, tantra is a form of yoga, using tantric mantra, mudras, yantras, and images as supports. This often involves kundalini meditation. *Shakti* is stored up, gained from the goddess's grace and presence, and from the vision of her mantric and imagistic forms. Men can drain this shakti in tantric sexual ritual, not only because the woman has lost her celibacy but also because there is believed to be a transfer of energy in sexuality. Men gain power, but women lose it (a reverse of the brahmanical notion that men lose their power as a result of sexuality). Some tantric texts support this view, speaking of women as yantras within which the man may find Shakti or

Devi. One meaning of yantra is "tool," and in this sense the women would be used by men in their search for power—clearly a Kantian ethical problem of means versus ends.

As to whether women were ever tantric teachers of men, there seems to be limited evidence for this claim in the Bengali Shakta tradition. We do have conversations between Shiva and Devi in the tantric agama and *nigama* texts, (in the agamas, Shiva speaks, and in the nigamas, Devi speaks). We could make the claim that this primordial couple represents the founders of the tantric tradition, and that Devi is a human woman teaching the tradition. There is no evidence, however, that Devi is anything other than a goddess on Mount Kailash, though she does occasionally incarnate in semihuman forms, such as Sati and Uma. In the puranic texts, where Sati and Uma also appear, they do not teach; they are subservient women, dedicated to Shiva. We do have the case of Bhairavi Brahmani teaching Ramakrishna Paramahamsa, though she seems to have taught as a celibate.

Women tantrikas are more highly respected as celibates, though they are more publicized as consorts in sexual ritual. Literal acting out of the rituals has less status than internalization of the ritual, and again we see that female classical tantrikas who understand ritual symbolically have greater social status than female folk tantrikas who actually perform rituals literally.

In this section we have noted the sensationalizing of tantra—that it is a corruption of religion, that it is an exciting avenue by which to subvert repressive Victorian and Indian notions of sexuality, that it is a form of sexual liberation for women. But although the sexual side of tantra is emphasized in other areas of India, in West Bengal the major tantric theme is death and its transcendence.

## Sitting on the Corpse's Chest: The Tantric Ritual of *Shava-sadhana*

Whereas other regional forms of tantra in India are famed for their real or imagined sexual rituals, the Bengali style of Shakta tantra is perhaps most marked by its emphasis on death. *Shava-sadhana*, or the ritual practice of sitting on a corpse, is one of its most important rituals. For many practitioners interviewed, it is the single most important ritual in Shakta tantra.

The corpse ritual contains the three strands of Bengali Shaktism: folk, tantric, and bhakti. But it is primarily a tantric ritual, and rarely performed in folk Shaktism or Shakta bhakti. From the folk perspective, the power of the corpse ritual leads to enhancement of life on earth. Challenging death leads to immortality, which is defined as *amarta*, nondeath, a situation implying long life, wealth, and power. From the yogic or tantric perspective, rituals in the burning ground lead to detachment from the physical world and union with a transcendent ground, as Shiva or Shakti or *brahman*. There is also a third interpretation for the ritual, which involves the incorporation of the devotional or bhakti perspective. From this angle, the ritual brings a loving relationship with a deity who has a form and personality, and gives salvation by grace. All of these are present in the ritual and literature of the *shava-sadhana* rite.

In the typical *shava-sadhana* rite, on a new-moon night (or the eighth or fourteenth day of the moon), the practitioner should go to a burning ground or some other lonely spot (a deserted house, a riverside, under a bilva tree, or on a hill). He (or she) should bring a corpse, young and attractive, low-caste, of a person who died by violence, drowning, or snakebite. The body is washed, and placed on a blanket, deerskin or tiger skin. The practitioner should worship it, and then sit on the corpse and contemplate the god or goddess. He or she will experience fearful images and sounds, as well as temptations, but he must remain emotionally detached—or else he may go insane. If he is successful, he may gain the power to use a mantra (*mantrasiddhi*), or become one with Shiva using the corpse as a mediator, or have a vision of the goddess. In the visionary case, she may appear to possess the corpse, or appear before the practitioner as a beautiful woman, a little girl, or a great goddess in the sky.

The origin of the corpse ritual is unknown. Shaivite Kapalikas and Kalamukhas early on made use of skulls and bones, and folk religion throughout India has used ritual sacrifices, including at times human sacrifices, to propitiate the gods and to make the ground fertile.[112] Kapalika practitioners worshiped the god Bhairava Shiva, and traditionally wore ashes from burned corpses as well as skull necklaces. The Kapalika carried a skull (*kapala*) that was used as an eating bowl, and wore a loincloth and animal skins. The word *kapalin* (skull-bearer) occurs in a third-century CE sutra (the *Yajnavalkya-smriti* 3.243), and Kapalikas are mentioned by name in texts from the ninth century CE onward.[113] They were known for their austerities and tantric practices. In Ramacandra's *Kaumudimitrananda*, a Kapalika offers oblations of human intestines into a ritual fire and revives a corpse (who then strikes the Kapalika).[114] In Somadeva's *Kathasaritsagara* (written between 1063 and 1081 CE), a Kapalika worships a corpse within a ritual circle or mandala, to gain power over a woman with whom he had fallen in love. Also in this text, a Kapalika brought a woman back to life while she was already on a blazing funeral pyre, and took her back to his cave by using his magical powers. Her husband followed, and threw the Kapalika's magical *khatvanga* staff into the Ganges. Somadeva comments, "Thus heretics, who make a mockery of the Shivagamas for the pleasure of evil accomplishments, fall [into ruin], as they had already fallen [into sin]."[115]

Narendranath Bhattacarya writes that this practice involves murder, for the tantrika gets a young *chandala* boy drunk and kills him, and uses him as the corpse in the ritual. Bhattacarya calls the practice "a typical and clumsy overgrowth of the primitive beliefs and rituals connected with fertility, death and revival."[116] I should note, however, that tantrikas with whom I have spoken say that the goddess must choose the corpse—indeed, finding the right corpse is proof that it is time to perform the ritual. To kill a person in order to create your own corpse would be to take over the goddess's responsibilities, and would displease her (and pleasing the goddess is the point of the ritual). Sadhakas with whom I spoke at the Shakta site of Tarapith reclined on piles of skulls and bones to address their devotees, and some of these bones had been used in ritual practices.

The use of corpses in ritual has also been associated with possession trance and asceticism. In the old Bengali *gambhira* rites (these forms are rarely seen today) there was a corpse dance, and the corpse was "awakened"—life was instilled, without visible signs. The corpse was purified by mantras, and placed in a pool or tied to high branches of a tree. A *hadi* or low-caste scavenger would then decorate it with wreaths and vermilion, and tie a cord around its waist. The presence of the corpse inspired the god Shiva to possess his devotees, and they would become strong with Shiva's own endurance and capable of withstanding various austerities: needles and nails driven into the body, through the tongue, and into the sides with cloths hanging that are dipped in ghee and then lit on fire. There was also possession by ghosts (*bhutas* and *pretas*) or by the goddess Mashan Chamunda Kali, and the participants would sing songs to avert evil.[117] The possession of the corpse appeared to have acted as the trigger or inspiration for these other forms of possession.

The corpse ritual is usually associated with magic and power in the world by writers, and its religious dimensions are neglected. Even in Mircea Eliade's *Encyclopedia of Religion*, André Padoux writes that, "Another 'secret' worship is done with a corpse. It is used to achieve particular goals, usually evil."[118] From this perspective, the *shavavada* or way of the corpse is understood as a ritual of black magic. Its practice is *nilasadhana*, here translated more as the dark practice rather than the ritual of Shiva. It may also be understood as fertility magic, whereby death brings life. The magical view of the practice is often seen in folklore. In a typical description from *Folktales of Hindustan*, King Vikramaditya encounters an evil exminister:

> He found the yogi seated in the midst of the fire, and before him lay a ghastly corpse. The dead body lay flat on its back, and a person, in whom the Raja recognised one of his discharged and discontented ministers, was sitting on the chest of the dead body. He was repeating some mantras, and now and then putting a flower immersed in red sandal paste, with leaves of bel and incense, into the mouth of the dead body. The terrible ceremony of raising the corpse was being gone through, and after an hour or so the ex-minister exclaimed, "Speak, O son, speak." Then Vikram saw to his terror the lips of the dead body move, but heard no sound. Again the ex-minister cried out:—"Speak, O son, speak. Thee, O my beloved son, have I sacri-

> ficed to mother Kali, in order to wreak vengeance on the ungrateful Raja. Speak, O son, speak." . . . Again, the cruel father and ex-minister cried out for the third time, but without success.[119]

As Jonathan Parry has pointed out, the corpse is viewed as polluting and dangerous, but also as an object of great purity, even a deity.[120] It is the auspicious sacrifice, said to be Shiva himself, and an extreme of both impurity and sanctity. Parry describes the *shava-sadhana* ritual as it is performed by the Shaivite Aghoris of Varanasi:

> According to the descriptions I was given, the corpse is held fast during the *śava-sādhanā* by a silken thread, which binds its wrist or ankle to a stake in the ground. It is then surrounded by a protective circle, within which the evil spirits of the cremation ground cannot penetrate, and outside of which are placed meat and liquor for them to consume. These spirits will try to engage the adept in a dialogue which he must at all costs resist. Provided that he is sufficiently resolute, they will eventually tire and accept the offerings he has left for them. This is a sign that his austerities will be rewarded. The corpse's mouth will relax, allowing the Aghori to feed it a tiny quantity of *khīr* [rice pudding]. He will subsequently decapitate it in order to acquire the skull, or cut a bone from the spine, and finally immerse its remains in the river. This is followed by a period of severe ascetic restraint which completes his mastery over the deceased's spirit. The *ojhā*, who is a specialist in the control over the malevolent dead, is also said to perform *śava-sādhanā* for similar ends. But while the Aghori sits on the corpse's chest, the *ojhā* sits on the stomach.[121]

According to this description, no religious transformations take place in the Aghori—he merely wishes to gain a skull, and control over a spirit, through whom he may communicate with other spirits.[122] *Shava-sadhana* here is a magical process in which evil spirits try to penetrate the protective circle, and the practitioner conquers by ignoring them. Eventually, by gaining the skull and performing austerities, he also conquers the soul of the deceased.[123]

In West Bengal, there are practitioners known as *pishacha tantrikas*, tantrikas who have gained power over *pishachas* or demonic creatures. Such power is often believed to be gained by practices at the burning ground. They are exorcists, and do a good business in protective amulets and intrafamilial revenge. One such tantrika interviewed in Calcutta had a back room full of dusty, grey-brown human skulls and bones, and I was told by informants that these objects had the most power (shakti) of anything in his supply. He had on the wall a picture of a skeleton sitting in meditation upon a corpse, with a red mandala of Kundalini at the navel area. In this image, the corpse was symbolic of the physical body, left behind during meditation.

These approaches to *shava-sadhana* are heavily magical, and do not appear to have a traditionally religious end in sight, such as proximity to a god or entrance into a state of liberation or *brahman*. However, there are other forms of this rite that are understood to be religious practices.

The corpse ritual is part of the tantric path known as *vamachara* (the way of the left or reverse practice) or *kulachara* (the way of a family group or religious lineage). The goal is loosening the person from the bonds of samsara—he or she is no longer attached, neither hates nor fears, is ashamed of nothing, and has gone beyond all traditional notions of good and evil. Such a person is in the state of *divyabhava*, beyond purity and impurity. It is a radical breaking of attachment, with both the world of samsara and traditional morality.

The Shaivite tantrika, who follows the yogic approach, seeks total concentration and conquest of fear, and worships the gods all around him and in the corpse. When the god dwells in his body for the fifteen years following the ritual, his own body is understood to be the body of Shiva, thus sanctified and treated as ritually pure. As David Kinsley writes, "Surrounded by death in the place of death, those aspects of reality that end in the fires of the cremation ground become distasteful . . . attachment to the world and the ego is cut, and union with Shiva, the conqueror of death, is sought."[124]

From the yogic perspective, the goal is to sit on the corpse and gain detachment from the fear of death and spiritual discernment, recognizing both world and self as finite, and even dead in comparison to the realm of *brahman*. This recognition should cause repulsion toward the physical world, and attraction toward infinity as Shiva or *brahman* or infinite consciousness. The tantric dimension can also include theistic elements and interpretation.

The devotional approach to the corpse ritual interprets the practice to be a sign of true love, and evidence of one's passion and dedication to the goddess. Indeed, the goddess is herself often seated on a corpse in her iconography. Shiva without Shakti is said to be a corpse, and the goddess (often in the form of Kali) may stand over him or sit upon him. The practitioner meditates upon Shakti in the heart lotus, wearing the dead bodies of two boys as earrings, with a belt made of dead men's hands, sitting upon the (spirits) (*pretas*) of Brahma, Vishnu, Rudra, Ishvara, and Sadashiva. They are dead, because they cannot act without her power.[125] She is naked, and surrounded by jackals. In her form as Ucchishtachandalini, she is wearing a red sari and ornaments, carrying a skull and a sword, and is sitting on a corpse. She is worshiped when the practitioner is in an impure state, with impure objects.[126]

Ideally, the corpse ritual brings about a vision of the goddess. As Woodroffe notes:

> In successful Śavāsana the Devī, it is said, appears to the Sādhaka. In Śava-sādhana the Sādhaka sits astride on the back of a corpse (heading [toward] the north), on which he draws a Yantra and then does Japa. . . . The Devatā materializes by means of the corpse. There is possession of it (Āveśa)—that is, entry of the Devatā into the dead body. At the conclusion of a successful rite, it is said, that the head of the corpse turns round, and, facing the Sādhaka, speaks, bidding him name his boon, which may be spiritual or worldly advancement as he wishes. This is part of the Nīla Sādhana done by the "Hero" (Vīra), for it and Śavāsana are attended by many terrors.[127]

The devotee sits upon the corpse to call down the goddess, who saves him when he is threatened by demons or ghosts. As the *Tantra Tattva* phrases it, "If her son is in trouble, Ma runs down from her golden throne on Mt. Kailāsa, without staying even to arrange her dress, and extends her ten fear-dispelling arms in ten directions, crying 'fear not.' "[128] The Mother's compassion toward her children is a well-known theme in Bengali song and story. The poet Dasarathi Ray states of the goddess as Jagadamba:

> Mother does not care for the children who mix with others
> And go about laughing and playing.
> She does not go to them, she rests instead
> [But] She takes the child who weeps on her lap.[129]

Here the tantrika is the child of the deity, overwhelmed by fear and love, who seeks to dwell in the lap of the goddess. This is the bhakti surrender of the devotee, who passes the ocean of birth and death to dwell in eternity with his goddess. The ritual of *shava-sadhana* is a powerful way to call down the goddess, for her power (shakti) is understood to dwell most strongly in corpses, burning grounds, jackals, and natural sites.[130] In this ritual, the corpse itself becomes the body of the deity, and the practitioner also becomes ritually sanctified. The goddess is often worshiped in other bodies, where the power of the mantra (*mantra-shakti*) reveals her true form. She may be worshiped as Kumari in the bodies of young virgins, as Uma in jackals, as Mother of Siddhis within the brahmani bird or kite.[131] She may enter the corpse itself, and speak through its mouth, or she may appear in a vision. The goddess descends as a savioress in the midst of fear, as Bhattacarya explains:

> When all earthly means fail . . . when in that terrible and pitiless great cremation ground, where horrors do a frantic dance, there is, despite the presence of the all-good Mother, nothing in all the infinite world which for our safety we can call our own; in that deep darkness of a new-moon night, haunted with destructive Bhairavas, Vetālas, Siddhas, Bhūtas, Vaṭukas, and Dākinīs . . . when the firm

> and heroic heart of even the great Vīra shakes with fear; when even the intricate bonds of the Sādhaka's posture on the back of the corpse which is awakened by Mantra is loosened; when with a fanning (*sic*) heart the Vīra feels as he sits the earth quake furiously under him; when without means of rescue he is about to fall and be crushed; when he is overtaken by the swoon of death—if even at such times the Sādhaka but . . . extends his uplifted hands, saying, "Save me, I pray thee, O Gurudeva!" then the Mother of the world, who is Herself the Guru, at once forgets all his faults, dispels all his difficulties with Her glance, and stretching forth ten hands instead of two, says: "Come, my child, there is no more fear," and blesses the Sādhaka by raising him to Her assuring bosom.[132]

Here danger is deliberately sought, so that the Mother goddess must come down and rescue the devotee.

One of the earliest stories of the Shakta form of the corpse ritual is the story of Sarvananda of Mehar. This story was told to me by several informants in Calcutta, and seems to be an important origin story for Bengali tantrikas. Sarvananda was believed to have lived in the late fourteenth or early fifteenth century, and to have attained *siddhi* by means of this ritual on new-moon night.

The story of Sarvananda begins with his grandfather, Vasudeva Bhattacharya, of Tipperah, in what is now West Bengal. He was a devoted Shakta, who went to Kamakhya in Assam to practice tantric worship of the goddess (*shakti sadhana*). He heard a voice say that he would attain liberation in his next life, when he would be reborn as his own grandson. He gave to his servant Purnananda an engraved piece of copper with his mantra (or according to some sources, a *yantra*), for worshiping the goddess.

Later Sarvananda, the grandson, was also attended by Purnananda, now an old man. The boy was uneducated, and both neighbors and family jeered at his lack of intelligence. While wandering about depressed he was initiated by a passing sannyasi, who told him to perform ritual practice with Purnananda. Purnananda told him about the most powerful form of practice, the corpse ritual.

Sarvananda and Purnananda assembled all the ritual implements, and only needed a recently dead corpse to serve as the seat of the tantric practitioner. Purnananda volunteered for this so that he might be blessed for his sacrifice, and Sarvananda agreed. Purnananda strangled himself, warning Sarvananda that he should be neither tempted nor afraid, and only ask for the vision of the Mother.

Sarvananda sat on the corpse of Purnananda; he saw horrible ghosts, terrible storms, beautiful heavenly dancers, and finally the vision of the Mother. He remained detached throughout. The goddess blessed him and revived Purnananda, and Sarvananda became a *siddha purusha*, a liberated person. The dark, new-moon night was miraculously transformed into a shining full-moon night. He also gained the power of *vak siddhi*, so that all of his statements became true. He was the first tantrika to see the goddess in all of her ten major forms in one night (the *dasha mahavidya*).[133]

Thus the corpse ritual evoked the goddess, who blessed Sarvananda with wisdom, and combined folk, yogic, and devotional goals (some of the most powerful Shakta stories combine these strands). His practice came by inspiration, but over time the ritual became suggested and even required, with a threat of hell for its nonperformance. As the *Kali Tantra* says of the practitioner:

> 12. He who worships [the goddess] Parvati without the corpse ritual will live a terrible life in Naraka [a hell-world] until the great destruction at the end of the world.[134]

Another famous practitioner of the corpse ritual was the eighteenth-century Shakta poet Ramprasad Sen. He performed this ritual on a funeral pyre using a *mala* or rosary made of human bone. He also performed it under a bilva tree, on a seat made of the skulls of five animals, including humans (*panchamunda asana*).[135] He too was blessed by a vision of the goddess.

According to Shakta folklore, it is the devotion of the practitioner that brings the goddess down to him. He is so loving that he is willing to risk the dangers of the burning ground, its ghosts and demons and jackals, to bring the goddess to him. She may enter his heart, or she may enter the corpse when it becomes a dwelling place (*murti*) for the goddess. Its head is said to turn around, and begin speaking affectionately (or sometimes terrifyingly) to the devotee. When the devotee asks for a boon, the goddess cannot refuse.

To bring the goddess Shakti into the corpse is also to bring life and power (shakti) into it, as Shakti is said to enliven Shiva. Some tantrikas compare the devotee's own body to a corpse, saying that the goddess must enter into the heart to enliven it. Others say that the practitioner himself becomes both the goddess and the corpse, realizing in him or herself both the divine spirit and the physical body.

In this practice, the corpse plays several roles. It may act as a ritual instrument, more an object than a subject (the individual soul of the dead person is of little or no interest here). From the folk perspective, the corpse is a magical battery—it stores energy (shakti). This is why its topknot of hair is tied: to hold the energy in during the ritual, and release it at the end (immersing the corpse in water serves this same function). From the yogic and tantric perspective, it is a warning; it motivates detachment from the physical world, destroys the fear of death, and brings union with the deity. From the devotional perspective, it may be a vessel or icon, into which the goddess descends for a temporary dwelling, or a favorite object of hers, which attracts her blessing.

Why should a corpse be capable of being possessed by a god or goddess?

Normally this state is reserved for living renunciants, professional oracles, and devotees. However, in this case, the corpse is not really dead.

In Indian tradition, there are two understandings of the moment of death. One is the moment of physical death. The other is the time of cremation, and more specifically the *kapala kriya*—the ritual midway through the cremation, when the chief mourner cracks open the skull of the burnt corpse with a staff, to release the *prana* or vital breath. There is thus a distinction between physical death of the body and ritual death of the soul. Death impurity begins at the release of the *prana*, and the *shraddha* rite of commemoration is performed on the anniversary of the burning of the body, not of the death.[136] Before the time of ritual death, the corpse is in a liminal state, neither fully dead nor alive, and thus an appropriate home for a deity who may exist on earth and in his or her heaven.

Despite the presence of deities, the religious elements shown in the corpse ritual (union with the god, devotion to the goddess) have not been emphasized by the few writers to discuss this ritual. Why? There are several possible reasons. The magical dimension has been sensationalized in the memoirs and exposés by writers in India, and associated with the criminal and perverse. Westerners, especially missionaries and Victorians, were repulsed by the whole tantric dimension and saw it as evil and demonic. In India, the corpse is associated by brahmanical Hinduism with impurity, the opposite of religion, and such impurity is threatening and perverse. Tantrikas respond with the desire to keep advanced rituals secret, and ignore the accusations or call their calumniators "spiritually primitive," like animals (*pashus*). For these reasons, and perhaps others, both tantrics and their opponents tend to suppress the religious dimensions of the ritual.

The goals for these variants of the corpse ritual are both religious and magical. From a folk perspective, the practitioner magically gains long life and power. The corpse is the personification of death, a challenge to conquer and later control. From the tantric approach, the corpse is used to facilitate detachment and identification with the deity—for Shiva, the god, is in many ways identical with *shava*, the corpse. Immortality is divine identity with a god and earthly identity as an *avadhuta*, one who has completely destroyed the passions, and the body of the practitioner becomes the body of Shiva. This destruction of attachment is echoed in the corpse as the destruction of life. For the devotional approach, the goal is intense love of the goddess, the enlivening of the passions, echoed in the corpse which comes to life under the benevolent gaze of the Mother, who gives her blessings to the devotee.

All of these understandings of the corpse ritual are followed by different tantric groups. *Shava-sadhana* is a central tantric ritual in West Bengal, and as such, it defines what it means to be a Bengali tantrika. It unites the folk, devotional, and yogic aspects of the tradition, and thus connects the tantric practice to the larger Shakta tradition.

To understand the role of ritual and doctrine in tantric tradition, let us look at the lives of some practitioners.

## Experiences of Shakta Tantrikas

### *Tapan Goswami*

There are several Kali temples in the Bolpur area in Birbhum, and one of them is on the edge of town, near the woods, with a cremation ground nearby. This temple is dedicated to Dakshinakali, a benevolent form of the goddess worshiped by householders. There is a large statue of Dakshinakali, with black skin and a smiling face, and her two assistants, Dakini and Yogini, are on either side. There are also life-size statues of Vamaksepa, Ramakrishna Paramahamsa, and his wife Sarada Ma. Behind and below the statues on the altar is a row of human skulls, painted red.

Dakshinakali is also called Bhairavi and Vaishnavi, and is merciful to her devotees. She is a goddess for householders. Renunciants and sadhus worship more powerful forms of Kali, such as Smasana Kali (goddess of the burning ground) and Vama Kali (left-side Kali, or Kali of the Forbidden). They offer her meat and wine, flesh and blood, in a skull. At this temple, offerings of meat and wine are made to Kali's assistants, Dakini and Yogini, but they are only offered outside of the temple.

The priest of this temple is Tapan Goswami, whose Vaishnava name reflects honors shown to his ancestors. He is a practicing folk tantrika, who learned meditation and ritual without initiation or lineage, and who worships the goddess Kali and meditates upon her. There are also some bhakti elements in his personal relationship with the goddess. He performs an unusual Shakta ritual—the feeding of skulls in order to gain spiritual allies. In tantric manner, he then uses the power gained from the skulls to help him in his meditation. Tapan and his family moved to Bolpur when it was much more rural. He spoke no English. Tapan narrated his story in a series of interviews:[137]

> I was born in a small village, about twenty kilometers from Bolpur. My grandfather was a temple priest and a tantric sadhu. There was a long drought in our village when I was young, and the crops failed. It was then that my family came to Bolpur, and moved near this temple. At that time the area was surrounded by dense forests, and people would hesitate to visit the temple. I came to Bolpur when I was six years old, and my father began to work as the priest of this temple. At the age of about ten or eleven years, I began to visit the temple at night, secretly. I was kept from going there in the daytime. But I could get the keys to the temple, and I went there at night,

even though often I was afraid. I felt that the goddess looked with favor upon me.

Here, we believe that on the new-moon night, people should offer incense and candles to the goddess. When I opened the temple door one new-moon night, I found that many types of offerings (*prasad*) were there. I ate them, because I was hungry, but then I was afraid that people would be angry at me, and I thought of not returning. But I had such a great longing to return, that I could not stay away, and after a few days I came back again.

When I was twelve or thirteen years old, some men came to our house and asked me to take them to the temple. After the rituals, they stayed outside late at night. I was sleepy, but suddenly I saw a large sweet [piece of candy] flying at me from the statue. It broke into pieces before me. I felt that there must be some power in that statue, and that I would have to find out about it for myself. The men left, but since that day I became more and more curious about the goddess's power.

To find the answer I began to visit many sadhus and sannyasis, especially those performing tantric practices. When I was about twenty-one years old, I met a sadhu who taught me about tantric practice. Then I went to study at the Ramakrishna Ashram at Siuri. I left for a while, to spend time at a village, and then attended Vishvabharati [University, in Shantiniketan]. While studying there, my interest in worship (puja) and religious practice increased. I went to work in Dubrajpur after I graduated, but I spend my spare time with the sadhus meditating on a sacred hill nearby. Later I returned to my own village, and I learned more about worship techniques from my father. He sent me to work at this Bolpur temple, but at the time there was a struggle going on between me and the goddess. I had many family problems, many financial problems. But in the end, the goddess helped me.

When I used to do the evening ritual, I would feel a cold wind blowing behind me, and it would extinguish the candles. I would shiver and my hair would stand on end. I would hear the wind, and know that there was power (shakti) in it. I felt it was the Devi's presence. One night, I came with my left arm broken, as there had been some fighting in the family. I prayed to the goddess at the temple, and even argued with her. My broken and twisted arm was healed by her grace that evening.

I began to meditate seriously, perfecting my knowledge and ritual practice. As I did this, I saw that I began to gain new power. I realized the power of spiritual practice, and that if any person could do it properly, he could gain perfection (*siddhi*). But it is difficult in daily life to balance family and spiritual practice. Families do not tend to encourage and inspire practice, and neighbors don't understand it; they look down on people who perform puja. This discourages practice. They are only interested in the goddess when they are sick or in need, then they will worship. Otherwise, they stay aloof. They only want immediate gains and blessings. I think that true spiritual practice can only be done in isolation, away in the mountains.

Here in town I only do vedic worship, but in the mountains I do tantric practice, as my grandfather did. Here I safeguard his property, and fulfill his unspoken dreams.

My grandfather was my main guru, and even after he died he continued to instruct me. I talked to him several times using a planchette after he died, but he told me to stop using it, and get instruction directly. His soul stays in the ritual seat (*panchamundi asana*) where he used to meditate, and when I meditate there I can speak with him. He comes to me like the wind, and I can hear the sound of his wooden shoes. Once, I was sitting here before the goddess and I heard the shoes and felt the wind at my back. It put out the candle. It was my grandfather's spirit, and he entered my body and I felt great bliss. I found myself chanting many mantras. I stayed conscious, and could see everything, but he was there too. He had told me that he would come that evening. The mantras made me feel full of power (shakti), and his presence was a powerful thing entering me. Once some people came and had cigarettes with some drug in them, and I felt myself becoming unconscious. I called on my grandfather for help, and he came to me and possessed me.

Many people have come here and tried to meet my grandfather in his subtle body. He was annoyed when some tantrikas wanted spiritual powers (*siddhi*), and built their own *panchamundi asana*. There should never be more than one at a sacred site at a time (for they would always be in competition). I speak with him often, but he would not speak with those people. My grandfather gained many powers as a tantrika. I have heard that he could cure people from deadly diseases and from snakebite. He had a guru, a guide who showed him the right way. He had great devotion for the goddess, and this is why we still have people devoted to the goddess in this family.

I was close to my grandfather, and I take after him. I never learned about meditative practice from my father, he only did ritual worship (puja). I had to learn on my own. I went out to stay with sadhus, and learned from them. I have taught my son worship, but if he wants to learn tantric practice, he will have to learn it for himself. It is up to him.

Really, *shakti sadhana* is becoming obsolete today because nobody teaches it. I do not want my own son to be a Shakta sadhu. I will teach others, but I will not teach him. I want him to work in an office. I had to go through much suffering in this practice, and I want to spare my son. If it is in his blood he will do it, and find a guru of his own. I want him to do worship, but not become a renunciant. It is a difficult life, and much suffering is involved. I had only my grandfather to help me.

An interesting incident happened many years ago. When my father was just a child, he was very ill, and he was declared to be dead by the doctor. My grandfather took him into the forest. There were hundreds of jackals and vultures surrounding him, but no animal came near or tried to attack him. My grandfather went into a meditative trance, and was full of devotion for the Devi. After three or four days, my father began to move, and he regained his life and his strength. The goddess saves people in her many forms—Durga, Kali, Tara—but it is my belief that my father was saved by the intervention of Kali.

The Devi gives blessings during life, and after death she can also help. She does not help directly, for such things are determined by karma. Those who did evil on earth are kept in hell in the forms of jackals or snakes, and they cannot leave immediately. If they didn't do much evil, they may move about their past family and friends in nonphysical form. But if the person dying had a good teacher, then he could act as a mediator for the person to reach heaven or Kailash, and Kali can help to show the way. If one wishes to reach the kingdom of the gods and goddesses, it is necessary to worship them.

It is difficult to describe. You see, in this world everything is both difficult and easy. It depends upon how you approach it. If a person has a proper guide, if he is given much instruction and experience, if his guru watches him closely, then nothing is difficult to attain. But the qualities inherited from previous lives are also important. Without the proper qualities, one cannot perform ritual practice. If a person was educated in this area in his previous life, then he could guide himself automatically, and would not need anybody else.

Ma has given me many favors. I remember once at night, I dreamt of a little girl (whom I believe was Ma) who came to help me. At that time I had little money and was renting a very small room. The girl came to me and took me to a new house for rent in my neighborhood. I awoke the next morning, and followed the path that we had taken in the dream-vision. I saw a house that looked exactly like the one I had seen. There did turn out to be a room for rent there, a spacious room that I could afford. So I believe she really did help me. Once she appeared as an old woman, perhaps eighty years old, and she patted my head, which was on her lap. At that time I was under much stress—my practice was not smooth, and I was disturbed by many bad events, which frightened me. But Ma saved me, and she gave me her blessings.

The goddess is normally invisible before us, but through meditative practice, we can see her. One ritual that I perform here is the feeding of skulls (*mundake khao nao*). Generally, they like puffed rice, though some like fried lentils, curries or wine. After an animal sacrifice, I feed them with meat. [Feeding in this case means offering a plate of food before each skull] The feeding is accompanied by a ritual fire (*homa*) and *yajna* [Vedic-style sacrifice]. After the feeding, I bathe them in ghee, yogurt, milk, and honey, and then I arrange them for worship. Sometimes I do this when I need more mental balance or physical strength.

Skulls are useful, because the dead person's soul often stays with the skull. The soul can predict the future, and help the sadhu. People used to do the corpse ritual (*shava-sadhana*) and sit on the dead body of a virgin girl. She would then become Kali, and the body would come back to life and talk. My grandfather performed the corpse ritual, but people today are afraid of it—if you make one mistake, you die or go insane. This sadhu in orange that you see roaming around here in the burning ground did the corpse ritual wrongly, and he was made insane by it. But he will return to sanity one of these days.

I feed the skulls on the altar, and they help me. I learned the skull-feeding ritual from my grandfather. When the skulls are fed, they are pacified and they become protectors. Then they are strong enough to fight off the evil souls (*atmas*) who wish to distract or harm the sadhu. When negative spirits (*bhutas* and *pretas*) try to disturb the sadhu's meditation, then the good souls fight the bad souls and keep the sadhu on the right path. Sadhus often have helpers. Sometimes the corpse ritual is performed with a woman, who is called the highest female practitioner (*uttara sadhika*). She is very skilled and helps the male through meditation if he is distracted by bad spirits. When the sadhu draws a circle around himself to protect him from these spirits, she is within the circle. Sometimes the sadhu may invite his guru in subtle form to watch over him and help him.

Today, it is widely believed that there are no ghosts, but really there are souls who do not die. They are always around us. Sometimes they may enter into our physical bodies, and cause problems or even tragedies. It is only by meditative practice, and by dedication to the goddess, that we gain control over them. Then they can work for our benefit. We become immune to fear, hate, and intense desire with their help. I show them loyalty, and they guard me.

The skulls in this temple mostly come from people who died in epidemics, especially cholera epidemics. Large numbers of people used to die, and there was no effective system of cremation at that time. Corpses would lie on the roadside or in the forests.

Under the altar of this temple there are 108 skulls buried. Some altars have 1,008 skulls. Skulls awaken the goddess, and make her present here. Male gods have stones or lingas, but goddesses have skulls. Some skulls are used for *panchamundi asana* [a ritual in which the practitioner sits on a seat in the midst of five skulls, generally of different types of animals and persons]. People use the skulls of a low-caste man [usually a Chandala], a jackal, a tiger, a snake, and a virgin girl. They must be young, and die suddenly by violence. Nobody wants the skulls of people who died of disease or old age. Some tantrikas have a relationship with the Doms [low-caste people who handle the dead] who work in hospitals, who notify them of appropriate deaths.

There are many forms of *tantrik sadhana*. There are three major styles (*bhavas*): sattvic, rajasic, and tamasic *bhavas*. The sattvic style is devotion (bhakti), and that is the best path to follow. The tamasic style can give one the presence of the goddess, but it does not last long. It stays for a little while, and then it ceases. It is very brief, and very fickle. Devotion lasts longer. One cannot get really close to the goddess without devotional love. Only bhakti justifies tantra.

I have practiced both vedic and tantric rituals. I do not call myself a tantrika—I don't take liquor, bhang, *ganja* [hashish] and that sort of thing. Tantra is a dangerous path—there is much possibility of insanity and brain damage. The tantric path to liberation is fast and easy, but it always has risks. The vedic path is longer, but the risks are fewer. I think that the feeding of skulls is the first stage of practice, where one learns to control *bhuta*s and *preta*s, and one gains immunity to [the bites of] snakes and dedication to the goddess. Then the goddess comes to protect her devotee, and vision comes, as well as telepathy and the ability to know the future.

I inherited this temple and burning ground, and now they are my property. I have given my village land and shares in the lakes to my brothers. I want to fulfill the wishes of both my father and

> grandfather. I have been here since 1979, for fifteen years. Ma developed the temple, and I have been her mediator. I have also been inspired by a sannyasini named Sangadevi, a distant relative of Rabindranath Tagore. I will be forever obliged to her. I hope that the temple will grow, and that more people will come to worship the goddess.
>
> What I want to do is stay at the beck and call of Ma, lay down before her feet, give her offerings and serve her, and also run my family and know about the outside world. Then my vision of her will be clear instead of fuzzy, and I can perform service to the world.[138]

Tapan's self-description differed when I visited him accompanied by different people. When I would come with a woman who was herself a Shakta and knew many renunciants (including a sannyasini whom he greatly respected), Tapan described himself as a tantrika who worked with skulls, and gave many ritual details. When I later came with a research assistant who was something of a skeptic, Tapan described himself as a Vedic practitioner, who emphasized bhakti devotion and love, as well as serving the world. He said that he was not a tantrika, and talked about his land and property instead.

Tapan is a good example of a tantric practitioner who has had to adapt to a difficult atmosphere. He incorporates both folk tantra (spontaneous meditative practice, feeding skulls to gain power and protection, seeking *siddhi*, communication with ghosts) and emotional Shakta bhakti in his practice. He had no formal initiation, and learned his practice from his grandfather—but only after the grandfather's death.

### *Jayashri Ma*

Jayashri Ma is a holy woman or *sadhika* believed by her disciples to be an incarnation of the goddess Adya Shakti Kali (Kali as primordial power). She describes herself as one with the Mother, alternately aware and unaware of the goddess, but having her soul (*atma*) permanently fused with the goddess. She calls the goddess by various names, including Adya Shakti Kali, Adya Kali, Adya Ma, and Adya Shakti Ma. She is included here because she is an underground female tantric guru, using both yogic and devotional elements. She has had a circle of devotees and a firm faith in her union with the goddess.[139]

Jayashri was born in 1948, in Darjeeling, West Bengal. She came from a Shakta family, and her father was a deputy magistrate and tantrika. He was a disciple of Taraksepa of Basirhat (in south 24 Parganas) and a visionary who had many religious experiences.

At the age of eight years, Jayashri met a friend of her father's, named Sudin

Kumar Mitra. He was an officer of the Indian Administrative Service (IAS) posted to Darjeeling, who came originally from Calcutta. He was also a tantric practitioner, and a year after she met him, Jayashri took initiation from him. He chose her as a disciple for her spiritual gifts, and she was his first disciple. She was fascinated by her guru, and described her love for him, which later was transformed into a love of Adya Shakti Kali.

Her guru Sudin claimed that he had been initiated directly by Adya Kali. At the age of seventeen years, he wished to have the Shakta guru Nagin Bagchi of Tarapith initiate him, but Bagchi refused. He said, "The Mother herself must decide, I am not your guru." After repeated requests, Bagchi finally told Sudin to bathe, fast, and remain alone in a room for the whole night. If Sudin were willing to do this, then Bagchi said he would initiate him the next morning. He went into the room at night, and at 2:00 AM the room was filled with brilliant light. He had a vision of Adya Shakti Ma, who said to him, "Chant these mantras along with me." He did so, and then she disappeared. He did not realize that this was his initiation.

The next morning, he ran to Nagin Bagchi to get initiated. Bagchi told him, "Don't you realize, you were already initiated by Ma at 2:00 AM!" Nagin Bagchi gave him two photographs, one of Bagchi himself and another one of Adya Sakti Kali. He told him to do a simple ritual of worship, offering incense to the photo, and praying for universal blessings. He was to say, *tomar jaya hok*, all victory to her.

Jayashri and her mother were both initiated by Sudin Mitra, but her father was not. Mitra told him that he was due to be initiated by another person, a sannyasi, who later turned out to be Taraksepa.

During her school life, Jayashri was close friends with her guru, and also with a swami named Bhaveshananda. By the age of ten years she would visit them, and do meditation with them. Mitra told her that Adya Ma was always with him, and that he had trouble sleeping at night because Adya Ma would keep him awake. He said that Jayashri would grow up to be a powerful woman, who would help many people.

At the age of thirteen, when Jayashri began going to temples for worship, she would fall into trances (*samadhi*). During worship she would see Tara Ma and Adya Ma before her. She was "drowned in meditation" (*dhyana*), subject to frequent visions and trance states. When Adya Ma would come, the world turned to light, and she would fall unconscious ("her senses would be lost"). She says that sometimes Adya Ma looks like her picture, and sometimes she appears in the image of Jayasri's body. She cannot really be described, but her power can be felt.

When she was seventeen years old, Mitra was transferred to Allahabad with the IAS, and he took her with him for a year. He instructed her in meditative practice, and they did mantra and visualization before Adya Ma on matching *panchamundi asanas* (tantric power seats made of five skulls). She sat next to him, and he transmitted his power to her. The power passed directly from heart to heart, and could only be felt; it was not mediated by sight or touch. After this ritual with her guru, Adya Shakti was there within Jayashri permanently.

About a year later, her father was transferred to West Bengal, and she went there to live with her family. She had wanted to take vows of renunciation (*sannyasa*), but her guru said that she had already become a renunciant inwardly, so no such vow was necessary. She was to be a householder holy woman (*grihi sadhika*).

After she moved, she became very ill with dysentery. This condition tuned into ulcerative colitis, which brought heart trouble. These have stayed with her to the present time. She obtained a college degree and studied classical music, but the illnesses restricted her movement and eventually made her stop her education.

She stayed after her father's death, but never married. She is now a primary school teacher, working with children. She is weak from her illnesses, and eats little food. The doctors she saw when she first became ill told her that she would be dead in ten years, but she has survived twenty-five years thus far. This is understood as a miracle by her devotees. Her guru prayed to Adya Ma to allow her to survive and help others, and she has done so. She rarely speaks of her religious experiences.

After her practice with her guru, she also developed some abilities at mediumship. She mentioned as major possessing entities the saints Mira Bai, Annada Thakur, Trailanga Swami, and Ramakrishna Paramahamsa. Adya Shakti Kali is always there, and Shiva often visits. These beings speak through her, and give information and suggestions to her disciples; she keeps a journal of their words. They speak a variety of languages, including English, through her. Normally, Jayashri speaks little English (and not a word during her interviews).

She also has a close relationship with her guru, though he is dead. She says, "Whenever I feel love, he comes to me. When I am sleeping, the guru comes and strokes my head. If I wake, I try to grab his hand, but I cannot. I always speak with him and see him. I feel that he has come now, even while we are speaking, and he is watching us." She said that the guru always knew when she was in pain from her illness, and often this would cause him pain.

A disciple described a past event, when she was writhing in pain from the colitis. Suddenly the pain ceased, and she began to speak—but it was the guru's words coming from her mouth. She was not aware of this, but she was aware that the pain had ceased. Instead of pain, she felt *ananda*, bliss, which showed its power by being able to erase pain.

Another disciple described a time when the Shakta saint Vamaksepa came to speak through Jayashri. He told the disciple that when he went to Tarapith (a Shakta sacred site), he should not eat at a certain hotel, because the brothers who owned the hotel were evil people who had murdered their own father. Instead he should fast, and go directly to speak to Nagin Bagchi, a respected sadhu at Tarapith. The disciple told Bagchi of the story that Vamaksepa told through Jayashri as medium, and Bagchi told him that the story was accurate, though not well known: the brothers had indeed murdered their father.

Jayashri often feels distant from the world. She says, "Now, I do not feel that I am in a human body. Instead, I am Shakti, I feel that I am Adya Ma. I am the mother, and all creation is my child. If you do meditation, you too can realize that you are really Adya Ma. Ma divided herself throughout creation, and everybody has a piece of the goddess inside. In the end, all will come back together again, and everybody will become the goddess."

This is to occur at the end of the Kali yuga, the time of universal destruction at the end of the era. Because this time is coming, Adya Kali has been withdrawing Shakta sadhus from the world—their prayers and meditation avert the time of destruction. The end-times may only come when there are no more sadhus to pray and meditate. Jayashri also noted that she is a goddess who appeared recently (she was popularized early in the twentieth century). Adya Shakti Kali did not wish to appear earlier, it was not her desire. It is possible that she has come to earth to preside over the end of the yuga.

Jayashri was initiated by a tantric guru, and her personal deity (*ishtadevi*) is Adya Shakti Kali. She finds tantra generally to be a good practice, for it denies hatred and accepts everybody and everything. She performs neither materializations nor initiations, and she avoids publicity, as most people who have visited her on the basis of her reputation have wanted favors—children, good marks on exams, new jobs. She spends her private life surrounded by photos of saints and pictures of gods, and finds her greatest happiness in meditation. She believes she has remained alive in spite of her illness and the pain it brings because her disciples need her presence and guidance.

Jayashri Ma tends to sit quietly while her mostly male disciples praise her, and she speaks of the goddess as latent in everyone. She pulled me aside, stared deeply into my eyes, and said that Adya Shakti Kali was deep within me, and that if I would meditate upon her, I would see her in my heart. She was my true self, and the true self of us all. She appeared to have no possessiveness in relation to the goddess.

Jayashri combined folk religion (in her possession trances), bhakti (in her devotion to the goddess), and yoga (in her meditative practice and training). All were important in her development as a female guru.

Both of the tantrikas interviewed here were folk tantrikas, who had some limited training in tantric tradition, but would not have been called scholars or *pandits*.

## Closing Notes

Although there are many kinds of Shakta tantra in West Bengal, I have described folk and classical types as the most important categories. For some easy differentiation, we find the following characteristic in folk tantra.

1. The *invocation* of minor or regional deities (or Vedic gods who are treated as regional), especially goddesses, as guides and as sources of power. Such deities may be understood in close relationships of family intimacy, or as enemies under ritual control. This opposes the classical focus on more Sanskritic goddesses.
2. The presence of *ancestors and the dead* as guides to hierarchies of spirit worlds, who can give power, protection, guidance, and direction. They may be contacted by ritual means or through possession. Classical tantra does not emphasize ancestors, though it respects Vedic sages and scholars.
3. The *transmutation* of energy, especially the energies associated with the sexuality and with death, into supernatural abilities (*siddhis*). Classical tantra tends to focus on knowledge and enlightenment rather than supernatural powers.
4. The performance of rituals involving *death and sexuality* to gain detachment, courage, and pragmatic ends. For classical tantra, such rituals are symbolic of philosophical concepts and transformation of consciousness.
5. A *shamanic dimension*, involving healing and prophecy for the community. Many tantrikas make their living by giving amulets, healing by gemstones, and predicting the future by astrology. Classical tantrikas tend to be scholars rather than healers or shamans.
6. *Communication* with the deity, often involving possession. Such communication allows the deity to empower mantras or physical objects, and help in cases of exorcism, disease, and other difficult situations. This communication often occurs in isolation, especially at the burning ground. In the corpse ritual, the deity is understood to possess a corpse, and speak through its mouth. Classical tantra tends to avoid mediumship and possession.
7. *Conquest of deities* (including ghosts and ancestors). If the supernatural being is hostile by nature, due to its personality or its means of death (often violent or unjust), then the tantrika needs to do more than communicate. He (or she) needs to use a mantra of a stronger deity to conquer the weaker one, and place it in the role of servant. Classical tantra does not support struggle with deities, unless they are symbolic of the person's lower nature.

8. *Dream initiation*, as an entrance into the tradition, rather than initiation by guru. The tantric guru is important if he can be found, but they are more and more rare, and many tantrikas are proceeding on their own without a guru. Classical tantra requires initiation by a guru who is a member of a lineage, and holds an empowered mantra.
9. *Dream instruction*, rather than interpretation of text and its commentaries or instruction by a guru. In this way, folk tantra may be called as a charismatic tradition. Classical tantra emphasizes knowledge of the tantric, and often the Vedic and devotional, literary traditions.
10. *Ascetic practices* to motivate chosen deities to possess the person, and thus create a bond that can later be used for communication. Offering blood or flesh, fasting and vigils, chanting mantras at the burning ground amid skulls and ashes in extreme weather, are all techniques that may motivate the god or goddess to descend. In classical tantra, such sacrifices are generally symbolic of surrendering the lower self to the higher self, rather than the means of coercing deities.

Although there are doubtless many influences on Bengali Shakta tantra, I suggest that two major influences have determined the development of folk and classical tantra. One is that folk Shakta tantra has its origins in the tribal traditions of Bengal's rural *ojhas* and *gunins*. Both share initiations at the burning ground, conquest of ghosts and spirits, and pragmatic results for meditation: healing, fertility, rain, prediction of the future. Both have practitioners who are visited in dreams by deities (and dream initiation is more important than a physical guru and lineage), and who can exorcize spirits and get rid of the evil eye. Both are concerned with supernatural powers (whether pacification of angry ghosts or the dark *shatkarmas*), and both freely violate brahmanical Hindu dharma. Neither is concerned with initiation into a particular lineage, caste, or education. However, the folk tantrikas make much greater use of yogic techniques (especially in mantra, mudra, yantra, and other ritual practices) than the tribal practitioners. I was told in interview by folk tantrikas of other folk tantrikas initiated by wandering *ojhas*, or who visited tribal *gunins* to sharpen their skills at curing snakebite and digestive disturbances. Even today, these two groups learn from each other, and take initiations from each other. This is an important connection.

I would also suggest that classical Shakta tantra has a different origin—the Sanskrit philosophical traditions of Advaita Vedanta and Samkhya. Both classical tantra and the philosophies share a concern with textual interpretation, Sanskrit linguistic analysis, theology, and metaphysics, and both understand *jnana* (wisdom) to be the path to *brahman*. However, classical tantra has a greater emphasis on ritual practice; several classical tantrikas interviewed described tantra as the active aspect of Vedanta philosophy (much as some yogis describe yoga as the active aspect of Vedanta). Both classical tantra and the philosophical traditions emphasize the importance of teacher and lineage, of proper education, and ritual suitability (*adhikara*). Whereas folk tantra has few problems with women and low-caste people taking initiation, classical tantra (especially as taught by brahmin gurus) is very concerned with this. Some tantras have long lists of requirements for both gurus and disciples, which include both proper family and education.

For those forms of classical tantra in which Advaita philosophy dominates, the theology is monist (all reality is one, *brahman*, as symbolically represented by the goddess), and for those in which Samkhya dominates, classical tantra is dualist (Shiva and Shakti are the primal forces of the universe, with Shakti as the force most immediately affecting human life and the physical world). Both of these philosophies are popular in the classical tantric or Kali-kula tradition.

If these are indeed two different tantric traditions with two different origins, how did they come to share the same name, and show up in different chapters of the same tantric texts? I suggest that they are linked by the value on esoteric yogic knowledge and practice, which can adapt to each. Tribal shamanism plus esoteric yoga equals folk tantra; classical philosophy plus esoteric yoga equals classical tantra.

There are many other influences, of course, and the major one is doubtless bhakti or devotion, which we shall examine next. Both forms of tantra have been variously affected by Mahayana Buddhism, Kashmiri Shaivism, south Indian Shri-kula tantra, Sahajiyas, Sufism, Nath yoga, perhaps even Chinese Taoist yogis and Tibetan Bon shamans. Now they are being influenced by ex-Rajneesh disciples roaming through India looking for the "real" tantra, and a variety of modern tantric groups looking for older traditions to graft onto New Age ideas (see chapter 5 for some examples of modern Western tantra).

Having two different tantric traditions with different origins clarifies the reasons for the tension between these two tantric groups, the different claims of authenticity and superiority, and the different values on brahmanical lineage and knowledge. It may be that, for both folk and classical tantra, the incorporation of esoteric yogic practice with an emphasis on meditative technique and supernatural knowledge developed in West Bengal into a common tradition of thought and practice for two radically opposed traditions. Eventually, the similarities of these perspectives came to outweigh their differences, and their contradictory aspects of yoga and *bhoga* (disciplined detachment and worldly pleasure) came to be shared.

In recent years, the most popular veil for tantric practice has been bhakti devotion. It is to some extent a defensive move—if tantrikas are persecuted, they can claim to be bhaktas. But it is also a legitimate part of some tantric practice. The traditions have become so fused that brahmanical Shakta devotees use tantric mantras to worship the goddess, while tantrikas perform bhakti ritual worship and sing devotional hymns. Let us look at the Shakta devotional tradition as a separate tradition.

# 3

# Shakta Bhakti

## *Devotion to the Goddess*

Shakta bhakti or devotional love is the worship of a single great goddess, Mahadevi or Mahakali or Parama Shakti, a goddess with many names. It may also be the worship of minor goddesses, who may not have the overwhelming power of the great goddess, but still can motivate the person to become a devotee. As one Kali devotee interviewed revealed, "I have taken refuge at Ma's feet. I want to be with her until I die. Day and night I live here at the temple, I never go anywhere. Here I am, and here I stay. Mother will give me shelter."[1]

The great goddess is without birth or death, eternal, independent, the soul of the universe. She is greater than the universe, yet at the same time smaller than an atom. She is both within samsara and beyond it, and her manifest forms includes the sun and moon, the winds, all humans and animals, the oceans and the earth. She is worshiped in such qualities as intellect, wealth, strength, mercy, modesty, forgiveness, peace, and protection.

We can describe four major types of Shakti bhakti in West Bengal. These are:

1. Folk bhakti
2. Emotional bhakti
3. Political Shakta bhakti or Shakta nationalism
4. Universalist bhakti or Shakta Vedanta

Folk bhakti is found in the *mangal-kavya* literature, the stories of goddesses who are divine outsiders, who enter the world to gain disciples and proceed to do so on the basis of reward and punishment. The male deities do not help them—these goddesses are on their own. Devotees must obey the summons to worship, or the goddesses will cause disasters. In this way, they differ from the group orientation of most tribal and folk goddesses. The goddesses of folk bhakti seek individual devotees, and a personal relationship with them. Sometimes these goddesses had once been human women, who had died and been transformed, and other times they are regional deities or Sanskritic goddesses who are worshiped as regional figures, such as the Kali of a particular buffalo shed or the Lakshmi of a particular field. In folk Shakta bhakti, a powerful goddess is made beneficent through the devotee's love, and devotion is the most important way of propitiating the goddess and gaining favors from her. Eventually the group may worship the goddess, but her passions (and sometimes her destructiveness) are focused on a single individual.

Followers of emotional Shakta bhakti focus on devotional love, and often tend to look down upon the folk aspects of Shaktism as involving only propitiation or economic exchange and lacking true love. Like the Bengali Vaishnavas, emotional Shakta bhaktas emphasize passionate devotion to the deity. She dwells both in her distant paradise (of Manidvipa or Kailash) and in the hearts of her devotees. She can bring earthly blessings, but also salvation from rebirth, life in her heavenly world, and final liberation to those devotees who desire it. Love of the goddess is shown through tears, laughter, song, and ecstatic symptoms.

Both folk and emotional bhakti are strongly experiential, and the ancient texts valued by scholars are often unknown to or ignored by devotees. As a result, Shakta bhakti is in many areas largely an oral tradition. Shakta devotees who do not read the puranas and tantras will listen to Shakta songs and read the biographies of Shakta saints or perfected ones (*siddhas*). For these devotees, the popular songs and biographies are themselves sacred texts, for they tell of experiences of the goddess. Shakta songs have been widely sung, and biographies of saints may come from published collections of saint lives, or from stories told within religious groups (such as *Kali-kirtan* groups, where hymns to the goddess are sung).

The third type of Shakta bhakti, Shakta political bhakti or Shakta nationalism, tends to be found in greatest measure in situations of political and social upheaval. The goddess is the Mother in her form as nature or homeland, and she needs to be protected from the evil behavior of invaders or outsiders. She is rescued by her children, who become her protectors and heroes in their own right. As in many family situations in India, the mother is supported by her children. This sort of devotion is primarily ethical, and the goddess is invoked as the justification for political or social action. Religious experience is found in feelings of patriotism and love of country and countryside.

The fourth kind of devotion, universalist Shakta bhakti or Shakta Vedanta, is a later development of the nineteenth-century saint Ramakrishna Paramahamsa's Shaktism, carried on through his disciple Vivekananda and his followers. It emphasizes the goddess's true nature as *brahman* rather than as a separate entity, with philosophy and ethics as the best way to understand her. She is an ideal form or representation of ultimate reality, and the sacred texts for followers of this approach would be the biographies of Ramakrishna as well as classical Hindu texts such as the Upanishads and the *Bhagavad Gita*. The goddess is understood to be present within all deities, and all religions are legitimate paths to her worship. However, the goddess's form represents maternal love, and is the sweetest and most appealing to practitioners.

All four of these subtypes may be widely found in Bengali Shaktism today, either independently or mixed with one another. In this chapter, we shall look at these various subtypes of bhakti, and examine some Shakta goddesses and their worship.

## Folk Bhakti: Coerced Devotion and the Goddess of Threat and Reward

The traditional image of Shakta bhakti is one that is similar to Vaishnava bhakti: a loyal and loving devotee and a merciful deity. However, Shaktism is a tradition with many aspects. As we look at its folk dimensions, we see that the devotee is not always loving; indeed, he may be complaining and even hostile. Nor is the goddess always merciful; indeed, she is often cruel and deaf to the devotee's pleas. Folk Shakta bhakti is a combination of folk Shaktism and bhakti devotion. It could be categorized as a subtype of folk Shaktism, but I placed it in the bhakti category because it emphasizes an individual's personal relationship with a goddess, and because it sometimes evolves into full-fledged devotional religion. In folk Shaktism, the goddess demands food, propitiation, and obedience. In folk Shakta bhakti, the goddess wants love and devotion from the devotee.

Folk pragmatism and bhakti devotionalism can create some unusual situations. We see in many traditions an attitude on the part of the goddess that might be called coerced devotion: "love me or you'll be sorry." Such goddesses feel neglected, and demand worship and worshipers. Sometimes they use threats, sometimes bribes, and they bend even devotees of other gods to their will. The role of the "woman scorned" is prominent here, and some folk goddesses are indeed angry because of poor treatment. Worship and ritual act to tame these goddesses, to chain their dangerous and malevolent energies and transform them into generosity and compassion. Frequently the stories have three stages:

1. The goddess enters the world, angry and neglected.
2. She shows her anger in vengeful deeds until her chosen devotee worships her, gives her offerings and calms her.

3. She renounces her hostility and becomes beneficent, giving blessings.[2]

Like the women who often are possessed by folk goddesses, the goddesses themselves have been seriously hurt or neglected, and are not willing to take the typical female role of being silent and submissive. Whether the goddesses are angry at low status in their divine households, neglect by their husbands, being used and abandoned, or some other reason, they come demanding respect from humans. There are no authoritative texts to encourage people to worship them; these folk goddesses must gain worshipers on their own.

A goddess in pain is dark and dangerous. Her anguish may show up in the form of poisonous snakes (in Manasa's case destroying the sort of happy marriage she could not have), or as demands for human sacrifice. Propitiation makes her calm but it is a temporary measure, and needs to be repeated over and over. In this section we shall look at an example of a Bengali goddess seeking love and devotees—Manasa.

### *Manasa, the Goddess of Snakes and Poison*

A well-known and classically demanding goddess is Manasa, the goddess of snakes. Manasa is widely worshiped, in both Adivasi (tribal) and Hindu low-caste groups; she is accepted as a goddess among the Oraons of Chotanagpur, the Kurmi of Hazaribagh District, the Santals of the Santal Parganas, and the Ho of Singhbhum. She is also worshiped by low-caste Hindu groups such as the Bauris, Bagdis, and Doms. Her worship has filtered into the higher-caste Hindu pantheons, where today she is often seen as a Hindu goddess rather than an Adivasi one.

Her stories emphasize her bad temper and unhappiness. She is kind to her devotees, but quite unpleasant to those who refuse to worship her. She was a goddess who had a difficult life: she had no mother, was lusted after and then rejected by her father, hated by her stepmother, and deserted by her husband. After this she decided to descend and seek love in the human sphere. She went out into the world to gain devotees but was easily angered, and would cause disaster to befall anybody who refused to worship her. Potential devotees had to be forced to worship her, for the other deities would not support her, and the persons whom she chose as devotees often had other gods whom they worshiped. She is a goddess who needs human love and will do almost anything to get it.

There are several long poems dedicated to the story of Manasa's life and adventures, called *manasa mangal-kavyas*. The term *mangal-kavya* refers to epic poetry that brings *mangala* or bliss, wealth, and good luck to its listeners. They were medieval Bengali poems that glorified the power of the goddess, and influenced the rise of Shaktism or the "Shakti cult." As Asutosh Bhattacharyya states, her cult develped because goddesses were thought to be more responsive than gods to human suffering:

> The Mangal kavyas no doubt originated in the setting up of Sakti as against this Siva who was callous and indifferent to the earthly miseries of the devotee. The faith that gained a footing in the society of Bengal in the wake of the Siva-cult was this Sakti-cult. But this Sakti-cult is something novel and composed of the purely national stuff of Bengal. It has not even the remotest connection with the Puranic Sakti cult. . . . [I]t is beyond doubt that the ingredients of the primitive notions inherited from the pre-historic ages of the country lie concealed in the characteristics of the Sakti cult of medieval Bengal.[3]

Some major *mangal-kavya* goddesses were Manasa, Chandi, and Sitala. The *Manasa-Vijaya* of Vipradasa was written in 1495, as a glorification of the goddess's victory (*vijaya*) over those who would not worship her. It includes elements from many older traditions. Manasa's origin was the divine equivalent of illegitimate:

> Days passed and one fine morning Śiva saw the birds mating at Kālidaha. He was excited at this sight and he cast his semen upon a lotus leaf. The semen was eaten by a male crow but he was unable to retain it. As advised by his wife he disgorged it on the same lotus leaf from which he had taken it. It then went down through the stalk and reached Pātalā, the kingdom of Vāsuki. There it fell like a thunderbolt on the head of Vāsuki. His mother, one of the sculptors among the Nāgas, realised that the seed belonged to Śiva. She therefore fashioned an image of a beautiful girl, which came to life when touched by Śiva's seed. The girl was named Manasā. Vāsuki's mother introduced Manasā to Vāsuki who accepted her as his sister and gave her charge of the entire stock of poison that was produced when King Pṛithu milked the Earth as a cow. Then Manasā held sway over the snakes, living at Kālidaha with the snake attendants.[4]

Manasa wanted to see her biological father. When Shiva encountered Manasa, however, he was sexually attracted to her. Manasa was terrified, and told him of her birth and proved that he was her father. He took her back to his house, where she did not receive a warm welcome. Shiva's wife Chandi suspected that Manasa was his concubine or co-wife, and Chandi yelled at Manasa and insulted her. Manasa tried to tell her that this was not the case, but Chandi refused to listen. Manasa was not welcome at her father's house:

> Then Manasa told the story of her birth and addressed her as stepmother. But Chaṇḍī was still suspicious. This irritated Manasā who replied hotly. Chaṇḍī lost her temper and jabbed a *kuśa* needle into

> Manasā's eye. Manasā took revenge by flashing her great power over Chaṇḍī from her other eye. Chaṇḍī fell down senseless. The news was reported by Ganeśa and Kārttikeya to their father Śiva. Śiva came and at his request Manasā looked again at Chaṇḍī, who then sat up. Then followed another quarrel between them. Chaṇḍī finally informed Śiva that she would not allow Manasā to stay at home.[5]

Shiva and Chandi had a turbulent marriage, as well as a history of attempting to humiliate each other in various creative ways, and Manasa was caught in the middle. Later, when Shiva was dying of poison, Manasa came to save his life. However, Chandi was there and attempted to kick her, so she looked at her through her poison eye and Chandi fell senseless. Manasa was able to cure Shiva, and later brought Chandi back to consciousness. Shiva finally arranged a marriage for Manasa with the sage Jaratkara, which did not work out well:

> After the ceremonies Chaṇḍī did not like Manasā being praised by the gods nor did she like to see her happy in her married life. Manasā was advised by her stepmother Chaṇḍī to wear snake ornaments on the bridal night. Jaratkara passed a sleepless night for fear of the snakes, whereas Manasā slept well. Chaṇḍī threw a frog into the room of the newly married couple, and all the snakes hissed together and ran towards the frog. The terrified Jaratkāra ran out of the house and took shelter in a conch in the sea. Manasā did not find her husband in the room in the morning. By her supernatural power she discovered what had happened to him, and bewailed her ill-fortune.[6]

Manasa's husband was terrified of her, and refused to live with her. However, he did come back for a few nights to perform his husbandly duty and impregnate her with a child, who was named Astika. The boy was sent to the snake-king Vasuki for his education soon after he was born. Having given up on anything resembling a happy family life, Manasa decided to get some human followers.

> Manasā was desirous of receiving homage from human beings. She therefore came down to earth in her chariot accompanied by her advisor Neto and began to appear to human beings in order to initiate and propagate her cult.
>
> She first appeared to some cowherds who laughed at her and called her a "blood-thirsty witch." She came to them as an old grey-headed Brahman woman carrying a basket, and begged milk of them to break her ceremonial fast, with a promise to help them. But they threw dust at her and a few of them beat her. Then she told them that she was a daughter of Śiva and was known as Manasā,

> the snake goddess. They did not believe her and challenged her to prove her identity, which she did by summoning the snakes before them. The terrified boys prepared to beat the snakes with their sticks, but Manasā disappeared and the snakes also.
>
> Later on, when the cowherds were going to drink water, all their cows fell into a marsh. They realized that such mischief had been caused by Manasā, who stood nearby and laughed at them. Then they fell at her feet, saying that they would worship her from then onwards. Manasā responded by rescuing their cows. Once again she demonstrated her power by milking a barren cow into her wicker basket; she then held it upside down and without spilling the milk drank from it. Having conquered the hearts of the cowherds, Manasā sat under a tree where, accompanied by Neto, she taught the boys the way in which her worship was to be conducted.[7]

The cowherd boys were Manasa's first chosen devotees, but they were not enough to satisfy her. When Manasa's worship was threatened by Muslims, she marched with her snakes against them and killed the Muslim soldiers. The Muslim ruler Hasan was convinced by this, and submitted to Manasa, and he became her devotee (consulting with brahmins to learn the proper way of worshiping her). Because of this, he was blessed with wealth, fame, power, and children, and his dead soldiers came back to life. She converted a number of different people from all walks of life, but ran into trouble when she tried to convert the merchant Chando.

Chando's wife Sanaka was willing to worship Manasa, but Chando insulted Manasa and profaned the worship. Chando was a devotee of Shiva, and Shiva's wife Chandi had told him not to worship Manasa. Chando also had some supernatural power given as a gift from Shiva, called *mahajnana* (great wisdom), and Chando and Manasa had numerous battles over this. Manasa stole his *mahajnana* while disguised as his beautiful sister-in-law. She eventually caused him to lose his wealth and be shipwrecked. He later found his way back home after much difficulty. Chando's youngest son Lakhindar (Lakhai) married the beautiful girl Behula, and Manasa sent a snake as her bridal present:

> Now, Lakhindar wanted to make love with Behulā, looked at her, and wanted to embrace her. Behulā was unwilling as this was not proper on the bridal night. Annoyed and disappointed, Lakhindar fell asleep. Manasā meanwhile discussed her plans with Neto. The snake Kāli was summoned and told to bite Lakhindar. But the snake did not dare to go without sufficient preparation. So Kāli was given Sleep and Drowsiness as helpers. Manasā followed her and waited at a distance. Kāli entered the room through the minute hole left by the architect and found the couple asleep. This scene aroused her

> sympathy, and she hesitated to bite Lakhindar. But finally remembering the order of Manasā, she did bite him. Behulā woke upon hearing the shout of her husband who was in great pain . . . Sanaka blamed Chando because through his neglect of Manasā, all his sons had suffered premature death from snake bite. Behulā expressed the same opinion.[8]

Lakhindar died of snakebite. Behula traveled up the river on a raft with her husband's corpse, and eventually ended up in Indra's heaven. There she promised that her father-in-law would worship Manasa if the goddess would bring her husband back to life, which she did. Toward the end of the story, after yet more adventures, she did finally get Chando to worship Manasa, and Chando begged Manasa's pardon and asked her to place her foot on his head in blessing. Behula and Lakhindar (who were really incarnations of the heavenly couple Usha and Aniruddha) returned to Indra's heaven, and Manasa got her worshipers.

Another version of the Manasa story, the *Manasa Mangal Kavya* by Bijay Gupta, tells of the growth of Manasa's worship and her coercion of Hindu devotees. The epic begins in a paradise world, during an earlier life of the merchant Chand Sadagar, a worshiper of Shiva. Chand accidentally came upon Manasa in a dense forest, while she was wearing only snakes for clothing. He frightened away the snakes, which left Manasa naked. She was angry, and cursed Chand to be born as a human being. He said that since she cursed him unjustly, as a result of an accident, her worship would never become popular on earth until he worshiped her himself. It was thus necessary for Manasa to gain Chand as a devotee, in order to gain other devotees.

Chand was born on earth, and later married Sanaka, who worshiped Manasa secretly. When Chand discovered this, he kicked the sacred pitcher with which Manasa was worshiped. Manasa decided to take revenge. She made his house fall down, and killed his relatives and friends with her poisonous snakes. Chand, however, had received supernatural power (*mahajnana*) due to his devotion to Shiva, and could return both people and property. Eventually Manasa stole his powers by deceit, and poisoned his six children. She then appeared to him, and told him that he would get back his children and powers if he worshiped her. He refused, and tried to hit her with a stick.

Sanaka went to pray to Manasa with two fishermen, and Manasa gave her the boon of having a son. However, this son was cursed to die of snakebite on his wedding night. Chand was preparing to go on a trading voyage when Manasa again appeared to him and asked him to worship her. He chased her away. Chand traded successfully, but on his way back she caused a storm that sunk his fourteen boats, and he was shipwrecked. He reached the shore of a distant land, and roamed about in poverty for twelve years.

When he eventually managed to return home, nobody recognized him, for he was emaciated and in rags. The townspeople were ready to kill him, but then his wife came and saw that it was her husband. By that time, his son Lakhindar was old enough to be married, and a marriage was arranged with the girl Behula. To protect Lakhindar on his wedding night, an iron room was built for the couple, but a snake came in through a tiny hole and bit Lakhindar.

His corpse was placed on a raft to float along the Ganguri River, as was the custom in that area. Behula decided to accompany her husband's corpse on its journey. She managed to overcome all threats, and eventually the raft reached the place where Neta, the celestial washerwoman, washed her divine laundry. Behula watched Neta kill her young son, and then bring him back to life. Behula approached her, and asked her to bring Lakhindar back to life. Neta answered that Lakhindar was killed because of Manasa's anger, and that she should go to Indra's court and ask the gods and goddesses for his life. Behula went to the heavenly court, and danced for the deities. They appreciated her skill at dancing, and offered her a boon. She asked for her husband's life. Manasa agreed to return his life, if Chand would worship her. Behula vowed that she would convince Chand. Manasa gave Lakhindar his life, and brought Chand's other sons to life as well. She also returned the ships full of treasure that had been lost in the storm.

They returned to Chand's house together, and Chand was thrilled to see how Behula's virtue and determination caused the return of his children and money. Behula told him of her journey, and also her vow to Manasa that Chand would worship her. Chand grudgingly agreed, but said that he would only worship her with his left hand (a form of insult), and with his back to her. A temple to Manasa was built at Chand's house, and she was worshiped with great ceremony. Because Chand had worshiped her (even with his left hand), Manasa's worship then spread throughout the world.[9] Once Chand could be coerced into worshiping her, worship from others could come easily. Again, Manasa got her worshipers.

As the account states, "Who can save the person when the goddess Jagatgauri herself has cast a poisonous look?"[10] This was his punishment. Even in alternative forms, Manasa will have her revenge upon those who do not worship her. She is not an easy goddess to love, but only love will calm her.

Manasa had to exert much effort in order to gain worshipers. Over time Manasa has undergone the Sanskritization process, having entered several puranas. These texts often serve as a social register of the gods, mentioning those deities that are considered respectable to upper-caste Hindus. She has become a high-caste deity, despite her mangal-kavya roots and interactions with low-caste people.

As an example of such upward mobility (and the Sanskritization process), we may look at Manasa's role in the *Brahmavaivarta Purana*, a Vaishnava purana with Shakta influence that was well known in Bengal. According to the *Brahmavaivarta Purana*, Manasa was the daughter of the *rishi* Kashyapa. She was a yogini and an ascetic, who worshiped Krishna for several yugas. She was also a student of Shiva. She had various powers, including granting immunity to poisons and bringing people back from the dead, and she was both virginal and the mother of a son. According to this puranic story, Manasa appeared spontaneously from Kashyapa's meditation, and she worshiped Shiva on Mount Kailash for one thousand years. Shiva taught her the Vedas and gave her the Krishna mantra. Then she performed long worship to Krishna, who told her that she would be worshiped in the three worlds. Manasa's father arranged her marriage with the sage Jaratkaru. Her husband did not touch her, and slept out under the fig tree. When Manasa saw him sleep past the time for the morning Vedic ritual, she awakened him. He was furious, and threatened her with the hell for disobedient wives. However, the Sun came to intervene, telling him that he was a wonderful and powerful brahmin. This made Jaratkaru feel better, but he still decided to leave Manasa. Then Brahma came down to tell him that would not be following dharma unless he gave Manasa a child. Jaratkaru touched her abdomen, thus impregnating her. He predicted that she would give birth to a son who would be a famous sage and a devotee of Vishnu. Manasa went to Kailash to be with her guru Shiva, and the unborn child listened to Shiva along with her. She gave birth to a boy whom she named Astika, and Shiva gave many gems as gifts to brahmins. He also taught the boy the Vedas. Manasa returned to her father's house, and brought the boy up there. Manasa later saved Indra's life, and he worshiped her.[11]

Manasa even got her own visualization (*dhyana*): she has white skin, wears jewels and a sacred thread which is a snake, she is wise and devoted to her husband, and a perfect yogi. She should be worshiped with flowers, incense, perfume, and other offerings. Her somewhat tantric mantra is *Om hrim srim klim Manasa Devyai svaha*, ideally to be recited 500,000 times.

As we may note, the dysfunctional family, hateful stepmother, and lustful father have been erased from the story, and Shiva has become her guru instead. Instead of her husband being afraid of her, he is angry for being awakened, and is an all-powerful brahmin. He curses her instead of running off and hiding in a seashell. Despite his erratic behavior, Manasa is devoted to him, and a proper orthodox Hindu wife. She would be almost unrecognizable to devotees familiar with her from the *mangal-kavyas*.

Not all goddesses of folk bhakti are threatening to their devotees. Sometimes goddesses are worshiped out of guilt rather than fear. In the village of Napukur (or Naopukhuria) in Murshidabad, we have an instance of a poor and low-caste woman who was metamorphosized into a goddess. Ma Dumni was a low-caste woman of Hindu or tribal origin. She lived in the jungle, and a feudal lord was attracted to her as he was passing through the area on a hunting trip with his courtiers. The king's followers arranged a rapid informal (*gandharva*) marriage with an exchage of garlands but no official rites (thus it was not a legal marriage). That night, the ruler and his party were stranded in a rainstorm, and became cold and hungry. The new bride chipped twigs of bamboo into small pieces that could be lighted for warmth, but her grace and skill at doing this made the ruler suspicious that she might be a low-caste Dom (a caste that which uses twigs for burning corpses), and he decided to desert her. The group left under the cover of darkness, and the woman awoke to find herself stranded and alone, in distress and despair. She wept enough to create a large lake (now called Dumni Daha), and nothing more was heard from her. Then, many years later, the local ferryman dreamed that the lost woman stood before him, saying that she had been turned into a block of stone lying unnoticed and forlorn, and he must rescue her. He did so, and set the piece of stone up as a goddess.[12]

The descendants of the ferryman have remained in charge of her worship, which occurs twice a week, and also in a major ceremony once a year. She has became a goddess who cures disease, protects stillborn children, and removes barrenness. She is offered goats in sacrifice, and her devotees perform penance for her blessings. They also suspend votive stones from strings on the branches of a banyan tree, beneath which is her statue, a four-armed icon that resembles the Buddhist Tara.[13]

Here we have deification following persecution and neglect, where the goddess's story evokes sympathy for the low-caste women deserted by selfish noblemen. Another deified saint is Rajballabhi of Rajbalhat in Hooghly district, in which she had her revenge for an attempted seduction. In her story, an elderly garland maker found a lovely little girl and adopted her. She grew up to be very beautiful. When a merchant passed by, making music on his fleet of boats, the girl came out to see them. The merchant decided to seduce her, and invited her aboard his boat to better hear the music. As she stepped onto it, the boat capsized, and as she stepped one after another onto each boat, it sank down into the water. The merchant lost several boats this way. An oracle revealed that she was a goddess, and the merchant bowed to her and asked for her forgiveness. She agreed to forgive him if he would build her a temple at that site and arrange for her regular worship. She then disappeared. As soon as he began constructing the temple, all of the capsized boats were salvaged with their merchandise intact.[14]

Not all people who worship goddesses in the folk tradition would wish to call their style of worship bhakti. As one Adivasi informant said,

> We do not believe in bhakti, we have no word for such devotion. We follow the calendar of life—of people, of cattle, of nature. We seek a balance. There are interactions controlled by unseen forces, and we seek reciprocity with them. Our goddesses and protectors give us hope in day-to-day life, and they bless us with fertility and happiness. We have love and respect, and we are dutiful toward them, and we worship them with rituals. We are grateful for their gifts. But we

> are not like the Hindu bhaktas. For them, bhakti is all gesture and drama, overly stylized and exaggerated. It is only for show, and the brahmins capitalize on it. There are phony claims of talking to gods, and the Krishna cult wants people to be slaves of gods and gurus, and build big temples. We only wish to be grateful, we don't want a public show.[15]

Folk Shakta bhakti shows an active world of goddesses who go out and interact in the world of humans, demanding worship and loyalty. Like Yahweh, they are jealous gods, acting in history and influencing the course of events. In their stories, they bring reward and punishment, revitalizing towns or destroying them, and they travel from one world to another with ease. Devotion is usually based on fear—the person loves and is loyal to that which is powerful. Though the goddesses often come from divine worlds they are not distant and abstract entities but here and now, demanding a response from the chosen devotee. The proper response is worship, offerings, and submission.

Folk bhakti often begins in response to a goddess's call. It is a prophetic call, in which the goddess appears to her often unwilling devotee and demands worship and sacrifice, and sometimes proselytizing. If this does not occur, the visionary will be punished, or the goddess will keep appearing until he or she is compelled to obey her. Even stubborn ones, like Chand in the Manasa *mangals*, have the patience of Job in the face of Manasa's destriction of his house, children, and wealth, but in the end even he must obey a divine decree. Once there is worship and the goddess is pacified, the danger and malevolence disappear. If we do not exactly have the redemptive power of selfless love here, at least we have the salvational power of ritual.

## Emotional Shakta Bhakti: Passion and Devotion for the Goddess

Whereas folk Shakta bhakti dates from at least medieval times, and is probably much older, emotional Shaktism really becomes dominant toward the second half of the eighteenth century. Tantric goddesses become more popular and benevolent, and Shakta poets write hymns to the divine mother, before whom they are children and devotees. The relationship that develops between goddess and devotee is intimate and personal, sweet or passionate, and very intense.

The most complex work on the expression of religious emotion has been done in India by the Vaishnava tradition, especially the Bengali Vaishnavas, but emotional Shakta bhakti has its own typologies of religious emotion. These are similar but not identical to those of the Vaishnavas. The Bengali Vaishnavas have five major devotional *bhavas* or moods through which to relate to the god Krishna (in West Bengal, Krishna is the high god, while Vishnu is one of his emanations). The god may be seen as the master (while the devotee is the servant), the friend (while the devotee is also a friend), the beloved (while the devotee is the female lover), the child (whom the devotee loves as a parent loves a son), or the god may be loved in the peaceful mood, in which god and devotee are united in a shared identity. The highest form of love is the selfless love (*prema*) between lover and beloved, best exemplified by the love between Radha and Krishna.

Among devotional Shaktas, the goddess tends to be loved in four major moods rather than five, for the role of the goddess as friend is relatively rare, and there is little literature that includes this relationship (it is seen in tribal and folk worship, however). The goddess in her majestic Great Goddess role would be Mother or mistress, with the devotee as child or servant. This corresponds to the god as master, the mood expressing the deity's majesty in Vaishnava theology. The goddess is also loved as a child, the young daughter of the household adored by her parents, though they know that before she becomes a teenager she must leave to marry into another household (this love of the young daughter corresponds to the love of the child Krishna). She is very rarely the lover, usually among the Shakta tantrikas, in which the play between the goddess and devotee is erotic as well as reverent (among Bengali Vaishnavas, such erotic play with the god is the highest form of devotion, experienced indirectly through the *manjari sadhana*).[16] And in modern, post-Ramakrishna bhakti, the goddess is understood to be the ocean of consciousness, and the mood of union with her overwhelms and absorbs the devotee's individuality.

The two most important moods for emotional Shakta bhakti, parental love and the child's love for its mother (or *vatsalya* and *prati-vatsalya*), have been described by Jahnavikumar Chakravarti. Here the child *bhava* is described:

> The devotee's emotion is like that of a child—his pouting and demands are aimed toward the mother. Sometimes he feels pride, sometimes he makes earnest requests, sometimes he feels anger or desire for her grace, sometimes [he feels] humility and fear, sometimes dependence. Above all, there is the agitated cry of the child, "Ma, Ma." It suppresses all other cries. [The devotee is] a mother-crazy child. At the end of his longest complaint, his final prayer is, "Brush away this dust, take me into your lap, Ma" or "Whatever is good, do that, Ma. I have set down my burden at your feet."[17]

A good description of the Mother's response to her often rather demanding child is described by Nigamananda Sarasvati in his book *Mayer Kripa* (The Mother's Mercy). She comes in her peaceful form to a sadhu who has been meditating at night in a burning ground, and she looks lovingly at him and tells him about devotion:

> The signs of devotion are seen when a person chants the names of the Mother, and listens to my hymns and songs of praise, when his mind is full of good wishes, and it flows toward me without a break, like a liquid. He worships without hope of reward, even [without hope of] liberation, for he desires to remain as my servant. . . . Because of his excessive love, his eyes are always full of tears, and his voice is choked. . . . When he attains the state of transcendent devotion (*parabhakti*), he cannot think of anything but me and becomes absorbed in my aspect as pure consciousness. This kind of devotee gives up all traditional observances and ordinary responsibilities, and he always calls for me, saying, "O Ma, O Ma." I come to him as the cow comes to the calf when it calls.[18]

The peaceful state of *shanta bhava* or united consciousness between deity and worshiper is considered undesirable in Vaishnavism because of its lack of sweetness and emotional intensity. However, the union of the goddess and her devotees through shared awareness, the closest equivalent of this Vaishnava mood in Shaktism, is often understood to be the highest Shakta goal (especially by Shaktas of philosophical inclination). For devotees of a more emotional style, being the child of the Mother seems to be most respected, and is the relational style for several of the most important recent saints of Shakta bhakti (such as Vamaksepa of Tarapith and Ramakrishna Paramahamsa of Dakshineswar).

The highest emotional state in emotional Shakta bhakti is often said to be *mahabhava*, the greatest state or perfection of *bhava*. *Mahabhava* is a devotional term, taken from Bengali Vaishnavism, and used by Shaktas to show total dedication to the mother. Bhattacharya speaks of this *bhava* for the mother as a love that is evoked by memory:

> The things of the Samsāra appear full of love to a lover because they are connected with the object of his love. The dresses and ornaments and even playthings of a husband or a wife or a son or a daughter who are absent become dear to us because of their connection with the objects of our love; otherwise, why is it that parents keep with great care things belonging to their children who live far away from them? Such articles are materials for the perfection of Bhāva in the domain of love. . . . Now, let Sādhakas consider what sort of a consummation of Bhāva there is if this love be centred not in wife and children, who are but, as it were, persons seen in a dream in this transient Samsāra, but in the beauteous feet of the Mother of the world, who is the centre of all love in the Brahmāṇḍa, full of love, full of Brahman, and full of bliss? How intense will be the climax of the consummation of Bhāva of him who has offered at the feet of the Mother all devotion, all love, and all affection for parents, wife and children. . . . The sight of everything in this world

> moves him to overflowing Bhāva. . . . Unceasing tears of love flow from his eyes in the plenitude of his tender feeling.[19]

Such states are described in many Shakta texts about the goddesses, especially the shakta puranas. According to the *Devi Bhagavata Purana*, devotional love is influenced by the three *gunas* or qualities of Samkhya philosophy (*sattva*, *rajas*, and *tamas*). Bhakti that is tamasic is present in the devotee who is full of anger and worships the goddess to harm others, and to induce pain and jealousy. Bhakti that is rajasic is present in the devotee who worships the goddess to gain personal advantage, such as fame or wealth, though he or she does not intend to harm others. Bhakti that is sattvic is present in the devotee who seeks purification, who renounces all karmas and sins, and surrenders totally to the goddess. Although this last is the best form of bhakti that is influenced by the *gunas*, there is still a higher type of bhakti, called supreme devotion or *parabhakti*.[20]

Supreme devotion is unselfish, for the devotee does not seek boons from the goddess. He or she recites the goddess's names and attributes, fixes the mind on her, has no desire to get rewards, and does not seek liberation. When he hears of her glory, tears of love flow from his eyes, his voice chokes and his hair stands on end, and he is filled with love when he hears of her stories and adventures. He or she recognizes the goddess's presence in all living beings. The devotee's mind is focused upon the goddess as on a continuous flow of oil, and he hopes for nothing higher than to serve the goddess forever. He or she is intoxicated with the goddess's love, and sings and dances with joy.[21] After death, the devotee spends time in her paradise, and may eventually gain liberation.

This shows the influence of Vaishnava bhakti, which also speaks of the mind flowing toward Krishna like oil, and such ecstatic symptoms as tears, choked voice, hair standing on end, and other such symptoms of intense love. As the *Devi Bhagavata Purana* asserts: "With hearts filled with love and with hairs standing on their ends, all should satisfy Me frequently with tears of love flowing from their eyes and with voice[s] choked with feelings and with dancing, music and singing, and with his whole body filled with joy."[22] The devotee should consider himself to be ultimately united with the goddess, and overwhelmed by the highest love, which is also the highest wisdom. "He sings my name loudly and dances, being intoxicated with My love, and has no idea of egoism and is devoid of his body-idea [or attachment to the body], thinking that the body is not his. He thinks that whatever is Prarabdha (done in his previous lives) must come to pass and therefore does not become agitated as to the preservation of his body and soul. This sort of Bhakti is called the Para Bhakti or the Highest Devotion."[23]

We also see this union of love and wisdom in the Devi Gita or Bhagavati Gita section of the *Mahabhagavata Purana*. The teachings of the Bhagavati Gita were revealed by the young goddess to her father Himalaya, lord of the mountains. She showed him her terrifying universal form, but her father was frightened, and asked her to take on her beautiful maiden form again. After she did so, she told him about bhakti as the best path to salvation. The goddess is really *brahman* or Para Shakti, pervading the world and existing in the forms of all of the gods. In the Vedas, she is *satchidananda* (the unity of being, consciousness, and bliss), and she is the origin of all creation. She gives liberation from the world, which is as illusory as a dream. The goddess originates all creation, preservation, and destruction, and she may be called by many names. While her ultimate role is *brahman*, she relates to her devotees through the forms of gods and goddesses, including Kali, Devi, Parvati, Shiva, and Krishna.[24]

One of the most intense emotional states in Bengali Vaishnavism is the *viraha* state of Radha, her state of loneliness and grieving for the absent Krishna. This occurred briefly in their separations during fights or during his unfaithfulness with other women (especially Radha's rival Chandravali), and in a more permanent way after Krishna left Braj to rule as a king in Mathura. We see a similar sort of Shakta grief over separation in the *agamani* and *vijaya* songs that have long been sung at Durga Puja time, when the goddess Durga is understood to be incarnate as the girl Uma. Such songs give insight into the emotional relationship of goddess and devotee, in which the devotee is the mother of the divine child. Uma's mother Menaka was left alone and sorrowful after Uma's childhood marriage to the elderly Shiva, and Menaka's songs of her sorrow at the loss of her daughter caused a strong response in listeners, as did Radha's songs of longing for Krishna. Both types of songs involved sorrow and love, as well as pride, pique, anger, denial, and other emotions. Whereas the erotic mood of lovers is most valued among Bengali Vaishnavas, it is the parent/child relationship that is most valued among Bengali Shakta devotees. Closeness to the mother returns the devotee to the love and joy that he felt in his own mother's arms, and it is the goddess's desire to return that state to the devotee. Such a state is joyful, as Gopinath Kaviraj explains: "But knowingly or unknowingly, [the true Self] wants nothing but joy. This search for joy is the aim of all our sadhana; i.e. to find our forgotten joyful Self—to regain the lost paradise. Mother wants to take us to the path of joy, every vibration of our mind and body is in search of [this] joy."[25]

The goddess may take on many forms to embrace her worshipers. As Shivachandra Vidyarnava Bhattacharya writes:

> Whatever form She may assume in Her aspect with attributes is but Her form. That Śakti alone who grants enjoyment, salvation, and devotion, is in all such forms. Now the Sādhaka may, if he so desires, know Her as Viṣṇu, Kṛṣṇa, Śiva, and Rāma, or as Kālī, Tārā, Rādhā, Durgā, Sītā and Lakṣmī, or please himself by calling Her mother, father, friend and well-wisher. It does not matter whether the Vaiṣṇava

> considers her as Viṣṇu in the form of Śakti, or the Śākta considers Her as Śakti in the form of Viṣṇu. . . . That Mahāśakti is everywhere the real giver of liberation, from whomsoever it may come, whether as Śiva, Viṣṇu, Durgā, Gaṇeśa, or Sūrya.[26]

Along the same lines, he quotes Maheshvari in the Durgagita section of the *Mundamala Tantra*:

> It is I who am Rādhikā in Goloka, Kamalā in Vaikuṇṭha, and Sāvitrī and Sarasvatī, the presiding Devī of speech in Brahmaloka. It is I who am Pārvatī in Kailāśa, Jānakī in Mithilā, Rukmiṇī in Dvārakā, and Draupadī in Hastināpura. I am Sandhyā and Gāyatrī, the Mother of Vedas, the objects of adoration to all the twice-born people. . . . I am Mahāvidyā formed of Hari and Hara, and I am also the worshiped of Brahmā, Viṣṇu and Śiva. . . . wherever there is Śakti (a female) there I am. O Mahādeva, know for certain that this is the manner in which I am best contemplated. Whoever forsakes this path of Sakti and proceeds along another path in search of me throws away the jewel which is in the palm of his had, and runs after a heap of ashes.[27]

Emotional Shakta bhakti is, however, not primarily a literary tradition, and does not have the focus on text and commentary that we see in Vaishnava bhakti. Such puranas as the *Devi Bhagavata Purana* and the *Padma Purana* are sometimes read, but the only really popular puranic text is the Durga Saptasati or Chandi section of the *Markandeya Purana*, which is read and sung every year at Durga Puja. Broadcasting this has become a tradition, and the same version is played each year on the radio in Calcutta. When a radio station brought in a version sung by new singers, it was deluged by phone calls protesting the change—and returned to its traditional Chandi with its traditional singers. Devotees also make use of tantric texts. Despite its questionable origin, the recent *Mahanirvana Tantra* is a very popular work, cited by both scholars and practitioners as a good source for Shakta devotion, while the *Kularnava Tantra* is a very important tantra for both groups as a manual for serious practice.

Shaktas whom I have interviewed love poetry—they read it, they write it, and they sing it. Although this may be related to an old proverb about Calcutta ("In Calcutta, throw a stone and hit a poet"), I have found the appreciation for poetic beauty throughout West Bengal. Many practitioners said specifically that they were performing Shakta spiritual practice in order to gain poetic inspiration. Some would focus on the goddess Tara for this inspiration, others said that any of the ten Mahavidya goddesses could give this boon. This poetry contains the popular theology of Shakta bhakti, and gives insights into those aspects of devotion to the goddess which are most important to her devotees.

In this section, I will present as examples of emotional Shakta bhakti some poetry of Ramprasad Sen and several other Shakta poets, and some poems traditionally sung during the fall holiday of Durga Puja.

### *Ramprasad Sen, Poet of the Shakta Revival*

Ramprasad Sen (1720–1781) has been called the main originator of the new Shakti movement,[28] and his poetry is still very popular in West Bengal. His poetic style was simple and emotional, and his epics were popular in their time (today, only his *Vidya-Sundar* and *Kalikirtan* survive in full). Many of his poems reflect the difficulties faced during his lifetime: the famine of 1770 (during which it is said that almost one-third of the population of Bengal starved to death), political and economic instability, and the decline of rural culture.[29] As with most Shakta poets, however, history was only a distant background for devotional poetry showing an intimate relationship with the goddess and concerns about death and salvation.

There is some confusion among scholars about which of Ramprasad's poems were written by the original Ramprasad Sen, of the Vaidya caste from Kumarhatta (now Halisahar), and which poems were written by a second Ramprasad, a Calcutta brahmin and younger contemporary of the first, who also wrote Shakta devotional songs. Shakta devotees do not tend to distinguish the songs of these two poets, however, and only speak of one Ramprasad who was a great devotee, and who died from an overdose of love of the Mother.

The original Ramprasad Sen was born into a Shakta family, and studied Sanskrit grammar and literature as well as Bengali poetry while he was young. He later studied Urdu and Persian, the languages of the Muslim rulers of Bengal. Though his father wanted him to follow their traditional caste occupation and become a physician, Ramprasad was more interested in the humanities, and he studied them throughout his teen years. He was initiatiated into the Kali mantra along with his wife Sarvani, by the family kula-guru, and he studied Shakta ritual practice with several other gurus. He spent much time in worship and meditation.

When his father died, it became Ramprasad's responsibility to support the household. He got a job as a clerk in Calcutta, but he would go into trances at work and write poems to Kali in his account books. He alienated his fellow workers, who saw him as lazy and absentminded, but his employer was impressed by his poetry when he examined the account books. He gave Ramprasad a small pension to stay home and write poetry.

Ramprasad spent hours in meditation, and he often did so while standing deep in the Ganges River. The river boatmen would listen to his songs as they passed by. As the story goes, one day the Maharaja Krishnachandra of Nadia passed Ramprasad and heard his evening hymns. He was impressed with Ramprasad's talent, and asked him to be court poet at his court in Krishnanagar. He gave Ramprasad thirty-three acres of rent-free land there, and the title of Kaviranjana (a sort of Poet Laureate). Ramprasad composed many songs and hymns for the court, and the Muslim nobles appreciated his Shakta songs. Initially his mother organized the household there, but it ran poorly after her death. There were bad crops and flooding, and the rent from others on the land was not collected. Ramprasad and his family often had no food, and he prayed to the goddess to save him from starvation.

He continued his spiritual practices, and worshiped the goddess at midnight on a seat of five skulls. He performed corpse rituals, and sat in a *panchavati* grove (containing five sacred trees). When his wife once perceived that his Kali statue was alive she fainted, and he worshiped his wife once with devotional songs, and both stayed in trance all during the night. After the maharaja's death, Ramprasad retreated from the world and from his family, and spent his time in meditation. He is said to have died as his Kali statue was being immersed in the river, with the vision of the goddess before his eyes.[30]

As examples of his work, the following poems are translations from the popular booklet *Ramprasadi sangit* or Songs of Ramprasad. This book is popularly sold at Shakta temples and *pithas* in West Bengal, for use by priests, singers, and devotees.

Ramprasad was considered to be love-mad (insane due to his love of the goddess) by his friends and family, but for Ramprasad their opinions were not important. Here he describes his ecstatic experience (*bhava*, a local abbreviation for *mahabhava* or highest state):

> O Ma Kali, wearing a garland of skulls,
> What an experience (*bhava*) you have shown me.
> You taught me how to call you,
> And at the moment I chanted "Ma"
> You drove me to ecstasy!
> Ma Tara, please tell me the source (of your sweetness)—
> Where did you get this name full of nectar?
> When worldly people look at me
> They call me mad from love;
> The members of my family
> Hurl curses and insults at me.
> But whatever people say, dark Mother,
> My faith will not waver.
> Let people say what they want
> I will chant the name of Kali forever.
> If you get rid of this illusory world,
> Insults and egotism are unimportant.
> I have made your red feet my goal.
> I am no longer concerned with worldly opinions.[31]

Imagery of death and salvation abounds in his poems. A partial version of this next poem was popularized in a recent film about the Thugee sect, "The Deceivers":

> Because you love the burning ground
> I have made a burning ground of my heart
> So that you, dark goddess, can dance there forever.
> I have no other desire left, O Mother—
> A funeral pyre is blazing in my heart.
> Ashes from corpses are all around me, my Mother,
> In case you decide to come.
> Prasad prays, O Mother, at the hour of death
> Keep your devotee at your feet.
> Please come dancing with rhythmic steps
> Let me see you when my eyes are closed.[32]

Several of his poems emphasize the value of devotion over the sort of states of unity and emptiness emphasized in Vedanta and in Buddhism, and use tantric imagery such as the chakras of kundalini yoga:

> O mind, think day and night
> Of the one with a frightening face.
> Mother is as beautiful
> As a sky full of blue clouds.
> She is naked, and her hair is wild.
> O mind, you do not realize
> She dances in the *sahasrara* and *muladhara* [chakras][33]
> She is in a state of bliss,
> Like a swan moving through a lake of lotuses.
> Place this blissful Mother in your heart
> And joyfully light the fire of wisdom
> To look deeply into her infinite beauty.
> Prasad says, she loves to fulfill the desires of her devotees.
> Tell me, what virtue can Nirvana have
> Compared with her love?[34]

Ramprasad worshiped Kali, the dark goddess, but some of his songs deny the darkness of the goddess. This poem is often attributed to the other (Dvija) Ramprasad:

> O mind, tell me what ritual you performed
> To find this black girl.
> When I see the radiance of this dark beauty
> Everything else disappears from my eyes and my mind.

In whose house did she live?
How did you bring her here?
She is not black, she is a full moon
Which floods the heart with light.
Her feet are as beautiful
As the rising sun which glows at dawn.
Dvija Ramprasad says, Those feet would be prettier
With an offering of red hibiscus (jaba) flowers.[35]

In this poem, Kali is the goddess of liberation (*kaivalyadayini*), and the human mind is compared to a kite—severing its string brings the person to freedom:

Ma Kali flies mind-kites in the market of the world.
The mind-kites are flying in the winds of hope,
Are tied by the strings of illusion,
And enclosed in bodies with bones and nerves.
She made the kites with intricate workmanship,
The string is toughened by the gum of worldly pleasure.
When one or two kites out of a hundred thousand have their strings cut,
O Ma, you laugh and clap your hands [to see them fly].
Prasad says, "His kite will fly away in the south wind [of grace]
Across the ocean of the world, and land on the other shore."[36]

Kali does not always answer prayers, however, and many songs are full of complaints by the devotee. The *bhava* of complaint is a popular mood for Shakta poetry. Here is one from the collection by Nathan and Seely:

I'm not calling you Mother anymore,
All You give me is trouble.
I had a home and a family, now
I'm a beggar—what will You think of
Next, my wild-haired Devi?
I'll beg before I come to You,
Crying "Mother." I've tried that
And got the silent treatment.
If the mother lives should the son suffer
And if she's dead, hasn't he got to live somehow?
Ramprasad says: What's a mother
Anyway, the son's worst enemy?
I keep wondering what worse You can do
Than make me live over and over
The pain, life after life.[37]

*Some Other Shakta Poets*

Another famous Kali poet and devotee was Kamalakanta Bhattacharya, who lived shortly after Ramprasad during the eighteenth century. He was initiated by a Vaishnava guru, but practiced tantra and yoga. He became a court poet and pandit, and wrote poetry for the raja of Burdwan. He later became the raja's guru. Like Ramprasad, he wrote songs showing emotional extremes, hating the world at one moment and loving it the next, because it is the goddess's dancing ground. Some songs pray to the goddess for salvation, and others ask for happiness and the goddess's love. Other famous Shakta poets include Antony Feringhee, who was Portuguese by birth and lived in Calcutta, following Hindu life and ritual, and Dasarathi Ray, who emphasized the universal nature of the goddess, as well as Narachandra Ray and Rasik Chandra Ray. The Muslim Shakta poets Kali Mirja (Mirja Hussain Ali) and Sayyid Jafar Khan are also well known. Such famous nineteenth-century writers as Michael Madhusudan Dutt, Girish Chandra Ghosh, Nabin Chandra Sen, and Ishvarachandra Gupta also wrote Shakta poems and short stories.

There are many poets who have not gained Ramprasad's fame but whose poetry is highly respected for its devotion. Their writing is collected in books called *Shakta padabali*, or poems to the goddess. Girishchandra Ghosh is a good exponent of emotional bhakti; he speaks of devotion as more important than knowledge:

> Ma, I have devotion, I do not understand books,
> I chant your name, Ma, with my heart open
> And all of my wishes are fulfilled.
> If you call out to Ma, and you are hot and anxious,
> Her peace will come to you like cooling water.
> Mother is filled with love, and she calls out to us—
> Brother, let us hear her call![38]

Such devotion requires only repentance, which evokes divine forgiveness. Mothers are believed always to forgive the children they love. Ghosh writes:

> I have done wrong, and I cried and repented,
> And Mother forgave me.
> She said, "Come onto my lap," and she wiped away my tears.
> Now I am no longer frightened, for Mother has taken care of
> everything.
> She has told me over and over
> I need only call out to her, and cling to her feet.[39]

Devotion may also bring madness, as Trailokyanath Sanyal writes (in the style of Ramprasad):

Make me mad, Ma Brahmamayi!
I do not want knowledge of right and wrong—
Let me be drunk on the wine of your love.
O Mother, you destroy the minds of your devotees.
Let me dive into the ocean of (your) love.
This world is your madhouse.
Some laugh, some cry, some dance in bliss.
Isha [Jesus], Musha [Moses], and the blessed Chaitanya
All have swooned, overwhelmed by love.
I will be blessed, Ma, when I come to you.
In heaven there is a fair of madmen, even guru and disciple
  [are mad].
Who can understand this play of love?
You are mad with love, Mother,
You are the maddest of the mad.
Make me rich with devotion,
For I am poor, and a slave of love.[40]

Often the god Shiva is himself understood as a devotee of the goddess (he is also her child, which makes their marriage an odd one). As Girishchandra Ghosh observes:

Mother, if Shiva is your husband
Why is he lying under your feet?
He looks up at you, full of fear,
And his chest is under your foot.
Is it because your foot is beautiful,
Is that why he places it on his chest?
[But if] you are mother to all beings
How can you have a husband?
The earth trembles from the weight of your feet.
Doesn't Shiva get hurt when you stand on him?
No, for he holds you
On the lotus of his heart.[41]

In this emotional bhakti poem by Rasikchandra Ray, the devotee uses the mood of conflict and struggle with the mother, and he will win his goal by defeating the goddess and gaining her blessings:

Come, Mother, join battle with me as I worship.
Let us see, Mother, who will be conquered, the mother or the son. . . .
Today the battle shall decide the issue.
What fear have I of death?
With the beating of drums, I will seize the wealth of salvation.

In battle after battle you have overthrown the Daityas.
This time, O Goddess, come and fight with me.
Rasikcandra your votary says: It is in your strength, Mother
That I shall conquer you in battle.[42]

In these poems, the devotee seeks the goddess's love, and hopes to love her and understand her (or, in the last poem, even conquer her). Devotees seek liberation, peace, and even greater devotion. The goals of folk Shaktism—wealth, healing, worldly power—are generally absent. These are emotional songs, as are the old songs of Durga Puja. These songs welcoming the goddess Durga and bidding her farewell are a special category of poems within the tradition of emotional Shakta bhakti.

### *Songs of Welcome and Farewell*

The *agamani* and *vijaya* songs welcome the goddess (called both Durga and Kalika) to her parents' home at the beginning of Durga Puja and bid farewell to her as the holiday ends and she leaves to return to her husband. These songs were widely sung during the nineteenth and early twentieth centuries, though today we hear only remnants of them. These songs are clear examples of the importance of emotional bhakti, for they are intended to involve the audience with personal emotions, with love and sorrow, toward a goddess in human form. They show more folk tradition than classical Hinduism, seeing the goddess as an unhappily married girl, her husband Shiva as a lazy drunkard, and her family as frustrated and concerned for her well-being. These are not high and powerful gods, but a human family with whom to sympathize, and the goddess is understood to be vulnerable rather than all-powerful.[43] In these songs, the deities are like people, and share human pain and sorrow.

The background for these songs can be found in the puranas, especially the *Kalika Purana*, which has long been popular in West Bengal. According to chapter 41 of this text, Sati had given up her life at the great sacrifice of Daksha (by yogic means, rather than by jumping into the fire), and she had also participated in the destruction of the sacrifice, along with her yoginis. She determined to be reborn so that she could return to her life with Shiva. Menaka was a devotee of the goddess, and worshiped her every day for twenty-seven years with offerings and austerities. The goddess then appeared to Menaka, and asked her what she wanted. Menaka asked for one hundred sons and a beautiful daughter full of good qualities, who would bring joy to all. The goddess agreed to this, and told Menaka that she herself would incarnate as Menaka's daughter, for the welfare of the world.

Menaka returned to her home, and gave birth first to Mainak, called "the greatest of the mountains," who is now said to live in the ocean. She then gave birth to ninety-nine other sons, and finally to a daughter. This daughter was born at midnight, amid showers of rain and flowers. Her skin was like blue lotus petals, and her father Himavat called her Kali. She was also called Parvati and Girinandini, the daughter of the mountain. Kali was playful and virtuous, and made her friends and relatives happy. She stayed close to her parents, until the sage Narada (troublemaker and gossip of the gods) came to visit.

Narada said that she must marry Shiva and no other, and that Shiva would have no other wife. Kali would shine like bright lightning, and be called Gauri. When Himavat objected to this, and said that Shiva had sworn to have no wife but Sati, Narada told him that his daughter was Sati reincarnated. Himavat and his wife were convinced by Narada's arguments, and agreed to have Kali marry Shiva.[44]

The *agamani* and *vijaya* songs accept this as the background, but then they begin to add details. Shiva is a poor husband, an aging alcoholic and drug addict, a tantric madman, who ignores his young wife and spends his time with ghouls out at the burning ground. It is an unhappy marriage, and Kali alternates between pretending the marriage is a good one and bemoaning her misery. She is called in these songs by a variety of names, including Durga and Uma.

Radhaprasad Gupta has described a Durga Puja organized by a zamindar named Gobindaram during the late 1700s.[45] It involved a welcome performed for two weeks before the Puja, involving songs of welcome to Durga.[46] The songs of welcome often deal with the mother's sympathy for the daughter's unhappily married state. Here Menaka sings to her daughter, Uma/Durga:

I have heard from Narada
That my daughter Uma
Spends her days in misery.
She roams the burning ground
Without thinking of her household.
If Shiva (Mirtunjaya) comes and talks of taking her back
Then we both, mother and daughter, will argue with him.
If we must, we will disown him
As the son-in-law.[47]

The songs of farewell (*vijaya*) speak of Menaka's sadness at having to lose her daughter once again, after her visit to her family's home:

O Navami night, you are so cruel
Because you will end, and I must send my daughter away tomorrow.
I tried to persuade Ṣhiva to let her remain with me
For more than three days,
But he wouldn't listen.
Uma has a face like a full moon,
But she rises and sets so quickly!

I hear the sound of drums in the distance.
O Navami night, you are merciless.[48]

In the songs of welcome and farewell, Durga becomes the beloved daughter, who is missed in her absence and welcomed on her return. As Gupta writes, "We invoke the mother with emotion (*bhava*) . . ." for intense emotion is appropriate to the dramas of love and loss. Some devotees feel these states so intensely that they dance in possession or ecstasy, reliving the events of the past. As Panchkuri Bandhopadhyaya says of this worship, "There is no fixed time or place for calling the daughter. You can call her any time and, responding to that call [as if] from her parents, the daughter will come dancing in, and she jumps onto the lap of her father with love and affection."[49]

He describes the environment of Durga Puja:

> For a fortnight before her coming, the sky and air of all Bengal would resound with songs of welcome. These songs were written over the centuries by the thousands by many village poets, and there is no record of them. . . . In these songs of welcome, there is a very beautiful picture of Bengali family life. The welcome given to the daughter and son-in-law, the daughter's affection for the parental house and the mother's love for her daughter, all of these are the particular characteristics of Bengaliness (*bangalitva*). These characteristics have been blended with mythological tales by the Bengali poets, and that gave rise to a wonderful poetry. . . . There was a time when it would have been almost impossible to find any Bengali ignorant of the exquisite feelings of the Bengali mother [as expressed through these songs].[50]

The songs tell of family life in Bengal, which was often difficult. Different aspects of the goddess are united in one beloved daughter, who is unhappily married to a poor and elderly husband. She is said to leave her husband's house to visit her natal family at the beginning of Durga Puja, to arrive on the sixth evening, and to stay until the tenth night, when her statue is immersed in the river. This immersion symbolizes the goddess leaving the physical world and returning to her husband. The young girl is described as beautiful, an incarnation of the goddess:

The daughter of the mountain moves gracefully,
Her feet are like the rising sun.
She walks sweetly, holding her mother's hand,
And the universe is full of unbounded joy, considering herself blessed.
O mind, worship this embodiment of the transcendent and inexpressible.

The eternal Parabrahman is born in the Himalayas.
She plays with her friends, [who] call out Kali, Kali, Kali.
Kalika has become the daughter of the mountain.[51]

Her father, called Giriraja, Girija, or Himalaya, and her mother, Menaka or Girirani, are close to their daughter, and unhappy at her marriage. Some poets describe her parents as royalty stricken by poverty, others have them as poor village folk, forced to marry off their daughter. The marriage was arranged by the sage Narada, the "ominous one-eyed matchmaker."[52] She was a young girl at that time, between eight and twelve years old according to most poets. She was married to the elderly groom Shiva, who is of high caste (brahmin Bandyopadhyaya) but who is wrinkled, poor, wearing ashes, rags, or tiger skin, and decorated with snakes. He rides a buffalo or roams the burning grounds on foot with disreputable ghouls, with whom he drinks alcohol and smokes hashish. Sometimes he is a Kulin brahmin, and has other wives, and Uma must face household feuds as well as poverty and an indifferent husband.

Her mother worries about Kalika, as her relationship with her daughter was close. But Menaka follows the rules of a good Bengali wife, who should not travel alone, so she cannot visit her daughter on her own. Instead, she coerces her husband into going to Shiva's home in Kailash and bringing their daughter home. This visit by the daughter is celebrated on the fall festival of Durga Puja.

Menaka mourns her time away from her daughter. As Jayanarayana Bandyopadhyaya writes:

You have gone to the home of Shankara, on Kailash
And you seem to have forgotten us.
You do not miss me, your mother,
To whom can I speak of this?
I have spent my days crying,
For my child Kalika is away from me.
Look at me, I am weak, and unable to move,
I am without Shakti, O wife of Shiva.[53]

Sometimes Menaka is more rebellious, saying that she will never send Uma back to live with her awful husband:

This time, when Uma comes, I will not send her back again.
Even if people condemn me, I won't listen.
She has been given to a husband
Who roams through the burning ground,
Who has ghosts for friends,
Who is an old man, and wears ashes.
My daughter is so young

He doesn't look after her properly.
When she comes this time [to visit]
I won't send her back again.[54]

Some poets link Uma and the goddesses together by having one turn into another. Uma's poverty and misery have turned her skin from golden to black—she has thus changed from Gauri (the golden one) to Kali (the black one), due to her anxiety. According to Harishchandra Mitra:

I spent the night thinking of my Uma—
It was hard to go to asleep.
At that moment [that I fell asleep] I could see her
Sitting here, near my head.
She had no ornaments, and her skin color had changed,
Her golden skin had turned dark.
It was difficult to recognize her.
My Uma is no longer the same.[55]

The poem also notes that Uma has no ornaments, implying that Shiva has sold them. Uma has become dark and emaciated, like the images of Chamunda Kali. Some poets describe Shiva as literally driving her crazy, for he stays in the burning ground and does not return home. So Uma too deserts her house, ignores her appearance, drinks alcohol, and wanders. As Ishvara Gupta laments:

Uma has been watching Shiva,
And her skin has turned dark through anxiety.
My daughter Uma is a princess,
But she has grown mad through sorrow.
She dresses strangely, and seems without modesty,
And now I hear she is drinking wine![56]

Other poems suggest that Shiva acts this way because he too has become mad due to his situation. He became blue-throated after drinking poison in an unsuccessful suicide attempt, for he could no longer stand the hunger and poverty he had to endure.[57] Shiva is always taking drugs, as Ramprasad complains:

O King of the Mountain, go and escort the bright one here.
How is my Uma doing?
It is over a year since she has gone to another's house.
I have heard from Narada that Uma is in great distress.
She wept bitterly before him, and she cried for her mother.
Her husband is addicted to hashish, and he has gathered
All of the hashish smokers in the land around him.
He sold Uma's clothes and jewelry to buy hashish.

My daughter is beautiful and perfect, and your son-in-law is always drugged.
I have heard that he [even] drinks liquid hashish with datura seeds.[58]

Few poets are sympathetic to Shiva as a married renunciant—most focus on Uma's difficulties. Menaka's neighbors all liked Uma and berate Menaka, having heard gossip of Uma's unhappiness. As Pyarimohan Kaviratna writes:

Though you were charmed by Narada's persuasions, O mountain-king's wife,
How could you just throw your daughter into the water
Without making proper inquiries?
You got her married to a husband who lives by begging.
There is no food or clothing in his home—
How unhappy your daughter must be![59]

Menaka was unable to convince her husband to bring their daughter back home—Himalaya was like a stone, and insensitive to the women's concerns.

Sometimes Menaka's husband would lie about his willingness to go and bring Uma home, and would pretend to send her messages and visit her, but eventually Menaka would find out about this. Himalaya was often compared to a mountain; he liked resting in one place, and did not like going off on long journeys. He would say that he had visited his daughter, and that she was fine and living well. But when Uma had not heard from her mother after a long wait, Uma came herself to visit her parents. Gadadhara Mukhopadhyaya writes:

Uma stretched out her arms, and embraced her mother.
She burst into tears of sorrow, and asked the queen,
"Why didn't you ever come to visit and bring me [back here]?
Your heart is made of stone, and so is my father's.
I realized this, so I came on my own.
But I shall not stay, I'll leave in a day or two."[60]

However, she is usually welcomed home with open arms, as Ramprasad observes:

"Today is an auspicious day for you!
Your daughter is coming home, go and greet her.
Come and see her moonlike face, and your misery will vanish.
Her bright smile is like nectar flowing."
On hearing this, the queen runs out with her hair and clothing loose.
She is so full of love that tears roll down from her eyes.
She leaves the king behind, and she hugs Uma and weeps with joy.
She puts Uma on her lap, and looks at her beautiful face and kisses her.

She says, "Your father is king of the mountain, but your husband was born a beggar.
You are such a wonderful daughter, and I have married you to naked Shiva."
Uma's friends are filled with happiness, they laugh and hold her hands.
They say, "How could you forget us for a year, when we love you so much?
Lift your face and speak to us, or we shall die!"
The poet Ramprasad laughs within himself, and is immersed in an ocean of joy.
When the Divine Mother comes [as a daughter], the people of the world are overjoyed
They cannot tell day from night, and forget even their [own] joy.[61]

Some writers have suggested that Menaka was overly concerned with Uma's welfare because she was still grieving over the death of her son Mainak. This son committed suicide—either due to conflict with the god Indra, or to his frustration at his poverty and lack of opportunity, or to upset at his sister's marriage. Uma was her only remaining child (the other ninety-nine sons mentioned in the *Kalika Purana* seem to have disappeared), and the only focus of love in her life. Rupachand Pakshi writes:

I am torn with grief from the loss of my son.
But I could forget it sometimes through having Tara (Uma).
Now if I have to lose her [too]
What reason do I have left to live?[62]

Some poets have Uma visit her parents on her own, and others have Himalaya go himself to bring his daughter home. Sometimes they travel on foot, sometimes by horse or elephant, but it is an exhausting journey. As Kaviwala Raghunatha Dasa writes:

Father, please tell me, how far are the Himalayas from here?
I can't walk any further.
The road ahead is difficult
And I am so tired of walking . . .
The scorching sun is burning me
And my pain is made more difficult
By the fires of hunger.[63]

Part of the reason why Himalaya doesn't like to visit the couple is because he dislikes Shiva. He considers his son-in-law to be old, drunk, and lazy, letting his daughter starve because he never works. When Himalaya does go to visit them, he generally leaves Shiva behind, and brings his daughter back with him. But Menaka realizes that Uma is unhappy about this, and suggests that Himalaya bring Shiva back. Menaka can see that Uma cares for her difficult husband. An anonymous writer claims:

> I have not forgotten what happened last time.
> I am a mother myself, and I know
> When I have hurt another mother [woman].
> When Uma arrived at the outer gate
> I placed her in my lap, and I said,
> "I hope that all is well with Shiva."
> Uma repled, "He is fine," and then
> She covered her eyes with the edge of her sari.
> She said, "What has happened to my eyes? What is wrong with my eyes?"
> I understood why she covered her eyes
> When I spoke of my son-in-law.
> The waters of the heart spilled from my daughter's eyes.[64]

Sometimes Uma denies that her marriage is a difficult one, and claims that her husband is really wealthy. As Kamalakanta Bhattacharya writes:

> Who says that Shiva is a pauper?
> Listen, mother, my house is full of gems.
> It shines brighter than a hundred suns.
> Since my marriage, I have never seen darkness,
> I cannot see a difference between day and night.[65]

There are several reasons why a new wife would not wish to admit misfortune. She might not want to lower herself before her mother, and lose what remnants of pride she possessed. She also might not want to admit the ill fortune that she herself had brought to the marriage, for it was believed the the new wife brings the luck of the household with her. A woman who cannot improve the situation shows her own faults, as well as those of her husband. Sometimes her mother may participate in this denial, to raise her daughter's status and her own. Rama Basu writes:

> I have heard good news from my daughter.
> At Kashi, Uma has become Annapurna [wealthy with rice]
> And my son-in-law has become a maharaja.
> Shiva came and told us, "See, Mother, things have changed.
> When I was first married, people called me mad.
> But now this madman is rich, and Kubera [god of wealth] is my treasurer."[66]

The goddess here is not demanding, like Manasa, but rather vulnerable, needing love rather than requiring it, and trying to appear wealthy and happy to deny her unsatisfactory life. For some devotees, this evokes the mood or *bhava* of protective parental love toward a divine child.

Shivachandra Vidyarnava Bhattacharya quotes a long *agamani* poem by Dasarathi Ray, who wrote of Himalaya as a Shakta, and his realization of his daughter's divine status (comparable to the *Gita*'s universal revelation of Krishna):

> Mountain began to worship Brahmamayī, knowing Her to be Brahman.
> He sat on his seat with a pure mind.
> In various places near Caṇḍī, the sacred book of Caṇḍī began to be recited.
> In the midst of this he fixed his meditation on Caṇḍī, his daughter.
> And putting a flower on his head, he worshiped Her with mental offering.
> Restless grew Mountain's mind as he saw Her.
> He saw that the infinite Universe was all His Uma's . . .
> The world was filled with the Daughter's daughters and sons.
> Millions of Brahmās, Viṣṇus, and of Śūlapāṇis [Shivas] lived under the protection of Her feet.
> The Queen of Śiva was Mistress over all.
> Giving up meditating, Mountain said, a hundred streams flowing from his eyes:
> "What have I, O Caṇḍī! with which to worship Thy feet?
> I am not in truth the monarch of this dominion. . . .
> Shutting my eyes, I see that all things in the Universe are Thine.
> What gems and garments shall I give Thee
> When the sea, which is the mine of gems, is Thy servant
> And in golden Kāśī thou dost live?
> O Īśvarī Annapūrṇē, who can say that Hara is a beggar
> When Kubera is the storekeeper in His house?
> The three worlds are beggars at the door of Thy three-eyed beggar."

Highly pleased, the Devi, with good cheer, said to Her father:

> "Finish the worship which you have resolved on.
> True, the infinite Universe is all Mine.
> The wealth I have given You is Your own."
> By Caṇḍī's grace Mountain worshiped the feet of Caṇḍī
> The seventh moon day ended, and night approached.[67]

Such songs are no longer sung on Durga Puja, as all-night Shakta poetry readings and popular *Kali-kirtans* have died out. This is partly due to the influence of urbanization and communism, partly due to the rise of love marriages and the decline of more traditional matchmaking. It is also partly due to different forms of music that have become popular (especially Hindi movie music, from movies that often glorify love relationships). In these older songs, many unhappily married young women could identify with the young wife, and many parents could identify with the difficulties of Menaka and Himalaya. Today, we do not see these songs of family happiness and unhappiness, of separation and grief and reunion, and it seems that no ritual for expressing family difficulties has risen to take the place of such songs.

### *Shakta Bhakti and Tribal Influences*

Where we do still see songs of welcome and farewell is among the Adivasi and low-caste Hindu groups, but the songs are to different goddesses. Rather than singing to Durga and Uma, we have songs to Tushu (the rice goddess) and Bhadu, who also come as daughters to visit parents on their holidays among the Jharkhand people of Purulia and Bihar. There are also other Adivasi songs which often include these themes, including the Jawa, Dhua, and Ahira songs. It would be very difficult to say whether the Hindu or tribal songs came first, as there are no histories of Adivasi goddesses, and little has been written on any of them. However, we can certainly say that there has been some Hindu influence on them, for the songs speak of the daughter returning to the parents' house, and some Adivasi groups who sing them have matrilocal marriage and brideprice (in which it is the husband who leaves his parents' house, and offers money to the woman's family for a bride). In Hindu tradition, the daughter usually leaves to live in her husband's house.

The tribal goddess Tushu is welcomed with songs when she comes as the daughter of the house, and there are songs of farewell when she leaves:

> When my Tushu must go
> My eyes fill with tears.
> Tushu, you have lived with us for thirty days
> And now you say you won't leave your mother
> But that isn't true—
> You are going away.
> On Paush Sankranti [day], the son-in-law comes
> And he will take you away.
> But we will quarrel with him
> We will not let him take you.
> We will not give you to him, or even admit that he is the son-in-law
> We will fight with him [for you].[68]

We also see such songs to Bhadu, who was a human princess. Bhadu puja is traditionally held on the last day of the month of Sravan, in mid-September, though some groups hold it in the month of Bhadra. According to the story, Bhadumani was the kind and beautiful daughter of Nilamani, the king of Kashipur. Her marriage was arranged with a prince from Birbhum, who was attacked by bandits and tragically died on the way to his wedding with her. She determined to mount his funeral pyre (though they were never actually married), and was transformed from a kind of *sati* into a folk goddess. She still comes to bless her people, and many songs are sung to her, celebrating her visit and mourning her departure. The festival is still celebrated, and is especially important to both virgin girls and prostitutes.[69] She is worshiped for her great love and compassion, as well as for her supernatural powers (some songs speak of her flying through the air, or helping people in distress). As Kishalaya Thakur writes in his article "Uṭsaber lokāyat ānginãya":

> At the time of the Bhadu festival held in the month of Bhadra, we see the same kind of impromptu composing of lyrics and singing them as with the Tushu mela [festival]. Bhadu is also a festival related to the rice harvest. This is the time for harvesting *aush* rice (during the monsoon). The goddess is Queen Bhadu (Bhadurani), imagined as a princess whose husband never came, or who was taken from her home. . . . Unmarried girls sing and dance all month, and each evening they gather at a particular spot in the village: "My dear, darling Bhadurani has come back home today."[70]

As celebrated among the Bauri group, Bhadu puja is a women's holiday, and her worship is performed only by women during the month of Bhadra. Sometimes she is worshiped in the form of a statue, which is made by a local artisan (*patua*). She is called down into the statue with three songs, but there is no particular song or mantra used. She is offered water, milk, plantain, rice, and other gifts, and after the ritual offering these are distributed among the guests. The major participants are barren women. This may continue throughout the month, or last for three days. On the last day, there are rich offerings and cakes, and singing and dancing throughout the night. On the next day is the immersion of the statue, and Bhadu's departure.

Many spontaneous songs to Bhadu are sung, often hoping that she will stay. Sometimes there is a touch of humor—here the daughter of the house ("my Bhadu" or my household goddess) is not a good cook:

> In the month of Bhadra is the worship of Bhadu
> [And] everybody makes cakes of molasses.
> But my Bhadu fed us with burnt cakes.
> O Bhadu, do not leave us!
> If you go away, our lives will also leave
> O Bhadu, do not leave us![71]

Sometimes an image of Bhadu is placed in a corner of the house, and children and other family members sing songs of welcome. Bhadu is offered sweets and clothing, and women who are ill treated by their mothers-in-law tell Bhadu about the situation. The women sing songs to her about everyday problems. In the districts of Purulia and Bankura, she was traditionally welcomed by dances and songs of unmarried girls; today the songs are sung by both genders:

> Bhadu has arrived at my home.
> Where should I offer her a seat?
> The seat should be placed under the piyal tree
> No, no, I shall take my golden Bhadu on my lap.[72]

The songs to Durga and to these regional goddesses show influences of other, earlier types of songs. In their background are Santal love songs and festival songs, and the *jhumur* songs associated with *kirtan* to deities. *Jhumur* love songs are popular at folk festivals in Puruliya and other rural areas. As the 1985 West Bengal District Gazetteer for Puruliya states, "the *jhumur*, in extempore dialogue form, offers the best medium of expression of the repressed desires and emotions of all men and women, especially peasants in open fields, without inhibitions."[73]

Another influence upon the devotional songs to the goddess are the *bhaoaia* songs of sadness and loneliness sung by the village girl to her distant husband. These also include songs of desire toward her lover. She may be a newly married girl who is lonely in an alien home, who cooks her food alone when her husband is away, and talks to the birds and insects about her problems. Her husband or lover may be a traveling businessman, a car driver, a musician, a buffalo or elephant driver. The songs of meeting and desire are very direct:

> O friend, where is your home?
> And what work do you do?
> Friend, tell me the truth
> Are you married or unmarried?[74]

The word *bhaoaia* derives from three terms: *bhava* or passionate feeling; *bhaoa* or the wide pasture lands for water buffalo, and *bao* or the wild wind that carries music from far away.[75] Such songs are traditionally sung in public by men, especially because of their themes of unmarried desire (*parakiya*). These songs have their own sets of rhythms, such as "the riding rhythm of the moving buffalo."

One subtype of *bhaoaia* song is the *chatka*, popular in northern Bengal. In this song, the girl is critical of her husband or lover, calling him unreliable and talking about the difficulties of family life.[76] Sometimes there are dialogues, with men and women in opposition to one another. We also see insults in the *gambhira* songs, in which the god Shiva is portrayed as a rather unimpressive human being. As one song puts it:

The naked old man is dressed like a clown
And he sits around in an outlandish manner.
The old man is completely mad,
And he is plastered with ash.
His tiger skin falls down from his body
[But] he remains seated.[77]

All of these sorts of folk songs contribute to the Hindu Shakta devotional song traditions, which emphasize earthly family life rather than celestial paradises and divine activities of distant gods. Bengali folk songs both sympathize with and satirize village life, and these themes also show themselves in songs to the high gods and goddesses of the great tradition. The human joys and sorrows of the *agamani* and *vijaya* songs are also reflected in the many other styles of religious and secular song found in West Bengal. The goddess is a young girl, a family member, to be loved and helped. She is vulnerable rather than powerful, unlike her other divine role as all-powerful mother. The songs are intended to evoke powerful emotions of sadness at separation from the daughter and joy at reunion, the saddest and sweetest aspects of emotional Shakta bhakti.

The various songs of emotional bhakti sometimes show the tension between householders who want a "normal" life for their daughters, and husbands like Shiva who are detached from the householder life, more interested in the yogic and tantric dimensions of life. It is often difficult for these values to dwell together, as it is often difficult for husbands and wives to live together.

Another form of emotional intensity is directed at the country of India, in its female form as Bharat Mata or Mother India.

## Political Shakta Bhakti: The Goddess as Homeland

The third type of Shakta devotion frequently seen in West Bengal may be termed political Shakta bhakti or Shakta nationalism. Like folk Shakta bhakti, this is basically a transformation of folk Shaktism. In this case, however, we do not have a goddess for a small village group—rather, we have Mother India calling to her billion people. The land is the Mother, and frequently she is in distress because of political difficulties. Her children (usually her sons) are her rescuers, who will save this damsel in distress. She calls upon them through the words of poets and writers, rather than through dream commands, to rescue her. The poets glorify her, asking her children to serve and protect her, and her children follow their exhortations.

Political Shakta bhakti is in many ways a return to the goddess's early tribal and folk dimensions, where she is involved with the lives of the group, and where she exists in nature rather than in temples and statues. The goddess reflects the suffering of her people in this poem by Jyotindranath Tagore, in which he uses the guilt of a son neglecting his mother to motivate political action toward freeing India:

> Awake, arise, children of India!
> How long will you sleep, forgetting your Mother?
> Remember the glories of India,
> How long will you remain closing your eyes?
> See the plight of the Mother—
> Sick and emaciated body, a mere skeleton.
> A demon assumes the form
> Of subjugation and ignorance,
> Rends the heart and sucks the blood.
> Selfish disunity is a monster
> Hacking the beautiful body.
> Tell me, is there a good son who can remain
> Unperturbed at a mother's suffering?
> The mother has suckled us all
> With milk-nectar in a hundred streams.
> Ignoring hardships, she has smilingly
> Nourished us with various foods.
> A child that forgets such a mother
> Has a stone for a heart.[78]

The goddess is also angry, however, especially at the injustices caused by British imperialism. Around 1890, we see the beginnings of religious nationalism in Bengal, and a desire to try and recapture the golden age of pre-Islamic India, with its independence of thought and behavior, and its focus on literature and art. By 1905, Kali and Durga became the goddesses of revolution, and devotees worshiped them for strength to fight the British rulers. Secret societies were organized by revolutionaries, who laid their weapons at the altars of Kali temples, and between the years of 1908 and 1917 over one hundred British officials were killed or wounded by members of such societies.[79]

Bengal was not initially associated with revolutionary fervor. Bengalis had a reputation for being intelligent and educated, but unassertive and even cowardly, talkative and lazy babus willing to work for conquerors without daring to confront them. Militancy was developed by means of literature and song, however, and patriotism grew through references to the homeland as the goddess.

Two books were especially influential. Bankim Chandra Chatterji's *Anandamath*, written in 1882, was based on the Sannyasi Rebellion of the 1770s. An army of ascetics, who called themselves *santans* (children) lived in a ruined monastery called the Abbey of Bliss. They were Vaishnava, but gave special devotion to the Mother Goddess as the Motherland. They sought to restore her from degradation and povery under Muslim misrule. There was famine in the land, but the government still demanded taxes. The children fought against the oppressors, but ended up accepting British rule as a stage toward the eventual resurgence of ancient Hindu tradition. The book gave Bengalis the phrase "Mother and Motherland are more than heaven itself," and the anthem *Bande Mataram*.[80]

In the most famous of the Shakta nationalist poems, *Bande Mataram*, the traditional image of the goddess as a temple statue is merged with a goddess who is the essence of nature, and also the savioress:

> Mother, I bow to you—
> Mother rich with streams, full of fruits,
> Cooled with breezes, and green with crops;
> Mother whose nights delight in white moonbeams,
> Clad in blossoming trees,
> Sweetly smiling, speaking kind words
> Granting happiness and boons.
> When seventy million throats
> Roar with powerful voices
> And hands of twice that number
> Hold sharp swords,
> Who says you are weak when you have such strength?
> I bow to the Mother
> Saviour with many strengths,
> And vanquisher of foes.
> You are knowledge, you are religion,
> You are mind, you are the holy of holies,
> You are the life in the body.
> You are strength in the arm, Mother,
> You are devotion in the heart, Mother
> Your image I make in one temple after another.
> You are Durga holding weapons
> You are Lakshmi roaming among lotus petals,
> You are the bestower of speech and learning,
> To you I bow.
> I bow to the prosperous, the pure and the peerless,
> Mother, I bow to you.
> Mother rich with streams, full of fruits,
> Mother green and sweetly smiling
> Adorning and nourishing the lands of the earth.[81]

Another influential text was a short tract called *Bhavani Mandir* (temple of the goddess Bhavani, a form of Durga).[82] It was published anonymously in 1905, though it is now believed by many scholars to have been written by

Aurobindo Ghosh (who later became famous as a guru in south India, though in his early days he was a Bengali revolutionary and spent time in the Alipore jail for terrorism). *Bhavani Mandir* was both a story of an ideal community and a philosophical and religious justification for nationalism. It spoke of a temple to be built in the hills for people who have renounced the world to work for the Mother. The goddess is full of shakti, strength and infinite energy, and her major manifestations were in war, wealth, and science. Worship of the goddess must be transformed into karmic action to save India and its traditional religion. The mother was "mighty Shakti," and the goddess's devotees must help the country through education, medicine, charity work, and industrial development, as well as fighting for freedom. India's destiny was to be politically independent, and to send out its Eternal Religion to unite mankind.[83] This tract particularly upset officials of the British Raj, and one called it "the germ of the Hindu revolutionary movement in Bengal." It glorified fighters who dedicated their lives to making India independent and powerful.

With the influence of these texts and others, terrorists came to be understood as religious figures in Bengal. When they were convicted and executed by the Raj authorities, the bodies were garlanded amid prayers to the goddess, given offerings of sacred food (*prasad*) and flowers, and there was fighting by crowds over the relics of bones and ash after cremation, which were thought to contain religious power (this motivated the British to get rid of the bodies very quickly).[84]

Since Independence, Shakta nationalism has periodically emerged in times of political stress. We have Bharat Mata, Mother India, a goddess not only for Hindu Indians but often for Muslim Indians as well.

In interviews in modern West Bengal, many informants spoke of Kazi Nazrul Islam as their favorite Shakta poet, and as the best writer of political Shakta bhakti. He was a Muslim, but a firm believer in Hindu/Muslim unity, and a freedom fighter hoping for a unified Bengal. He wrote both Hindu and Muslim devotional songs, and many of his poems followed the writing style of Vedic hymns. His rallying songs for Hindu nationalists often used Shakta imagery, and he was said by many informants to most truly embody the mood or spirit (*bhava*) of Shakti.

Kazi Nazrul Islam was born in a small village in Burdwan, West Bengal, in 1899. His family was extremely poor, and he was named Dukhu or sorrowful one. His father died in 1908, and in 1909, he took a job as muezzin and keeper of the local mosque (he was then ten years old). His uncle wrote songs for a traveling troupe of folk musicians. Nazrul began to write songs for them, and started studying acting, singing, and dancing. He left his job to travel with a troupe of actors, and this began a series of many years of erratic travel, temporary study, and a variety of short-term jobs. He was supported for several years by a local landowner so he could attend school.

Nazrul was profoundly impressed by the revolutionaries he had met during his travels, and in 1917 he enlisted in the 49th Bengalee Regiment for two years. He went to Calcutta, and became interested in politics. He composed and sang revolutionary songs during a 1921 strike in Calcutta. He was arrested, and continued to write songs supporting the cause of Indian independence. He began a newspaper called *Dhumketu* (Comet). It was immediately popular—its first issue sold out in two hours. In 1922 he published an issue calling for complete Indian independence, with his famous poem calling upon the goddess Durga to enter the struggle. The poem was called "Anandamayir Agamani" or "The Arrival of the Goddess Durga." In it, he shows the folk Shakta bhakti emphasis upon the wrathful goddess who has been neglected and who seeks revenge:

> How long will you be concealed
> Inside that clay image, O Mother?
> Our paradise has been conquered
> By a tyrant, an evil monster.
> The divine children are being whipped
> Our young heroes are hanged daily
> All India has become a slaughterhouse.
> O goddess of catastrophe, why do you delay? . . .
> Who else but you can come to the battleground
> Holding your sword of lightning?
> I listen to the slogans of peace, and my heart bleeds in fury.
> Peace has been trampled in this land of atrocities. . . .
> Save me, Mother, save me.
> Speaking of nonviolence in a nasal voice is an old woman's way.
> Sever their heads, Mother!
> Destroy the love of the impotent hypocrites.
> Bring the war, and the sword, and teach the sacred hymns.
> Only you should be at the front, with your sword in your hand.
> Remove their effeminate weakness, let the blood flow and be shed.[85]

Here he protests against the nonviolence of Gandhi. This poem angered the British, who arrested him and Comet's publisher. He was jailed for a year, and spent a month of that time on a hunger strike. After leaving jail, Nazrul secretly married a Hindu girl. Her widowed mother objected, but sixteen-year-old Promila was already pregnant. He continued to be politically active, and his books of poetry, *The Flute of Venom* and *Song of Demolition*, were banned. He almost died of malaria, but later managed to start a new political party, The Workers and Peasants' Party of Bengal. He also wrote articles against Muslim extremists, for which he was branded a *kafir* or heretic by many Muslims.

He continued to be a controversial writer, but he was very prolific, and there were many people who agreed with his views. He wrote poetry, music, and newspaper articles, translated Omar Khayyam's *Rubaiyat* and thirty-eight chapters from the Qur'an, and wrote Hindu devotional songs. He became music director for several films, and worked for a variety of recording companies. In his first movie he was the director, musical director, lyricist, vocalist, and an actor. It was very successful, and his records sold well. He also wrote plays and did research in classical Indian music. He produced several radio programs on music, and for his "Mabarag Malika" program he created twenty-one new classical modes (which he named after Hindu deities). He wrote thirty-six books of poems, nine plays, three novels, and worked on ten movies, as well as writing songs, short stories, essays, and children's literature.

Though he became successful, his life ended tragically. His son died, and later his wife became paralyzed, and Nazrul sold everything he owned (including his copyrights and royalties) for her medical treatment. He spoke out against the division of Bengal by the Muslim League, and sank himself into his work. In 1942 he had a total breakdown. He became violent, and was sent to a mental hospital, but he remained mute after shock treatments. Many treatments were tried and were unsuccessful. He stayed mute and unaware of his surroundings for over thirty years, until he died of pneumonia in 1976. Bangladesh observed two days of national mourning for him, and both houses of the Indian Parliament held a minute of silence to honor him.

Some of Kazi Nazrul Islam's poems demonstrate emotional Shakta bhakti, not just political bhakti, as in this poem where he looks forward to death:

Shyama's name has lit the incense of my body.
The more it burns, the further spreads the fragrance.
My love is like incense, rising ceaselessly
To touch mother's lovely feet in Shiva's temple.
With that holy fragrance my soul is sanctified.
Oh, Mother's smiling face floats in my mind
Like the moon in the blue sky.
When will everything of mine be burnt and turned to ashes forever?
I'll adorn Mother's forehead with those glory-ashes.[86]

Sometimes his poems are primarily nationalistic. Bengal is a goddess for him, as Palli Janani (Village mother):

See how lovely she is, Bengal my deep-green mother.
Her beauty overflows mountain and cave, forest and field
And the lonely wastelands.
She moves like a shadow in the rice fields, and through the forest clearings
And she plays her *vina* like a hermit at the bend of a dusty path. . . .

Like a flower among lotuses her face gleams from the darkness of a pool.
She wanders wild in the forest, with tigers and bears as her playmates.
She joins in the dance of the storm, under her spell the snake dances. . . .
Her skirt billows in the young green crops
And the clash of her anklets is the cricket's tune.
Her boat-song echoes in the ebbing tide
Her *baul* songs are chanted in the rustling fields.
And sometimes by the burning-ghats on the Ganges
Her breast is wet with tears.[87]

Nazrul's poem "Woman" is an ethical challenge to Indian tradition. In it, he criticizes the system of purdah and calls for women's liberation—it is a poem to challenge both Hindu and Muslim traditions, which encouraged the separation of women. Women were kept as cooks and housewives within the home, and hidden from the larger world. Shakta imagery is the background (he makes reference to Sarasvati and Lakshmi), and the divine nature of the woman is the reason that she should be respected and admired. It is an interesting poem to be written by a man of Muslim background, and it shows the ethical concern which runs throughout Shakta political bhakti:

I sing of equality
In my eyes there's no difference between man and woman.
Man is responsible for half of the great, noble, everlasting things of the world
And the other half goes to the credit of woman.
Again, for half of the sin, sorrow, grief and tears of human life man is responsible
While the other half is wrought by woman.
Who is he that hates woman as if she were a Hell?
Tell him the [source of] original sin is no woman, it is the male Satan
Or say, sin and Satan are neither male nor female, but a neuter gender. . . .
Woman is the goddess of wisdom, the goddess of music, the goddess of golden corn
Woman is the queen of beauty, who beautifies the sights and sounds. . . .
Every great achievement of the world, every great campaign
Bears the stamp of magnificent sacrifices by a mother, a sister, a wife.

In each war, the blood given by men has been written
But how many women gave the vermilion point from their foreheads
Is not recorded by its side.
How many mothers have torn away their hearts
How many sisters have rendered service
Nobody has engraved this in the martyr's monuments. . . .
Woman has infused love, affection, kindness and tenderness into her child—Man
And cruel Man has paid the debt in a strange way:
He has imprisoned her who kissed and nourished him at the breast
Within the four walls of Purdah. . . .
Listen, dwellers of the Earth!
The more you oppress others, the more impotent you become.
O woman! Tell me the tyrant who has imprisoned you
In the demon's palace of jewelry.
You have lost your genius for self-expression
You are now a coward, languishing in the background
Speaking from behind the screens.
You do not look me full in the face.
There are bangles on your wrists, and anklets on your feet.
O woman, tear off your veil, break your chains to pieces
Throw the veil that makes you a coward to the four winds!
Strip off those ornaments and dresses which are symbols of slavery. . . .
The day is not far off
When the world shall sing the glory of woman
Along with that of man.[88]

Nazrul's poetry shows the syncretism and political awareness that have often become a part of urban, activist Bengali Shaktism. Since the time that India attained its independence, however, political writing has tended to be separated from religious poetry (though the recent party of Rama has used religious imagery in its advertising and public relations).

It may also be noted that as well as poems to Bharat Mata or Mother India there are poems written today to Ma Ganga, the Ganges River. Like Mother India, she nurtures her children, and also like Mother India, she has many problems. Currently, one of her major problems is pollution, and songs have been written to the children of India asking them to protect their eternally pure Mother Ganges, who suffocates from the chemical and other waste flooding into her each day.

## Universalist Bhakti: Ramakrishna Paramahamsa and the Goddess as Consciousness

While emotional bhakti tends to be the most important form of goddess worship in West Bengal, we see in more urban areas a mixture of devotional love and Vedanta philosophy, which may be called universalist Shakta bhakti or Shakta Vedanta. It emphasizes worship of the goddess, yet says that she is *brahman*, as well as other deities—including Western ones. Shakta universalist bhakti is a tradition without a real name. It is sometimes called Neo-Vedanta, synthetic Vedanta, Shakta universalism, or Ramakrishnaism, and is a modern tradition based upon the life and sayings of the late nineteenth-century saint/avatar Ramakrishna Paramahamsa of Dakshineswar. It is quite widespread in the Calcutta area, and informants throughout West Bengal claimed to be followers of this tradition, and sometimes initiates into various Ramakrishna lineages.

Ramakrishna Paramahamsa was a priest of the goddess Kali throughout his life, until he died of cancer at the age of fifty-six years. He was born of a Vaishnava brahmin Chatterji family in the village of Kamarpukur, West Bengal, in 1836. Both of his parents had visions of gods and goddesses, and his sister and aunt were believed to be possessed at times. Ramakrishna was nicknamed Gadadhar, after a vision that his father had (his official name was Shabhu Chandra) and as a child he had visions and fell into trances. He enjoyed playing dramatic roles in his youth, and dressing in women's clothing. At the age of nineteen he was appointed priest of a new Kali temple at Dakshineswar. It had been built by Rani Rasmani, a low-caste widow, and it had been difficult for her to find a priest for the temple because of her caste and situation.

Ramakrishna began his Shakta practice there, worshiping in the grove of five sacred trees behind the temple, and he was given Shakta initiation in the Kali mantra. He had intense religious experiences, which often included paralysis, burning sensations, and the experience of beings entering and leaving his body. He said that visions came to him constantly, and that for six years he was unable to shut his eyes or sleep. He experimented with various forms of nontraditional spiritual practices. At one point he decided to commit suicide, and had picked up a sword with which to kill himself, for the goddess would not appear to him. This threatened suicide motivated her to appear. According to his biographer Mahendranath Gupta:

> I determined to put an end to my life. When I jumped up like a madman and seized [a sword], suddenly the blessed Mother revealed herself. The buildings with their different parts, the temple, and everything else vanished from my sight, leaving no trace whatsoever, and in their stead I saw a limitless, infinite, effulgent Ocean of con-

> sciousness. As far as the eye could see, the shining billows were madly rushing at me from all sides with a terrific noise, to swallow me up! I was panting for breath. I was caught in the rush and collapsed, unconscious . . . within me there was a steady flow of undiluted bliss, altogether new, and I felt the presence of the Divine Mother.[89]

Ramakrishna's experience of Kali as *brahman* became the foundational event for the Shakta Vedanta tradition.

Ramakrishna continued to have visions of Kali. As priest, he saw her statue as alive, and he would laugh and dance with it, joke with the statue and hold its hands, and lie down next to it at night. Sometimes he identified himself with Kali, and he would decorate himself with flowers and sandal paste. His employers and relatives though that he was mad, and tried different strategies to cure him: Ayurvedic medicine, exorcism, even a prostitute (in case the madness was due sexual frustration). They also arranged a marriage for him with a young girl. His visions and trances continued, however.

Ramakrishna practiced a variety of tantric rituals under the instructions of Yogeshvari, also called Bhairavi Brahmani, a woman who felt that his states of apparent madness showed sainthood. He also fell into extended trances under the teaching of the Vedantin Totapuri. He practiced various Vaishnava rituals and entered into states of strong religious emotion (*bhavas*). He also briefly practiced Islam and Christianity (for about three days each). However, he remained a Shakta and a priest of Kali all his life, dancing and talking with the goddess, and acting as her beloved son. Many of his actions and statements echoed those of Ramprasad Sen, an earlier Bengali Shakta devotee.

Ramakrishna had many visions and mystical experiences with the goddess at Dakshineshwar, near Calcutta. He was said to have attained Vedanta enlightenment with Totapuri in one day, though there were several days of preparation prior to this, and Totapuri stayed on for almost a year after this (until he had a vision of the goddess Kali, and realized that she was present everywhere).[90] Followers of Shakta Vedanta have chosen to focus upon these latter practices and experiences, claiming Ramakrishna to be an expositor of the philosophy of the Upanishads who used colloquial language so that its ideas would be accessible to the common people. In their beliefs, the Vedantic perspective dominates the Shakta aspect, to the point that they will claim that Ramakrishna was never really a Shakta (the goddess was only symbolic), or that he was only briefly a Shakta (it was a stage that he went through), or that after his initiation by the Vedantin guru Totapuri, Ramakrishna ceased to be a Shakta, and instead became fully liberated and a Vedanta philosopher.[91] According to this perspective, having become enlightened through Totapuri, he then becomes a deity himself, called Ramakrishna-deva or the god Ramakrishna by devotees.

Affiliation with Vedanta has many advantages, for the Upanishads are a highly respected set of texts, and association with them raises the person's religious status among the educated. As a Vedantin, the person can claim to be Western, accepting a generic monotheism (*brahman* is all gods in one), and can also accept Christianity as a spiritual path (at least those forms of Christianity that can be harmonized with Hinduism). Like the Brahmo Samaj, Shakta Vedanta incorporates Western values into Hinduism, dismissing folk Hinduism as a less-evolved form of religion (among the liberals) or as rank superstition (among the conservatives). This view is widely espoused by Ramakrishnaites, as well as by many Hindus in the United States. It is "India for export," denying the more regional emphases of sectarian Hinduism or characterizing them as symbolic or primitive. For some followers it describes a sort of reverse colonialism or evolutionary religion: Christianity, because of its historical and particularistic focus, is a primitive form of Vedanta, and when Christianity evolves it will develop the proper universalist perspective, which the Hindus already possess. Vedanta thus becomes a more advanced religion than Christianity, and contradicts the claims of Christian missionaries about the superiority of Christianity to Hinduism.

Among urban, educated Bengalis with religious sympathies, I have found Shakta universalism to be the dominant perspective (though there are large numbers of Bengali Vaishnavas, and communists who hold other religious perspectives).[92] Much of the responsibility for the development and redefinition of Ramakrishna's religious tradition must be laid upon the shoulders of Ramakrishna's major disciple Vivekananda. Whereas Ramakrishna danced with Kali's statue, Vivekananda was conscious of India's status in relation to the West, and wished to develop both a unified set of Hindu ethics and a philosophy that could stand international scrutiny. To do this, he chose to downplay Ramakrishna's Shakta focus, and emphasize instead his universal role as Vedanta sage to the world. The textual focus moved from stories about devotion to Kali to the Upanishads and the *Bhagavad Gita*. A focus on strength and social service grew to substitute for devotion, and Vivekananda spoke of bhakti at times as "effeminate nonsense," forgetting Ramakrishna's love of the goddess (as well as downplaying Ramakrishna's ecstatic and visionary states). Ramakrishna's dancing and singing with Kali were forgotten, and his followers became renunciants who were scholars and chanted Sanskrit stanzas. As Vivekananda said of the religion that he was forming, "together we conceived that his ideal had to be spread. And not only spread, but made practical. That is to say, we must show the spirituality of the Hindu, the mercifulness of the Buddhists, the activity of the Christians, the brotherhood of the Mohamaddans, by our practical lives. We shall start a universal religion now and here."[93]

"Ramakrishnaism" as a religion came to be based on the philosophy of Neo-Vedantism or Synthetic (*samanvayi*) Vedanta, which claimed to be different from more traditional forms of Vedanta because it was based on Ramakrishna's experiences. As he practiced and demonstrated the value of other religious traditions (however briefly), this opened up the possibility within Neo-Vedanta for members of other religious faiths to be practitioners.

However, the later followers of Ramakrishna could not eliminate Shaktism entirely if Ramakrishna was to be their divine incarnation. Despite theological claims that Ramakrishna was really a joint incarnation of both Rama and Krishna (thus making him Vaishnava instead of Shakta), his devotion to the goddess Kali was simply too pervasive. So the tradition grew up as a mixture of Shaktism and Vedanta, with Kali as the personification of universal consciousness, and her followers reading the Upanishads, doing meditation on Vedic mantras, and working in society performing service.

In its philosophy, Shakta universalism is a transformation of Shakta classical tantra, with the addition of devotional bhakti. The general outlook remains, with the goddess as infinite consciousness, who in her formless (*nirguna*) aspect is ultimate and a great ocean, but in her *saguna* form likes worship, especially puja and visualization. In Shakta universalist practice, however, the philosophy recedes into the background, and bhakti comes to dominate—both for the goddess as *brahman* and for Ramakrishna himself. He is recognized as an incarnate god or an avatar (we see this view in his titles, such as Ramakrishna Deva, or Bhagavan Shri Ramakrishna). According to informants, he is understood variously as Kali's beloved son, her lover, her full incarnation, or her partial (*amsha*) incarnation, whom she possessed at certain times. For many Shakta universalists today, Ramakrishna is a living spiritual guide who comes to them in dreams, or a god or inner guru who lives within the heart. While all religions are one, Shakta bhakti is the best and sweetest way to worship the infinite as mother, and worship of Ramakrishna as ideal devotee, guru, god, or avatar gives access to the devotion and dedication that he possessed.

Some devotees continued to emphasize Ramakrishna's love of the goddess Kali. As Swami Gambhirananda writes:

> Mother Kali was never to him a mere image. She was the veritable living Mother of the universe; and now he longed to be ever in Her loving presence. The delay in the revelation caused him agony. He cried, he implored, he writhed and rubbed his face on the ground like one in gripping pain. At last when he had reached the limit of human endurance, the veil lifted, and he had a beatific vision of the Divine Mother. . . . From that day the Divine Mother never left him. She became a living presence to him. He saw her moving about before his very eyes, and from Her he took his directions at every turn.[94]

Other devotees chose to emphasize the brahmanical nature of Kali, however. A text published by the Ramakrishna Math, the *Sri Ramakrishna Upanishad*, clearly links Ramakrishna with the nondualist tradition of Advaita Vedanta. It quotes Ramakrishna's words as *bhakti shastra*, as sacred words understood through devotion. As Ramakrishna is stated to have said to an Advaitic scholar, "What harm is there in meditating on God and worshipping Him? I worship the Devi. She stands before me as the manifold *jivas* [souls] and objects of this universe. Bhagavati and Isvara are one. Is the diamond different from its lustre or the sun from its rays? You cannot see the one without seeing the other. The Devi whom I worship is the Brahman, the one without a second."[95]

Devotion is not only philosophical, it is also ethical, with concerns like sin and salvation. As the *Sri Ramakrishna Upanishad* advises:

> When your heart is unsteady pray to the Divine Mother of the universe. She will protect you. She will save you from the sins hidden in your heart. Tell yourself constantly that Iswari is beside you. If you do so, you will shrink with shame from evil thoughts and evil deeds. . . . [Such a person] is wise among the learned. He can also argue well like others. He behaves towards his parents with love and respect and without any flaw. He is loving to his friends and relatives. He is sweet of speech and helpful to others, and will earn the love and esteem of everyone. . . . The Devi stands by you; fall at Her feet; you will get whatever you want; She will save you from sins.[96]

This Upanishad supports such traditional Hindu Shakta ideas as sacred places of pilgrimage that hold merit due to the spiritual practices of devotees:

> The milk of the cow permeates her whole body and is mixed with her blood. But can we get milk if we press her ears? No. It is from the cow's udder that we get milk. It is true that the whole world is filled with God. But its holy places are like the cow's udder. Devotees go there, receive into their hearts the devotion that swells up there like a fountain and reach god. God easily gives *Darshan* [vision] in those holy places where many devotees for countless generations have performed penance and meditation. Here are deposited the penance, chanting, meditation, worship and prayer of innumerable devotees. . . . Even stony hearts will melt in these places which have been hallowed by the song and dance of devotees.[97]

There has been a strong humanistic influence on the Shakta universalism of the Ramakrishna Mission, however. Swami Lokeswarananda's *Practical Spirituality* is a text that shows the more modern Ramakrishna mission perspective on religion (the book's essays were originally published in the Mission's bulletin), and it is clear that the attitude toward Kali has changed since Ramakrishna's death. Lokeswarananda writes in a chapter called "The Divine Mother":

> Those who worship God as Mother feel her presence all the time, feel She is looking after them, attending to their needs. They depend upon Her completely, just as a small child does upon its mother. They have no wish of their own, they do not ask for anything lest they ask for something they should not have, they want Mother to decide what they should have and what they should not have. They ask Mother to help them so that they may do nothing wrong, nothing that she may not want them to do. It is the most satisfying relationship that one can imagine. Satisfying, but also demanding, for nothing should be done that may hurt Mother.
>
> But where is religion in it, in particular, how can this help an individual in his religious life? At best, it may give him some false hope and courage, false because the existence of such a mother is doubtful, apart from what she can do or can't do. He may imagine anything he likes, he may imagine that he is being protected by an unseen mother, but he may soon realize that he has been a fool, nobody is protecting him, he has to protect himself.[98]

Swami Lokeswarananda recognizes the humanistic adaptations that Swami Vivekananda gave to Ramakrishna's ideas; as he writes of Vivekananda, "In all he said and did, Swami Vivekananda's chief concern was man. He described man as "the only God I believe in." "Man-making is my mission," he used to say. Man, according to him, has immense possibilities, there being almost no limit to his growth . . . strength, courage and self-confidence—these, according to him, are the essence of religion, all other things are peripheral.[99]

Is this tradition true to Ramakrishna's religious insights? He spent forty years as a Kali priest, and practiced Islam and Christianity for less than a week. He claimed to reach the highest states in these traditions, but he had little background in Western religion, and his insights about Western religion were curiously Eastern.

Jeffrey Kripal, in his recent study of Ramakrishna, emphasizes that Ramakrishna was not only a Shakta but also an unadmitted tantrika (in the sense that tantra is a link between sexuality and spirituality).[100] He clearly supports identification of Ramakrishna as a Shakta, and not a Vedantin: "The truth of the matter is that, although Ramakrishna certainly preached a type of universalism, such concerns were at best peripheral to his deeper desires and in actual fact inspired few, if any, of his numerous visions and ecstasies . . . it was Kālī of the Śakta tradition that was the focus of Ramakrishna's life, not the abstract *brahman* of Vedanta and the Brahmos. The center of his teaching was ecstatic love for a personal deity, not formless meditation on an impersonal Absolute."[101]

Although Ramakrishna found Vedanta dry and "boring,"[102] Vivekananda's new movement based on Ramakrishna emphasized it, and rejected the "female" aspect of Ramakrishna in favor of Vivekananda's more male and activist religion. According to Kripal, the early biographies of Ramakrishna were censored and hidden in favor of later, biographies more acceptable to his monastic followers. He notes that accounts of Ramakrishna's life written earlier than his most popularized biographies barely mention his time with Totapuri or any interest in Vedanta; even his biography, the *Kathamrita*, in its Bengali version discusses his conquest of Vedanta through love of the goddess: "I fell into the clutches of a knower [Totapuri]. He made me listen [to Vedanta] for eleven months, but the seed of devotion did not go away. Turning around, there was that very 'Ma, Ma.' "[103]

M. D. McLean has argued that Ramakrishna was a Shakta bhakta, in the bhakti tradition of Ramprasad Sen. Ramakrishna was inspired by Ramprasad's spiritual experiences throughout his practice at Dakshineswar, and Ramprasad's songs made him desire the vision of the Mother so much that he threatened to kill himself. He himself sang Ramprasad's songs to explain his own devotion, and one of Ramakrishna's most famous statements about his relationship to the goddess ("I want to taste sugar, not become sugar") was from a song by Ramprasad.[104] It may also be noted that Ramprasad meditated in a grove of five trees (*panchavati*), and worshiped his wife as an incarnate goddess, as Ramakrishna did later.

Walter J. Neevel, Jr., argues that Ramakrishna was not only primarily Shakta but also a Shakta tantric:

> We will suggest that his tantric sadhana was much more than casual or formal, and that in interpreting his teachings we can understand them more adequately in the categories of tantric thought and practice than in the concepts of Sankara's *advaita* which the biographers primarily employ. . . . As we have seen, at or near the beginning of his twelve years of intensive sadhana, he was initiated as a sakta temple priest, and his first period of undisciplined sadhana was dominated by his intense bhakti toward the sakti, Kali. Adding to this first period the time spent under the *Bhairavi*, we see that at least two-thirds of this twelve years was devoted to a sakta variety of tantric sadhana.[105]

It was his gaining of the Mother that allowed him to move from being in a continual state of divine madness to his later role as a sage and guru. Although Totapuri came to see him in 1864, Ramakrishna is quoted in several of his biographies as later rejecting the knowledge of *brahman* (*brahmajnana*). Twenty years later, in 1884, he said, "O Mother, do not plunge me in the knowledge of Brahman and take away my consciousness!—Do not give me Brahmajnana; I am but Thy child.—I have fears and anxieties! I do want my Mother!—A thousand salutations to Brahmajnana! Give it to him who wants it, O Mother."[106]

Ramakrishna remained a Kali priest throughout his life, and a devotee of the Mother until the end. Modern Shakta universalism was not Ramakrishna's philosophy, but rather the development of his experimental perspective in a syncretic fashion that absorbed both Eastern and Western ideas. Like that text loved by modern worshipers of Ramakrishna, the *Bhagavad Gita*, modern Shakta universalism attempts to unite many conflicting paths into a new whole. Its sacred texts are the traditional texts of Vedanta philosophy, as well as the biographies of Ramakrishna, which have become sacred texts to the devotees of Ramakrishna. They give insight into Ramakrishna as a god who is worshiped, and as a spiritual guide who visits in dreams to guide his devotees toward the Mother or toward *brahman*. In an odd way, it becomes Shaktism once removed—the worship of Ramakrishna is the worship of a Shakta who himself worshiped the goddess.

A strong point of Shakta universalism is its ability to absorb and incorporate the ancient and modern, village and urban, local and foreign religious traditions. Of the various forms of Shaktism, it has the most commonality with Western philosophy. However, its tendency toward an evolutionary perspective causes Shakta universalism to obscure or reject its own roots (both in village Shaktism and in Ramakrishna's practice) as primitive and superstitious, and to seek the status gained through orthodox Vedanta universalism that is accepted by the West. It thus tends to lack respect for its own origins, and comes to resemble liberal Protestant theology in its embrace of science, ethics, and humanism.

## Experience in Shakta Bhakti: Premik Maharaj and Annada Thakur

### *Premik Maharaj and the Andul Kali-kirtan Samiti*

Andul is a village in the Howrah area, across the Ganges from Calcutta, with banana plants, lakes overgrown with water lilies, and an old raja's mansion with great Roman-style pillars and an ancient courtyard. In Andul, there is a group that has been performing *Kali-kirtan* for over one hundred years: the Andul Kali-kirtan Samiti. This biographical sketch of its founder comes from interviews with current group members and a biography written by the group.[107]

This group or "club" (the English word is used) was founded by a Shakta devotee named Mahendranath Bhattacharya, more popularly called Premik Maharaj. He composed many *Kali-kirtan* songs, with his friend Krishnachandra Mallik adding the music and rhythms. During Premik's time there were about fifty singers and musicians in the group, and it was patronized by Andul's royal family. At present, the group has about thirty-five members.

Premik was born in Andul in 1844. His father was a philosopher, a *pandit* of the Nyaya school, and his grandfather Ramaratna was a scholar and sadhu. Ramaratna was said to have died by his own will (*icchamrityu*), sitting on the shore of the Ganges and doing mantras until his life-force left his body (his two wives died willingly on his funeral pyre).

As a child, Premik studied Sanskrit with his father, and later at college gained the title Kaviratna, Jewel of Poets. His father suggested that Premik recite from the "Chandi (or Devi-Mahatmya)" and vow not to drink water until he could compose one poem daily. He married early, and later became head *pandit* at the local English high school, but his real enthusiasm was for spiritual practice. He let his wife and sons handle his earnings and household decision making, and eventually he left his job to do meditation full time.

Premik was first given initiation by his mother, as was his family's tradition, and he took Shakta initiation from a holy woman in Birbhum named Jote Ma, who had become an ascetic and never married through fear of widowhood and love of the goddess. Her personal deity was Kali, and Jote Ma was said to be able to grant miraculous healing and fertility to barren couples. She would walk on water to collect flowers for worship services, and it was said that she did not die, but disappeared into a temple. A few years later, Premik took advanced initiation into the tantric *kulachara* lineage from Kulavadhuta Purnananda Natha. This included study of classical tantric texts. He received the initiation name Kulavadhuta Vashishthanandanatha. Premik spent most of the day in worship, and after eating would return to meditating at night. On many nights he would not sleep, but sat instead doing ritual worship and visualization of the goddess.

Premik also wrote several plays, some of which were performed by local drama groups, and Baul songs (these songs later acted as a basis of the Baul lineage of Shibpur). However, he was best known for his poems and songs, understood by devotees to have been written while he was in a state of *bhava*. His songs are still sung by the *kirtan* group today. Premik was a contemporary of Ramakrishna Paramahamsa of Dakshineswar, and was invited to sing by Ramakrishna's chief disciple, Vivekananda.

The *Kali-kirtan* group at Andul showed me a variety of Premik's songs. Many of Premik's songs show his concern with salvation at the time of death, and are reminiscent of Ramprasad's style of writing. He combined the passion of emotional Shakta bhakti with classical tantric study and initiation. His songs focused upon his love of the goddess; I include a few in translation:

> O Ma, I am very much afraid
> Thinking of whether I shall be delivered.
> I do not know, O dark Mother
> Whether you will appear to me on that day
> When with a frightful look
> Yama will come and grab me!

O Ma, I don't have anyone of my own
Only you, in all of the three worlds.
There are shades of illusion (*maya-chaya*)
In the form of son and daughter
And they can fill the senses.
Because I am conscious, things are easy
When I lose that consciousness
I'll be pulled down,
Into the vortex.
People will say too easily
"His time is up, and he is dead."
O Ma, giver of strength
Shelter me with your third eye.
And look after me on that day, Ma,
So that I am not tricked by Time, and pulled away.

This next song is also concerned with salvation, though there is a touch of coercion toward the goddess at the end of the poem, implying that the goddess must help him, or she will lack worshipers on earth:

When shall all of life's troubles end
O Dark One, for how long must I stay here?
On the oceans of life
There are great, surging waves,
And I am frightened.
Be merciful to me, Ma.
Because when the day ends
This poor soul will drown.
"Bhavani" is the most important word in my life
And thinking "Ma" is the most essential thing.
I have lost my relatives
And now [like a river] I will lose my banks
I am adrift.
Please take me to the shore, O wife of Shiva.
O Tara, you are the deliverer of lowly ones
Won't you save this lowly person as well?
Accept this devotee.
For who else will take the name of Tarini
On this earth?

Sometimes Premik takes the role of Kali and Shiva's son, and seeks salvation on his mother's lap:

The lotus of my heart is trembling,
My maddened mind is enjoying the fun of it.

The madman [Shiva] and madwoman [Kali] have gathered together
A whole crowd of mad people
And look, Anandamayi [Kali] is dancing in bliss!
All of my sense organs and instincts watch in amazement.
And during this chaos
The doors of wisdom swing open.
Premik the madman says,
You cannot fool me, Ma, with these events.
If one's parents are mad
How can they expect their son to be sane?
Listen, Ma Tara, you relieve us of our burdens
I give you a special appeal.
At the end of my life
When I float on the waters
Lift me up onto your lap
As your son.

The current *kirtan* group sings on special occasions, the large goddess puja celebrations (especially Durga, Kali, and Jagaddhatri), the birth celebrations of sannyasis and saints, temple openings and when invited by families (especially at births). For performing, they wear reddish Shakta robes, with wigs of matted hair (*jata*) hanging down toward the ground, in the style of traditional tantric ascetics. Singing begins with an invocation to the goddess, praising her. They give about twenty to twenty-five performances a year, in West Bengal and in other areas of India. Other *Kali-kirtan* groups in and around Calcutta include the Siddeshvari Bagbazar Kali Kirtan group, the Mauri Kali Kirtan samiti, the Jhodhat Kali Kirtan samiti, and the Salkia Vinapana Kali Kirtan samiti. Such *kirtan* groups demonstrate the more social side of the Shakta tradition, opposing the renunciant tantric strand with its emphasis on isolation and death.

### *Annada Thakur: Adya Shakti and Photo-bhakti*

Many small shops on Calcutta streets have a common picture hanging from the top of the stall or sitting in a wall niche. It is the photograph of a black, tribal-looking goddess, with a crown and four arms, standing upon a prone Shiva. Storekeepers said that the picture was of Adya Shakti, and that it had much power. The photograph itself was widely venerated. Indeed, the goddess herself had decreed that her photograph rather than her statue was to be worshiped. She is the goddess of a new Shakta *pitha* near Dakshineswar, called Adyapeath Dakshineswar Ramakrishna Sangha.[108]

Adya Shakti or Adya Shakti Kali, in the form of a black stone statue, was discovered by Annada Thakur around the turn of the century. I would describe her as a goddess of Shakta bhakti because of her personal relationship with Annada Thakur, though her story has folk and tantric elements as well.

Annada Thakur, accepted as a major prophet and saint by the Adyapeath monastic community, was born of a brahmin family in Chittagong, and came to Calcutta to study Ayurvedic medicine. His family did not approve of this decision, considering such work impure for a brahmin. However, he graduated Ayurvedic college, though he never practiced as a doctor. He wished to remain celibate and possibly become a renunciant, but his mother on her deathbed said that Annada must either declare lifelong celibacy then and there, or he must have a marriage arranged for him. He left the decision to her, and she arranged a marriage for him with a young woman named Manikuntala. After the marriage, Thakur's mother made a remarkable recovery, which was attributed to the auspicious influence of the bride.

Thakur began a business in Calcutta manufacturing Ayurvedic remedies, but he was subject to visions and trances that made work difficult for him. In his autobiography, he speaks about his first significant vision, when he saw a statue of Kali carried by four girls through the streets. Nobody else on the street saw them, however, and he was told by the people he questioned about the vision that he was crazy. When he later did meditation on Kali, he fell into a week-long trance state in which he had continuous visions of her play (*lila*).[109]

When his normal state of mind returned after a week, his friends told him that he had gone mad. During that time he was cared for by his friends Girish and Shachin, even though he had beaten Girish during this period of insanity. He asked them not to tell his parents about it. While in trance, he had narrated poems to Kali, Krishna, and Ramakrishna, which revealed to his friends that he was a devotee. A few days later his father came to Calcutta and took him back to his family in his native village. There he had many dreams of renunciants.

His mother was also subject to revelatory dreams, and claimed to know herbs for medicines from her dreams. When Annada had a severe illness as an infant, and doctors had given up hope, she sat before a statue of Mangala Chandi and had a vision. She saw a woman beckoning, who said that Annada would be cured if she would offer her puja; she later recognized this figure to be the goddess Adya Shakti Kali. When Annada returned home, his mother had a dream in which her personal deity appeared, telling her to let Annada go away to be a sadhu. She cried the next day, but let him leave Chittagong.

Annada came back to Calcutta, and once again tried to work at the Ayurvedic dispensary. Ramakrishna Paramahamsa appeared in a dream, however, telling him to shave his head and bathe in the Ganges. Then he told Annada to bring back the statue that he would find hidden at Eden Gardens, a park in Calcutta, beneath linked pakur and coconut trees. He was to take along three other devotees, observe silence, keep the image as concealed as possible, and follow future instructions. He took three friends along, and went out early in the morning to Eden Gardens. He found the trees by the water's edge, and the statue was lying in the mud beneath the water. He stayed silent and covered it with a cloth, and Annada and his friends returned home.

The statue turned out to be made of black marble, a nude Kali about one foot high. Though covered with mud, it was intact. She had her hair in three matted locks, and wore a crown and carried a scimitar. People in the vicinity heard about it and came to see it. They said that the statue was alive, and that its eyes were sparkling.

Annada did puja to the statue, and gave out the goddess's sacred food (*prasad*). Suddenly he perceived that everybody in the room had become an image of the goddess, and even children looked like her image in miniature. His friends feared that he would go insane again. When his friend's wife Bimala Ma put a garland around the statue, he cried out and prostrated himself, and stayed in the room for two days. He was fed the goddess's food by his friends, but his mind was elsewhere. He got up and locked the statue in a trunk, and again fainted.

He saw a dream vision of Kali in the form of a sixteen-year-old girl. Her eyes were as bright as those of the statue, and she wore a red-bordered sari and shell bracelets. She gave him a command, ordering him to immerse the statue in the Ganges the next day. He awoke, and refused to do it, and dreamed again of Kali as a woman with loose hair and bloodshot eyes, angry and dreadful, with a newborn baby in her lap. She acted like a folk Shakta goddess and threatened him, telling him that disaster would befall him if he did not immerse the statue. She dashed the child against the floor, breaking its skull, so that it lay in a pool of blood. This, she told him, would happen to him. Then she appeared in the form of his aunt Choto Ma, whom he had always liked. She told him to get the statue photographed, and then immerse it afterward. When he asked why, she said, "I do not like to be worshiped at one place only. So I won't remain installed at a particular place [as a statue]. I shall be with all my devotees. Have me immersed in the Ganga. . . . I do not want to be worshiped according to the Shastric rites alone. If anyone pays homage and gives offerings to me, saying in the simple and sincere language of the heart, [something] such as 'O My Mother, take this food, wear this garment' and then uses those things himself, it will be regarded as an act of worship. The prayer of a simple and sincere heart constitutes my worship."[110] She told him that he could not keep the statue, however, and she threatened him. She said, "I am your antagonistic force; if you keep me, the strength of your enemies will increase, your [goals] will not be fulfilled . . . and your family line will be[come] extinct."[111] She did relent a bit, saying, "If you desire to worship me in this particular form, go to Varanasi, build a new temple there and have an image like this made of eight metals installed in the temple and then worship that image. . . . If you do so, I shall reveal myself there in that image. . . . I will reveal myself in any image you may invoke me in with devotion."[112]

He announced his decision to immerse the statue the next day, and was met with resistance from his friends and their relatives. Some of them told him to keep the statue and get money from the people who would visit it, and some museum representatives came and said that the statue was ancient and from Buddhist times, but he refused to give it to any of the museums. He had the statue photographed professionally, and word spread quickly that it was to be immersed. Many local people came to worship it, among whom the prostitutes showed great devotion.

He went to immerse the statue, followed by a large crowd of people, and he sang, "Dwell in my heart, O Mother Bhavani." He threw the statue from a boat into the middle of the Ganges River. He fainted afterward, and was in bed for three days. He was periodically awakened by his friends, who fed him, and then he went back to sleep. The goddess appeared to him in a dream, again in the form of his aunt Choto Ma, and announced, "My name is Adya Shakti. I should be worshiped as Adya Ma."[113] She then narrated a hymn to herself which he was to write down, and tell to others. When he awakened, he told his friends about the dream. They said that many people who had taken photos of the statue had had dreams telling them to immerse the photographs in the Ganges.

He planned to go to Varanasi and set up a new temple to Adya Shakti there, as she had suggested he do earlier. However, the goddess changed her mind. She appeared in a dream in the form of a sixteen-year-old girl, telling him that serving parents is the duty of a son. "Father is religion personified; father is as high as heaven itself," but "Superior even to father is mother, for bearing the child in her womb and bringing it up. So the mother is the greatest object of reverence in the three worlds."[114] She told him not to go to Varanasi but to stay in Calcutta and worship her there.

Again he obeyed her, and he stayed in Calcutta and periodically visited his parents. He attempted to practice medicine, but he came to the conclusion that he was unable to be a physician. Indeed, he stated that he was frightened and cried and felt suffocated when he thought of following that profession. He tried writing as an occupation, and wrote a play that was to be performed, but he went temporarily insane during this period, and the play was never staged or produced.

He lived mostly with friends as a sort of informal house priest, and he would pray for the good of the household. In one case, when a child fell ill he used the goddess's technique of coercion. He prayed, "Oh Mother, if any calamity befalls this household then you also will get involved. Your holy name shall be disgraced; and nobody will keep your photo nor worship you any longer."[115] Adya answered him in a dream, appearing as an old woman with ragged clothes and dishevelled hair. She said, "I am meting out the punishment they deserve for keeping me neglected. They took my picture for worshiping; but they left it in a most wretched condition; how can they avoid the consequences thereof?"[116] He later found the neglected photo under a pile of clothes, partly eaten by white ants. The picture was framed and worshiped, and the ill son recovered.

Annada also had dream revelations that predicted births and deaths, and showed cures. He made little mention of his wife in his autobiography, saying only that she would be upset when he fell into trances. The relationship appears to have been a celibate one. His major emotional involvement seems to have been with Adya Shakti Kali.

Further information on the origin of the Adya Shakti statue came to Annada during meditation. He saw his sacred thread catch on fire and he pulled it off, and then he fainted. Annada awoke finding himself being cared for by a sadhu, who told him to stay alone and meditate for three days. He did so, and had a dream revelation. In the dream, he learned that the statue that he found at Eden Gardens was originally called the Mother of Gayadham, and presided over a temple on a hill in Gaya, a holy city in Bihar (near West Bengal). An epidemic broke out among the hill tribes, and the hill men threatened to shatter the statue and burn it if the Mother would not save them from the disease. He saw the same sadhu who had cared for him in this dream, in his previous life as a sadhu who had lived in Gaya. The sadhu had received a dream command to save the goddess's statue and take it to Bengal. He did so, and hid it in the jungle that later became Eden Gardens. It remained hidden there until it was found by Annada Thakur, and revealed to be Adya Shakti Kali.

Annada traveled throughout India, visiting both Shakta and Vaishnava religious sites, and he bemoaned the infighting and hostility between these two groups. He spent six years in Varanasi. Toward the end of his life, Annada had a dream vision of Ramakrishna, who told him that his life would soon end. Annada asked how he might best serve humanity, and Ramakrishna told him to serve his parents for ten years and be a householder, and then practice meditation while living on the banks of the Ganges. He also told Annada to establish a temple.

In the dream vision, Ramakrishna showed him a complex image of three temples. The first was on the back of a large swan, with a golden spire and gems in the walls. On the altar was a living statue (*jagat murti*) of Ramakrishna. The second temple was on the chest of Shiva, who was lying like a corpse, and Adya Shakti stood upon him. The third temple was on Garuda, with Radha and Krishna standing within the OM symbol (he emphasized that this temple was "not inferior" to the previous two). The three temples then merged into one temple, and the three images at the altar fused into one joint statue. Ramakrishna was at the bottom, with the word "Guru" written, then in the center above him was Adya Shakti, with the words "Knowledge and Work," and on top were Radha and Krishna in the OM, with the word "Love." The temple was made of marble. Ramakrishna said that the temple should be built in West Bengal, in "Kalisthan" (the land of Kali), between the temple of Nakuleshwar Shiva at Kalighat and Dakshineshwar Shiva at Ariadaha. He said that it would establish faith in people, and that at least three devotees a year would see manifestations of the divine there.[117]

He gave instructions for how temple ritual should be handled, and how a variety of other buildings should be built. Whereas the images of the Guru and Radha and Krishna might be of wood, stone, metal, or clay, the Adya image must be made of a combination of eight metals. Ramakrishna predicted that when religion fades from the world, only Adyapitha will remain as a place where God might manifest. And it must be built in Bengal, for "devotion still pervades the land there," and it is the only land that responds to the divine call.[118] Ramakrishna also told Annada to cut down his penance to one year with his family, and then one year on the Ganges with his wife. After that, he should start building the temple.

Ramakrishna also gave a vision of the future temple to Annada's friend Dhiren, who drew up the plans. In 1913, the first religious festival to the goddess was held on Makar Sankranti day, on land held temporarily. Annada set up a missionary society, the Ramakrishna Sangha at Dakshineswar, and officially established Adyapeath in 1914.

Land was bought at Dakshineswar, and the foundation was laid in 1920. All sorts of people contributed toward the fund raising. One year later, Annada Thakur died. There was chaos immediately afterward, but the building continued. His wife oversaw work on the temple, and added a Matri Ashram for elderly woman renunciants. In 1926, they began building the marble-faced temple, and in 1959 the images were consecrated and installed. Many more buildings have been added. It has become a major tourist attraction, part of the "holy trinity" of religious sites (as one informant phrased it) of Dakshineswar, Belur Math, and Adyapeath, along the Ganges near Calcutta.

Adyapeath, also known as the Dakshineswar Ramkrishna Sangha, is considered by devotees to be a modern addition to the numerous *shakta pithas* of West Bengal, sanctified by the will of Adya Shakti Kali. It is a large temple complex, with a central temple and a new hall next to it. This is the Mother Theresa hall, large enough to feed two thousand people in long rows on the floor each day. Meals cost about two rupees, and the destitute eat for free; meal tickets are sold by monks. There are marble floors, inscribed with the history of the place and the names of donors (there are over a thousand names). Surrounding the two central buildings is a courtyard, and around them are other lemon-colored buildings: offices, orphanages (separate ones for older and younger boys, and older and younger girls) which are called ashrams, and housing for the renunciant monks and nuns. The oldest area includes Annada Thakur's house and temple, with a pond, near a banyan tree; and later buildings include the library, offices, kitchens, and meeting halls (including a Vanaprastha meeting hall for older people), as well as parking areas and other living quarters under construction. The monks refer to each other as brother (*bhai* or *dada*), and the nuns as sister (*bon* or *didi*). It is run by a general secretary, who is also called brother, and the position rotates every few years. Major decisions are made by the Temple Committee.

All members dress in lemon yellow robes, and the orphanage girls wear yellow saris with red borders. It is run largely by donation, and its public functions are attended by Bengali politicians and businessmen (one celebration that I attended included the governor of West Bengal, the chief justice of Calcutta High Court, the ministers of commerce and labor, the director general of the police, and various heads of businesses as speakers).

Fundraising is very important, and most monks spend time at it. Funds are often donated for specific purposes: paint, food, cars, buildings. One Bombay singer donated a jeep to carry medicine (which is not for the use of the renunciants). Monks and nuns do prayers at dawn, evening, and night, give lectures, work at the clinic, teach religion classes at the school, take classes (especially Sanskrit), edit their journal (called *Matri-puja*), cook and serve meals, and clean. Only brahmins work in the temple. More than five hundred people live and work at Adyapeath, ranging in age from about ten years on.

Adyapeath sponsors pujas and prayers, and they open up their triple statue to public view twice a day—for half an hour in the morning, and half an hour in the evening. Hymns to Kali (*Kali-kirtan*) are sung by groups of devotees during this period. There are *homa* fire sacrifices twice a day, with vegetables and milk products, and large yearly pujas for Durga and Kali, with high attendance. There are offerings of bananas, vermilion, rice, and sweets, and on Durga Puja there is immolation of a statue of an *asura* or demon made of flour. Devotees perform vows (*manat*) and ask for boons, usually dealing with wealth, fertility, and health. People meditate in front of the goddess, and repeat her name or chant hymns. Adya Shakti Kali was believed to have spoken to Annada Thakur, and to be willing to speak with other sincere devotees. The current general secretary has said, however, that he has not had people report their personal experiences to him. Adyapeath is unusual in being a worship site for both Shaktas and Vaishnavas. Shakta traditions such as animal sacrifice are not performed, in order not to alienate the Vaishnava worshipers.

Both Annada Thakur and his wife Manikuntala are worshiped at Adyapeath, and a variety of hymns have been written to them by devotees. Adyapeath has published a book of songs, *Guruguna Gan*, which contains a variety of hymns. In one, called "Annadakirtana," Annada is portrayed as an emotional bhakta and as virtually an incarnation of Adya Shakti Kali:

> Let us all sing the song of Annada
> And cry while chanting his praises.

He gave the treasure of Adya Ma
By [the grace of] his guru Ramakrishna.
He was a child in the lap of his mother
He would laugh, weep, dance, and sing
He lost himself in the mother, and gave the mother's mantra
He gave the mother's love to earth.
It was [really] the mother who posed as Annada
Mother Adya was in the form of Annada
[She came] to console her children.
She wanted her created beings to do karma yoga and *shakti sadhana* . . .
O mind, remember the words of Annada, which bring us merit:
"You will have countless experiences of devotional love (*prema bhakti*)
Your purified mind will be filled with love
Because you have done meditation in the mood of the mother (*matribhava*)
You will see the image of the couple[119] before your eyes."[120]

The song "Matritarpana" is dedicated to Annada Thakur's wife Manikuntala Devi. It is also implied that she is a goddess:

Come, all who are devotees of the mother, disciples and servants
Sing the mother's glory.
Annada's devotee, Manikuntala Devi, lovingly called Mamami
Was both a householder and a yogini.
Chant her praises from the center of your heart.
She married Annada at the will of his dying mother
Because of his devotion to the mother[121]
When her mother-in-law saw her standing to the left of Annada
The critically ill woman was cured.
The world became full of joy
And Yama [lord of death] left the village. . . .
Mother, you are an equal partner in Annada's spiritual life
Have you left [Mount] Kailash to come to earth
To help this suffering world?[122]
You have given your life in sacrifice.
History states that the Rajput women
Would send their beloved husbands to war
To win heroic victory, and follow their *dharma*.
But mother, you have humbled the pride of those kings and queens
You allowed your husband to go to the forest
To do spiritual practice, and attain his goddess (*ishtadevi*) . . .
You are another form of Thakur

You are equal to him in love and religious experience (*bhava*).
As your husband is Thakur, so you are Thakurani.
[On earth] you flashed like lightning
Why did you leave us so soon?[123]

Partly due to Annada Thakur's influence and the large number of pilgrims visiting Adyapeath, Adya Shakti Kali has become a popular deity in West Bengal. Although Annada Thakur had stated that Adya Shakti Kali herself had wanted worship through her photograph (or "photo-bhakti" as one informant phrased it), clearly the tradition of worshiping through statues is preferred by many Shaktas. However, photos are very convenient, and in many urban areas have taken over the areas that used to hold larger altars and statues.

We see in Annada's story the major types of Shaktism: there is folk Shaktism (in the goddess's demands upon Annada Thakur and her dream commands), there is tantra (in her *mantra*, and her role as Mahavidya goddess), and there is emotional bhakti (seen in Thakur's ecstatic responses to the goddess's presence, and his loving worship).

## Closing Notes

These various forms of bhakti—the folk type involving coerced devotion and obedience to a local goddess, the emotional type involving passionate love of a devotee for a loving mother or daughter, the political type involving idealism and patriotism toward Mother India, and the universalist type involving love of a goddess who is infinite consciousness—have all been very important religious traditions in Bengali Shaktism. Although they may be found in pure form in literature and poetry, in ritual practice they are often strands that are braided together. Many Shakta songs and rituals also show the influence of Bengali Vaishnavism.

The Bengali or Gaudiya Vaishnava tradition is largely monotheistic, with Krishna as the high god who originates or emanates the other Vaishnava deities (including Vishnu and Rama, as well as his consort Radha), and has Shiva and Kali as his devotees. It has a long tradition of emotional poetry, and many rites in both temple and home. One Vaishnava rite is the dressing of the god, which has been adopted into Bengali Shaktism. It is a classic bhakti ritual usually performed by Vaishnavas, the *raj-besh* or dressing the deity in royal robes. The Shakta version places the goddess in the role of queen, with the priest as her handmaiden or dresser. The audience watches, to appreciate the richness of the sari and jewelry and to show love and respect. I saw this ritual in a home worship for Adya Shakti Kali that I attended in Calcutta on Kali Puja night, 1994.

Devotees often worship Adya Shakti Kali as a goddess of love and compassion, with a photo or statue in the home. I attended a Calcutta ritual in which a house image of Kali was in the form of the original statue found by Annada Thakur. This statue was a dark stone, with strong lines and a grim expression, but it was being treated with full-fledged bhakti devotion. This statue had black skin and four arms: one hand raised peacefully, one with a sword, one open, one holding a head by its hair. The statue was dressed in a green-and-red sari shot with gold, and a garland made of marigold flowers. Her shrine was white, and hung with tinsel decorations. A *linga* on the left had a cobra over it, and was draped with flower garlands. On the right was a large picture of Ramakrishna Paramahamsa in ecstasy, also hung with flower garlands. Another picture nearby had Ramakrishna and Sarada Devi with a red hibiscus (jaba) flower between them. It had the Bengali letters for "Ma" in the center, and a jeweled Kali rising from the flower.

As I walked in, the priest was seated before the goddess, wearing a long white dhoti and sacred thread, in meditation. He was on a white dais strewn with rugs, on which were trays of ritual implements: brass pots, conch shells, incense, and a large white fly whisk with a chased silver handle. The whole room was a sort of tent inside the house—red-and-white striped, with a central flower design, hung with tinsel balls. The doorways were draped with marigolds and long leaves.

Rather surprisingly for the inside of a private house, the goddess was behind bars. Deity cages are often seen in public places, where it is feared that either the jewelry or the statue itself might be stolen. The heavy iron and heavier locks and chains are for the deity's protection (though upon first seeing these "gods behind bars," I wondered if they were being symbolically jailed).[124] The bars at the Kali puja were painted red, and the locks were opened for the worship. The ceremony went on behind the bars, however. The devotees sat on a cloth on the floor, with the women in front. A calendar hung near the front showing a large Kali with a child Shiva in her arms; on his chest was a disembodied foot. This image is widespread in West Bengal, for Kali as Adya Shakti is the mother of everything, even her husband Shiva. The foot on the child's chest was there to show her dominance, according to several informants; the story of Kali being embarrassed at accidentally stepping on her husband did not tell the whole story. According to other informants, the posters that show an adult Kali with a younger Shiva do not really represent their ages, but rather their importance: the older figure always deserves greater respect.

During the ritual dressing of Adya Kali, the priest slowly stripped the statue of its original sari and garland, waved incense before her, and lay his head at her feet. He then got an expensive new red Benarasi sari, held it up to the audience, and slowly cut off first the price tag and then the blouse piece. The statue was dressed with Vaishnava care, first in a red ruffled petticoat, then with the sari and bracelets, necklaces, earrings, nose ring, crown, and a necklace of small golden skulls. She was all in red and gold, like a bride or a beneficent goddess. The dressing in jewelry and garlands continued until her grim expression was almost invisible—she was a small mountain of silk, gold, and flowers. Her dark face was hidden by the symbols of devotion, and even the severed head that she held barely poked through, looking like a friendly elf.

When Kali was fully dressed, the priest let her look at herself in a pink mirror, and put Western perfume on her (from a gold spray bottle). The tape recorder played songs to Kali (*shyama sangit*), mostly by the well-known *Kali-kirtan* singer Pannalal Bhattacharya. But when the ritual of offering light (*arati*) began, the tape switched to Vaishnava songs. The lights were circled before the goddess to the the song "Jaya Jagadisha Hare" (which is part of Jayadeva's famous poem to the avatars of Vishnu). This was the end of the ritual, and people began to leave.

I asked why a Vaishnava song was being played to a Shakta goddess, and one of the older devotees answered, "All gods are the same—the name doesn't matter. Well, maybe for Vaishnavas it matters, but not for us. Hari, Durga, Kali, Shiva—they're all the same. It doesn't matter which name you use." Another devotee added that though this ritual might look Aryan, it was really non-Aryan, and had nothing to do with Vedic tradition. He said, "The Aryans like *homa* and *yajna*, but it is non-Aryans who use statues (*murti*). Aryans don't like images, and non-Aryans don't like abstractions. They are really different, though it may look as if they have merged together."

There is Vaishnava imagery in the ritual, and also in the *shyama-sangit*, the songs sung to the goddess. They express passion, respect, devotion, submission, and reconciliation to the goddess's will, as well as pouting and demands for boons. The goddess is almost literally covered with sweetness, transformed from terrifying to domestic by getting new clothes. The various types of Shaktism merge together, creating new combinations, and including new metaphors. Here, a folk and tantric deity becomes a bhakti goddess.

Such creativity and adaptation has happened with many Bengali Shakta goddesses—including the two most important ones, Durga and Kali.

# 4

# The Great Bhakti Goddesses of West Bengal

## *Durga and Kali*

In order to understand Bengali Shaktism, it is important to know the major goddesses that inspire devotion and awe, and their history and origins. The great bhakti goddesses of West Bengal are Durga and Kali. There are other important goddesses, such as Sarasvati, goddess of music and literature, and Lakshmi, goddess of wealth and fortune. Each of these has devotees, but their prominence and their celebrations are small in comparison. Durga and Kali are perhaps unusual as bhakti goddesses, for they have roots in folk Shaktism, though their more brahmanical devotees claim exclusively Vedic and puranic origins. Although their dominant aspect today is bhakti, it is clear that they have many other dimensions as well, and we can trace the strands of Shaktism by examining their worship and histories.

### Durga: Folk, Warrior, and Bhakti Goddess

We bow down our heads to the Primal spirit who covers the universe. We bow down to the feet worshiped by the world—We bow down to the Protectress of the world. Save us, O Durga. Thou art the only way in the forest, in wars, in the midst of enemies, in fire, ocean, deserts or in courts of justice. We bow down our heads to the savior of the world. O Durga, save us. We are sunk in the great and unfathomable sea of danger and thou art the only way to salvation. We bow down our heads to the savior of the world. O Durga, save us.[1]

Durga is a goddess with several important aspects: the folk dimension of fertility and threat, a military and royal aspect, a Sanskritic side, and an ethical dimension. There are many types of devotion associated with Durga. In her modern and urban aspect, Durga is the goddess of courage and strength, who remained pure when tempted by demons and was able to conquer them, restoring the power and dominion of the Hindu gods. In myth, she is preeminently Mahishasuramardini, as shown in the "Devi Mahatmya" section of the *Markandeya Purana*. She is the killer of the demon Mahishasura, the force of good over evil, the goddess who is celebrated and worshiped in the largest annual festival of West Bengal, Durga Puja. Ethically, she represents virtue and honor.

Durga grew to this lofty status over time. She absorbed many traits from the gods and goddesses around her. As the gods all gave her weapons to kill the demon in her puranic origin myth, on a subtler level village deities gave her many qualities that were later incorporated into her stories. In her earlier form she is Shakambhari, a goddess of vegetation and fertility (plants grow from her body), but she is also the daughter of a Vedic king as well as a creation of the major Hindu gods. She is a defender of purity, a personification of courage and will who conquers the demon of lust. She is a young bride, who visits her parents for three days each autumn. She is a wrathful and destructive goddess, the threatening Ugrachanda Durga and the fierce Durga Katyayani. She is an agricultural goddess who lives in trees and is ritually represented in the nine plants combined at Durga Puja (Navapatrika). She is a loving mother to her children who call upon her.

According to the medieval *Bhavishya Purana*, she is a goddess of tribal and low-caste people worshiped thoughout India: "Durga is worshiped by various groups of mlecchas [foreigners], by all *dasyus* (thievish tribes or outcaste Hindus), by [foreign] people from Anga, Vanga and Kalinga, by Kinnaras, Barbaras [non-Aryans] and Sakas."[2] According to the *Harivamsha*, Durga was worshiped by such tribal groups as the Savaras, Barbaras, and Pulindas.[3] These groups are scattered throughout India. In a variety of Shakta puranas, Durga is associated with many other goddesses: we have her manifestations as the nine Durgas (Nava-Durga), Pada Durga, Gupta Durga, Kanaka Durga, and other Durgas. These have a strong folk dimension—they are dangerous goddesses, though they can be propitiated. Sometimes they are understood as devouring nature goddesses who have been conquered by tantric spells and made benevolent. In her traditional iconography, one Durga tends to be the central figure (generally the multiarmed figure of Mahishamardini), and she is surrounded by eight smaller figures, also with multiple arms. Shulini Durga is a black warrioress with eight hands, carrying weapons and a lotus; her four attendants hold maces. Jayadurga is also black with four hands, and she was said to be worshiped long ago in tribal Savara style with naked dances and worshipers hurling curses at the goddess if she did not fulfill their desires. Jayadurga has three eyes and crescent moon, and likes offerings of burnt fish.[4] Durga is also Jagaddhatri, who holds and preserves the universe.

As an agricultural goddess, she is called Vana (or in West Bengal Bana) Durga or Shakambhari. Vana Durga is goddess of the forests, and she is often worshiped there in outdoor shrines that have no roof over them. In her folk form, she is sometimes seen as a *budi*, an old woman or ancestress figure. In the ritual of Budir Puja (worship of the old woman) practiced in some villages in northern West Bengal, offerings of milk and sugar are made to the sheora tree, in which the goddess Vana Durga is understood to dwell. This worship would occur annually, at the time of Durga Puja, and village women would visit the tree accompanied by musicians, with worship articles in wicker baskets. Vana Durga was offered rice boiled in milk by a brahmin priest, for the welfare of women and children. Pregnant women and mothers of children who had died when young would tie pieces of new cloth dyed in turmeric to the tree after the worship.[5] In Birbhum District, Vana Durga is also called Gundi Thakurani, or the goddess who lives in the tree trunk. She is worshiped by Adivasi or tribal groups without brahmin priests, and birds and pigs are sacrificed to her. She is offered the eggs of ducks, hens, and pigeons, which are marked with vermilion. Sometimes animals offered to her are not killed but simply tied up for a day and then let free. She has special worship on new-moon days, and picnics for women and girls twice a month (these gatherings include widows, who are usually not allowed to attend religious events in brahmanical Hinduism because they are believed to bring bad luck). Vana Durga is traditionally worshiped by women at all major events in a child's life.[6]

In Mymensingh in Bangladesh, she is called Rupasi or Rupeshvari, and worshiped at the foot of a sheora tree for the welfare of women and children. If the tree could not be found locally, a branch would be planted in the village, and worship done at its base. After first worshiping the goddess Shashthi at home, the woman concerned for her child's problems would come to the tree accompanied by other women, singing songs and carrying a winnowing fan with various offerings in it. The woman would hug the tree as if it were a friend, and give it the offerings (including ducks' eggs, which are broken at the foot of the tree). In Assam as well, Rupeshvari is also called Vana Durga or Durga of the forest.[7]

Sometimes Vana Durga is worshiped in the form of a statue, showing Hindu influence on her Adivasi worshipers. Between the rivers Ajoy and Damodar in West Bengal, she is worshiped on the first day of Durga Puja without a brahmin priest, with birds sacrificed to her, but on the second day of Durga Puja a priest is invited and her statue is worshiped in a more traditional Hindu manner. She is understood to live in both the sheora tree and in the statue, which has ten arms and a terrifying face with three eyes. However, the tree roots are marked with vermilion, and called the original seat of worship. Sacred pitchers are placed at the roots, and lamps are offered there. The goddess is called "she who lives in the sheora tree" and "goddess decked with wild flowers." Worshipers ask the goddess of the tree trunk for sons, rice, and ploughs.[8]

The sheora tree is small, and tends to grow unattractively and crookedly. It is called "ghost tree," and in Bengali folklore it is said to be a place where female ghosts and demonesses live. It has no sanctity in the brahmanical Hindu tradition, and is usually found in the jungle or in solitary places. Chaudhuri speculates that this is to prevent the negative influence of the goddess from affecting the village, for Vana Durga is also Jatapaharini, a demoness known for killing babies. He suggests that she has been gradually transformed from a demoness into a protectress.[9]

Vana Durga is also sometimes called the mother of the *danavas* or demons, which also shows her separation from the brahmanical Hindu traditions. She is associated with the fierce mothers who lived in trees, who were called the *vriksha matris.* These goddesses were said to be worshiped long ago by priestesses. The trees were protected, and no branch was cut. These trees were worshiped for safe childbirth and other boons (often with rags dipped in turmeric and vermilion). Pupul Jayakar suggests that this transformation of fierce goddesses into protectresses occured due to the use of yantras by women;[10] tantric yantras are believed to have the power to transform malevolent female spirits into protective goddesses—sometimes this occurs by having a person bury the yantra under the goddess's image. Such tree goddesses arising from the folk traditions have both positive and negative sides. As the *Mahabharata* states of the *vriddhika* tree goddesses, "Those desiring children should worship the tree-born goddesses, the *vṛddhika*, who eat human flesh."[11]

Vana Durga is also seen during the Bengali rituals of Durga Puja. On the right side of some Durga statues is a plantain tree covered with cloth. This tree is called Vana Durga, and it is worshiped along with Durga and the other deities in the pandal or shrine during Durga Puja. As B. C. Mazumdar writes, "As to whence this Vana Durga came the Puranas are silent, and the priests offer no satisfactory explanation. That this Vana Durga was a goddess of some wild tribes seems pretty certain. . . . That in addition to the image of Durga a Vana Durga has to be set up and propititated, shows that there was something in the origin of the Puja which recognised a goddess other than the consort of Siva."[12]

The agricultural Durga was also known as Shakambhari, or she who feeds the starving with vegetables from her own body. Worship of Durga as Shakambhari is rare today, but it does survive. In the village of Majigram in Burdwan, Shakambhari has both daily and yearly worship. She is called Mother of the Universe, and her statue is understood to be alive. According to one story, during the time of invasions, when Bhaskar Pandit was destroying the land of Bengal (or Radha), Shakambhari was worshiped in the village of Edua. When that village was attacked, the priest fled with the statue. He arrived at Majigram, but there was no place for the statue to be established, so he kept it under the water of a pond. He died without a temple being built, and the statue stayed underwater for many generations. Then a man of the Bagdi caste went fishing in the pond, and found a stone in his net. He left the stone on the bank, but he got a dream command from it that night: "I am Shakambhari, and that [rock] is my image. Arrange for my worship." He brought the statue to the village priest, where it has received worship since that time.[13] The statue has four arms, rides a horse, and is made of black stone (this is unusual, for Shakambhari traditionally stands holding a lotus with bees in her hands, as well as various plants and flowers). Puja is performed with the visualization of Jayadurga, with offerings of fish, leafy vegetables, and rice cooked in milk. At the annual festival in the month of Asadh, the goddess is carried on a wooden throne to a special temple, and offered goat sacrifices.

The goddess Shakambhari has an unsuccessful wedding that is also celebrated yearly, to Deuleshvar Shiva. It maintains the old tradition of fighting that is associated with weddings.[14] The members of the Bhattacharya clan represent Shiva's family, and members of the Batabyalas represent Shakambhari's family. A strong young man from the Bhattacharyas takes Shiva in the form of a *linga* to his wedding, accompanied by his friends. They go in procession through several villages, and they are challenged at each. People blockade the roads and refuse to let the group through, and they must struggle and often come to blows in order to leave the village. But when the man holding the groom (the Shiva *linga*) fights his way past the group or darts through an opening in the crowd, all hostilities cease. When Shiva finally reaches Shakambhari he is welcomed, and there is a feast and music. But another fight breaks out, an argument that the bride is too dark, and the groom is too old. The marriage is canceled, but the wedding food is eaten, as it is already on the table. Then the deities are returned to their respective temples.[15] Thus we have a fertility deity who remains unmarried, much like the traditional independent tribal goddesses.

In the nineteenth century, there was greater worship of Shakambhari at the Durga Puja festivities. On the day of the goddess's arrival, women would be possessed by the goddess, and carry on their heads large pots with newly planted grain, as another form of Durga Shakambhari, goddess of vegetation. There would be processions to worship Shakambhari carrying water, rice, banana leaves dipped in Ganges water (specifically the Hooghly River), and other plants and fruits.[16]

On rare occasions, Durga is worshiped in animal form. Ward tells a story of Durga incarnating as a jackal, and rescuing the child Krishna when he fled King Kamsa, and of Vamachari Shaktas (Shakta tantrikas who deliberately violate dharmic tradition) who feed jackals daily, and call them by the goddess's name. Sometimes the statue of a jackal is worshiped alone, and at other times it is accompanied by statues of Durga and Kali of the Burning Ground.[17] Jackals or hyenas are animals associated with the burning ground, for they are scavengers and eat the dead.

In some of her darker forms, Durga has been a goddess of the burning ground, sending out possessing spirits and requiring human sacrifice. In the eleventh-century collection of stories *Dashakumaracharitam*, a sage tells of her temple. "After some days I came to a small temple of Durga, where a party of Bheels were about to make the child an offering to the goddess, in the hope of obtaining success through her favour, and they were then deliberating in what manner they should kill him, whether by hanging him on the branch of a tree and cutting him to pieces with swords, or by partly burying him in the ground and shooting at him with arrows, or by worrying him with young dogs."[18]

We see Durga as a punishing goddess in this text in the story of Pramati's mother, who tells him about her past, and being cursed by the goddess: "Bewildered by unreasonable jealousy and anger, I abandoned my husband, your father, Kamapala; and for that sin I was cursed by Durga, who condemned me to be possessed by an evil spirit for a year. That year, which seemed to me like a thousand years, is ended; and I am now come from the great festival of Siva, where I have met my relations, who had assembled there, and have received full pardon from the goddess . . . who said: 'You are forgiven; the curse is ended; go and be happy with your husband.' "[19]

Durga has both agricultural and orthodox Hindu dimensions. R. P. Chanda distinguishes them with an evolutionary perspective:

> From this sketch of the traits of the goddess it is possible to distinguish two different strata—one primitive and the other advanced. The primitive form of Durga is the result of syncretism of a mountain-goddess worshiped by the dwellers of the Himalaya and the Vindhyas, a goddess worshiped by the nomadic Abhira shepherd, the vegetation spirit conceived as a female, and a war-goddess. As her votaries advanced in civilisation the primitive war-goddess was transformed into the personification of the all-destroying time (Kali), the vegetation spirit into the primordial energy (Adya Sakti) and the savioures from *samsara* (cycle of rebirths), and gradually brought into line with the Brahmanic mythology and philosophy.[20]

Durga was adopted into the Hindu pantheon as a warrior goddess—there are images of her slaying a buffalo by the fourth century CE, and descriptions of her in the puranic texts by the sixth century CE.[21] Although she has several origin stories in the puranas (as a form of Parvati, or as Vishnu's power of illusion), her major story comes from the *Markandeya Purana*, in the section known as the "Chandi Saptasati" or "Devi Mahatmya." In this story she is both a created being, given power by the gods to defeat a demon who had a special boon (that he could never be killed by a man), and a preexisting force, the supreme, primordial Prakriti, the active opposite of the inert Purusha. As the Devi Mahatmya describes her, "She creates this entire universe, both moving and unmoving. It is she who, when propitious, becomes a boon-giver to human beings for their final liberation. She is the supreme knowledge, the cause of final liberation, and eternal; she is the cause of the bondage of transmigration, and the sovereign over all lords."[22]

Though she is created, she herself also emanates other goddesses, such as Kali and the fierce *matrika* goddesses or Mothers. Accompanied by these goddesses, she conquers the demon army (which is exclusively male).

The story of Durga in the Devi Mahatmya revolves around three battles: Durga fought with Madhu and Kaitabha, with Mahishasura and his armies and Shumbha and Nishumbha and their armies. Her role was a minor one in the first battle—she merely emerged from Vishnu's eyes, mouth, nostrils, arms, heart, and breast, so that he would wake up (she is here called Yoganidra or the power of yogic sleep) and kill the demons. He did wake up, he fought the demons, and he won.

In the second battle, which is best known, there was a war between the gods and their ruler Indra, and the demons (*asuras*) and their ruler Mahishasura. The demons won, and Mahishasura became the lord of heaven, expelling the gods. Brahma, Vishnu, and Shiva concentrated their anger into a great light, and they were joined by the other gods; this light united like a blazing mountain, and then coalesced into a woman's form. The lights from the various gods became her limbs, and she was given weapons, jewelry, and armor by the gods, as well as a lion to ride. Her crown touched the sky, her feet shook the earth, and her thousand arms went in all directions. She conquered the armies of demons, even those who danced and fought after their heads had been chopped off. She is called various names in the battle: Chandika, Durga, Ambika, Bhadrakali, Ishvari, Bhagavati, Shri, and Devi. She fought the demon king Mahishasura, who could shift forms at will. Though he became a lion, an elephant, and a buffalo, she conquered each form, and in the end he emerged from his slain buffalo form as a man. She is again praised by the gods as the origin of the worlds, as primordial Prakriti, as supreme knowledge, the cause of liberation, and the origin of the Vedas. Pleased by the hymns, she promises future boons, especially salvation in times of danger.

This boon is taken up rapidly—at the beginning of the next chapter. The demon kings Shumbha and Nishumbha also conquered Indra's heaven, and took away his sacrifices and his heavenly bureaucracy (Vayu, Agni, and the other gods lost their jobs). The gods remembered that the goddess had granted them a boon, so they again sang hymns to her. Parvati came, and divided into two bodies: a dark one called Kalika, and bright one called Ambika. The lower-level demons Chanda and Munda saw Ambika, and reported back to the demon kings that they should possess this woman. When a matchmaker came, Ambika/Durga responded that she could only marry the man who conquered her in battle. The demon kings sent their armies, which she conquered, and then sent Chanda and Munda. When Durga saw them, her skin became black with anger, and Kali emerged from her forehead (it is not clear if this is the earlier Kalika, or a different goddess). Kali devoured elephants and riders, ate weapons, and killed Chanda and Munda (Durga then gave her the name Chamunda, as conqueror of Chanda and Munda).

Then the demon kings and their remaining armies came out, and surrounded Durga. At that moment, the creative energies (shaktis) of the various gods came forth in female form, as an army to fight the demons. When drops of blood from the demon Raktabija fell to earth and created new demons, Kali drank all of the blood so that no new demons would arise, and Raktabija was conquered. When Shumbha accused Durga of being dependent upon her female army to win the battle, she absorbed them all back into herself, saying that they were only her own powers. Both demon kings were slain in the battle.

The gods once again sang hymns to her, as the cause of liberation, as Narayani and Vishnu's *maya* (Vishnu's power of creating form in the illusory world), as Queen of the Universe. Again she offers boons, and predicts her future incarnations. These will be to slay future demons, and to maintain the world with plants from her own body (in the form of plant goddess Shakambhari) until the rains return. She also states that people will be blessed when they hear this story, especially in the autumn festival. Listening to it will protect people from evil spirits and planets and from nightmares; it will conquer fear, and give protection from all dangers.

Durga saved the gods and the world, and stated that she would incarnate on other occasions when necessary. She would respond to the prayers of her devotees in times of danger, such as forest fires, war, capture by enemies, storms at sea, threats by wild animals, or when they are generally afflicted by pain. She will also respond if the devotee is robbed or imprisoned or in danger of execution.[23] She shows that willingness to give boons to disciples by granting one devotee kingship and another liberation, after they have prayed to her for three years (and offered her their own blood).[24] She maintains an ambiguity of creation and destruction, protecting the world now but destroying it at the end of the age. As the Devi Mahatmya states, in times of prosperity she is Lakshmi, who brings wealth and happiness to human homes, but in times of misfortune she becomes the goddess of misfortune Alakshmi, and brings ruin and misery.[25]

Though today Durga is popularly linked with Shiva, in the *Markandeya Purana* she is closer to Vishnu. She defends the cosmic order, as does the god Vishnu, and she intervenes in times of danger and chaos. As Vishnu incarnates in avatar form, so will Durga, and as Vishnu became a bhakti god loved by his devotees (especially in his role as the mischievous child Krishna), so Durga was transformed from a cold and distant warrior goddess to a loving mother and eager daughter. This transformation was important, for a warrior goddess may be beautiful but is also merciless. She represents purity and courage, but never sensuality—as may be seen in the statues of Durga that fill Bengali cities during Durga Puja. Though the goddess is beautiful, she is not portrayed in a sensual fashion. And even as a married goddess her husband is in the background, quite literally—in most of the Durga Puja pandals, Shiva is almost invisible, painted as a tiny head in some dark corner of the backdrop; he is not shown in large three-dimensional form as are his wife and children.

As a bhakti goddess, Durga is clearly positive and auspicious for women and children. She unites women and children in her worship; she is concerned for pregnant women and those with a difficult history of childbearing, and women who miss their young daughters married to husbands in distant villages. We see this female community in her worship as a young bride who comes to visit her parents during Durga Puja. Women get together before her statue, talk to her, feed her, bemoan the fact that she must leave, and invite her back again next year. They douse each other with *sindur*, the red powder that brings good fortune and is associated with marriage. Women exchange news and talk over their problems, and Durga is the daughter who listens and shares in their concerns.

However, she is also herself a strong, and from a Western view perhaps over-involved, mother, who keeps her children close to her. It is said that her son Karttik would not marry, lest his future wife should starve his mother Durga.[26] Shiva, the under-involved father, is emotionally distant and usually off meditating somewhere.

Durga is a goddess with many faces. During the Durga Puja festival, the Navaratra or nine nights, Durga is sometimes worshiped as a different warlike deity on each night (largely following her roles in the Devi Mahatmya). On the first night she is Mahakali, who destroyed the demons Madhu and Kaitabha through her power of creating illusion. On the second night she is Mahishamardini, the goddess who killed the buffalo-demon who had conquered the three worlds. On the third night she is Chamunda, who killed the two demon brothers Chanda and Munda. On the fourth night she is Kali, who destroyed the demon Raktabija by licking up his drops of blood that fell to the ground. On the fifth night she is the daughter of Nanda, the herdsman, who predicted the death of Krishna's evil uncle Kamsa. On the sixth night she is Raktadanti, goddess of the bloody teeth, who bit a demon to death. In the seventh she is called Shakambhari, who fought the demons of famine and protected the world for a hundred years. On the eighth night she killed the demon Durga, and got her name Durga after this event. On the ninth night she is Labhramari, who killed the demon Aruna.[27] Thus she is both Shakta and Vaishnava, with tribal imagery of boons, fertility, and destruction, tantric illusory creations and magical use of blood, and bhakti defense of her devotees and the world.

Most versions of Durga's story include the origins of the *asura*'s buffalo identity. According to the *Vamana Purana*, a brahmin demon king named Rambha was promised an invincible son, who could change forms at will. This son was born and grew up, and "was seduced by" an attractive three-year-old buffalo named Shyama. Shyama became pregnant, and gave birth to a light-colored buffalo who could take on other forms. In another variant of the story in the same purana, her husband dies and the pregnant buffalo enters the funeral fire as a *sati*. Her son survives the pyre, and becomes powerful.[28] According to the *Kalika Purana* version of the story, Rambha wanted to have the god Shiva born to him as a son in three births, a son who becomes famous and victorious over the gods. Shiva agrees to this, and takes on the form of a cow to have sex with the demon king. Shiva is then born as the son, Mahisha. Shiva is thus wife, mother, and son in this story.[29] The kinship concerns here are later complicated in the struggle with Durga, the virgin goddess often called the wife of Shiva, and mother of his children. The *asura* is a form of Shiva, so in the great battle, Durga thus kills her husband (though it is often said that he will be reborn in her paradise).

With the rise of bhakti, the warrioress Durga came to represent the power of good over evil in brahmanical Hindu society, and of dedication to virtue over such weaknesses as lust and desire for power. Many informants told me that this was the real meaning of the statues displayed on Durga Puja, showing how a woman's virtue can conquer the lust of even an all-powerful demon. Sometimes there is an ethical explanation, and sometimes a more allegorical one. Durga has also come to symbolize yogic concentration. Swami Jyotirmayananda writes of the victory of the Devi over demons, and relates it to yogic victory over the mind:

> The subtle implication of victory is important for an aspirant to understand. Human life is a struggle in which the Divine in each of us is battling against the demoniac. Only in the state of liberation does life become free of conflict. . . . In the mystical plan of yoga, as presented by Hindu culture, there are three types of obstacles that must be overcome on the way to attaining this victory over the mind: *mala*, *vikshepa*, and *avarana*. *Mala* refers to gross impurities of the human personality; for example, excessive attachment, pride, jealousy, greed, and hate. *Vikshepa* refers to the distraction cause by subtle desires of the unconscious. And the third is *Avarana*, which refers to the veil of ignorance.[30]

Jyotirmayananda discusses Durga destroying impurity in two demonic forms, Madhu and Kaitabha, which represent attachment and hatred (Madhu means "honey," and Kaitabha means "bitter"). These two demons came out from Vishnu's ears, thus showing that "when your mystical ears are 'stopped up' you can't listen to anything with steady concentration. Attachment and hatred then arise."[31] Durga and her associated goddesses, Sarasvati and

Lakshmi, purify the devotee and encourage the growth of divine qualities. Durga gives courage, purity, and conviction. As the same author states, "Worship of Durga, therefore, implies that you gain insight into adversity and the impurities of the mind, and you develop a willingness to overcome the gross impurities of your personality."[32]

A more psychological interpretation is given by Carmel Berkson in her *The Divine and Demoniac*. She analyzes the complexities of the Mahishamardini myth, noting that Mahisha represents human struggles, while Durga controls the powers of the unconscious:

> We present the hypothesis that Mahisa is [an] anthropomorphic hero-symbolic of the psychic struggles and fantasies of the mythmaker, the devotee and the artist-who dramatizes a predictable sequence of life events and rites of passage. . . . Mahisamardini is a functioning symbol. The symbol operates as a defence system which protects the individual from the ravages of dominating instincts liable to spring capriciously from the unconscious; it harnesses potential dangerous drives and the onrush of random discharges always at the brink of consciousness. Projected and organized into recognized interacting myths, ritual prescriptions and plastic and dramatic representations, the chaotic raw material of the unconscious is controlled, both releasing and protecting the person from the tyranny of the crushing forces within, even while the energy charge is conserved.[33]

Mahisha had a tragic birth, from a humanoid father who was attacked and murdered, and a mother who was a buffalo cow and went onto the funeral pyre while pregnant to mourn his loss. Mahisha was born from the pyre, an orphan at birth, "a monster who is, nevertheless, prince charming."[34] Alone as a child (though in some accounts raised by earthly nature spirits or yakshas), he practiced austerities to gain power. He gained power from the god Brahma, conquered the demon kings, the human kings, and eventually the gods. He took over the wives of the gods, and also the sacrifices offered to them by humans. The gods could conquer him, so they create Durga, the goddess, from their combined powers. Only she was able to conquer him. Their fight is part of a universal pattern, the royal sacrifice of the demon child to the devouring mother. Berkson also mentions a Freudian interpretation of the struggle, that Durga is a neurotic mother who will not allow her children to leave, and destroys them instead.

Whereas for Berkson, Durga is a devouring and even sado-masochistic mother, for her devotees Durga is a paragon of virtue, who represents the conquest of good over evil. As a more classically bhakti goddess, who is concerned with her devotees in a personal way, Durga may also be a daughter as well as a mother, and this is seen in the modern festival of Durga Puja.

Durga is worshiped in several forms, and one that is popular in rural West

Bengal is that of Jagaddhatri. The name Jagaddhatri came from a title given to Durga in the Devi Mahatmya, after she killed the demon Mahishasura. The gods sang her praises and worshiped her with divine flowers, and she was called the sustainer (*dhatri*) of the universe (*jagat*), thus Jagaddhatri.[35]

According to one story, Krishnachandra Raya, the raja of Nadia District, introduced the worship of Jagaddhatri. When he was released from the prison of a Muslim ruler, Krishnachandra was returning by boat from Murshidabad to Nadiya. This was at the time of the autumn Durga Puja. He heard the sound of the drums on the boat, signifying that it was the tenth or last day of the puja, and he was depressed at missing the festivities. Later that evening, he had a vision of the goddess Durga, who appeared before him in the form of Jagaddhatri and told him to worship her in one month, on the ninth day of the bright fortnight in the month of Kartik. Krishnachandra ordered an artist to create a statue of the goddess Jagaddhatri, and he worshiped it with great splendor at the appointed time. If this story is true, worship of Jagaddhatri was introduced during the middle of the eighteenth century. As the contemporary literature does not mention the puja however, it is likely that more public worship was begun later.[36]

Jagaddhatri is generally described as strong and beautiful, like Durga. However, she has more tantric associations than Durga. Narendranath Bhattacharya states that Jagaddhatri's worship was introduced into tantra by the fifteenth-century writers Srinath and Brihaspati.[37] If this is so, it would have been secret worship, and known to few. In the well-known tantric compendium *Tantrasara* of Krishnananda Agambagish, a visualization of Jagaddhatri is given: "Riding on a lion, adorned with jewelry, is the four-armed Mahadevi. She wears a snake as a sacred thread, her two left arms hold a conch and a bow, and her two right arms hold a wheel and five arrows. She wears red clothes, and her skin is as red as the early rising sun. Her lotuslike navel is beautiful in the three folds of her belly, and she sits on a lotus that blooms on a throne in the island of gems. She is worshiped by sages such as Narada. Meditate upon that wife of Shiva."[38]

These are classic tantric goddess images: red clothing, a snake for a sacred thread, and multiple arms. Jagaddhatri puja is similar to Durga puja, except that her image has four arms instead of ten, she is seated without the figure of Mahishasura being present, and she is accompanied by the demigoddesses Jaya and Vijaya rather than the deities Lakshmi, Sarasvati, Kartikeya, and Ganesha. She is also associated with the land and fertility, as are most folk goddesses, and as is Durga. In his novel *Anandamath*, Bankimchandra Chatterji described Jagaddhatri, Kali, and Durga as three different states of the motherland of India. He represented Jagaddhatri as the image symbolizing ancient India, Kali as the impoverished Mother India under the British rule, and Durga as the future Mother India, victorious over her enemies.

Jagaddhatri is often worshiped as part of Durga Puja. Pratapachandra

Ghosh, in his 1874 book *Durga Puja*, describes a set of prayers used at the festival which use both vedic and tantric imagery:

> We seek as our refuge the goddess Durga, fire-colored, burning with heat, daughter of the sun, who is sought after for the reward of rites, and who is liberal [in bestowing them]. The broad-eyed goddess, the destroyer of the demons and the protector of the gods, is impetuous, we adore her exceeding swiftness. She is divine knowledge, accessible through the Sruti. She is divine lustre, she is Usha. It was after quelling the arrogance of Vayu, Indra and Agni (that) she imparted divine knowledge to them and explained the apparition. She is prime and highest knowledge, she is the progenetrix of this world, whom those who are learned in the Agama [Tantra] worship as Jagaddhatri, the supportress of this Universe. . . . As fire she conveys the sanctified butter to the assembly of the gods and nourishes them plentifully. May that Durga confer prosperity upon us.[39]

Sometimes Jagaddhatri is worshiped in the form of a dhatri or amalaki tree, rather than in a statue (worship in this form may reflect her folk/tribal roots in Vana Durga). Her devotees cleanse their courtyards with cowdung and water, and bring a dhatri branch (representing the tree in which Jagaddhatri resides) and plant it in the middle of the courtyard. They give offerings (flowers, fruits, betel, threads dyed red and yellow) at the foot of the branch. Near the branch is a white gourd, in which a hole has been made, and something put inside. The thing inserted is kept secret, and called "secret treasure" (*gupta dhana*). After giving the offerings, the devotees circumambulate the branch seven times, circling the threads around the branch while a priest chants mantras. Any remaining thread is tied around the devotee's hand with a prayer for wealth and fortune.[40]

In some puranic texts, Durga is styled as a Vedic goddess, representing many universal qualities. According to the *Brahmavaivarta Purana*, she is the eternal goddess who presides over creation, worshiped by Brahma and the other gods and sages, and herself the image of Brahma. She imparts virtue, truth, piety, salvation, and pleasure, and destroys pain, grief, and sorrow. She helps the oppressed and gives success to those who strive. She gives intellect and delusion, hunger and satisfaction, sleep and consciousness. Her virtues are infinite.[41] When the universe dissolves at the end of the Kali yuga, only she as primordial Nature will appear as real. Showing her bhakti aspect, she gives salvation to all creatures and release from life, death, and old age. She is the mother of the universe.[42]

Durga is also present in some versions of the *Ramayana* story. For instance, according to the Rama story in the Bengali *Mahabhagavata Purana*, Ravana was a devout worshiper of Durga, and worshiped her each day in his Devi temple in Lanka. Rama was also initiated into the Devi mantra, by the sage Vasishtha. When Ravana kidnapped Sita (who was one of the incarnations of the goddess), Durga became angry with him, and she shifted her loyalties toward Rama. When Rama and his armies came to rescue Sita, Rama was terrified, and Brahma suggested that he should worship the goddess, who would give him courage. Rama stopped to worship her at a bilva tree, chanting the Devi Sukta and tantric mantras to evoke her presence. She appeared to Rama, and gave him the boon of being able to kill Ravana. She assured him of victory. Since that time, it has become traditional to worship the goddess in the autumn (she was previously worshiped in the spring). Rama was able to kill Ravana with a weapon received from the goddess, and he recognized that his victory was due to the goddess's grace. In this story, Shiva was born as Hanuman, and a variety of other gods were born as monkeys.[43]

Durga is best known as a warrior queen, and her fierce independence and her refusal to submit to the unwanted attentions of a lustful demon make her a natural icon for emerging India feminism. Informants told me of feminist groups who worshiped her, and *Manushi* magazine (an India feminist journal) spoke in an article about the importance of women putting on the "Durga *rupa*" or acting like Durga when men demeaned or harrassed them. The Durga *rupa* or form represents Durga's personality, strength, and virtue. Thus, women should have the courage to defend themselves from men who wish to harm them. Durga's abilities at warfare may derive from her tribal aspect, in which many women are protectresses, and understood to be as fierce as male warriors. In a Hindu culture where the ideal woman is devoted and submissive to her husband and family, the warrior Durga of the Devi Mahatmya has neither parents, children, nor husband. She is beautiful and powerful, and stands on her own without family support. That power and independence is reflected in her festival, though a family has been added as well.

In West Bengal, Durga Puja is also a celebration of daughters. Durga is not only the warrioress but also the delicate young girl given early in marriage and missed by her family. Durga Puja welcomes the return of the girl who has married and left her family, and her sweetness and love are given reverence by the whole family. They miss her while she is gone in her husband's house, and value her three-day visit to her parental household. It is a time of appreciation of her virtues and sympathy for her problems. We see this shown in the *agamani* and *vijaya* songs that have traditionally been sung at Durga Puja, the songs of welcoming the goddess and bidding farewell to her. These show her domestic aspect, which today has come to dominate over her martial and agricultural aspects.

We see in the worship of Durga the three strands of Shaktism: she is the folk goddess Vana Durga of the forest, she is the four-armed Jagaddhatri worshiped with tantric mantras, and she is the loving daughter welcomed home with bhakti devotion by parents and friends, as well as the revered virgin mother who protects the good and defeats evil. She is welcomed in West Bengal's biggest and most ornate festival, Durga Puja.

## Durga Puja: Worship of the Goddess as Daughter and Mother

Durga Puja (or Durgotsava, the Durga festival) is traditionally celebrated on Navaratra, from the first to the ninth of the bright half of the autumn month of Ashvin (September/October). Some texts say that it should be celebrated in both the spring and the autumn, but it is the autumn holiday that has become the major time of celebration. The rituals of Durga Puja are documented in the dharmashastra texts, in handbooks, in ritual texts, and in other sources. P. V. Kane notes that there is a "voluminous literature" on Durgotsava, involving "every digest on vratas, tithis and puja" (religious vows, time periods and ritual worship) as well as a whole series of special treatises.[44] Durga is called down to dwell temporarily in a statue to visit her worshipers, and after several days she leaves them and returns to her heavenly home.

Durga puja is *pandal* time in Calcutta. A *pandal* is a large, temporary enclosure that contains an altar or stage to hold one or more deities, usually in the form of statues. They may imitate temples, well-known urban buildings, huts, or skyscrapers, with a Potemkin-village style façade added on to a single room. The room may be large, and some have twenty-foot ceilings with crystal chandeliers. Each year, there are hundreds of major *pandals* in urban Calcutta competing for prizes, not to mention the numerous smaller and less elaborate shrines with statues and pictures spread throughout the city. One prizewinner, the Adi-Ballygunge *pandal*, was styled after a village hut, complete with a muscular mannequin in a short loincloth playing a drum to call the devotees to worship. It was next to a small temple to Shiva and Kali, with Shiva as a black *linga* with a face painted on it, wearing a silver crown. Such *pandals* are used for the major goddess festivals in West Bengal—for Durga Puja, Kali Puja, Lakshmi Puja, and Sarasvati Puja. Durga Puja and Kali Puja are the two biggest festivals, with the most elaborate statues and celebrations.

Plans for erecting *pandals* begin about three months prior to the holiday celebrations. *Pandal* makers and organizers discuss design, materials, and cost. They are much more elaborate than the marriage *pandals* that one sees at other times of the year, though traditional materials like bamboo and wood are used for both types.[45] The *pandals* are lit up with neon and Christmas lights at night. They are built on foundations made of bamboo, and often are built by Muslim construction workers, though Hindu artisans generally make the statues (this illustrates the kind of equilibrium that has often been reached between the two religious communities). There are prizes in the newspapers for beauty and design, and hordes of people make their way from one *pandal* to another, especially during the evening and into the night. The buses and trains are packed with devotees and curious visitors, dressed in their holiday clothing, going to greet the goddess. Each statue is understood to show the goddess in a different mood, with variations of clothing and background. The faces on the goddess statues do not tend to be emotional, however, but rather detached and subtly smiling. It is the demon, Mahisha, who is most active and passionate—either full of lust and aggression or fear and submission.

There are often storms on Durga Puja. Observers at the *pandals* discussed how there is always a disturbance when the Mother comes—whether earthquakes, rain or hurricane. The timing of the thunderstorm in 1993 was perfect—it occurred just at 5:30 AM, when Durga was astrologically determined to enter into the statues. The mixing of worlds is a dangerous time, but it is believed by devotees that Durga would always help them so that none would be injured. Worshipers in Calcutta were called by loudspeakers from 4:00 AM on, by music and drumming, occasionally accompanied by the sound of a conch (the traditional announcement of the deity's presence). The loudspeakers would play Strauss waltzes (*Tales from the Vienna Woods* was frequently repeated), Indian ragas, and Hindi movie music.

Durga has the biggest annual festival in West Bengal generally and in Calcutta particularly—Durga Puja. This is odd, because Durga temples are very rare in West Bengal, and she is not generally discussed outside of her holiday season. However, the tremendous focus on her worship at this time makes her an important goddess. Durga is worshiped both in public, with large statues and crowds, and in private, in home services in which a smaller statue is set up. She is portrayed as strong and beautiful, with ten arms.

Such worship is said to be important to the goddess. As the *Kalika Purana* states, "Whoever, through laziness, hypocrisy, hatred or stupidity, does not celebrate Durga Puja, has his desires frustrated by the angry Devi."[46] She should be worshiped in order to please her, for the devotee to gain happiness in that year, for the destruction of evil spirits and demons, and to gain delight.

On the holiday of Navaratri, the nine-nights festival, the final three days are celebrated in West Bengal as the major nights of Durga Puja. Some Shaktas worship a different manifestation of the goddess on each of the nine nights. These manifestations vary, but a common list might be: Mahakali, Mahishamardini, Chamunda, Kali, Raktadanti, Nanda, Shakambhari, Labhramari, and Durga. Some celebrants worship Durga on the first three nights, Lakshmi on the next three, and Sarasvati on the final three nights.[47] There are group chantings of the "Devi Mahatmya" section of the *Markandeya Purana*, which describes the goddess Durga's conquest over the demon Mahishasura. These songs involve a rather bloody description of her victory, but they still generate devotion in both the singers and their audiences. Sometimes a chorus of little girls sings the Devi Mahatmya story, shrilly and enthusiastically.

There is much discussion among modern informants of how Durga Puja has become commercialized, has lost the devotion with which it began, and become a month-long school vacation accompanied by visiting relatives and gift-giving. Real devotion is not associated with public *pandals* and temples, according to many informants, but rather with small ceremonies in the home, where the goddess is treated as a visitor and welcomed. The temples and street *pandals* tend to be more of a social occasion, for meeting friends, dressing up in new saris, seeing processions of political figures, and traveling around Calcutta by taxi (at least for the growing middle class).

Whereas the earlier Durga Puja statues were aniconic slabs of stone or wood, later images were made of clay or metal, with four arms and then ten arms, to protect the devotee from danger in all ten directions.[48] Sometimes these arms were associated with the ten great wisdom (*mahavidya*) forms of Kali/Durga. Modern *pandals* usually have the multiarmed Durga in the center, killing the demon Mahisha with a trident as he emerges in human form from the body of a decapitated buffalo. Durga has golden skin and three eyes, and is beautiful and calm. She holds many weapons, and rides upon a lion; she is accompanied by her children Lakshmi, Sarasvati, Ganesha, and Kartikeya. Shiva, her husband, is not usually present in statue form, though he may be a small image painted somewhere on the backdrop. Her children are often said to represent the four castes that are united in her worship: Sarasvati, goddess of learning, for the brahmins; Kartikeya, god of power, for the kshatriyas; Lakshmi, goddess of wealth and fortune, for the vaishyas; and Ganesh, god of labor and success for the lowest-caste people, the shudras. According to the *Kalivilasa Tantra*, Durga should be surrounded by these four deities, as well as Jaya and Vijaya (goddesses of success and victory), the god Brahma, the mouse and peacock (vehicles of Ganesha and Karttikeya), and the Navapatrika or Kalabau (a collection of nine plants wrapped together).[19]

Image makers, who work in centers like Kumartuli and Patuapara in Calcutta, make these statues from a straw and bamboo skeleton. Clay and rags are added in layers, and the final layer has clay mixed with jute. The dried clay heads may be sculpted individually, or molded from casts. The surfaces are sanded, primed, and painted or varnished, and backgrounds are added. The clothes may be sculpted on, but usually they are added later: saris and dhotis, hair made of jute, tin weapons, *solapith* ornaments,[50] and tinsel jewelry.[51]

Although there are generally the same traditional figures in all of the *pandals*, many modern additions are made to the images of the goddess and their backgrounds. The Bengali newspaper *Ajkal* had an interesting article on a new version of the statues:

> According to Shastra and the rulings of the almanac (*panjika*), the goddess Durga will be arriving this year riding on a swing. But in the worship area (*puja mandapa*) of Yuvak Sangha in central Calcutta, the Devi will descend with her family this year from a helicop-

> ter. The object is the same—killing the demon. But she will come armed with ten weapons in her ten hands. In Madhu Gupta Lane opposite Shraddhananda Park, the Devi carries only one weapon—a remote control system. When she presses the button of the remote control device, the demon will be instantly destroyed. This will be preceded by several other events, like a stage drama. The demon (*asura*) will come in riding in a submarine, and waves of the sea will hit the boat. The Devi will come in by helicopter. They will argue, but not facing each other—they will argue by satellite. This will cause a war to begin, and the Devi will target the demon's submarine by missile. [When it hits] the submarine will break into pieces. But the "Submarinasura" [the demon or *asura* in the submarine] is immortal. . . . The beautifully hand-painted backdrop and an extraordinary sound and light show will draw the attention of all Calcutta.[52]

Some images also involve social commentary, as in the Durga image at Shyambazar (also reported by *Ajkal*):

> Another daring instance of [commentary on] social degeneration is seen in the Durga image of Navin Sangha at Shyambazar. Here the Devi fights with two terrifying demons. Lakshmi and Ganesha are tied up and held by the demon Black Marketeer. On the other side, Sarasvati is held in the grip of the demon Illiteracy. Under the feet of Black Marketeer are people who lie trampled [beneath him]. Under the claws of the feet of the demon Illiteracy lies a student breathless under the weight of scholar (*pandit*) and syllabus. Amulya Pal, the distinguished artist from Barasat, has given an extraordinarily meaningful expression of social problems in this image of Navin Sangha. All over Calcutta, variety and aesthetic expression have added new forms to the images and shrines.[53]

During the year that Yuri Gagarin went into space, Durga appeared in a space suit standing on a rocket. During the wars in Vietnam and Bangladesh, there were violent backdrops, and Durga carried rifles and submachine guns. In his article "A Goddess in Our Hearts," Dipak Rudra describes Durga's arrival on horseback or on an elephant, on a boat or palanquin. She is sometimes helped by Muslims and Catholic priests.[54] In recent years, her *pandals* have imitated famous buildings: the Calcutta High Court, the White House, the Konarak Sun Temple, the India Gate, and the *Statesman* newspaper building.

Every year, Durga is understood to be awakened out of her sleep for the holiday. This is called "worship at an inappropriate time" (*akala puja*), during the autumn. Durga is said to be sleeping soundly from the time of the summer solstice to the winter solstice, when she normally awakens. This is why the earlier worship of Durga was in the spring, and called Vasanti Puja. However, the celebration was moved to the autumn because of Rama. According to the *Kalika Purana*, Rama began the autumn worship (*sharadiya puja*) in order to conquer Ravana, the demon king of Lanka, and recover his wife Sita. He prayed and fasted for Durga to help him in his upcoming battle with Ravana, and Brahma sympathized with Rama and woke her up. She watched the fight between Rama and Ravana for over a week, and finally with her blessings Rama conquered Ravana on the ninth day (*mahanavami puja* day). On the next day, Rama celebrated his victory. Over time, it became a custom to begin all important undertakings on this day.[55]

Thus began the habit of waking up the goddess at about midnight. As Brahma could not always be depended upon to act as mediator and alarm clock, the ritual of awakening or *bodhana* was introduced. Some informants say that when she is awakened, the appearance of the goddess makes the skies blaze with red, white, and blue lights, and that she is like a burning mountain (but one must have spiritual eyes opened to see this). The statue of Durga is installed on a dais on the sixth day of Navaratra, with hymns and drumbeats, under a bilva tree. Durga is called down from her heavenly rest into the tree by means of Vedic hymns and tantric mantras (thus mixing the folk tree goddess, the tantric mantras, and the bhakti celebration). The performer should state his intentions, worship the bilva tree as Durga, and then establish a ritual pitcher for her. He awakens Durga with a mantra, and reminds her of her awakening by Rama. He takes offerings (earth, sandalwood paste, flowers, fruits, vermilion, gold, silver, etc.) and places them on the tree, so that it will be an auspicious place for the goddess.[56] Later a branch of the bilva tree is taken to the place of worship, and Durga is transferred from the tree by the ritual of endowing life (*prana-pratishtha*) into the statue. A long passage from the *Kalika* or *Matsya Purana* is then chanted, describing her physical attractiveness and her weapons. She is also established later in the combination of nine plants, Navapatrika. The performer states, "O blessed Durga! Come, enter into the [sheaf of] plants; this is your place in the mortal world; I throw myself on your mercy."[57]

Navapatrika is a collection or sheaf of nine plants which together form one entity, the Kalabau or banana-wife (it is also called the Nava-Durga or nine Durgas). It is organized around a young banana or plantain plant, which is wrapped by an aparajita vine with a variety of other plants (usually bilva, turmeric, arum, pomegranate, barley or manaka, rice, jayanti, and ashoka) and dressed as a married woman. Some informants say that the plants represent different parts of Durga's body: head, hair, breast, nose, and so on. The leaves of the banana or plantain are twisted like a woman bowing her head, with turmeric as Durga's skin when she was incarnate as the golden Uma, and paddy rice representing Durga's aspect as fortune or Lakshmi.[58] Pratapachandra Ghosha mentions the various goddesses worshiped in Navapatrika: Kalika in the arum plant, Durga in the turmeric plant, Brahmani in the plantain,

Karttiki in the sesbania, Shiva (the goddess) in the bilva tree, Raktadantika in the pomegranate, Sokarahita in the ashoka tree, Chamunda in the mana tree, Lakshmi in the rice plant.[59] After sunrise on Saptami Puja day, the Navapatrika is taken in a procession with music to be bathed and covered with a new silk sari (usually in yellow or white edged with red). She is carried by a priest, and placed next to Ganesh. In prayers, the Navapatrika is addressed as an alternative form of Durga, though the sheaf is popularly thought to represent Ganesha's wife.[60] She is praised when she is given offerings: "Om, O patrika [leaves], O nine forms of Durga, you are the darling of Mahadeva [Shiva]; please accept all these offerings and protect me, O Queen of heaven. Om, adoration to Durga dwelling in the nine plants."[61]

It is likely that the most ancient aspect of Durga Puja is that involved with harvest and fertility, its remnants reflected in the Navapatrika. S. R. Das discusses the image's change from folk origins to bhakti deity thus: "The plantain-plant-lady is also worshiped (in some parts of Eastern Bengal) during the Durga Puja [and] is no other than Vana Durga or Durga of the forest, who was originally a primitive deity, and when the rite at a later date was hinduised, she was given a place at one corner of the puja mandap."[62] We also see the agricultural theme in the pitcher that is installed by the priest as another dwelling place for Durga. Ghosha describes how fruit and vegetables are put into the pitcher along with Ganges water, and it is set upon dough that has five grains scattered on it. The priest chants a prayer, and the grains are equated with the life of the gods and long human life, the nectar of immortality of the gods.

On the next day, Ashtami day, Durga was thought to have killed Mahishasura, and animals (usually goats, occasionally buffaloes) are sacrificed. Many devotees fast on this day, and visit temples such as Kalighat in Calcutta. Sometimes there are competitive sports events. Mazumder notes the older tendency to sing obscene songs on this day, especially in the villages.[63] In older days, there would be gunshots announcing the beginning of the puja and the sacrifice, and women would pray in groups, holding in each hand a clay plate of burning resin. There was worship of young virgins and elderly married women, by bowing before them and asking their blessings. On the following Navami day there is ritual worship with lamps, incense, and food offerings, and dancing with drums and music. All animal sacrifices must be finished by this day. On the last day, Vijaya Dashami day, devotees bid a sad farewell to Durga with sweets, red powder (*sindur*), and other offerings. She is ritually called from the statue, which then becomes an empty shell, a dead body whose soul has fled. In the evening, her statue is taken to the nearest river or lake, and immersed with hymns, songs, and music. Sometimes the statue is taken out on a boat and thrown into the water midstream. The goddess has returned to her home, and the statue being thrown in the waters is only a corpse.

Durga Puja also involves home worship, in which wealthier houses can afford their own statues, and Durga is welcomed in a more personal manner as the daughter of the household who has come for a visit. Because a daughter would often leave her natal family at a very early age in an arranged marriage in which she went to live with her husband's family, there was a great sense of loss on the part of both the daughter and her parents. Durga Puja represents the time that the daughter could return to her parents' house, and was a time for happiness and reunion. Families welcome their own married daughters back by honoring and worshiping the goddess Durga. When Durga (and daughter) leave, at the end of the festival, the married women of the family or neighborhood typically gather in the household and walk around the goddess in a circle making the noise of ululation (a trilling sound of farewell), and then wipe away the goddess's tears with betel leaves (she cries because she is leaving her loving household). She is offered consecrated food, and red *kumkum* powder (vermilion) is put on her forehead, symbolizing her return to married life. The women may also mark each other with *kumkum*, in a playful way.

The men then take the goddess, to the music of drum and cymbals, to a truck or cart that takes her to be immersed in the river. They chant in Bengali, "the goddess will return again next year" in deep voices, and happily go to the river, beeping their horns and making noise in various ways. It was suggested by one informant that the men were happy that their (symbolic) sister was leaving, for now they have their mothers' full attention again; Indian sons in extended families are traditionally close to their mothers, and may become jealous of the attention toward their sisters.

The 1993 Durga Puja ceremonies at Belur Math, a monastery and center of learning associated with Ramakrishna Paramahamsa and the Ramakrishna Mission, were crowded with hundreds of worshipers. The monks appeared to have their own drum corps, and there was much drumming as the statue of Durga was marched out of the temple and toward the shore of the river. There was ecstatic dancing and a procession by the monks as the statue moved toward its immersion, and a man danced before the Durga statue while holding hot, smoking pots of coal and incense, a form of ritual asceticism often seen with religious *manat* vows. Though Belur Math emphasizes Shakta universalism rather than theistic Hinduism, some of the older rituals remain.

There is currently criticism of Durga Puja by the Communist government of West Bengal, which says that the money could be better spent in a poor culture. It tolerates such religious ritual, but with suspicion and often with newspaper attacks. Such attacks, however, seem unlikely to derail a celebration as popular as this one.

We see both in the imagery of Durga and in the Durga Puja rituals the uniting of the three strands of Shaktism, harmonized together into Calcutta's major festival.

## Kali: From Buffalo Protector to Burning Ground Goddess to Mother of the Universe

*Jaya Kālī Calcutta walī*
*Bhūter nāch bāje tāli.*

Victory to Kali, Mistress of Calcutta
The spirits dance to the sound of clapping.

Chant to Kali, often sung by the Indian Native Regiments at the sound of the evening gun

Although the origin of Calcutta's name in the terms Kali or Kalighat has been debated, it is certain that Calcutta has a special relationship with the goddess Kali. It is she who watches over the city, allowing its survival in the face of economic disaster and massive unemployment, political corruption, epidemics, and the immigration of poverty-stricken refugees. She is also the figure who grounds the city in its religious tradition, as it is challenged by computers, skyscrapers, communist ideology, and STAR television (broadcasting *Dynasty* and *Baywatch* over Asia). She may be seen on the dashboards of taxis, protecting the drivers from accidents, and inside homes for personal devotion.

Kali is the great goddess of Calcutta. The song at the beginning of this section salutes Kali as Mistress of Calcutta, who is queen of the spirits who dance around her. According to S. C. Banerji, she is the most popular deity in West Bengal, and there are almost no towns or villages in Bengal where Kali is not worshiped in some form or image. In many temples and private homes she receives daily worship.[64] Although Kali is seen throughout India, Bengal has traditionally been her home. She has often been a minor goddess in other areas, so that the Reverend Eyre Chatterton could write in 1901, "And yet Kali, in spite of her proved pre-eminence in Bengal, is after all but a local goddess, for it appears she is but little thought of in other parts of India."[65] Whether this was true at the time it was made, today it is clear that Kali has also become a pan-Indian goddess, and she is worshiped by a variety of different castes and tribes. She ranges from being a folk village goddess who protects a small area, and an ancestress who grants boons, to a tantric and yogic goddess who gives liberation to her devotees, and a loving mother who gives them protection (as Raksha Kali) and entrance to heaven. The stories that follow show these three aspects.

As a village goddess, Kali tends to be a protectress of a particular city or locality. Among many Adivasi groups, she is called Kali *bonga* and offered goats as sacrifices. Among the Oraons of the Sunderbans (a jungle and swamp area south of Calcutta), she is called Bankali, the forest goddess (possibly related to the Muslim forest goddess Banbibi). She is the presiding goddess of the Sunderbans, and she is invoked before cutting trees, collecting honey, and performing other work there.

The tribal Oraons of this area also worship a form of Kali who is a guardian deity, especially for buffaloes. Kali's worship is celebrated as a form of buffalo-blessing. The goddess is worshiped in the buffalo shed, without a statue. The head of the family washes the hooves of the buffalo, and organizes the offerings (including vermilion, rice, chicken, a lamp, and rice-beer). He puts a pile of rice on the ground, feeds the chicken with it, and chants the name of the deity. He then sacrifices it, and the chicken is cooked with rice by the women. The meal is first offered to Kali, and later distributed to the extended family. The heads of the buffaloes are marked with vermilion, as are the shed and the house. A feast is then given to guests who have assembled for the worship. The buffaloes do not work that day.[66] The moody goddess is made benevolent by this worship.

There are also folk understandings of the goddess Kali that deal with tribal magic. Among the Oraons in West Bengal and the Chotanagpur area, Kali Mai has traditionally been the major goddess of the village black magician (*mati*). She has attendant spirits who bring the black magician any spirit he wishes to see, and she is invoked in the magician's worship of any other spirit or deity. The major god of the village witch finder (*bhagat*) is Mahadeo (Mahadeva or Shiva). Thus, we have the socially acceptable shaman with his deity Shiva, who seeks out and condemns the black magician with his unacceptable goddess Kali Mai (here Shiva and Kali are enemies). When Kali Mai's power is sought by such a magician, he sets up a mud altar for her. Three pieces of earth are set on it, and the magician places an iron trident on each of them as her symbol. They are daubed with vermilion, and offered areca nuts and copper coins. A red chicken and a black goat are sacrificed to her, and she is offered rice-beer. The altar is smeared with whitish clay each morning, and she is offered flowers. She is given many other offerings, and the black goat's blood is daubed on the altar.[67] She will then give the magician what he wishes.

There are many Shakta tantric elements in tribal worship, especially in tribal magic. Here the tribal Kali of the *mati* receives goat sacrifice, alcohol, red offerings, and blood, much as the Hindu Kali does, and she can give the control over spirits sought by many tantrikas. Both tribal magicians and tantrikas may propitiate her, or seek to control her.

Among the low-caste Hindu Bauris, Kali is worshiped both on an individual daily basis and in group fairs and festivals. Individually, the deity may be placed in a mud hut in a courtyard, or in a part of the house. Festivals usually involve offerings to Kali (food, flowers, incense, goat sacrifice, music and dance, and immersion of the clay pitcher into which she is invoked). Kali is worshiped in summer, autumn, and winter, sometimes with a statue. In one 1964 ceremony reported by K. C. Shasmal, there were fireworks and verbal duels by the village poets, with other caste groups (Bagdis, Mahishyas, Goalas, Sadgops) attending.[68] Kali was invoked by a low-caste priest, who worshiped her with sincere devotion rather than mantras.

Sometimes Kali is said to appear in human form, and later become a stone statue to be worshiped. In the village of Kaiti, there is annual worship of a Kali statue that was believed to have originally been an outcast girl. According to the story, a high-caste villager was returning to the village from a long pilgrimage, and he encountered an orphaned Santal tribal girl. Out of compassion, he took her back to the village and gave her a job as a cow-keeper in his brother's house. One day, one of the cows escaped her care and trampled a neighbor's rice plants. The neighbors chased the Santal girl to punish her. The frightened girl found refuge in an oil-grinder at a nearby oilman's house. They searched for her everywhere, but she disappeared from the village. A few days later, the brahmin who had brought her to the village learned in a dream that she was really the goddess Kali in human form, who had chosen to stay in his house. The goddess told him in the dream to search the oil-grinder, and he would find a deity carved of stone within it. He did find it, and told the villagers about it, and a temple was built in that oil-grinding room and daily worship was arranged. Over time, a larger statue of the goddess was created and installed. The old statue from the oil-grinder is still used today for worship.[69]

The Karunamayi Kali statue of Vishnupur had also originally appeared as a human child. A man named Krishnachandra Hota, who worked for Nawab Alivardi Khan, had no children. He saw a young girl crying in the street and pitied her, and he brought her home with him and raised her as his own child. He named her Karunamayi. When she grew old enough to be married he tried to find a husband for her, but without success. When he was going to work one day, Karunamayi wanted to go with him, and she hurt her leg on the way and had to return home alone. When his work was finished, Krishnachandra went home, but could not find his daughter. He asked for her everywhere, and at last when he reached the burning ground of the village near the river, he heard a heavenly voice. It said that his adopted daughter Karunamayi was really the goddess Kali, and that now she had transformed herself and was living in a hole in the banyan (vata) tree at the cremation ground. Krishnachandra found the tree, and saw a four-armed stone image of Kali there. He took it home and installed it in his house.[70] According to another variant of the origin story, the statue was carried off from south India by a fleeing refugee, who was threatened by the Muslims when he reached Murshidabad. In order to save the statue, he threw it into the river. The statue was carried by the current of the river to the vata tree, where its roots caught the statue. The villagers began to worship it, and soon the goddess became popular for her kindness to her devotees, and she was called Karunamayi Kali.[71] This means merciful one, or Mother Kali full of compassionate love.

Some statues of Kali are believed to have more power than others, and the Kali statue at Kalighat temple in Calcutta is said to be especially powerful. This Kali is believed by many folk and tribal people to be very active. She appears in dreams to help and advise. In a Chamar song that is sung during healing rituals, a meeting between the tribal Kali and Kali of Calcutta is described:

> My [tribal] Kali Devi ascended a palanquin
> And proceeded to the market of Kalipur [in Calcutta]
> Having met the Kali [there]
> She returned in the palanquin.[72]

Because folk Kali statues tend to be associated with specific physical locales, the incarnate Kali within a particular statue may become a wanderer when that statue is taken from its home. For instance, the protecting Kali of Dacca in Bangladesh was Dhakeshvari or Ramna-Kali, and she looked kindly upon her devotees. However, Dhakeshvari is now a refugee, like the Hindus who were forced to move as she was during Partition, and she has resettled in West Bengal.[73] But she is still a refugee goddess, far from her true home.

Another folk Kali is found in the village of Ranjana.[74] The temple of Kali Budi (Old Woman Kali or ancestress Kali) was originally a temple to the god Dharma, but over fifty years ago a man of the Sadgopa caste had a dream of Kali, who said that she wanted to be installed there. His own ancestors had long ago dreamed of her as a rock that wished to be dug out of the ground and placed near their household, which they did. Now she wanted a change of scene. She was placed in the Dharma temple, where the priests liked her, for she was alive and granted boons, whereas the god Dharma was irritable and malevolent. However, this Kali did have a bad temper. When ten people took and ate a goat that had been dedicated to her, she was angry, and they all died the next day. A Muslim woman threw hot gruel on another dedicated goat, and found her own skin covered with burns—which only healed after offerings to Kali and Dharma. When a Bagdi man saw a vision of Kali walking at night, he thought that she was his girlfriend, and he pursued her and she ran away to the Kali temple. When he had nearly caught her, he suddenly felt pain and burning all over his body. He prayed to Kali, but ended up dying.[75] As with most Shakta folk deities, the goddess can be both helpful and dangerous. Insulting her requires propitiation—and it cannot be guaranteed to work in all cases.

In the village Badabelun in Burdwan, Kali is worshiped in her form as Bada Kalima (Elder Mother Kali or Big Mother Kali; the term implies power as well as age and size). While the age and size show folk influence, the revealed style of worship was tantric. When the patriarch of the Bhattacharya family, Bhriguram Vidyavagisa, was on his deathbed, he called his sons together. He told them how Kali appeared to him and had told him to move from Ketugram to Badabelun early in his life, and how she had recently appeared to him in his dreams, telling him to prepare to die. She wanted her worship to continue, and he needed to inform his sons how to worship her. He told them how to perform her worship in a long poem, emphasizing tantric rites rather than the Vedic *homa* fire or the puranic *arati* or worship with lights; they were to use tantric mantras and offer animal blood in a skull:

> On the new moon of Kartik, sit [in meditation] through the night
> Worship Mother with devotion, after building her image.
> It should be fourteen cubits tall
> Worship it according to tantric rites.
> Put earth on her body on the full moon of Asvin
> Make her tongue from a winnowing tray.
> Offer her three bags of rice, and sweets
> Then be seated and keep a steady mind.
> Offer her a banana, and the blood of goat and buffalo in a skull
> But do not perform *homa*-fire or *arati* to the Mother.
> Light torches at the time of worship
> And offer red hibiscus flowers at the Mother's feet.
> Then give her sweets, rice and lentils, and meat offerings.
> Continue to worship her until dawn.
> Do not immerse her pitcher [in which she was installed]
> But keep it inside the house, and daily offer it loving worship
> On the third day after Kali Puja.[76]

He also told his sons about his experiences of Kali. After he had moved to Badabelun due to the goddess's dream command, he collected a set of five skulls and buried them at the local cremation ground, and sat there in tantric-style meditation. He built a statue of Kali himself, and he would worship her at the burning ground, with vultures and jackals roaming about. He would call her "great bliss" (*mahananda*), and spend long hours before the statue. One day he went off for a bath, and when he returned he found that the image on the altar was not the one he had built. He had made a peaceful goddess, but when he returned he saw a terrifying figure. She had become very old, and was standing on a corpse with a terrible face, full of blood and horrifying to see. He was frightened to see the image, and was about to run away. However, the goddess spoke to him reassuringly, saying "My name is Elder Mother. This image will be worshiped for ages. Anyone who worships me with devotion will never have to worry about the next world." She told him to marry, for someone had to serve her after he died, and she suggested a bride for him. She told him that on the next new moon, the daughter of a brahmin would die of snakebite, and her relatives would bring her to the burning ground. He should take a handful of ash from the funeral pyre and put it into her mouth, and it would bring her back to life. He should then marry this reborn woman and start a family.

He agreed to do this, and on the next new moon he saw the funeral party.

The girl's father wept like a madman, and he went over to Bhriguram and begged him to bring his daughter back to life. Bhriguram followed the goddess's advice and put the ash into the girl's mouth. She sat up and said "Goddess," and stretched as if she had just awakened from sleep. Bhriguram then told her father of the goddess's command, and he agreed with the proposal for marriage. This was the beginning of Bhriguram's family, and the reason for the necessity of maintaining the goddess's worship.[77] Tantric worship emphasizes the goddess's power over life, death, and liberation—in this story, she is clearly a conqueror of death.

In these stories, Kali is understood as an urban goddess of Calcutta, a village tribal goddess who gives local revelations, and a tantric deity who brings back the dead.

## Kali and Her Origins

Most historians seek the origin of the goddess Kali in the Sanskrit Great Tradition, preferring textual rather than village sources. As Sasibhusan Dasgupta writes, "We have a tendency to trace the history of all goddesses from the Vedas."[78] In the Vedic texts, Kali has been associated with the goddess of night Ratri (based on the "Ratri Sukta" of the Rig Veda), and with the fearful Nirritidevi of the Shatapatha and Aitareya Brahmanas. The name of Kali is first found in the Mundaka Upanishad, where Kali is one of the seven tongues of the sacrificial fire or *yajna*. However, here she is only a flame and not a goddess.[79] Kali is later mentioned in the *Mahabharata*, seen by Ashvatthama when he entered the Pandava camp at night to kill the soldiers. She had bloodshot eyes, wore red garlands, carried nooses, and was of terrifying appearance. There is some question of whether this image came with the earliest writings of the text or was a later addition.[80] Her skin is dark, and some writers say that Kali's four arms represent the four Vedas.

In early Sanskrit literature, Kali is negative and devouring. As Bana's *Harsha-charita* describes her, "The tongue of the goddess of Doom's night, black like the charcoal of the funeral piles and covered with blood, licks up the lives of living beings, like a cow that licks her calf's shoulder—eager to swallow all creation as a mouthful."[81]

In the *Khila Harivamsha* we find a goddess fond of meat and wine, being worshiped by Adivasi and low-caste groups, and in Bhavabhuti's *Malatimadhava*, a terrifying goddess is described who is worshiped with human sacrifice. She is dark and violent (*ugra*), and her temple is in a burning ground.[82]

In the medieval puranas, there are many stories of her origin. Kali's origin is described traditionally as an emanation from the goddess Durga in the Chandi section of the *Markandeya Purana*:

> 5. Thereupon Amibikā [Durgā] became terribly angry with those foes, and in her anger her countenance then became dark as ink.
> 6. Out from the surface of her forehead, fierce with frown[ing], issued suddenly Kālī of terrible countenance, armed with a sword and noose.
> 7–9. Bearing the strange skull-topped staff, decorated with a garland of skulls, clad in a tiger's skin, very appalling owing to her emaciated flesh, with gaping mouth, fearful with her tongue lolling out, having deep-sunk reddish eyes and filling the regions of the sky with her roars, and falling upon impetuously and slaughtering the great asuras in that army, she devoured those hosts of the foes of the devas.[83]

Many stories of Kali's origin are variants of her emanation from the anger of the warrior goddess Durga in this text.

In the *Linga Purana*, Shiva asks Parvati to destroy the demon Daruka, who can only be killed by a woman. Parvati enters Shiva's body and takes the poison that is stored in his throat. With this, she is transformed into the terrifying Kali. Accompanied by cannibalistic spirits (*pishachas*), she attacks Daruka and his armies. Kali defeats them, but becomes so maddened by the battle that she threatens to destroy the world. Shiva comes to calm her, and the world is saved. Also in the *Linga Purana*, Kali is part of Shiva's army as he goes off to defeat another demon. She wears skulls and an elephant hide, and holds a trident. She has been drinking the blood of demons.[84] She is called the daughter of Himalaya, thus linking her with Parvati and Uma (this link is seen later on in the *agamani* and *vijaya* songs). In the *Vamana Purana*, Shiva calls Parvati "Kali" because of her dark skin. Parvati is angered at this, and performs austerities to gain a light complexion. When she succeeds, her skin becomes golden and she is called Gauri, but the dark skin that falls away retains consciousness, and becomes the dark and violent Kaushiki, who then generates Kali.[85]

However, there are also oral traditions that have her arise for different reasons. According to one story told to me by an informant in Kalimpong, Sikkim (which borders nothern Bengal), Kali arose out of Durga's grief and anger at the death of her child:

#### HOW DURGA BECAME KALI THROUGH GRIEF AND ANGER

> One day, Ma Durga rubbed the dirt from her hand, and made a young man from it. She told him to guard her while whe was taking a bath, and not to let anybody in. Her husband Shivaji was off on his ice-mountain praying to Indra, but he finished and came home. When he came to the door, the young man told him, "Ma is bathing, I am her bodyguard Ganesha, and you may not enter." Shivaji tried to enter three times, and then finally he chopped off Ganesha's

head with his trident. It went flying off out into the ocean, and it sank down deep into the waters.

When Durga came out from the bath, she saw the dead body of her son and became maddened with grief. She told Shivaji that he had killed their son, and she flew off to go looking through the world for his head. She was unable to find it, and turned dark from rage. She started eating men and drinking their blood as she flew through the world. The gods then called her Kali Ma.

As she flew in grief and anger, the world became full of earthquakes and lightning, and the people became afraid. The gods held a meeting, to determine what to do. Naradamuni came, like the postman, and he brought the news from Shiva Bhagavan's house. In this way, the gods learned what had happened there. The gods decided to revive Ganesha, and cut off the head of a white elephant and put it on to Ganesha's body. They did so, and he came back to life. But they also needed to bring peace to the world.

Narada told Shivaji, "This is a problem of your house, you must make peace there." Shiva went off to think about it. That night, Kali was drunk on blood, and she staggered from house to house. By accident, she went into her own house, and she stepped on Shiva, who was asleep on the floor. He called out, and she recognized him, and stuck her tongue out in embarrassment and shame [touching her husband with her feet is an insulting act]. He said to her, "If we stay married, if you stay my wife and I your husband, then you will get your child back." He said that Ganesha was now alive again, and she should calm down. She did not believe him, but Vishnu [who was well known for his honesty] came by and verified it. Then she became calm, and was no longer dark.

The informant added that "Durga is a good mother to people, and Kali is a bad mother to them, but really Durga and Kali are the same person—they just appear to be different."[86] Good mothers may become devouring, and then return to being good again.

We also see Durga turning into Kali in this myth about how Durga killed the demon Mahishasura. In this situation, she becomes angry at the gods for creating her to be a sex object for a demon. According to this story, by an informant of mixed Bengali and Oriya background, she became Kali out of the combination of anger and shame:

#### HOW DURGA BECAME KALI THROUGH SHAME AND ANGER

Durga was created by the gods to kill the evil demon Mahishasura. But she noticed that he was fast, and able to avoid her in fighting. However, when he fixated upon her genitals (*yoni*), he stopped moving. Only when he was staring at her *yoni* would he stay still, and was she able to kill him. So she did kill him while he was staring, but she was angry at the gods for creating such a situation; she was humiliated that she could only kill Mahishasura if he stared at her in this way.

After she killed him, this anger grew stronger and made her insane. She turned into Kali, and danced a dance of destruction, which would have destroyed the worlds. The gods needed to stop her, so they had Shiva lie down before her as she danced. His *linga* stretched out, and entered her as she danced over him. Her tongue stuck out in shame, and feeling Shiva's *linga* made her stop dancing. Thus she was stopped from destroying the world, and as she calmed down, she returned to being Durga.[87]

In each case, Durga is transformed into Kali through an excess of emotion, especially anger and shame. Kali is associated with wild and uncontrolled passion. In the first story, Durga grieves over her dysfunctional family, in which her husband kills her son. She becomes violent and cannibalistic because of her rage and sorrow over the death of the child. In this case, it is the gods who repair the damage and bring Ganesha back to life. Only with the return of her child does she calm down and return to her peaceful role. In the second story, it is Durga's pride that is wounded. She is angry at this trick of the gods, who created her to slay a demon but only if she acts like an immoral woman, allowing a man who is not her husband to stare at her with lust. She dances in anger, destroying the worlds, so the gods send Shiva to have sex with her and thus pacify her. When she feels him penetrating her, she calms down, becoming a submissive wife. Again, she is Kali in her active, destructive, and emotional role, and Durga in her submissive and dutiful role.

Kali's origin is also sometimes mentioned in Vaishnava literature. In the *Adbhuta Ramayana*, a version of the *Ramayana* story popular in West Bengal, Sita on her return to Ayodhya tells the assembled sages that there were really two Ravanas. The junior Ravana had ten heads, and he was killed by Rama at Lanka. However, the senior Ravana had a hundred heads, and ruled the island of Pushkara, where he played with the planets like balls. He was much more powerful than the junior Ravana, and Rama and the sages declared war on him and invaded his capital. Rama was unable to conquer him, and fainted from the exertion in his chariot. Sita was with him, and felt it necessary to rescue him, so she took on the form of Kali and fought the senior Ravana. She had female power-emanations (*matrikas*) come out from her body to help her in the battle, and they fought the hundred-headed Ravana and his armies. Sita (in the form of Kali) killed the hundred-headed Ravana and his armies, and returned in triumph to Ayodhya.[88]

When Sita turned into Kali and killed the hundred-headed Ravana, Rama saw her in the form of Kali: "Here is Kali with four arms and a fiery tongue, standing on Shiva Mahadeva who is a corpse. She is naked and drinking blood, with her eyes deep set in her sockets. She wears a garland of human skulls, and she is ready to swallow the universe."[89] This is a rather different image of the gentle and patient Sita than is usually seen. Brahmananda Giri's *Tararahasyam* also mentions Kali's destruction of Ravana. William Ward writes in 1815 of the story of the *Adhyatma Ramayana* that he had heard, which includes another Kali tale. In this description, Sita took the form of Kali to kill the thousand-headed Ravana, while Rama wept at his inability to conquer him. She fought Ravana for ten years, eventually killed him, drank his blood, threw his limbs around and danced madly with joy. The gods called upon Shiva to stop her, and he threw himself at her feet. When she encountered him there, she turned into Sita again, and went home with Rama and his brothers.

This Bengali *Ramayana* portrays Rama as ineffective, and shows how his wife (Sita in the form of Kali) is the true warrioress. This is quite different from the *Ramayana*s from northwestern India, the better-known *Ramayana*s of Tulsidas and Valmiki, in which Rama is the hero who saves the delicate Sita.

There has traditionally been rivalry between Shaktas and Vaishnavas in Bengal, with Vaishnavas calling Kali a cannibal and a black witch, and Shaktas calling Krishna immoral, lustful, and a liar. Sometimes, however, there are stories of the deities getting along with each other. In Shankarnath Roy's modern biographical series *Bharater Sadhaka*, the author describes a story about the Shakta tantrika Krishnananda Agambagish. One day as he was wandering through the garden next to his house, collecting offerings for his midnight worship of the goddess, he saw a bunch of ripe bananas in a nearby grove. He decided to use them to worship the goddess that night. But when he went back to the garden in the evening, the bananas were no longer there—his younger brother, a Vaishnava, had offered them to the Gopal (young Krishna) statue that he worshiped. Krishnananda was upset, and he did the offering without the bananas. He was still disturbed when he left the prayer room and walked into the courtyard. He saw a light in the small hut where his brother had worshiped Gopal, and he entered the hut. There he saw his Kali holding the young Gopal in her arms, feeding him with those bananas. This vision gave him a new insight; after this, he felt that Kali and Krishna were really the same.[90] Certainly, they were not enemies, as their devotees sometimes were.

This insight into their unity works both ways: sometimes Krishna is really Kali, and sometimes Kali is really Krishna. According to the *Mahabhagavata Purana*, Kali incarnated deliberately as Krishna. Shiva had told Kali that he had a desire—he wanted to make love with Kali in a male form, and himself in female form. This could best be done by his taking a human birth in female form, and her taking birth in a male form. Kali kept this in mind. When Brahma came to her and worshiped her as the goddess, and asked her to get rid of such demonic tyrants as Kamsa and Duryodhana (for they were disturbing the goddess Earth), she agreed to become incarnate on earth. She would be born as Krishna, and save earth from the demons. Shiva could then be incarnate as Radha, Rukmini, and other of Krishna's wives and consorts, and he could get his wish fulfilled.

Kali was born as Krishna, the son of Vasudeva and Devaki (who were Kashyapa and Aditi reborn), and Devaki knew of his true identity as Kali. To prove his/her power to his parents, Krishna overcame a variety of dangers (taking on his original form as Kali when he fought). He made love to Radha, who was Shiva in human form, and who was married to the impotent Ayana. He also made love to Radha and the *gopis* in the *rasa* dance. Krishna/Kali later helped the Pandavas win the *Mahabharata* war and destroy the Kauravas, for the Pandavas in this version of the story were worshipers of the goddess.[91]

We also see Krishna turning into Kali. According to a story narrated by a village singer-artist or *patua*, Krishna turned into Kali in order to save Radha's reputation.[92] Thus, from this Vaishnava perspective, Kali is a form of Krishna, and he takes on her form for the sake of drama and variety.

According to some practitioners, Kali's major emotion or *bhava* is anger, and we see folk elements where she must be continuously appeased by ascetic behavior:

> When Durga had to kill the demon, she became transformed into Kali. She was very angry, and her rage would have destroyed the world. People wished to pacify her, to avoid destruction, so they decided to torture themselves. This would make her feel better. They put bamboo splints through their skins, and swung by hooks in their backs, and they rolled around temples and sacred places many times. The goddess was calmed by this, and her anger left. People remember this, and still do these practices today.[93]

Although we might view this as the "misery loves company" perspective, informants generally say that a mother becomes worried by the pain of her children, and becomes benevolent and forgiving toward them.

The goddess helps her own children, showing up in times of danger and despair. One informant told me the story of Kankalidevi, a local form of Kali who showed up in the courtroom to save her devotee:

> Ramdasa Chaudhuri was a worshiper of Kankali Ma, from a small village in Birbhum. He was said to be a descendant of the poet Chandidas. He was a devotee of Kankalidevi from childhood, and eventually he became her priest at Kankalitala (a *sakta pitha*, or site sacred to the goddess), having been given the role by the previous priest, Jogindranath Chaudhuri. However, a landowner who lived in a nearby village one day appointed a different priest, who disrupted the worship of Ramdasa. When Ramdasa asked the landowner why

he had done this, the landowner told him that he owned all the land in the area, and would appoint whom he chose. He forbade Ramdasa from worshiping at the temple. When he could not drive out Ramdasa, the case went to court.

The landowner had many witnesses to testify for him, but Ramdasa had none. However, when the lawyer asked Ramdasa for witnesses, he put a red hibiscus (jaba) flower (sacred to Kali) on the witness chair, and said that it would tell what the goddess desired. The people in the courtroom laughed, and the lawyer said that a flower could not act as a witness, this was madness. At that moment, a beautiful girl appeared beside Ramdasa, and said in a high voice, "I am a witness for Ramdasa, and he is the right priest for Kankali Ma." Then she disappeared. The observers were amazed, and the court was adjourned.

That night, the judge had a dream in which Kankali Ma insisted that he support Ramdasa in this case. The judge followed the dream's command, and the court declared Ramdasa to be the offical priest of Ma Kankali's temple.[94]

## *Kali in Tantra and Bhakti*

There are many visualizations or *dhyanas* of Kali, which describe different aspects for the devotee to contemplate. According to one visualization in the tantric encyclopedia *Tantrasara*, the four-armed Kali is smiling and full of blood, with three red eyes, and she stands on Shiva's heart. He is lying like a corpse, yet he is involved with her in reverse (*viparita*) intercourse (in which the woman squats over the man).[95] In another visualization in the *Tantrasara*, Kali wears a sacred thread that is a snake, and is drunk on alcohol, standing within a cremation fire and having reverse sex with Shiva.[96] In other descriptions she is soaked with a shower of nectar, wearing matted hair, and making a loud roaring noise. Sometimes she stands on an ordinary corpse, and sometimes she stands on Shiva as a corpse. In some places in Navadvipa there are statues of Shavashiva (Shiva as a corpse), in which there are two forms of Shiva: Mahakala is lying flat on his back on top of Shiva, who is a corpse, and Mahakala is having reverse intercouse with Kali.[97] At Podatala in Navadvipa is a statue of Kali seated on Shiva's chest, in which she is addressed as Bhavatarini (the savior from danger).[98]

Like Krishna in the *Bhagavad Gita*, and reminiscent of Purusha in the *Purusha Sukta* of the Rig Veda (10.90.1), Kali may also reveal her universal form (*virat rupa* or *vishvarupa*). In the *Kurma Purana*, Kali/Parvati revealed her universal form to her father Himalaya. As her father was frightened, she assumed her original form, with the fragrance and complexion of a blue lotus.[99] In the Chandi, she expanded her form to frighten the demon Mahishasura:

38. Then he saw the Devi pervading the three worlds with her lustre.
39. Making the earth bend with her footstep, scraping the sky with her diadem, shaking the nether worlds with the twang of her bowstring, and standing there pervading all the quarters around with her thousand arms.[100]

In some puranas, the goddess is described in a frightening and destructive manner. According to the *Skanda Purana*, Shiva told Devi to destroy the world at the time of universal destruction.[101] She hesitated to do this because of her feminine compassion, and Shiva yelled at her to do it, with a great roar. She took the form of Mahakali, expanding like thunder and lightning. She became full of lightning, her eyes were like burning pits of fire, and she was difficult to see. Her giant figure covered the three worlds, she roared and breathed fire and laughed, wearing a tiger skin and a snake for a sacred thread. In this form she destroyed the universe. In the *Devi Gita*, the goddess is huge, with a thousand heads, a thousand eyes, and a thousand pairs of feet.[102] In the *Devi Bhagavata Purana*, as the gods looked at the Devi, she appeared to have one thousand eyes, one thousand hands, and one thousand feet.[103]

While sitting at the burning ground, the Shakta sage Krishnananda Agambagisha had a vision of the goddess Kali. She told him that Shakta tantra in Bengal flowed like an underground river, but now it was becoming polluted, and he needed to cleanse it. He was to worship and popularize a new form in which to worship her. When he asked which form he was to worship, she told him that it would be the image of the first woman that he saw the next morning.

When he awoke at dawn the next morning and walked toward the Ganges, he saw a woman with dark skin at the entrance of her hut. One foot was on the step of her hut, the other was on the ground. Her right palm was full of cowdung, and she held her hand to make sure that the cowdung did not fall—a position that had the fingers in the mudra of fearlessness. Her left hand applied a coat of wet mud on to the wall. Her dark hair hung long, and she wore a short sari. When she saw Krishnananda standing in front of her, she stuck her tongue out in embarrassment and turned away.[104] This became the popular image of Kali, with an image of Shiva lying under her feet added later on. It may be noted that the image described (especially the short skirt and dark skin) would better fit a tribal woman than a high-caste Hindu woman.

The meaning of Shiva lying at Kali's feet has been much debated. The popular view is that Kali is a good wife who touched Shiva with her foot accidentally, a violation of respect and purity, and is embarrassed at this breach of etiquette (showing surprising delicacy for a woman who dances naked in battlefields and drinks blood in burning grounds). Upendrakumar Das says that Shiva fell at the goddess's feet in wonder when he saw her create and destroy the world. And at the end of time, Kali dances upon the corpse of the world and the power of time, thus she dances upon Shiva, who represents the corpse of the world.[105]

Kali is an important goddess for Shakta tantrikas. Many tantrikas are also emotional Shakta devotees, and their practice mixes bhakti and tantra. One approach to tantric Shakta bhakti is described in Shivachandra Vidyarnava Bhattacharya's *Tantra-tattva* (translated into English as *Principles of Tantra*), in which knowledge of the goddess as an abstract quality (whether as Kali or Durga) is insufficient to gain happiness and freedom from fear. Only her vision will suffice:

> I am a Jīva [soul] scorched by the fire of the three forms of sorrow [from self, material, and supernatural worlds]. My mind and life are constantly on the rack of the terrible troubles of Samsāra. Suffering miserably under the influence of the poisonous exhalations of the world, I cry day and night, "Save!" At such a time the fact of Her being everywhere does not remove my burning pains. . . . I am completely surrounded by the fearful huge fire of Samsāra, and have no way [to] escape. Scorched on all sides by the burning heat of this circle of fire, I in despair, throw up my arms, and with heart-rending and deeply plaintive voice cry: "O Mother of the world! where art Thou? I die—I die! O merciful Mother save me! Come, O Mother! Come, O Mother! Come, O Mother, Mother of mine!" Instantly, while these words are yet in my mouth, the Mother, the charmer of the heart of Bhairava, grieved on learning of Her son's sorrow, forsakes Her golden throne on Mount Kailāsa, and, without even staying to arrange Her dress, hastens to and stands before me, extending Her ten fear-dispelling arms in all ten directions, and crying "Fear not! fear not!" Then only will my sins, my diseases, my griefs, my troubles and my sins be for ever at an end. My distress will not be relieved without the aid of this merciful and gross manifestation, even though I should possess the knowledge of Her subtle existence as the all-pervading Devī. Digambara, has, therefore, said: "The Mother of the Universe pervades the Universe, but still, when I am overwhelmed with sorrow, I say: "Come O Brahmamayī, save me!"[106]

In the Kali-kula lineage of Bengali classical Shakta tantra, Kali gives liberation to her devotees, and is the origin of all things. In the *Mahanirvana Tantra*, a questionable yet influential text,[107] Shiva calls her the source of the world, the origin of all form, formless yet with form, the Supreme Adya Kali who existed as darkness before the beginning of things.[108] She is called Adya or primordial Kali because she originates all things and in the end devours them. She is the creator, preserver, and destroyer of the universe, and the source of the power of the gods. Although the tantra includes chants that seek to bring Kali under the tantrika's control (4.82), most hymns are devotional in nature. The tantrika seeks refuge or asks for Kali's mercy, adoring Adya Kali whose beautiful face is radiant, and offering red hibiscus flowers with great devotion, saying, "O Adya Kali, who abides in the innermost soul of all, you who are the innermost light, O Mother! Accept this *japa* of my heart. I bow to you."[109]

In chapter 7 of the *Mahanirvana Tantra*, the Adya-Kali-Svarupa prayer calls upon the goddess as terrifying and beneficent, devourer of Shiva, ocean of the nectar of compassion, of infinite mercy, liberator from desire who grants all desires, the joyous one who gives blessings and is seated on a lotus.[110] Chanting this hymn leads to union with *brahman*, for one of Kali's tantric names is Kaivalyadayini, giver of liberation.

It is Kali who saves, whether by her compassion to bhaktas or by her giving liberation to yogis and tantrikas. We see this liberating role of Kali in the life of Ramakrishna Paramahamsa, where the goddess appeared to him in his famous vision of *brahman* as an ocean of consciousness. It is likely that Ramakrishna's understanding of Kali was strongly influenced by the Bengali Kalikula tradition.

While the goddess Kali traditionally threatens order and stability, she also represents a transcendent order, beyond *dharma* and the expectations of an earthly life. In the texts she is ugly, with black and emaciated body, matted hair, and snakes, but in her statues and posters she is young and beautiful, with flirtatious eyes, large breasts, a narrow waist, and a big smile. She may be deep blue, sky blue, or even white (with delicate pink hands and feet)—all are beneficent and auspicious forms of the goddess. Informants say that this beautiful form is her real and inner form, and the ugly image is only to frighten the unworthy and the evil. If you are her enemy or do not respect her, the black Kali of the burning ground will drink your blood (much like the angry folk goddesses). But if you are devoted, she is the beautiful white Kali, whose graceful form will come to you at the time of your death, and she will smile lovingly as she takes you to Kailash (Shiva's heaven) or Manidvipa (the Island of Jewels) to dwell on her lap forever. Kali's heaven is a beautiful place.

As a devotional goddess, Kali is Mother of the Universe, and the beloved parent of Shakta poets like Ramprasad Sen. She is described with love, and her dark side is justified by the presence of death in nature—Kali represents what is true, not what people would like to see. She is described as loving, sweet, and compassionate in her poetry—but she is also capable of saving her devotees from their own karma, sweeping them out of the ghostly worlds between incarnations and taking them to her paradise.

According to the *Mahabhagavata Purana*, Kali's heaven of Kalisthan is surrounded on all sides by an ocean of sweet water. It is full of precious jewels, and surrounded by walls with four gates in the four directions. In the middle is a throne placed upon lions, full of gold and jewels. The goddess sits on it, served by sixty-four yoginis, and she makes love with Sadashiva. Toward the north is a forest full of flowers and singing birds, and in the east is a lake full of golden lotuses and other flowers.[111] According to the *Devi Bhagavata Purana*, Kali's heaven is only open to women. During earthly worship, the devotee should give offerings to brahmins, young girls and boys, the public, and the poor, seeing all of them as forms of the goddess. When the worshiper dies, and he goes to Kali's heaven of Manidvipa, he must take on the form of a woman, to echo the form of the goddess.[112] The book mentions a visit to the goddess's paradise by Brahma, Vishnu, and Shiva, all of whom were turned into women. They spent a hundred years standing in female form and dress, admiring the goddess dressed in red and her throne which was brighter than a million suns, and they were accepted by the goddess's attendants as companions (*sakhis*). They were so happy in this form that Shiva begged the goddess not to give them their masculine forms again, for they wished only to serve the goddess forever.[113] They worshiped the goddess in her heaven, and received many revelations from her.

A popular form of Kali worshiped in Calcutta is Adya Shakti Kali, or Kali as primordial power. Some writers believe that she is a joint deity, mingling together several goddess images. Sudhakar Chattopadhyaya writes of the mixture of Uma, Kanya-Kumari/Katyayani, Vindhyadevi, and Ishtar: "Thus in the Adyasakti of the Hindus we find an admixture or merging of a Himalayan, a Dravidian, a Vindhyan and a Mediterranean deity, all coalesced together into one. It is also probable that a Proto-Mongoloid Mother goddess of the Kirata tribe also merged into the Mother cult."[114]

We also see Bengali myths and stories about Adya Shakti. A medieval myth about Adya Shakti and her relation to Dharma Thakur or Niranjan was cited by Asutosh Bhattacharya. In this story, she is not a primordial goddess but rather the daughter of Dharma Niranjan (who is sometimes equated with the Buddha). She is an unhappy goddess who attempts suicide but fails and ends up pregnant instead. This has the positive result of having her give birth to the Hindu gods:

> The Lord (known as Nirañjan or Dharma, obviously meaning here the Sun) descended on the great void and thought of creating the universe. First of all, the Lord created air out of the great void. He seated himself on the bubbles, but they failed to bear His weight and were broken to pieces. Then again the Great Lord wandered through the great void. . . . In the course of time the Lord created Ādyā Śakti (the Prime Energy) out of the perspiration of His body. He accepted Ādyā Śakti as his daughter. Leaving her alone, the Lord with his mount went away for penance. . . . The Lord returned but grew anxious on finding his daughter grown up and of marriageable age. But where to get a bridegroom for her? He asked Adya to wait for some more time and started again for Ballukā [a river]. He left

> nectar in one vessel and poison in another. Ādyā asked, "What should I do with them?" The Lord said, "Do as you like with them."
>
> The Lord on his mount returned to the bank of Ballukā. Time passed but He did not return to his daughter. Ādyā, finding her youth unbearable, drank the quantity of poison left by the Lord for her with an intent to commit suicide. She did not die, but became pregnant instead. In [the] course of time she gave birth to Brahmā, Viṣṇu and Śiva. They were all born blind. They went to the shore of the sea Kāraṇa and devoted themselves to meditation. The Lord wanted to test their sincerity of devotion, and came floating before each of them in the form of a corpse. Brahmā and Vṣṇu turned their faces against the stinking corpse. But Śiva took it out of the water and began to dance, carrying it on his shoulder.
>
> The Lord was pleased with him and rewarded him with eyesight. He also rewarded him with an additional eye. At the request of Śiva, Brahmā and Viṣṇu also got eyesight by the grace of the Great Lord. Now all of them returned to Ādyā. The Lord asked Brahmā to created the Universe, Viṣṇu to preserve it and Siva to destroy it whenever he felt it necessary. Now the Lord turned to Ādyā and asked her to devote herself to [the] creation of mankind. He said to her, "Thou shalt take rebirth and in every rebirth Mahésa [Śiva] shall marry thee. By him thou shalt beget children in every new birth." Thus through the union of Śiva and Ādyā the earth became populated.[115]

According to the *Shunya Purana* of Ramai Pandit, Adya drank the seed of Dharma instead of poison, and that is why she became pregnant. As the story goes in that text, Adya (here also called Durga and Jaya) generated the god Kamadeva, personification of lust. He went over to where Dharma was meditating and filled him with lust, and Dharma left his seed on a dish and put it into Adya's temple. Adya mistook it for poison, and swallowed it. She promptly become pregnant, and gave birth to triplets in three different ways: Brahma came out by piercing the crown of her head, Vishnu came out through her navel, and Shiva was born in the natural way.[116] She later saw her son Shiva begging for alms and walking around naked, and suggested that he become a farmer, so that he could grow all the necessary bananas and crops for the worship of Dharma.[117] Both versions imply incestuous relationship: here Adya drank her father's sperm and became pregnant by him, and in the previous story she was to marry her son Shiva and populate the earth.

Sometimes Adya is understood as a Buddhist deity, who was only later converted to Hinduism. The medieval *Shunya Purana* emphasized her Hindu identity, equating her with Durga and Kali. It called Adya by the Hindu name of Durga, and described her as decorated with red hibiscus (jaba) flowers, and as having devotees sacrificing goats before her (both of these are part of Bengali traditional worship of Kali). Sarkar finds the origin of this conversion in her marriage to the god Shiva, and its results in the yearly Gajan and Gambhira festivals:

> Hence it is clear that in the time of Râmâi the worship of the Buddhist deities was converted practically into that of the Hindu Shiva and Durgâ. This was done in the following way. At first in Dharma's Gâjan, Âdyâ sat as the presiding deity, Shiva and the other gods attending as spectators only. Then, when the prediction of Râmâi to the effect that "Mahesha will marry her (Âdyâ) in the next birth" came to be true, Shiva received the worship of the Gâjan votaries, with Âdyâ as wife on his left side. Here must be sought the beginnings of the modern [rituals of] Gâjan of Dharma and the Gambhîrâ of Âdyâ, the latter among the Brâhmaṇic Hindus and the former among the Hinduized Buddhists.[118]

In the *Dharma-puja-paddhati* attributed to Ramai Pandit, the marriage of the Buddhist figure Dharma Niranjan to Adya Chandika, the daughter of Adi Buddha, has been transformed into a marriage of Shiva and Adya during the Gajan festival. During the festivities, Adya sits on the left side of Shiva, and Dharma Niranjana has been invited as a guest. The marriage was celebrated in Hindu style:

> The women made Âdyâ put on bracelets of conch-shells and a new piece of cloth. After the ladies have thus welcomed the couple and observed the traditional ceremonies not enjoined in the Shâstras but somethow or other accepted as inviolable by them (and known as *strî-achâra*, lit. female custom), the Brâhmaṇas commenced reciting the Vedas. . . .
>
> Seating Maheshwara on a gold seat (called *pâta* and nicely decorated for the purpose), the ladies joined together in taking round Âdyâ. (Then) a hundred ladies seated Shakti on a (similar) seat and with words of benediction on their lips, took her seven times round Maheshwara, seated or standing under a gold canopy.[119]

Adya Shakti is also present in some tantras, especially the *Mahanirvana Tantra*. In her tantric identity, she is no longer an unhappy girl—she is the wife of Shiva, Adya Shakti Kali, and equal to him. There are many meditations that focus specifically upon her. In chapter 4, Shiva speaks of her formless nature:

> 32. Because you devour Kāla, you are Kālī, the original form of all things, and because you are the origin of and devour all things, you are called [the] Ādyā Kālī.

> 33. Resuming after Dissolution your own form, dark and formless, you alone remain as One, ineffable and inconceivable.
> 34. Yet having a form, you are formless; though yourself without beginning [you are] multiform by the power of Māyā, you are the beginning of all, Creatress, Protectress, and Destructress that you are.[120]

There are hymns of praise to offer the goddess, and in typical tantric fashion, the *Mahanirvana Tantra* emphasizes the benefits of following its rituals to Adya Shakti Kali:

> 37. He who, on a new moon night, when it falls on Tuesday, worships the great Ādyā Kālī, Mistress of the three worlds, with the five Ma-kāras, and repeats her hundred names;
> 38. He becomes suffused with the presence of the Devī, and for him there remains nothing in the three worlds which is beyond his powers.
> 39. He becomes in learning like Brihaspati himself, in wealth like Kuvera. His profundity is that of the ocean, and his strength that of the wind.
> 40. He shines with the blinding brilliance of the Sun, yet pleases with the soft glamour of the Moon. In beauty he becomes like the God of Love [Kama], and reaches the hearts of women.
> 41. He comes forth as [a] conqueror everywhere by the grace of this hymn of praise. Singing this hymn, he attains all his desires.
> 42. All these desires he shall attain by the grace of the gracious Ādyā, whether in battle, in seeking the favour of Kings, in waters, or in disputes, and when his life be in danger. . . .
> 46. O Devi! He who with firm devotion meditates upon the Paramā Māyā—image of the most excellent Kālī—is without a doubt relieved of all dangers.[121]

According to modern worshipers of Adya Shakti Kali, interviewed in Calcutta, Bolpur, and Suri, she is a *yuga devi*, a goddess of the apocalypse. Historically, there have been four great yuga goddesses, one for each of the great spans of time or yugas that make up the past of the universe. During the golden age or Satya yuga, the presiding goddess of the age was Adya Sundari. During the silver age or Tretya yuga, the presiding goddess was Adya Bhubaneshvari. During the copper age or Dvapara yuga, the goddess was called Adya Tarini. As one of her devotees explained:

> We are now in the Kali yuga, the age of iron that represents the end of the universe and the close of time. Our presiding goddess is Adya Shakti Kali, who revealed herself late in the yuga to preside over the great disasters of the end-times. The evidence that the end of time is

> close is in the destruction of social order in India: the brahmins work in shoe stores and handle leather, temple priests eat chicken and goats, children no longer obey the rules of the caste system (*varnadharma*) and marry out of caste and subcaste, the political leaders are corrupt, girls wear blue jeans and cosmetics, the Communists forbid the teaching of religion and persecute the sadhus, and so on.[122]

Kali is worshiped by many Shaktas to help them in the afterlife—to bring them to her heaven, or to give a good rebirth. However, not all devotees believe that Kali will save the person at the moment of death. As one tantrika interviewed said, Kali is concerned with the number of her own devotees (it is a rivalry that she has with Krishna): "Kali gives us everything in this world—she is the air I breathe, the food I eat. But I wouldn't trust her in the afterlife. If I went to her heaven, she would just throw me back to earth again, so she could get more worshipers. She wouldn't get me liberated—that I must do on my own."[123] Yet for most devotees, one must have faith, even in the face of existential uncertainty. As R. K. Dasgupta writes, "For the Shakta Kali is clothed in death and wears a garland of skulls, for thus alone can she promise immortality. She is dreadfully dark, for one must face darkness to reach the light behind. To love a loving mother is inferior devotion. The Shakta loves his cruel Mother, capricious Mother, for he must bear with her unkindnesses as but an earnest of some delayed benificence. And the love remains even if that benificence never comes."[124]

Kali worship shows the three strands of Shaktism: she is the tribal Kali bonga or Kali Mai, as well as the folk Kali Budi or Bankali; she is the tantric Adya Kali and the four-armed Kali of the *Tantrasara;* and for the devotee she is the protective and loving Kali who is also the Mother of the Universe. Rather than the black burning-ground Kali, she is the light blue or white auspicious Kali, looking with happiness at her devotees. Her various aspects are celebrated at her new-moon puja festival.

## Kali Puja and the Night of Magic

Coming several weeks after the end of Durga Puja, on the night of the new moon, Kali Puja has much in common with Durga's holiday. Both have the *pandals* (temporary shrines) on the street corners of every neighborhood, and the statues of the goddess that are understood by devotees to be alive after ritual invocations. Both have music and noise and crowds at night, following the paths lit up by neon and flickering incandescent lights through the smoky air. Both have richly dressed and decorated statues of the goddess, and people go "*murti*-hopping" from one pandal to another to absorb the moods (*rasas*) and view the fashions of the different images. Some people comment in an animated way on the goddess's form, clothing, and jewelry, others stand in silent contemplation, while children run and play hide-and-seek behind the visitors. As with Durga Puja, food is often placed beneath the raised altar/stage which holds the statues, so that it may be blessed.

Kali Puja night is a time for magic shows and theater, for very loud fireworks and celebrations, but also for animal sacrifice to the goddess and contemplation of her importance in this world and in the universe. For most devotees, she is not merely Shiva's wife but rather the origin of the universe, and her night reminds devotees of the fragility of their lives and their dependence upon a goddess who is alternately ruthless and compassionate. Many informants emphasized how careful one must be in worshiping Kali, for an error in worship could bring down her wrath. As she is a goddess of both creation and destruction, her anger could mean anything from the loss of a job to a death in the family.

Her images are varied in the different street-corner shrines. Some shrines are the size of small camping tents, made of rattan or bamboo, with small Kalis like voluptuous dolls or withered old women, with white ornaments made of *solapith* and bright crepe-paper streamers. Large shrines have beautiful Kalis standing on white Shivas, dressed in silk or gold lamé or imitation tiger skins. I did not see in 1993 the politicized style from 1983, when Kali and Shiva represented different cultural values; I vividly remember a tribal-style Kali wearing animal skins and a fierce expression stepping on a blond Shiva dressed in a three-piece Western business suit, holding a briefcase. However, there were some Kalis at the 1993 Kali Puja with dark skin, large noses, and kinky hair, politically correct Kalis looking like the Adivasis or tribals of West Bengal rather than Aryan invaders or Western imperialists.[125] Some Kalis were bright blue, voluptuous, and smiling happily, rather mature at an ideal sixteen years old. On a street corner in a winding urban street was a beautiful white Kali with red palms and splashes of vermilion, with a white Shiva beneath her. Her (male?) attendants had both breasts and curled moustaches this was auspicious Kali, who could bring the devoted to heaven.[126] In the larger and more well-funded community *pandals* were giant statues, fifteen feet high or more, with piles of offerings all around.

Kali Puja is also a time for spontaneous expression, especially for gangs of teenaged boys with fireworks. I was warned over and over by friends, informants, and total strangers not to be out on Kali Puja night. However, the crowds were at the temples and *pandals*, and the streets were largely deserted. I saw two different Kali Puja rituals in private homes (considered "safe" by my informants), both of which were brahmanical in style and quite devotional. The earlier ritual, a ritual dressing of Kali in her form as Adya Shakti Kali, was performed in the house of a male Kali devotee. Most of the second floor of the house was a worship room, with a statue of Kali wearing a silk sari and full of expensive jewelry. The other ritual was on the other side of town, performed from late night to early morning. It was directed by an elderly woman who had informally become a renunciant, and lived part-time in the joint family home. At other times, she performed pilgrimages to various shrines, temples, and sacred mountains. She was greatly respected by the family members, and considered herself a devotee of Kali and of Ramakrishna Paramahamsa. The family had hired a brahmin priest to perform the rituals, but he kept making mistakes and she kept correcting him. He took the criticism well, and adapted to her suggestions. He was the priest, but she was clearly in control.

In earlier days, Kali Puja (like Durga Puja) seems to have been a wilder holiday. However, whereas Durga Puja was celebrated with dancing girls and devotees dancing in mud and blood, Kali Puja seems to have been more of an ascetic's holiday, with mortification of the flesh as a way of showing devotion or gaining folk or tantric boons. Writing in 1907, John Campbell Oman describes a ritual of hook-swinging to Kali. This ritual was more frequently seen in older Bengal (it is now illegal) as a form of worship of Kali's consort Shiva:

> In the case I saw, the man who undertook to be swung in honor of Kali, had the muscles of his back terribly stretched by the hooks. . . . As the man was whirled aloft high above the heads of the excited onlookers, he threw down amongst them small pieces of cocoa-nut and sweetmeats resembling comfits, while the drums made a deafening noise, and the multitude shouted, "Victory to Mother Kali." Votaries, less bold than he, passed skewers or canes through the muscles of their sides and hands, and even through their tongues, all for Kali, to whom no offering could be made more acceptable than blood, and in whose honor they danced about in wild enthusiasm.[127]

A nineteenth-century observer describes the austerities undergone by devotees of Kali:

> Towards the wall there were stationed several blacksmiths, with sharp instruments in their hands. Those of a particular group, that carried the rods, canes, and other implements, now came forward. One would stretch out his side, and, getting it instantly pierced through, in would pass one of his rods or canes. Another would hold out his arm, and, getting it perforated, in would pass one of his iron spits or tubes. A third would protrude his tongue, and getting it, too, bored through, in would pass one of his cords or serpents. And thus, all of a group that desired it had themselves variously transpierced or perforated. When these had finished, another group was waiting in readiness to undergo the cruel operation; and so another and another, apparently without end. . . . And those who were

> transpierced began dancing in the most frantic manner,—pulling backwards and forwards, through their wounded members, the rods and the canes, the spits and the tubes, the cords and the writhing serpents, till their bodies seemed streaming with their own blood! All this was carried on *simultaneously;* and that, too, within a briefer period of time than has now been occupied in the feeble and inadequate attempt to describe it! Again and again would the loud shouts ascend from the thousands of applauding spectators—shouts of "Victory to Kali! Victory to the great Kali!"[128]

Often the only way that these people could stand the pain was to be in a state of possession, usually by Kali or Shiva. Such possession may be performed in the folk tradition for worldly favors or to repay a deity's grace, and in the tantric tradition to gain supernatural powers or yogic detachment. It also served as anesthesia in these rituals, to guarantee detachment from pain.

Kali Puja or Shyama Puja takes place on the same night as the all-India holiday of Divali or Dipavali, the festival of lights. An early reason for the use of lamps on Divali night is to help the ancestors see where they are going when they visit from the lands of the underworld. This is why traditional Indian houses are cleaned and the lamps are lit—to welcome the ancestors back. Often family members will stay up all night to receive them.[129] Divali is also associated with fertility rituals and offerings to snakes (who are associated with the ancestors), and with Rama's victory over Ravana, and Krishna's victory over Narakasura.

In Gujarat it is the Kalaratri (the black or witches' night), when careful people avoid the evil spirits of those who have died violent deaths and who walk the streets on that night. More motivated people greet the ghosts by giving cake offerings at crossroads, or make a circle guarded with iron and water, and use mantras to gain control of a spirit who will act as a servant for the coming year.[130] Low-caste Chamars believe that both male and female witches prowl, riding on tigers and alligators, endangering the community. In some areas of India there are sham fights between good and evil, often using lighted fireworks, and sometimes ending in riots.[131]

Modern *pandals* for both Durga and Kali Pujas are built by puja committees and local groups (*sanghas*) who gather money in each neighborhood for the local *pandal.* Extortion apparently is involved in some neighborhoods, with life and limb threatened by the local gangs unless the householders give large donations. (Of course, there is a theological justification: the gangs would only be expressing the goddess's justifiable indignation at their unwillingness to support her statue and *pandal.* After all, winning a prize for best *pandal* glorifies both the goddess and the neighborhood.) Some *pandals* are sponsored by criminals (*goondas*) who control extortion, prostitution, illegal liquor sales ("hooch"), and organize riots to deliberately create civil unrest. The problems of the festivals are perhaps best described by an editorial in the Calcutta *Statesman* newspaper:

> If people in this part of the country look forward to Durga puja, followed by Kali puja and Diwali, they also dread certain unsavoury practices which have over the years come to be associated with the festive season. First and foremost is the nuisance of the strong arm tactics adopted by many organizers of community pujas when collecting subscriptions. Something that ought to be a voluntary and pleasant gesture by an ordinary citizen is made to degenerate into a reluctant act prompted by intimidation, not ruling out threats of physical violence. The Calcutta Police as well as the police force in the districts of West Bengal have in previous years, gone through the motions of discouraging the use of force by puja committees, but with neither sincerity nor anything resembling determination. In fact, the suspicion that policemen were rewarded for "cooperating" with anti-social elements was not always unfounded. The result was predictable—rather than seek police help, ordinary people fought back their anger and just paid up the amount demanded, whether they could afford to do so or not. But the picture was refreshingly different during the recent Durga puja. Complaints about forcible collection were taken seriously and in many cases remedial measures, often calling for firmness, taken. The grateful citizen breathed a sigh of relief, sending up a hopeful prayer that there would be a repeat, commendable performance come Diwali.[132]

Apparently the payment of protection money has grown over the past few decades; local teenagers go from house to house, demanding money for the neighborhood statue, lighting, and *pandal* construction. If sufficient donations are not forthcoming, trouble is promised. Sometimes the damage is passive—they will convince the landlords or local politicians not to help the family if there is trouble. Sometimes the damage is more active, and they will threaten to wreck the house or harm its inhabitants. Some informants say that the changes occurred with the rise of the Naxalites (communist revolutionaries who were bombing buildings and assassinating political enemies in the 1960s and 1970s) in West Bengal, and some say it began before that, with the loss of respect for Hindu traditions and deities that resulted from colonialism and commercialism in the nineteenth century.

According to an article by Tanmay Chatterjee, violence and extortion have been a part of Kali Puja since the times when dacoits (thieves) gained power. It is also a time of theft, gambling, and drunken brawls; as a deputy commissioner of the Calcutta police said, "Community Kali pujas are basically by the goondas (criminals), of the goondas, and for the goondas." Muslim gang leaders, too, reportedly donate generous amounts for Kali Puja subscriptions.[133]

The goddess herself is not understood to be in favor of crime, but she is morally neutral and as such will not punish criminals who are her devotees. The time of Kali Puja marks the beginning of the cold season, when the mud and slush of the rainy season are gone and the roads are open again. This is also the time that the predatory gangs have traditionally begun their annual raids. The best known of these was the Thugee sect, a Hindu/Muslim criminal organization that used the worship of Kali as an organizing principle to strengthen the cohesion of their group and a corrupt theology to justify their business of robbery and murder. Members of the two religions got along so well that Thugee has sometimes been called by historians the best historical example of Hindu/Muslim unity.

The Puja celebrations of Durga and Kali are the largest Shakta festivals of urban West Bengal. They reflect the importance of the Bengali bhakti or devotional tradition, but incorporate historical change: Durga in a British bonnet, Durga in fatigues with a machine gun, Durga with her finger on the nuclear trigger. Then there is Kali in a tiger skin and Shiva in a grey flannel suit. They are both religious art and social commentary. They have long been under attack by the Communist authorities, who write newspaper editorials arguing that the pujas are wastes of money and time. Nevertheless, Shakta devotees often say that even if they have only one handful of rice remaining, they will offer it to the goddess.

## The Great Wisdom Goddesses: The Ten Mahavidyas

Some important goddesses of both tantra and bhakti in West Bengal are the ten Mahavidyas, or wisdom goddesses, who are usually understood to be forms of the goddess Kali. These goddesses create a sense of the depth and richness of Kali's roles in the Shakta tradition. They are specialized for boons in certain areas, and each has her own priests who have one Mahavidya form as personal deity (*ishtadevi*). I first saw these goddesses vividly in a large shrine in Calcutta set up for Kali Puja.

This Kali Puja shrine (*pandal*) was sponsored by the South Calcutta Amara Sabar Club, and had the ten Mahavidya forms of Kali in the form of large statues standing on a stage about thirty feet wide. Each of the ten statues was made with great care, and draped with marigold garlands and necklaces of red hibiscus (*jaba*) flowers. The central figure was Shyama Kali, much larger than the other figures (about fifteen feet tall). She was dark and smiling, wore a crown, and stood on a white Shiva who had brown matted hair and a rising cobra. A jackal stood next to her on its hind legs, drinking the blood dripping from her necklace of severed heads. Two of her hands blessed, one held a sword decorated with eyes and skulls, another held a severed head with Shaivite markings in red. Next to her was Tara Ma, who stood over a dead white Shiva wearing rudraksha beads. He wore a tiger skin and held a trident. Tara had dark blue skin and a necklace of white skulls, and four arms. Her long, kinky brown hair hung down in matted strands of *jata*, and the bun at the top of her head was fastened with skulls and rudraksha beads. She looked like a tribal goddess, and wore only a tigerskin loincloth. Her breasts were covered by her matted hair. In either direction were statues of the other Mahavidya goddesses.

Crowds visited these statues and bowed before them, giving offerings that were placed beneath the raised stage. There were multicolored designs painted in rice paste (*alpana*) before the stage, and the remains of incense and other ritual objects. These were tantric goddesses, but everybody could visit them and ask for blessings.

The ten Mahavidyas are forms of the goddess Shakti, Kali, or Sati, and were said in the puranas to have originated at the time of Daksha's great mythical sacrifice. According to the *Brihaddharma Purana* (Madhya 6.12), Sati wished to go to Daksha's sacrifice, and Shiva did not want her to go. Fire flashed from her third eye, and she was transformed into Kali (Shyama). When he saw this, Shiva was terrified, and he tried to escape. However, all of the ten directions were blocked by the emanated forms of Sati. These were the ten Mahavidyas.[134] Sati's transformation into Kali is described vividly in the *Brihaddharma Purana*: "As Shiva stared at Sati, she gave up her golden complexion, and her skin turned as dark as night, as dark as collyrium. Her whole body trembled. In a state of intense passion, the high-breasted Sati ignored Shiva. She became the lotus-eyed Shyama [Kali], naked, with wild hair and four arms. She stood full of courage, her body shaking like an earthquake."[135]

A longer description comes from the *Mahabhagavata Purana*. According to this text, Daksha's daughter Sati was not invited to her father's sacrifice, and wanted to go anyway, Shiva told her it would cause great trouble and he refused to allow her to go. To emphasize her desire to go, she split into ten forms, and frightened him into agreeing that she should go. However, Shiva was right—it did cause great trouble, including Sati's suicide. As Bhattacharya tells the story:

> Pondering thus in Her mind for a moment, the daughter of Dakṣa opened Her three fearful eyes, and overpowered Śaṅkara with illusion. Śambhu (Shiva) stood still at the sight of the Devī, with Her lips parted in anger and eyes shining like destructive fire. On being thus looked at by the frightened Maheśvara, the Devī suddenly displayed the terrible teeth in Her terrible mouth and laughed aloud. On hearing that frightful sound of laughter, Mahādeva was paralyzed with fright. Opening His three eyes with great effort He saw (but once) the world-terrifying aspect of Jagadambā. When He looked upon Her, Her body immediately lost its golden colour, and took on that of a dark mass of crushed eye-paint. She appeared na-

> ked as space, with dishevelled hair, with a lolling tongue, and four arms. She was langourous with desire, terribly furious, bathed in sweat (caused by her anger) and of frightful countenance; garlanded with skulls, bearing on Her head a brilliant crown and a crescent moon, shining like ten milllion suns. Her voice thundered loudly.
>
> In such a fearful aspect Satī dazzling by the mass of her own brilliant energy, stood before Mahādeva, and uttered loud peals of laughter. Seeing the wonderful appearance of the Devī, Mahādeva lost all self-control, and, bewildered with fright, sought to flee in all directions . . . he frantically rushed again in flight in every direction. Seeing her husband so overcome with fear Parameśvarī was moved to pity, and with a view to restrain Him stood for a moment before Him at each of the ten quarters of the Heaven in the form of the ten Mahāvidyās. In whatever direction He ran with haste he thus saw a fearful form standing before Him. In fright He fled in another direction, only to be again confronted by another such form. After having thus run towards each of the ten quarters of the Heaven he saw that there was none without danger for him. Then, feeling altogether helpless, he sat down on earth and shut His three eyes.[136]

Shiva asked why she had become black and fearful, and who these terrible forms were. Sati explained the situation to him. She had promised Shiva long ago to bless him for his austerities, and thus incarnated as a beautiful girl in order to marry him. She took on these terrible forms only to convince him that she needed to go to Daksha's sacrifice, and the fearful aspects are for the destruction of the sacrifice. Shiva humbly asked her pardon for any offenses that he had committed, and agreed with her desire to go to the sacrifice. Here we see a common Bengali Shakta theme, of pan-Indian male gods being inferior to the goddess and acknowledging her greatness.

Kali is always the primary Mahavidya goddess of the Bengali Kali-kula, but there are various lists of Mahavidya goddesses.[137] The *Niruttara Tantra* divides the Mahavidya goddesses into two groups—those belonging to the northern Kali-kula, and those belonging to the southern Shri-kula.[138] Each of the Mahavidya goddesses has a set iconography, a set of abilities and powers, and a literature and yogic style of her own. The most important of the Mahavidya goddesses in West Bengal are Kali and Tara. Kali is the one who grants liberation (*kaivalyadayini*), the highest primordial wisdom. She is Adya Vidya Kali, the ultimate image of the bliss of *brahman*.

According to the *Mahakalasamhita*, some deities give blessings in the Satya yuga, some in the Treta yuga, some in the Dvapara yuga, and some in the Kali yuga. But the ten Mahavidyas give blessings in all four yugas, and Kali is most important for the Kali yuga.[139] She brings new rules (*nava vidha*), which all must follow. Kali is Adya, primordial Kali, who swallows the past and future. She is the goddess from whom all gods emerge, and to whom they all return. Adya Shakti Kali is the basic form for all other forms of the goddess, beyond comparison or competition, and unique. According to various sacred texts of the Kali-kula tradition, Kali gives both pleasure and liberation during the Kali yuga. She is worshiped by gods and sages, and her worship is necessary for any spiritual accomplishments. According to the *Tararahasya*, seeking liberation without worshiping Kali is like trying to satisfy hunger without eating, or like trying to see oneself in a mirror while keeping both eyes closed.[140] As a sea is vast compared to a river, so Kali is vast compared to the other deities, and all of the Mahavidyas that were generated from Adya Kalika also lie eternally within her. Although Kali is black to our eyes, because we cannot see her light, she is radiant in her true form, which is great brilliance (*mahajyoti*).

Sometimes Kali is called the great Kali (Mahakali), who represents absolute night and the power of time. Mahakali may have five or ten faces, each with three eyes, and carries a collection of weapons. She is the darkness into which all colors dissolve, and her brilliance is veiled by the darkness of ignorance. She is time which destroys all things, swallowing them up into her mouth with her long tongue, and she stands on the copse of the universe, representing the unity of life and death. Adya Kali is the origin of all things, and her consort or *bhairava* is Mahakala. She can also be a yogic or tantric goddess and grant liberation. For some devotees, the goal of devotion is not heaven with the goddess, but *brahman* or *kaivalya*. As one of her tantric devotees explained, "Mahavidya Kali takes her devotees from death and darkness to life. She controls death, and she can give freedom from bondage. That is why she is called Kaivalyadayini—she who gives liberation. Those dedicated to her will not be reborn, they will get salvation, and they will be with Ma Kali in the five heavens (*panchakasha*), or they will go to Shivaloka. Acceptance by Ma means that both men and women will become free (*mukta purusa* and *mukta nari*). They will be able to cross the waves, and never come back."[141]

The Mahavidya goddess Tara is also very important, especially for those tantrikas who wish to follow the more classical forms of tantra and be knowledgeable in the literature (shastra). Tara gives both divine and earthly wisdom, and as Jnanodayini gives all knowledge by intuition, without the necessity of study. Tantrikas devoted to Tara tell of past renunciants who gained all knowledge overnight, simply by Tara's grace. Her devotees become poets and literary authorities, they gain all desires, such as health, popularity, and good reputation. She also chooses special devotees as her children, of whom the best known is probably Vamaksepa of Tarapith.

In the *Tantrasara*, Tara is described as young, fierce, short, and large-bellied. Some of her more important forms include Ekajata, whose matted hair holds the god Rudra; Nilasarasvati, with deep-blue skin, associated with meditation and austerities; and Ugratara, who stands on a corpse, wearing brown matted hair and fierce snakes; she places the whole world in a skull-cup.[142] She is associated with knowledge and poetic ability, and as Nilasarasvati gives power over speech (*vak shakti*). She lives in the burning ground, and protects from danger and violence. She is worshiped on battlegrounds, in solitary forests, or in Shiva temples.[143] She sometimes wears eight serpents for ornaments, which represent the eight supernatural powers (*siddhis*) that she can grant.

Tara gives wisdom, and is viewed by her devotees as a spiritual guide. She gave great wisdom to her beloved saint Vamaksepa, and in her worship instinctual urges are destroyed by fiery knowledge. As one of her priests said, "Tara is supreme divine knowledge. She is a Mahavidya, but I call her Mahavid-Ma. She gives knowledge of brahman, and thus she is called one who gives knowledge (*jnanodayini*). She gives knowledge of the solar system, of palmistry and astrology, and of the arts. Her name refers to both star, which she teaches people about, and the eye, her third eye of knowledge. She gives inspiration, and her name is part of the Baul stringed instrument (*ektara*). She is Brahmavidya Devi, the most important of the Mahavidya goddesses for writers and poets."[144]

In West Bengal, the other Mahavidya goddesses are less important. The third one is Shodashi, also known as Sundari or Tripurasundari. In south India she is better known as Shri Vidya or Lalita. She is a friendly goddess, described as young and beautiful; she wears red robes and sits on a red lotus. Her image is as bright as the morning sun, and she has four hands and three eyes. Often she is shown sitting over the navel of the god Shiva, wearing a golden crown and a garland. In the Shri Vidya tradition, she is a goddess of vedantic knowledge, ruler of the states of consciousness and the goddess of the Shri yantra, which arises from the mantra OM and is the pattern that lies below the visible universe. She is also called Rajarajeshvari, supreme ruler of the universe, for she controls its creation and destruction. She is portrayed as a sixteen-year-old girl who represents the rising sun, before the heat comes. Her consort is the five-faced Shiva. She is rarely invoked in Kali-kula tantra.

Bhuvaneshi or Bhuvaneshvari is a protectress, shining with light like the rising sun, with three eyes and a smiling face. She wears a moon on her forehead, and red clothing (as tantrikas traditionally wear). She sits cross-legged upon a red lotus, and holds a noose and bonds in her hands. She represents the cosmos, the directions of space, the essence of illusion or *maya*. She bestows wealth and power.

The fifth Mahavidya, Bhairavi, can also be a protectress, though she is a warrior and has the power of destruction. She too wears red clothing and ornaments, and a crown or crescent. She is beautiful, and has three eyes. She has a variety of forms, which carry rosaries, manuscripts, trident, sword, noose, bow, and other objects. Her hair is loose, and there are bloodstains on her breasts. In her more wrathful forms, she wears a garland of human heads or skulls. She is the power of death—the fearful goddess, also called Tripura Bhairavi or Dakini. Her consort is Rudra or Kala-Bhairava.

Chinnamasta fulfills the desires of her devotees, despite her rather unusual appearance. She stands over the the goddess Rati and the god Kama, who are embracing each other, and she is young and well built, naked, and fierce in appearance. Her skin is as red as a jaba flower. She holds her own severed head in her left hand, and she drinks the blood flowing from her own throat. Sometimes she wears a garland of lotuses. Her companions Dakini and Varnini stand near her, and they are also drinking her blood. Dakini has three eyes and wild hair. Varnini has red skin, and holds a beggar's bowl and a sword. Both have a knife and skull-cup. Chinnamasta is a figure of radical transformation, a great yogini. She is the self-sacrifice (*atma-yajna*) that allows for transcendence, the end of the world that swallows up the forms of creation. By this destruction, she destroys attachment to the physical world and the mind, allowing the person to travel beyond it. Her consort is the headless Shiva. She is the power of sacrifice, as the continuity of the world depends on destruction and sacrifice, for all life feeds on other life.[145]

The seventh Mahavidya goddess, Dhumavati the widow, is an unattractive character. She is angry and coarse, her robes dirty, and she has few remaining teeth. She is elderly and tall with pendulous breasts, harsh eyes, and a big nose. She is always hungry and thirsty, and quarrelsome. She holds a winnowing fan, and her chariot is pulled by a crow. She is haughty, shrewd, and quick tempered. Her mantras are used in war. Called the Smoky One, she has the power of poverty, and as a widow she has no consort. She is surrounded by smoke from the burning and destruction of the universe. She is associated with Alakshmi, goddess of misfortune, and seen in beggars, lepers, the diseased, in hunger and thirst, in mourning, and in scenes of destruction.

Bagalamukhi is young with golden skin, three eyes, and four hands. She sits upon a corpse and holds a club, a noose, and a thunderbolt, and she holds the tongue of an enemy. She is a warrior, and can combat enemies. She wears yellow robes and garlands, and golden earrings. She helps her devotees against thieves, during wars and quarrels, and in illness. Her mantras are said to fly like the wind, and she is associated with magical powers, especially the power of paralysis and subtle forms of killing. She is the crane-headed one, whose power is cruelty, and she is said to be deceitful and happy in suffering. Her consort is the one-faced Rudra.

The ninth Mahavidya, Matangi, has dark skin and three eyes, and she sits on a jeweled throne. She is young and attractive, wearing necklaces of pearls and coral, and conch earrings. There are various forms of Matangi, which have red or black robes, hold a skull and knife, and sit upon a lotus or a corpse. She is associated with the sixty-four arts. She is the elephant power, the power of domination. She establishes the rule of peace, and calm prosperity. Like a forest fire, she consumes the abode of demons, and she chases away the terrors of the night. Her consort is Shiva Matanga.

The tenth Mahavidya, Kamala or the lotus goddess, is associated with Lakshmi and Shri, and has golden skin. In her iconography, she is seated or standing on a lotus. She has four arms, two of them holding lotuses, and two signaling the granting of boons and allaying of fears. She is bathed in a stream of nectar by four white elephants, and she wears silk robes and a jeweled crown. She has eight major forms, including Gajalakshmi, Mahalakshmi, and various forms of Viralakshmi. She has the power of wealth, and her consort is Sadashiva.

According to Madhu Khanna, Kali represents the power of time and evolution; Tara represents the power of hope and spiritual ascent (potential actualized through transformation); Shodashi is the power of perfection and sustenance; Bhuvaneshvari is the power of projection of space and consciousness, and the supporter of existence; Chinnamasta represents the consummation of the life-cycle and the end of existence; Bhairavi is the power of destruction that dissolves the world; Dhumavati is the ultimate destruction, the night of cosmic slumber; Bagala is the tendency toward illusion and paralysis; Matangi is the power of domination and the dispensing of justice; and Kamala is reconstituted unity, and good fortune.[146] The ten Mahavidyas hold the key to the psychic transformation of the seeker, and represent the processes of life-variety, contradiction, change, and multiplicity, the dynamic unity of existence.

Sometimes the Mahavidya goddesses are further divided into Mahavidyas, Vidyas, and Siddha-Vidyas. The Mahavidya is composed of pure bliss, the Vidya is composed of pure spirit (*sattva*), and the Siddha-Vidya gives special powers. Some writers have gone into great detail on these subcategories.[147]

## Closing Notes

Bengali Shakta tantra involves the worship of many forms of the goddess, of which the Mahavidyas are important examples. The Mahavidyas are late medieval goddesses, who show ten aspects of the cycle of existence, of divine day and night, and they are the energies of which the physical universe is the outer expression. The Kali-kula goddesses are associated with the dark fortnight and the new moon, whereas the Shri-kula goddesses are associated with the bright fortnight and the full moon. Sometimes they are worshiped together in a single mandala, which has images of each. However, Shakta devotees often focus upon a particular Mahavidya to worship. I have interviewed worshipers of the Mahavidya goddesses, and include two descriptions here: from a devotee who worshiped a form of the goddess Tara, and a priest of Bagalamukhi.

Outside the town of Navadvipa, a large Vaishnava center, live many Shakta practitioners. Santosh Kumar Raya inherited a statue from his father, Pancanan Raya, of the goddess Nila Sarasvati. The statue is small and beautifully made, of a seated goddess with typical Vajrayana iconography, holding a thunderbolt (*vajra*) and skull cup. However, he understood the goddess to be Hindu rather than Buddhist. He told of his worship of the goddess:

> Nila Sarasvati is a form of the goddess Tara. She has eight forms: Vajratara, Chamunda, Ugratara, Kameshvari, Kali, Mahagra, Sarasvati, and Nila Sarasvati. I worship her in the early morning, in the open air. She is my Nila *ishtadevi*, my personal goddess. I worship her by chanting mantras, and by using yantras and this statue.
>
> As my meditation mantra, I use her description in Sanskrit: "The goddess is standing upon Shiva with a smiling face. She laughs out loud. She has four arms, and holds a skull, and a blue lotus, and weapons. She was created by a wish of Brahma. Her hair is saffron in color, and she carries a snake. She destroys the inertia of the world." I close my eyes and concentrate upon her image. I have practiced in this way for fifty-five years. Such meditation can be dangerous, for if a mistake is made, the worshiper can go mad. If you chant the wrong way, you must fall down before her.
>
> My father, Panchanan Raya, got this statue from Vamaksepa. Somebody had brought it to him from Tibet. This goddess is handed down from father to son; I got it from my father when he was on his deathbed. I was five years old then.
>
> I have no guru, but my father owned many books. I read his library, and practiced what the books said. I have done spiritual practice since childhood. I think the most important book is the *Tantrasara*, though the *Cinacara Tantra* and other tantras are also important. My mother helped in my father's practice.
>
> When I first wake in the morning, on my left side I visualize a guru shining with white light. He represents consciousness. On my right side, I see the guru's consort (shakti), who shines with red light. They are in the highest chakra. I see a moving lake (the *kula kunda*), and a still lake (the *maha-kunda*). Shiva dwells in the still lake, eternal and changeless. Sometimes I feel so [distant], and I cry, feeling great separation. I do internal worship to the guru and consort in the *sahasrara* chakra, and then descend to the heart center. This is the place of the individual soul. The downward lotus faces upward and opens. I see my goddess, Nila Sarasvati, visualized in the heart. I worship her, and her statue form dissolves into a yantra, the great yantra with a triangle in the middle. It represents the union of desire, knowledge, and action.
>
> I project my goddess into events in the world. You should always project the goddess into the eyes of those with whom you speak; this causes a positive result, both worldly and spiritual. You

> should see the goddess in the eyes of others. If you want a spiritual life, your eyes should be educated to project inner beings into other people. When I used to lecture, I would see the goddess in the eyes of the students. Pray to the goddess to stay within the eyes of people, and within objects. You should say, "Please emerge with power and beauty. Do not play hide and seek, especially in this world. I know that all people that I see are really you, the only being. Please leave your hiding place. Nothing here is stable, everything changes, let me see you, my prayer is eternal. Do not hide from me."[148]

Like many practicing tantrikas, this informant did not learn about tantra from a guru, but rather from his father's library. Many tantrikas do not wish to teach disciples; they say that if a person is really dedicated, he will learn without a guru. In his days as a professor, he could see the goddess in his classroom, and within the students; thus he could balance the physical and spiritual worlds. His tantric Mahavidya goddess was also a bhakti goddess worthy of worship.

Satyananda Giri is a priest of a temple to the goddess Bagalamukhi in Calcutta. He declared that the Mahavidya goddesses help during the process of yoga, as well as at other times:

> During kundalini yoga, the Mahavidyas can appear to the practitioner and help him. I am a priest of Bagala, but the other Mahavidyas can help also in this process. The Mahavidyas are themselves a form of yoga. There are eight hidden Mahavidyas: Jagaddhatri, Jayadurga, Mahishamardini, Karnapurna, Nitya, Shorashi, Mahasarasvati, and Bagala. But Bagala is best for a sadhu in trouble, for she has the power of resistance. It is she who returned the Vedas to India.
>
> When the Vedas were stolen, Narayana went to look for them. Bagala came to help him, and she turned herself into a fish. Narayana went inside of her, and they went down under the ocean. Where the Indian Ocean and the Arabian Sea meet, there was a giant named Shankhachura, and he had stolen the Vedas and put them in a cave. The giant was resting before the cave, and he saw Bagala as a lovely fish he wished to capture. But the fish vomited out Narayana, and Bagala told Narayana to chop off the head off the giant. Narayana did so, and recovered the Vedas and returned inside the fish. He was going take full credit for the return of the sacred books, but Bagala announced her identity: "I am Bagala, one of the ten Mahavidyas, and I helped you to accomplish this."
>
> The goddess must always be worshiped by visualization, by meditation upon the figure of the deity. Goddesses have different forms, and you must concentrate upon the form of the one you

> wish to see. Her mantra is Om hling Bagalamukhi. . . . Hling is the initiate's name for Bagala. The other lines mean that she will wash away all trouble, she cannot be grasped by the hand or captured in words, she resists evil, and brings paralysis to those who threaten, and her inner nature is *buddhi* (consciousness).[149]

He also stipulated that the "hidden" Mahavidya goddesses should only be contacted by serious practitioners. Though some of these were well known as bhakti goddesses, their Mahavidya aspects were secret. If worshiped in tantric fashion, with proper mantras and visualizations, they can lead the practitioner to the union of Kundalini and Paramashiva, and bring various forms of ecstatic trance.

This priest of Bagalamukhi told me of her rituals and many of her mantras, and emphasized how she would help in times of emergency when other deities would not. He said that these figures were generated from Kali for each of the ten directions (though some devotees told me that they were also the wives of Vishnu's ten avatars). It is clear in his story that there is some tension between the classical Narayana, who wished to take all of the credit for the rescue of the Vedas, and Bagala, who resented this impulse on his part. Her action thus involves her with the Vedas (she becomes Vedic in a most tenuous sense), as well as with a god of brahmanical Hinduism. These gain her respect in the mainstream Hindu religious tradition.

The Mahavidya goddesses are ritual specialists, to be contacted if certain goals are desired. They are also associated with astrology, and can bless or obstruct life events. For some Shakta tantrikas, they are mediators between humble devotees and the distant and powerful creator goddess. For others, they are experts and teachers who can bring specific types of knowledge and power.

For the most part, Shakta belief and ritual have not spread to other cultures, as have other types of Indian religion, such as hatha yoga. However, we do see some limited influence on the West by the Shakta traditions, often in quite altered form. We have examined Shaktism in its native context—let us observe some of its global and transnational aspects.

# 5

# Shaktism and the Modern West

## *Kundalini Vacations and Tantric Honeymoons*

Attitudes toward Indian religion have changed drastically in the course of a century, especially in that mixture of disparate (and often mutually exclusive) ideas called New Age religion. Rather than the older interpretations of Indian religion as primitive or heretical, it has instead been considered a source of valuable ideas and images, a tradition older than Christianity that gives a more varied set of images and metaphors for pathways to the divine. The goal for much New Age practice is not historical accuracy but rather a set of religious ideas that seem appealing or inspiring or exotic to people today.

In the New Age religions, there are influences from both popular Indian religiosity (in such concepts as karma, reincarnation, chakras, yoga, and mantras) and from various traditions of goddess worship. Though Shaktism as practiced in West Bengal has never really gained a major following in the West, it has migrated and been transformed in a variety of ways. In its initial migratory form, as Shakta universalism, it became popular through Ramakrishna and Vivekananda; their followers set up Vedanta Centers in the gUnited States and Europe, and published a variety of books on Hindu tradition. Other forms of Shaktism followed.

Over time, we see three major transformations of Hindu Shakta traditions in the modern West.

1. *Shakta tantra* has become a religion of hedonism, with an immanent goddess recognized as dwelling within the woman, and sexuality understood to be a spiritual path.
2. *Kundalini yoga* has become popularized, Westernized, and

fairly widespread, bringing bodily health, relaxation from stress, and occasionally religious insight and knowledge of past lives.

3. *The worship of Hindu goddesses* is sometimes seen, but is less prominent; it focuses primarily on Kali as a sort of Freudian goddess bringing catharsis from past traumas. Goddess worship is seen in some New Age books, largely by feminist writers, in which Kali has been transformed into a personification of female rage, and there are special rituals for incorporating her energies and accepting one's darker side. Other Hindu goddess, such as Lakshmi and Sarasvati, are largely ignored. The aspect of bhakti that has become strongest is Shakta Vedanta, in which the goddess is a symbol of all religions and beliefs.

These new religions and interpretations have partly come from Indian practitioners who have visited the West and gained groups of disciples, and partly from Western writers and syncretistic groups (some of them outgrowths of the Theosophical Society), who have come up with their own interpretations of these traditions. This section will not be a comprehensive view of all New Age adaptations, but will show a sample of Shakta mixing and matching in these three areas.

## Shakta Tantra

Tantra in the West has largely lost its theistic and ritual dimensions; Shakti is now understood primarily as power, rather than as a goddess. Whereas Shakta tantra in West Bengal has both devotional and folk dimensions, Shakta tantra in the United States and Western Europe largely ignores these, and tends to have only one dimension: that of sexuality. Rather than giving up attachment to the world for the sake of the goddess, here we have people immersing themselves in the world to find her. She has become immanent rather than transcendent, full of self-satisfying earthly lust (*kama*) rather than self-sacrificing spiritual love (*prema*). Religions change as they travel and become popularized, and the United States has a strong Protestant tradition of denominationalism: if you are dissatisfied with your church, start a new one. This is exactly what immigrant tantra has done; it has started new denominations. Probably most popularized by Rajneesh, tantra in the West has become sectarian. We have Neo-Tantra, Hawaiian Goddess tantra, Oceanic tantra, "Red Indian" tantra (or Quodoushka Cherokee tantra), Ipsalu tantra, Erotic Magical tantra, the Esoteric School of Tantric Shamanism, the House of Bods, Pantra Sex and Spirit Workshops (encouraging people to "align and aloin"), Opening the Heart of the Womb workshops, Sacred Tantric Journeys, Transformational

Tantra, Celebrations of Love, Dance of the Kundalini, Omega Pathways Sexual Alchemy, Tantra House (specializing in occult and psychic powers), and SkyDancing Tantra, as well as a variety of others.

Probably the major popularizer of tantra in the West, and the origin of many of these tantric offshoots, was the late guru Bhagavan Rajneesh. He was not Bengali Shakta, but his teachings have shaped Western understandings of tantra. He was born in 1931 as Chandra Mohan Jain in Madhya Pradesh, central India, of Jain parents. He was the eldest of eleven children, and a sickly child who almost died of smallpox and asthma. From the age of seven, when his grandfather died, he was fascinated with death. He spent time with dying people, watching their relatives and following funeral processions to the burning grounds. At fourteen, he spent a week in a deserted temple waiting for death, in order to conquer it. Several years later, the girlfriend that he loved died. He started having severe headaches, and was unable to eat or speak. His parents believed that he was going insane, and took their son to a variety of doctors. He would lie on the floor counting to one hundred over and over again.[1]

At the age of twenty-one, he had a religious experience that he called his enlightenment, in which he felt a "new energy" and freedom, and he said that he was "mad with blissfulness." He felt weightless in a "storm of light," and stated that he had gained detachment. He continued his education and got his M.A. in 1957, and he spent several years teaching philosophy and psychology at the University of Jabalpur. He traveled through India giving talks and having debates, aggressively challenging traditional religious and political views, and he read widely. He rebelled against his family religion of Jainism, calling its ascetic tradition masochistic, and he emphasized the sexuality that Jainism believed in regulating and suppressing. He came to condemn all organized religions as dead, life-denying, and perverted in their rejection of the physical world.

By the late 1960s he began to develop his system of Dynamic Meditation, a state of induced chaos that he said would cleanse the body of its anxieties and stresses. He began initiating people into the order he was creating in 1970, and established an ashram in Poona, India, in 1974. A large number of visitors from the West came to learn from him, wearing orange clothes and a *mala* (set of beads) with a locket that contained Rajneesh's picture. The 108 beads were said to represent the 108 forms of meditation to be taught at his ashram. He called his followers tantric neo-sannyasins, who were not rigid and life-denying like traditional sannyasins, but rather "joyous creatures, rebels and dancers." He was the Tantric Master, making sex the meditation of his disciples.[2] He believed that since Westerners cared most about sex and money, these should be the emphases for Western Tantra. In 1981 he established another ashram in Antelope, Oregon, known as Rajneeshpuram (or Rancho Rajneesh), which ran into trouble with the local authorities. Rajneesh changed his name to Osho, and continued to experiment with meditation and encounter groups. He died in 1990, in India.

Rajneesh redefined tantra—it was no longer a system of disciplined meditation and ritual, but rather a rebellion against all ritual: "Tantra is freedom—freedom from all mind-constructs, from all mind-games; freedom from all structures—freedom from the other. Tantra is a space to be. Tantra is liberation. . . . Tantra takes all disciplines away."[3] He disagreed with the traditional yogic and ascetic dimensions of tantra. He wrote that ascetics are people with severe psychological problems: "Something very antagonistic to life—very life-negative, very life-denying—has entered into the bloodstream of humanity. And it has come through those so-called ascetics. These ascetics are neurotic people; they are masochists, they torture themselves. Their only joy is in creating more and more misery."[4] Rajneesh's Tantra encourages sexuality, which he believed would generate love and religious experience: "The greatest, most intelligent people are the most sexual people. This has to be understood, because love energy is basically intelligence. If you cannot love you are somehow closed, cold; you cannot flow."[5] However, a tantric neo-sannyasin must not cling to one partner, for that simply causes more bondage. Traditional marriage is a bad and stifling idea. God has appeared in millions of forms—why cling to one?

His Western tantra denied all religious institution, and is not based on tantric texts. Surprisingly, he even denied the existence of both tantric texts and rituals: "Tantra is not a religion in the ordinary sense because it has no rituals, it has no priests, it has no scriptures. It is an individual approach towards reality. It is tremendously rebellious. Its trust is not in the organization, its trust is not in the community; its trust is in the individual. Tantra believes in *you*."[6]

Rajneesh's transformation of tantra has maintained certain traditional ideas, and jettisoned others. The focus on individuality, the lack of conformity, and the avoidance of institution is quite traditional for Shakta tantra, and not rebellious at all. The focus on the presence of the divine within the material world is debatably found in Shakta tantra, which allows a few semi-hedonistic rituals leading toward a basically ascetic goal (identification with Shiva and Shakti), and the rejection of family ties and obligations is found in the ascetic and yogic traditions (which may substitute the tantric kula as one's family or lineage). However, the lack of deities (his Shakti is an energy, like Reich's "orgone energy," and not a goddess) and his acceptance of various therapies and belief systems takes the syncretism of the Shakta tantric traditions and greatly exaggerates it. And most forms of tantra have a strong yogic dimension, which emphasizes disciplined practice.

Rajneesh's understanding of tantra as a rebellion against organized religion, free sexuality, and experimental spirituality has generated and influenced a variety of other Western tantric groups. Charles and Caroline Muir, who have created a popular school of tantric yoga, follow a similar path, though they place more value on long-term romantic relationship. In their book *Tantra: The Art of Conscious Loving*, there is a variety of myths about tantra that have been adapted for the West. The book jacket defines tantra as "an affirmation of our monogamous choice" (carefully ignoring the "ritual wives" that tantrikas have often taken as consorts for only one night). They write that tantra is "a spiritual system in which sexual love is a sacrament,"[7] and speak of tantra's emphasis on love, ignoring the lack of the word love (*prema*) in the tantric texts. They discuss how people operate with a "passion deficit" due to fear of AIDS in the modern world, and how tantra can solve this problem. They do admit to interpreting some tantric teachings "from an end-of-the-twentieth-century point of view," but then emphasize the antiquity of the tantric tradition, claiming that it goes back nearly five millennia. They are relentlessly upbeat, calling tantra a "therapy for psychosexual wounds"[8] and a way of letting go of disharmony in "tantric communication." Overlooking the ascetic emphasis of most original tantric texts, the Muirs describe tantra as "fun": "The early Hindu practitioners of tantric yoga experienced and taught sexual play and sexual union as an act of joyful celebration, as a demonstration of connectedness, as a symbolic affirmation of the unity inherent in a couple's relationship, and as a means for achieving spiritual sublimity."[9] Of course, this could be done more easily in ancient times, as "sexual 'hangups' were not prevalent" at that time, as they are today (ancient India being something like southern California). They equate tantra with Taoism, emphasing the male as light and hot, and the female as dark and cool: "When Tantricas exchange sexual love, they draw on their separate impulse centers or bodily chakras to balance yin and yang, feminine and masculine, negative and positive . . . it uses love as a salve, as a tonic, as a panacea for sexual wounds."[10]

There is an unspecified goddess involved in tantra. When the Goddess of Tantra is fully realized, according to these writers, she will cause women to release their "orgasmic energy" which will bring in the New Age (again, not the Hindu Kali yuga but the Age of Aquarius): "We believe that the Goddess began her reawakening in the 1960s, during the period we know as the Sexual Revolution, and that she is still in the early stretching stages of waking up. . . . Soon she will step out into the light, and her radiance will illuminate all humankind. When this happens, when women awake from their slumber and their enormous orgasmic energy is released to the world, we will have attained the new Age, the Age of Truth."[11] Such a release of this orgasmic energy may bring unlikely events: "Tantra describes the female power of shakti as limitless . . . if the woman releases her fluid while her lover is outside of her, it may burst from her in a fine mist, or explode like a fountain, high into the air—up to six feet high."[12]

In order to create such fountains on a greater scale, these two ex-yoga teachers have begun the "Hawaiian Goddess Source School of Tantra Yoga," with tantra taught in weekend seminars or on seven-day "honeymoon style" vacations. There are also home-study courses available, such as "Freeing the Female Orgasm/Awakening the Goddess." The focus is a popularized sex therapy and alternative form of healing, dealing with "physical, emotional and psychological scars that women have experienced in their lives." Information on interpersonal communication and lovemaking skills are said to open the woman to creative energy and "new levels of personal power and ecstatic pleasure." Clients are taught muscular exercises and instructions from the *Kama Sutra* (which is not, incidentally, a tantric text). The advertising for Hawaiian Goddess Tantra does not emphasize its religious dimensions (no traditional Hawaiian goddesses are invoked), and it redefines religion as a form of pleasure, and as a therapy.[13]

Another modern form of tantra is Oceanic Tantra. Oceanic Tantra emphasizes "dolphinbreath and undulatory movement" as a means of generating and manipulating sexual energy, to gain health and longevity, and show "ways [that] men and women can be multi-orgasmic." Various workshops and seminars make use of dance, music, theater, visualization, "love in the sensuous waters," and performing breathing and wave movements that generate "interspecies communication with dolphins and whales" (they also allow one to feel the "Tantric pulsation of the universe"). Rather than seeking an encounter with Shiva and Shakti, the goal has shifted to identification and communication with various animal species. If tantra is said by the New Age to speed up evolution, it is curious that its focus seems to be downward, toward communication with less intelligent forms of life (though perhaps the claim might be that these species are equal or superior in intelligence—if only we knew how to speak with them).[14] Begun by a musician ("a master of the art of Music Healing") and a psychotherapist at their Kahua Hawaiian Institute, the goal of this form of tantra is to create "passionate and dynamic ways of bringing greater consciousness into the areas of sexuality and spirituality." Their live performances include "Tantric Wave" and "Sex Magic Rituals." The advertising for this institute describes the "Tantric Experience you'll treasure forever" in terms usually used for kundalini yoga: "As sexual energy rises it can rejuvenate every cell in our body. By connecting with the heart it becomes prayer; rising up into the mind we can experience visions and revelations; and ultimately we can experience communion with the divine. This fulfills a deep yearning in all of us to experience our own divinity."[15] However, the term *kundalini* is not used here; perhaps it has been trademarked. While the altered states of consciousness of Hindu Shakta tantra generally involved an understanding of the subtle body and direct awareness of the gods or of ultimate consciousness, those forms of Western tantra have taken a sideways turn, emphasizing this-worldly alternatives, such as increased sensuality and animal consciousness.

Another form of Western tantra is Chuluaqui-Quodoushka or "Cherokee spiritual sexuality," called Red Indian Tantra in Europe. It was said to be revealed by a *metis* (a Cherokee-Irish medicine man), and it causes the human sexual relationship to be a reflection of the sexual relationship of Grandfather Sun and Mother Earth. Its founders call it a "Mystery School of the American Indian," mixed with teachings from other cultures and also other planets and galaxies. These include the Pleiadian Emissaries of Light (ancestors who teach the rituals of the "Dolphin Starstreams") and the Sirian Archangel Leagues. Success at the practice brings healing (to self and planet) and a variety of psychic abilities. On their Fall Equinox weekend, they "Experience medicine teachings, exercises and sweat lodge ceremony to heal the 1st energy vortex (chakra): Being the Elements, clearing energy channels of old beliefs, psychic contracts, releasing anger and programming, igniting our animal totems, aligning our essence and higher self channels along with communication using sexual energies of visualization and touch."[16]

Quodoushka uses a sexual Medicine Wheel, which integrates the person with nature, and recognizes the body as the temple of the God/Goddess. It is ostensibly based on the Tantras, which they accept as texts, and which another pamphlet claims were written by women: "Tantras: Written scriptures founded thousands of years ago in India by women of a secret sect; originally called Tantrism. Women were thought to possess more spiritual energy than men; consequently, a man could attain realization of divinity only through sexual and emotional union with a woman."[17] It is taught in workshops by a Fire Medicine Person, and includes "lost ceremonies of sexual magic" and "sexual rites of passage." Leaders take semi-Native American names, such as Lone Eagle and Rainbow Lightning Elk. According to one rather disillusioned informant, sexual interaction is mandatory at these workshops.

Another tantric variant is Ipsalu tantra, which describes itself as "An Accelerated Path toward the Mastery of Sexual, Emotional, Physical and Mental Energies." It is also called Tantric Kriya Yoga, and described as "scientific mysticism." It advertises its ability to create modern *siddhis* or supernatural powers: it lets you amplify and transmute sexual energy, clear away old karma and primal trauma memories, rejuvenate the body and keep it young ("by prolonging the arousal state in lovemaking or self-pleasure, you bathe your body cells in youth-maintaining hormones"), honor and balance your inner male and female (in order "to save our planet from its current self-destructive course"), take responsibility for your life, and gain enlightenment ("Masters have described enlightenment as a perpetual orgasmic state").[18] It teaches techniques you can perform in the privacy of your own home ("Discover how to be transcendent and orgasmic simultaneously!")[19] Except for the occasional references to enlightenment, this is much like folk tantra, in its more pragmatic goals: *siddhis*, eternal youth, fulfillment of desires. Tantric *kriyas* are traditional meditative practices, but they generally require an ascetic context.

Miraculous powers are gained by practice of the Cosmic Cobra Breath, which transmutes sexual energy. It is a secret practice, revealed only to initiates. Initiation takes fifteen minutes, and should be done in a weekend intensive, and never written down. However, motivated souls can be initiated by telephone. There is also a correspondence course available. One such retreat advertised a sweat lodge, another a Tibetan Tantric Rebirthing.

This practice was attributed to a revelation by Babaji, a Hindu sage who was said to have been born in 203 CE and who gained physical immortality in his body. He is an avatar (though it is not specified of whom he is an avatar) who came to earth to reveal this form of tantra. Practitioners may also get channelled or "guided" information from the deceased Osho (Rajneesh), and Kuthumi of the Theosophists (who is here equated with Pythagoras), as well as Mother Earth (the Shakta goddess for this variant). Such appearances are described as pleasurable, as one teacher describes: "By the end of Saturday, I was so swept away I could barely verbalize enough to bring the class to a close. We chanted three OM's to finish, but nobody moved. After several minutes of being transfixed, I found myself saying, 'We are not alone. There is a Presence.' Wave after wave of orgasmic energy began coursing up my body, breaking at the heart. I was absolutely in rapture. This went on for about 45 minutes. Several in the group said they saw Babaji there. Certainly everyone felt his energy."[20]

A subcategory of Ipsalu Tantra is Agni Yoga ("firebreath orgasm"), which allows the person to "redistribute the lifeforce." There is also Yoga Nidra available ("Self-Programming Theta Threshold Audio Course"). As necessities for this form of tantra, there is a Personal Vibrator Kit for Chakra Stimulation, and a Wand of Perpetual Youth. Another tantric organization, the SkyDancing Institute, advertises its Tantra Love and Ecstasy Trainings. Its brochures use a variety of styles of imagery (Buddhist yab-yum line drawings, Zen bamboo, Gustav Klimt paintings, African sculpture), but its philosophy and practices derive from the Neo-Tantra of Rajneesh. As a brochure's introduction states, "Our activities provide a gateway into the Tantric way of life by helping you to awaken to your ecstatic potential, embrace your own vital powers, create a more fulfilling love life and to enliven your sensuality as well as your spirituality."

Tantra, or "the yoga of love," is democratized here—it is no longer only "the cherished practice of Asian nobility." Anybody interested can practice it, assuming that he or she wishes to pay for a workshop. SkyDancing tantra claims to integrate "the ancient spirit of Tantra" with humanistic psychology and clinical sexology, to present the "Tantric paradigm." It also incorporates some other traditions, such as American Indian and Taoist traditions (which are said to possess "holistic sexuality"). A variety of other practices are added: bioenergetics, NLP (neuro-linguistic programming), massage, and communication skills. There are workshops in which sexual energy is used as a magical tool; people visualize their desired situations and the visualized image is charged with "orgasmic energy" in order to manifest it in the world. The original meaning of the word *tantra*, associated with the warp and weft of a loom, is seen in the goal of "weaving a Tantric network" together with other practitioners, a network made up of their combined energies. The brochure claims "scientifically documented benefits," and describes the main instructor's combination of "French erotic humor, American pragmatism, and Indian mysticism."[21] While most workshops are for couples, there is also one for males only—the Circle of Shivas.

SkyDancing tantra is primarily taught by traveling workshops and short-term training seminars, either by its originator, Margo Anand, or by teachers who have been certified by the program. One advanced technique is called "riding the wave of bliss." Anand argues that tantra is really a form of recycling, and should be practiced more widely because it is ecological:

> Since the industrial age, we have been taking from the Earth, plundering our planet, and then just throwing away. People now are understanding that this is not the way and that there is a need to recycle our material resources. In Tantra, there is a parallel awareness with respect to the human body. We have a human personal ecology that has unknowingly been abused. Sexual energy is not something you take, then you throw it away. This is the prevalent experience of sexuality in Western culture; sexuality is associated with violence and it always ends with an ejaculation. Tantra teaches the gentle way, the more balanced way between masculine and feminine. Practitioners learn to recycle the sexual and vital energies, recirculating these resources to various energy centers throughout the body. . . . This ecological balance of the self is why I think Tantra will become more and more popular.[22]

Such sensual recycling leads to mystical insight: "The ecology of the body is the same as the ecology of the planet, and both are the same as the ecology of the universe. In the experience of ecstasy, we are linked to the cosmos and the cosmos is within us. In this way we understand that we are divine and that there is no difference between God/Goddess and each of us."[23]

The Sunrise Center in Corte Madera, California, has a variety of semitantric events associated with their "Celebrations of Love." Workshops include the Erotic Magic Tantric Ritual ("Ancient wisdom remains within us, encoded in our cellular memory ready to be reawakened"), Secrets of the One-Hour Orgasm (somewhat more self-explanatory), Tantra and Sexual Energetics, Tantra Healing and Sacred Sexuality ("Release blocks to feeling a deeper level of self-love and personal intimacy. . . . Revitalize and rejuvenate with chakra toning, meditation and body drumming"), and Tantric Touch. There are also potluck Tantra Community parties involving Sufi, tribal, and disco dancing. Tantric practices also involve hot tubs, massage, Grof breathwork, massage (including Sacred Spot Massage), past life regressions, sensual education, and music ("ragas, chants, Tantric gospel, and baroque").[24] As tantra here is a modern and continually evolving practice, it also has an Internet address.[25]

Along similar lines, the author Ashley Thirleby writes of tantra as a sort of magical hedonism: "Tantric sex is the ancient key to unbelievable sexual pleasure and psychic power, attained through a set of very special sexual rituals practiced by the 'Hindu Cult of Ecstasy.' It is a kind of 'sexual magic' which brings pleasure, power, energy and control."[26] As such, both the theistic and meditative dimensions are either ignored or rejected, allowing the person to gain religious benefits without religion: "Tantra is not 'meditative.' Tantra pointedly avoids the usual forms of 'meditation,' which it considers a 'repressive, passive act.' Without meditation, without yoga, and without the strict dogma of religion, you will be able to attain, through the Tantric Sexual Rituals, all that meditation, yoga, and so many religions promise—and have a much more enjoyable time in the process."[27]

Some writers accept tantra as including meditation, but to some rather surprising ends. In *New Age Tantra Yoga: The Cybernetics of Sex and Love*, tantra is the meditative union of magnetism and electricity: "The woman is magnetic, and the man electric. The two combined create an electro-magnetic field of force. If the proper combination is effected, the sparks literally fly . . . they act like a lightning rod, drawing to them in the sexual embrace the cosmic energy that exists about them . . . the body becomes sensual, the mind telepathic, and the soul intuitional."[28] The practitioners must be good conductors, or they can be electrocuted in this process; as the author states, "sex can also destroy." Tantra unites mind, emotion, soul, and body into a "single indivisible stream of cosmic force" via "nude yoga," which encourages the movement of these energies. Tantric practice unites biological function and cosmic pulsation, and its long-term goal is "the expansion of love-consciousness" thus "extending the Divine Plan of the Elder Brothers of mankind for regenerating the race and restoring Cosmic Order to the Earth."[29] This brotherhood is not clearly described, but it helps practicing tantrikas, allowing them entrance "into the ranks of the Immortals." Tantrikas thus gain cosmic social status, they "walk with the Nobility of the Earth, and their initiation confers every protection under Karmic law."[30] This brotherhood gives tantrikas abilities at telepathic communication, immortality, and fusion of the practitioner with his/her partner, creating a magnetic aura that fulfils desires. They gain access to "Shamballa, center of the Interplanetary Government of Earth." Eventually, they will bring about a New Race of perfected humanity, following the Divine Plan to reconstruct human beings and human civilization. They will also bring about the rebirth of Lemuria and Atlantis. The author speculates that tantra may have been imported from another planet.

Although this may sound more like a computer game than a religious treatise, it follows the ideals of folk tantra: supernatural powers, telepathy, immortality, the ability to gain all desires, communication with supernatural beings, and attainment of cosmic power. However, rather than *siddhas* or yoginis, these tantrikas contact a cosmic brotherhood, who intend to perfect all of humanity rather than the single practitioner.

These interpretations of tantra, from Rajneesh on, adopt the name of "tantra" and describe a quite different history and belief system. These writers deny tantric texts, ascetic rituals, and meditative practices, and develop goals that are quite different from traditional ones.

Some writers associate tantra with a sort of Western Shaktism as worship of the female principle, a combination of nature mysticism and a belief in Jungian archetypes. In his *Tantra, The Cult of the Feminine,* André van Lysebeth states that tantra is not a religion but rather a perspective, which allows one to unite with cosmic principles concretely within the body. He suggests that the reader consider a beautiful young woman as a process stretching from birth to death rather than an individual at a particular stage of life:

> A male Tantrist feels the impact of her beauty, for him she embodies Cosmic Femininity, but at the same time he sees her as a process. As if superimposed upon her, he visualizes the baby she once was and the wizened old woman she will become. He also envisions her coupled with a man, taking his semen and perpetuating the process. Infertility would not matter because, come what may, she is part and parcel of the process called "humanity" which is itself included in the eternal process of cosmic and planetary life. Moreover, a Tantric man's attitude would be the same in front of a crippled old woman: he would visualize her as young and beautiful but also as an embryo or even a fetilized ovum in her mother's womb. Considered as a process, her life did not begin at the moment of conception and will go on, after her.[31]

Tantra is associated with worship of the feminine principle, which is the principle of life within the woman: "Lying dormant within her, involute, is the entire experience of all past generations through the entire evolution of humankind, even pre-human life."[32] Tantra returns to the earlier worship of the Mother, which he claims as humankind's original religion. Although he does not cite Jung, his description invokes Jungian archetypes, especially in Jung's understanding of the anima:

> Women's mystery is not restricted to her sex: it pervades her entire being, including (and perhaps most of all) her psyche, her mind. Women are intuitive because they are in tune with their senses and attuned to cosmic rhythms. They know the secrets of life and health, of plants, of flowers. . . . A woman understands the human soul's wellspring, for in her unconscious mind and through it, she is directly linked to the major currents of the mind which bear us and

> carry us forward. She both attracts and terrorizes. Each man holds within him the image of the ultimate, absolute Woman, but if he were actually to meet her, it would be tantamount to being struck by lightning: more powerful than love at first sight, he would remain forever attached to her.[33]

He understands Shakti as nature's creativity, which brings him back to archaic times when people lived in a magical, sacralized universe, amid benevolent and hostile forces. This was a better time, which was not as sterile as the modern world, and the tantrika becomes a sort of medium possessed by that ancient worldview:

> A non-Tantrist taking a stroll in a forest may feel in harmony with nature. Great! But if I put on my Tantric "glasses" I see in this mighty beech tree the Shakti, universal creative and organizing dynamism: the forest suddenly becomes a gigantic swirl of vital energy. A swirl in which each tree, each blade of grass, each living being is an extraordinary force field, a whirl of intelligent, pure energy in the infinite ocean of life, an ocean where all borders are dissolved. My own body is also this primordial energy. Energy and Wisdom! . . . Borne and guided by it, I feel safe and secure: it protects me at all times against the onslaughts of the outside world. It keeps me alive for it is Universal Life expressing itself through "me."[34]

For another author, Maryse Cote, tantra is primarily a form of therapy. She also writes from a semi-Jungian perspective, and finds that tantra explains how to help women out of difficult situations: "Today's women carry the traumatic imprints of millenia of injury and humiliation on a cellular level in our wombs and our bodies. These memories are reaffirmed as women experience painful childbirth, abortions, forceful sex and unfulfilled, incomplete orgasms. . . . How do we, as women, reclaim our sexual power?"[35]

The answer to this question is tantric practice, in which the woman can overcome these past events and experience her own shakti:

> My first true initiation into Tantric yoga began at a nontraditional Tantric ashram in India, in the late seventies. A series of intense initiations there, including major illnesses, transformed my life forever. At that state, I started to awaken to my powerful gift as a healer. At an ashram I received a special facilitator's training in *Breath Therapy/Rebirthing*. That education immediately took me to my core wound. Intense catharsis started to release me from a very rigid, sexually oppressive and dysfunctional Catholic upbringing.
>
> Letting go of the extra psycho-emotional baggage prepared me to experience *mahamudra samadhi*, a deep merging with all that is, for the first time in my life. Then my heart opened through sex with

> a partner. I felt totally ecstatic. In this way I identified my ecstatic nature through lovemaking. I soon realized my ecstatic nature could express itself on its own, independent of sexual union with a partner.
>
> Being able to keep experiencing my ecstatic nature through my shakti energy has been such an awakening and a powerful reminder of who I truly am. It feels like a deep reconciliation between my body and spirit, a merging of the male and female within myself.[36]

This former high school teacher has developed programs in "Raising Tantric Energy" (for men) and "Sacred Sexuality" (for women), and she considers herself to be a tantric "initiatress," restoring the sanctity of rites of passage with "erotic dancing, sensual rituals, shared sisterhood and play." Women embody the Divine Feminine, as "healers, sacred prostitutes, temple dancers, mothers, lovers and priestesses," and in tantric worship she teaches women to recognize the Divine Feminine within them.

The definitions of tantra have expanded to the point that the word has become almost meaningless. "Tantra: The Magazine" had a letter column, "Dear Tantric Goddess," which suggests that people who write in should first invoke the goddess of their choice, and then write in about questions or problems dealing with Tantra. They had tantric issues on Sufism, Egyptian religion, Tara, Sophia, Pele, Sekhmet, Hsi Wang Mu, and others. They advertised tantric flower essences, tantric statues, tantric tapes and videos, tantric love seats, tantric massage, tantric teachers, tantric love-potions, tantric tools (such as the "sacred G-spot stimulator"), tantric classes and workshops, tantric radio dramas (such as "The Adventures of Doc Kunda and Lini—a Tantric Couple"), and tantric vision quests and other trips. The theistic Shakta side of Tantra has been suppressed in favor of a few chosen rituals, and the traditional ritual context has all but disappeared. The focus is on sensuality rather than detachment or possession by deities, and the death and corpse rituals have also disappeared.

In these forms of New Age tantra, we see a Western projection on the Mystic East, which is believed to be more sensual and world-affirming than Western culture. These writers and practitioners are inventing something new, but claiming authority based on the old, giving knowledge and authority without study or effort. Tantra becomes a sales gimmick, whose aspects of renunciation, transcendence, and yogic meditation are largely forgotten, as are its devotional and philosophical aspects. The closest New Age approach to ideas of Shakta tantra would probably be in Jungian ideas of the archetypal feminine.

## Kundalini Yoga

We see a similar problem with the second area, kundalini yoga, another tradition that has reached the West and been transformed. As described earlier in this book, Bengali kundalini yoga focuses upon a goddess who is understood in both theistic and nontheistic ways. Sir John Woodroffe was one of the earliest writers published in the West on kundalini yoga. He wrote from a classical tantric and Shakta universalist perspective, to which he had been exposed by his tantric circle of friends and teachers in Calcutta. He wrote on kundalini during the early twentieth century. At this time there were also members of the Theosophical Society exploring Indian thought, and reinterpreting Indian ideas according to their doctrines. The Theosophical writer C. W. Leadbeater wrote his own interpretations of chakras, which were based on his personal visions rather than on Hindu tradition. Woodroffe was very critical of Leadbeater's claims, and this split between traditional Hindu understandings of kundalini and Western occultism with its auras and chakras has gone on from early in the twentieth century. As kundalini yoga has been adapted to the West, its goals and practices have changed from its ascetic roots. We see writings on scientific studies of kundalini energy, on its relationship to stigmata and to UFOs.

Leadbeater's book on chakras showed pictures of his own visionary images of these centers. Another early theosophist, George Arundale (president of the Theosophical Society from 1934 to 1945), also wrote a book on kundalini. Arundale lived in India, but for him, Kundalini or Serpent-Fire was a universal force, a power in the earth and the solar system:

> Is there a Kundalini chain linking the constituent elements of our own solar system, and another chain linking the various solar systems? Surely so, and speculation is no less interesting as to the nature of the centres of a solar system and on their vivification by cosmic Kundalini. The Earth has its centres—whirling wheels of fiery energy—and it would appear that one of the functions of some of the Lords of Evolution is the regulation of distribution and intensity of Kundalini. This is a reason why even Their work has been described as hazardous, like the work of those who bring ammunition to the front line trenches in time of war.[37]

These Lords of Evolution are members of the Great Brotherhood, or Great White Lodge, souls who have become members of the Inner Government of the World ("compared with which all outer governments are but toy governments"). New members become linked with this brotherhood by kundalini energy: "The mighty force of the Kundalini of the Brotherhood flows through these centres and through each member, so that admission to the Brotherhood involves participation in this great flow; the gradual uniting of the consciousness of the individual with the consciousness of the Brotherhood as a whole, involving a progressive uniting of the two Kundalinis. The Kundalini of the individual begins to enter the stream of the Brotherhood Kundalini."[38]

Although Arundale does not speak in theistic terms of Kundalini as a goddess, he has not entirely lost the imagery: "Kundalini sings to the student with the voice of all that lives . . . she can be heard by those who have the ears to hear. She is substantial, even though yet more spatial, and can be seen by those who have the eyes to see. Kundalini is no mere fanciful abstraction. She is no mere theory, no mere externalization of an imaginative outpouring. She lives. She sings. She arrays herself in scintillating colors."[39]

Other Theosophists and occultists emphasize the universal nature of kundalini—it comes not only from India but from other countries as well. Kenneth Grant claims an Egyptian origin for tantra and kundalini, which he says are based on the Draconian or Typhonian cults of ancient Egypt. He writes that Kundalini is the Fire Snake of the African Ophidian cults, and worship of Shakti is the exercise of the Fire Snake. Its goal is altering the physical body, and creating a subtle body:

> The ability to function on the inner, or astral planes, and to travel freely in the realms of light or inner space, derived from a special purification and storage of vital force. This force in its densest form is identical with sexual energy. In order to transform sexual energy into magical energy (*ojas*), the dormant Fire Snake at the base of the spine is awakened. It then purges the vitality of all dross by the purifying virtue of its intense heat. Thus the function of the semen—in the tantras—is to build up the body of light, the inner body of man. As the vital fluid accumulates in the testicles it is consumed by the heat of the Fire Snake, and the subtle fumes or "perfumes" of this molten semen go to strengthen the inner body . . . [Kaula] initiates have methods of preventing the deposit of semen in the testicles, and urine has curative properties as well as being a stimulant; the tantras give instructions for its use in the rejuvenation of the physical body. Of far more importance, however, is its value as a bisexualizing agent which, if ingested at certain times of the month, creates a condition, wherein the initiate becomes androgynous and without fear.[40]

We also see the use of kundalini in religious traditions brought to the West by Indian religious leaders. Yogi Bhajan brought White Tantric Yoga, or 3HO (the Happy, Healthy, and Holy Organization) to the West, with himself as the Tantric Master who teaches kundalini yoga. Yogi Bhajan was raised as a Sikh in the Punjab, and later came to the United States and became a guru. He is believed by devotees to be the only legitimate kundalini guru. According to one informant:

> Tantric yoga is practiced by 3HO. But only Yogi Bhajan can be the Tantric Master, and when he dies nobody else can perform initiations. Only he can oversee the exercises. Under the guidance of the

> Master, white tantric exercises can cleanse the aura of crap—past life impressions, karma, blockages, garbage, even marks left by poor diet. People sit in rows—men on one side, women on the other, facing each other. You do exercises, breathing, and mantra, for several hours. People almost always look into each other's eyes. Some exercises are strenuous—you might have to hold your hands in the air for half an hour or forty-five minutes. The guru meditates while this goes on, and guides the participants. Tantra is any exercise done between men and women, under the guidance of the Master, to cleanse the aura and erase past impressions. You would never have men doing tantra with men, or women with women. It requires a balance of male and female energy.[41]

Despite Yogi Bhajan's claim to be the only legitimate tantric master and teacher of kundalini yoga, other Indian gurus and teachers have taught and written on the field. These include Amrit Desai, teacher of kundalini as Kripalu yoga; Swami Rama of the Himalayan Institute; Swami Sivananda, Swami Radha, Sri Aurobindo, and Swami Muktananda, among many others. It was also mentioned by Ram Dass in his popular 1971 book *Be Here Now*. Western interest at the popular level in kundalini yoga was probably most influenced by the writings of Gopi Krishna, in which kundalini was redefined as chaotic and spontaneous religious experience. Gopi Krishna wrote about his kundalini experiences in strictly experiential terms:

> The sensation again extended upwards, growing in intensity, and I felt myself wavering; but with a great effort I kept my attention centered round the lotus. Suddenly, with a roar like that of a waterfall, I felt a stream of liquid light entering my brain through the spinal cord. . . . The illumination grew brighter and brighter, the roaring louder, I experienced a rocking sensation and then felt myself slipping out of my body, entirely enveloped in a halo of light. It is impossible to describe the experience accurately. I felt the point of consciousness that was myself growing wider, surrounded by waves of light. it grew wider and wider, spreading outward while the body, normally the immediate object of its perception, appeared to have receded into the distance until I became entirely unconscious of it. I was now all conscious, without any outline, without any idea. . . . I was a vast circle of consciousness in which the body was but a point, bathed in light and in a state of exaltation and happiness impossible to describe.[42]

However, although Gopi Krishna had many positive kundalini experiences, he also suffered many difficult side effects: anxiety, sleeplessness, loss of appetite, hallucinations, nightmares, fevers, physical and emotional pain, depression. It was a warning of the dangers of using kundalini meditation as a spiritual path without guidance. It also predicted the rise of New Age books on experiential, nontraditional religions (especially the generic "shamanism") with the main character as an innocent who does not understand what is happening to him, and who must learn slowly over the years to understand the meaning of his religious experiences.

For some practitioners of kundalini yoga, its association with Indian religious traditions has disappeared completely. This approach may be a result of Gopi Krishna's influence. Kundalini has become understood as a spontaneous spiritual (as opposed to religious) event, which requires no teacher or tradition. As John Selby writes, "The reason kundalini meditation is such a remarkable process for spiritual awakening is that it is not based on complex theological arguments, or culturally defined religious concepts. Kundalini meditation is focused instead upon the immediate, ultimate experience of the divine within all of us, not upon belief systems regarding that divinity. Therefore, regardless of our particular religious upbringing and theological beliefs, all of us can employ kundalini meditation to aid in our spiritual evolution."[43]

He calls kundalini energy the Christ-consciousness, the Truth that sets you free, allowing a person to reenter the Garden of Eden, and encounter Christlike Inner Masters. It thus becomes an alternative to the third person of the Trinity, the Holy Spirit.

Many New Age writers feel free to separate what they view as essential to a tradition from its cultural context, which they consider to be unnecessary baggage. The basis for this decision-making is personal experience and inspiration, or occasionally some promptings from Inner Masters. Barbara Condron, another Western practitioner, discusses how Kundalini energy induces out-of-body experiences and telepathy with the dead. It arises due to the evolution of mankind, appearing only in mankind's most recent incarnation, the fifth root race:

> It is only with the development of the individual soul during the fifth root race that man achieves the elevated consciousness required to use the Kundalini energy. Earlier root races enjoy this flow of creative energy which enables physical procreation to occur, but they lack the necessary experience and understanding to harness her spiritual powers. By the time reasoning is developed, the thinker can realize his individual ability to guide his evolutionary development through the choices he makes. . . . This prepares his consciousness for the conscious use of the Kundalini energy.[44]

The chakras recycle the Kundalini energies throughout the body. Such energies are not unique to India, however, as we also see them in the New Testament. Jesus' feeding the multitude with loaves and fishes also symbolizes the chakras:

> The five loaves are symbolic of the five lower chakras. These are the chakras that directly affect and work with the reenergizing of your conscious and subconscious minds. The two fishes are symbolic of the two higher chakras that work with the recycling of energy into the superconscious mind. The twelve apostles represent the twelve major aspects of the conscious mind. Jesus is usually in control of the situations described during his life. This symbolizes the ability to give direction to the many aspects of Self.[45]

In the New Age literature, kundalini energy has become a way of understanding strange and often chaotic experiences that happen to a person without any previous practice or education. It is a major cause of "spiritual emergencies," when sudden visions or sensations disrupt normal life. Many writers have spoken of their encounter with kundalini energy, and some associate it with goddesses from other traditions. For instance, Vicki Noble writes in *Shakti Woman*: "In early 1978 something happened to me that I understood afterward as a Kundalini experience, because I found a book that described similar kinds of states. I was awake in the middle of the night . . . when suddenly I simply flew out of the top of my head and dissolved into the black space of the night sky. Inside my head was ringing the message, 'I am one with all witches through all time.' "[46] She saw images of witchcraft, shamanism, and sacred animals, and heard supernatural messages. She associated the snake images with female shamanism, which she believes to be based on menstruation: "The snake is linked to both menstruation and Kundalini, and both of these are connected with the female ability to receive information from the spirit realm and express it in the form of oracular speech. Yoga was probably invented by women menstruating, who learned to master the tremendous energies and forces available to them during this sacred, profound time of the monthly cycle."[47]

Such events occur because the Dark Goddess is trying to make herself known through certain human women, whom the authoress calls "shakti women": "Shakti women are human females who are feeling the call of the Dark Goddess—the deep, serious will-to-life arousing from within the body of the planet. This demanding energy of the Death Goddess—she who would destroy the old forms in order to make way for the new—is pushing through us for healing and the realignment with Nature that needs to happen at this time."[48] Although this goddess often comes in Indian forms (especially those of the Dakini and the goddess Kali, who makes Shiva appear dead because she puts him into a trance state), the Dark Goddess is really an archetype and shape-shifter who can take any form. Noble likes the original tantric practice (she defines tantra as "the sexual practices of ancient and contemporary Indian Goddess worship"), but does not approve of New Age tantra: "Contemporary Tantra in the West focuses almost exclusively on how-tos and step-by-step technical performances designed somehow to stimulate her G-spot and bring the couple together in the Big O, now known as the Valley Orgasm."[49] However, the right sort of tantric practice evokes kundalini, whose spiritual heat rises and purifies, bringing deity possession: "Sometimes in this magical space I have seen and felt the deity enter my partners—the male God into my husband, the Goddess into my female partner—or I have embodied them myself. When I 'am' the serpent woman, or Aphrodite, or Kali with a male partner, it is unforgettable and wondrous, and when I have 'become' Dionysus with a female partner, it has been awesome."[50]

While a more traditional tantrika might object that the wrong deities from the wrong traditions are possessing the wrong genders, modern Western practitioners easily overlook such details.

Some traditions simply like the chakras, and see no reason for them to be associated with kundalini yoga. There are many popular books whose ideas about chakras derive not from the Indian kundalini yogic tradition but rather from the mixings and matchings of the Theosophical literature. This literature does not link the chakras to Shiva and Shakti but rather to the correspondences of Western esotericism, where chakras are variously associated with Tarot cards, astrological signs, Kabbalistic sephiroth, colors, and flowers.

Some writers have also been influenced by various feminist "back-to the-goddess" religions. As an example, *The Women's Book of Healing* by Diane Stein links chakras, "aura work," and color healing with the "matriarchal reverence for life and birth" as opposed to "patriarchal conquest, competition, mechanization, corporate mentality, and death-worship negativity."[51] Inner spiritual practice "reclaims the lost goddess and the goddess-within"[52] leading to "re-attunement with the goddess Earth." The body has various aura levels and energy bodies, connected by a silver cord (described in much the same way as the silver cord of astral projection). These bodies are connected by pranic energy, especially in the "etheric double," and the double and the chakras can be cleansed by colored gems and visualization. Such cleansing is necessary, as chakras are "the immune system of the body."[53] There are seven aura layers corresponding to the seven chakras, and each has its own body, style of healing, direction, color, and gem. In chakra balancing, faint or clouded chakras need more color, while overly active chakras need to be "shut down" with the properly colored stone. The *prana* that is thus manipulated is "the life force that comes from the goddess," and the kundalini it generates is "positive enlightenment, oneness with the goddess, and the connection of the four bodies."[54] The author cites as her sources three famous theosophists (Helena Blavatsky, C. W. Leadbeater, and Annie Besant) and also W. J. Kilner, known for his descriptions of healthy and diseased auras (which he saw through lenses coated with chemical dyes). She describes her understanding of healing: "Brief mention is needed here on the sources women link with for healing. Some women heal by looking within themselves and/or connecting directly with the goddess in meditation. . . . Seeking within or reaching to connect with the goddess is called *animism*, and is the experience of most Western women healers. These women seek the goddess as a Be-ing within as well as beyond themselves, the goddess as all of life and all of life's processes everywhere."[55]

Here we have chakras and goddess worship, yet it is a far cry from the Indian perspective on kundalini yoga. Again, the theistic side is lost, kundalini becomes a power rather than a specific goddess, and experience rather than tradition is the key to all understanding. The chakras are understood not as locales for deities but rather as localized centers of instincts. There is neither asceticism to gain detachment nor devotion to a deity—instead, the goal is to attain Shakti as intensity of experience, which leads to a sensual bliss which is the equivalent of enlightenment.

## Worship of Hindu Goddesses

The worship of Hindu goddesses in the West has never really caught on with the New Age. Worship among modern feminists and syncretists has tended primarily toward the classical goddesses of Greece and Rome, and the Celtic goddesses which have been glorified in modern Druidism and Wicca. It is curious how many feminist groups lament the dearth of living goddess traditions, yet ignore the actual living goddess traditions in India in order to recreate the dead goddess traditions of Europe. Most serious members of the women's spirituality movement would accept that their goddess traditions are "reconstructed" from the remnants that can be found from other cultures. The limited use made of Indian goddesses also involves reconstruction—usually of the goddess Kali, though occasionally we run across a reference to Lakshmi, Durga, or Sarasvati.

Kali is often associated with dark goddesses from various cultures—the Greek Hecate and the Gorgons, the Celtic Morrigan and the Babylonian Anath, the Egyptian Isis who unites the powers of sexuality and death. She is a union of Jungian opposites, creation and destruction, and a popular image of her comes from the vision of the Bengali saint Ramakrishna. He saw her as a dark goddess rising from the water, holding in one hand a baby to which she had just given birth, and in the other a sword with which to kill it. For New Age goddess worshipers, Kali trampling her husband under her feet shows female empowerment, and her potential destruction of the world shows female anger. For worshipers who do not believe in academic religious history, and instead follow a "spiritual history" that is revealed in dreams or by charismatic individuals, Kali becomes a dangerous woman, a goddess to be invoked in times of stress who fills them with power. Although their knowledge of actual Kali traditions in India is limited, bestowing power is one of the functions that we see for the goddess in folk Shakta bhakti.

As the history of the goddesses is rewritten, the "patriarchal establishment" comes in for much blame. Feminist writers analyze the behavior of men of the Bronze Age (who were an establishment even then); they were not merely warriors who oppressed matriarchal societies, but also theologians, who distorted the worship of a single all-powerful goddess into the worship of her fragments:

> Male priesthoods made the shift [to a split image of the goddess] by concentrating more and more on the Negative Goddess. Once her devotees, they expressed increasingly obsessive fears of the sexual and death dealing powers of the Great Mother. They did not, as women priestesses had always done, identify with the dark side. . . . Thus Kali, the Hindu Great Mother, became "dark, all-devouring time." . . . She also has her benevolent aspect, but the functions became increasingly severed: *Paradox is split into dualism, an act characteristic of patriarchal consciousness.* No doubt as men engaged more and more in wanton slaughter of their own kind for plunder and power, the more they needed to project this split in their own psyches onto the Goddess. The benevolent Kali becomes virtually a separate pale goddess, a passive mother, a sex-partner without power. . . . the Bronze Age Kali is split into the Death Goddess, or the Sex Goddess, or the Mother Goddess—but is no longer the one cosmic process containing all aspects and polarities. And it is only as the terrible destroyer, time, that she has any authority or power left.[56]

The authors here have great confidence in their knowledge of Bronze Age theology. For such "spiritual histories," secular or academic history is considered to be biased or simply irrelevant—it is the experiential or archetypal dimension that comes to dominate. Many of the feminist writers use Jungian concepts, and recast archetypal conflicts as historical ones.

Hinduism in the New Age was probably most publicized by Ram Dass (Richard Alpert), a psychologist and associate of Timothy Leary who went to India, took a Hindu guru, and popularized Hinduism as a spiritual path rather than an institutional religion. Many Westerners followed his lead and went to India, searching for spirituality. One Westerner whom Ram Dass met in India was Bhagavan Das, a tall Californian who wandered and sang Baul songs. Das wrote of his vision of Kali while sitting at the cremation ground next to a burning corpse with a tantric yogi named Mashani Baba:

> Then what I saw gave me chicken skin and made every hair stand on end. Mashani Baba's skin color darkened to black and his eyes became large and wild, like a tiger's. He extended his thin dark arm down into the flames and pulled up a piece of human flesh and began eating it. At that moment his teeth became fangs and I noticed

> he had large breasts and a vagina. He had completely transformed into Mother Kali and was feeding on death which gave him life.
>
> "Mashani, Mashani," I cried as a violent shaking of my body began, the kundalini shakti beating in my solar plexus like a drum. My gaze was frozen on the Goddess Mashani [Smasana Kali] as I felt the energy move up my spine like lightning. I was now centered in my head and could hear the sound of Om like a wind in my ears, opening up my third eye. The bliss was beyond the beyond, greater than any sexual experience of my life. It was a pure communion of flesh and spirit as the Cosmic Mother drank the hot blood of ego from my skull. My body had completely disappeared and I was just a severed head in Kali's hand. The sound of Shiva's double hand drum echoed in my inner ear as I inhaled the pungent incense of burning flesh.[57]

Here his teacher, a householder yogi, was transformed into Kali in Bhagavan Das's vision, and later threw burning coals at him. However, it is rare for Westerners to immerse themselves in that way into the Indian tantric tradition. A more popular and less intimidating approach is that of the Ramakrishna tradition, into which Lex Hixon was initiated. Shortly before his recent death, Hixon wrote his book *Mother of the Universe (Visions of the Goddess and Tantric Hymns of Ramprasad)*, expanding Jadunath Sinha's translations of Ramprasad's Kali songs. He states that it was in the tradition of Bengali Shaktism that he "first encountered God, or Ultimate Reality, addressed and experienced as Mother," and for him Mother Reality or Mother Wisdom is a universal tradition. "The Great Mother is humanity's most primordial, pervasive, and fruitful image of Reality. . . . Through the Goddess tradition, alive everywhere on the planet, she guides, protects, terrifies, chastens, heals, liberates and illuminates. Her relation as Great Mother to the cosmos and its innumerable life forms is as tender as her relation with each precious human soul. . . . The Goddess always remains the uncompromising Warrior of Truth—not primarily a nurturing mother figure but a Wisdom Mother who educates and liberates, gradually removing all limits."[58]

However, he also recognizes that goddesses and their statues have different moods or *bhavas*, an idea most often described in Vaishnava bhakti, and he can describe the modern mood of Ma Kali:

> The Dakshineswar Kali, in vivid contrast with the Goddess presence at Kalighat and Tara Pith, looks and acts like an attractive, enlightened young film star or rock star. She is blissfully playful, and comes forth from her temple to communicate directly with pilgrims from the strange realm of modernity. She does not draw the veil of ancient power around her as at Kalighat, or consume all veils in mystic blackness as at Tara Pith. She is the Kali of contemporary,

> revolutionary, evolutionary humanity. She wants to play with us, to dance with us, to awaken the whole world, not just the relatively small circle of hereditary Mother worshipers who are privileged to be near her geographically and culturally.[59]

Hixon finds her deepest style of being through a Shakta universalist understanding, as pure awareness: "As intimacy with the Goddess develops, she becomes the primary guide and eventually the sole Beloved, appearing everywhere and speaking through all creatures. Religious rites and yogic disciplines become outmoded. True delight is not to be obtained by any complex strategy, whether worldly or religious, but simply by abiding as original awareness, prior to and beyond the process of projecting and reflecting. . . . The phenomenal world, however, is none other than Mother's own infinite awareness. There is no duality."[60]

But knowledge of India is not necessary for visions of Kali. David Alan Ramsdale had his vision of the Mother before a Kali statue in a Vedanta temple not in Calcutta but in Hollywood. He had no previous knowledge of or attraction to this goddess (though he did like Lakshmi), and was quite surprised by her vision:

> I had been sitting quietly for about fifteen minutes when I began to feel another presence in the temple. I looked around. The other pilgrims had left. I was the only person there. Then I realized that the presence did not have a location in space. It seemed to be everywhere. There was a crackling sound like lightning, and I turned to see its source. The statue of Kali Ma suddenly stood out in my vision, as if she had been hiding before and had just leaped out into full view. My eyes fixated on her face, for her smile seemed alive and warm like that of a living person. A light danced in her eyes. I was transfixed.
>
> What happened next can perhaps be best described as telepathy. No longer able to deny that I was experiencing a living yet disembodied presence that filled the entire temple with its power and love, my attention shifted to my spiritual heart in the center of my chest. Instantly I was aware of her presence there. Paradoxically, her impersonal love for me felt so intimate that I felt she was closer to me that I was to myself. I actually felt embarrassed. If she was in my heart, then she was aware of all my greeds and hates, my selfishness, my hopes and fears.
>
> "Finally!" she said. The words appeared in my head, but they were in a husky, firm yet friendly feminine voice accustomed to giving orders. "You have no idea what it took to get you here. No idea!" The intensity of the last two words vibrated through my body like an earthquake. "Let's get down to business," she continued. "I am Kali.

> You are mine. If you are to worship any other goddess I will guide you in her direction. Do you understand me?" I nodded humbly.
>
> Sensing my mild state of shock, she stopped talking and sent me another radiant smile. Rings of light rippled out from her black and red statue. In that moment, she became the most beautiful female form I had ever seen. She was woman. The essence of change, the very power of the universe, driven by unfathomable, infinite love. In the conversation that followed, she revealed how she would be playing a much more obvious role in the healing and awakening of the planet.[61]

Kali continues to play an important role in his life. "My relationship with Kali Ma remains as dynamic and fresh as at that first meeting. . . . I have never sat down and channeled Kali Ma. Nor have I given much thought to this boon she has given me of hearing her voice. Since I have done very little to manipulate these events, I tend to take them at face value. She is, apparently, always right. Anytime she gives me a command—her 'advice' is invariably in the form of an action she wants me to take—the results are exactly as she predicts."[62]

Whereas Kali appears to some Western shaktas in statues or in transformations of other people, to others she appears through the arts. Le'ema Kathleen Graham, a dancer and teacher, says that the Dark Goddess began to appear in her dances in midlife, filling her life with depth and intensity:

> I realize now that Kali has had a hold of me most of my life. Kali has sunk her fang-like teeth into me and will not let go until she devours me whole. I feel her chasing me with sabre in hand, keeping me on the conscious path. Since my path is the dancing one, I created a devotional dance to this goddess with many aspects: Lover, Creatress, Mother of All, Destroyer of Falseness, Purifier, Awakener.
>
> In the form of classical East Indian Kathak, my dance to Kali depicts her in her aspect as a warrioress brandishing the sword of truth. Holding real fire in my hands, I make my entrance onto the stage. I sit in meditation and invoke Kali's presence by chanting her mantra: "Om Namo Kali Om," allowing myself to be filled with her, becoming one with the deity. Then the dance begins with fast and furious footwork to music by Ravi Shankar. Kali dances in the fire, the light of truth. Her truth can be fierce. Though it heals, the truth like a sword can hurt.
>
> Enacting Kali's fierceness through dance fills me with a sense of purpose and clarity, and the ecstasy of divine madness. Kali has the power of lightning, and my *mudras* illustrate her wide and wild eyes with lightning bolts darting from them. Kali's striking lightning bolts are the "ah-ha" insights I receive when, in the midst of a chaotic situtation, I get a flash of inspiritation that liberates me from a

> stuck place. I am set free to proceed with a fresh outlook. Kali is the great liberator of suffering. She is teaching me that it is only my attachments and expectations that create anguish. Through her quick lightning bolt action she transforms me.[63]

Part of Kali's appeal for this dancer lies in the goddess's acceptance of instinct and impurity. Kali is an immanent goddess:

> Kali is a force that says "Yes!" to primal instinctual energy. To me Kali is very much a goddess of the body. She is not some lofty, out-of-reach, intellectual, out-of-body deity. She is not removed from the human condition. I see Kali in the flesh, blood, bones and bowels of humans. Each time my baby sucks my breast for milk, or I water my garden with my sacred menstrual blood, or I feel my lover's lingam inside my yoni uniting us in Tantric bliss, I know that I am enacting Kali's holy rites. And I rejoice! Thank Goddess!
>
> I sing praises to Kali, the only goddess capable of sanctifying housework: ". . . Om Namo Kali Om . . . Oh Kali cleanup home . . . Om Namo Kali Om . . . I praise You when I mop the floors . . . Om Namo Kali Om . . . I praise You when I scrub the toilet . . . Om Namo Kali Om . . . I praise you when I turn the compost heap . . . Om Namo Kali Om . . ."[64]

Certainly this is not a typical orthodox Hindu view of the goddess, which still retains ideas of purity and impurity. However, the New Age allows for all sorts of original associations. Kali also represents anger and power: "My devotion to Kali has helped me see that even my anger is divine—and that it is okay to have an emotional body that responds to injustices of every kind. Kali has shown me that it is okay to go to the edge of death and come back a deeper person for having touched her blackness. Kali has taught me that saying 'no' and ending what no longer serves me or does not contribute to my truth, health, and well-being is absolutely appropriate. Kali tells me that it is okay to be a force to be reckoned with—to be a powerful woman!"[65]

The writer Cassia Berman grew up Jewish and in the Bronx, yet was attracted from an early age to various forms of the Divine Mother:

> Over the years, she has revealed to me with humor and grace many different aspects of herself—her beautiful faces as the goddesses of Hindu and other religions, as women of the past and present through whom she has incarnated, as a presence of light, and as a sweeter essence within me than I generally have let myself feel. . . . "It came as surprise when Mother Kali appeared in my life one summer day, and I felt her as that same sweetness in my heart that I have come to associate with gentler aspects of the Divine Mother. Her entrance, I slowly realized, was but an unveiling of a power,

> with all her images of seeming goriness and destruction, that had always been part of my inner iconography."[66]

She appreciates Kali's imagery, the naked woman dancing with heads and sword:

> Although women in our time have been actively tearing down the old stereotypes, exploring and rebuilding themselves psychically and psychologically, nothing in our culture really prepares us for the complete freedom and outrageous imagery with which Mother Kali is portrayed. The image of Mother Kali, wild hair flowing free, cutting off the heads of limited ideas so human beings can discover and experience for themselves the inherent freedom within, is a vision both men and women can benefit from and use as a guide.
>
> Through this powerful and provocative image, the seeming violence, negativity and incomprehensibility of life in this world is seen and personified as a beneficent, even delightful, dancing force. The often painful process of growth, change and movement is shown to be nothing more than the loving game of illusion the Mother of Consciousness plays with her children as she helps them shed the fetters of the false perspective to which they cling, that they may dance in freedom, too.[67]

While these sorts of prophetic calls usually come to Westerners from Kali, they sometimes appear from other goddesses. An ex-student of mine had a call from Durga, during her time as a Wiccan priestess (which in retrospect she figured was the closest thing that the West had to offer in terms of goddess worship). Durga's presence was initially introduced by dreams of Ganesha:

> I spent nearly ten years celebrating the Great Mother in the Neo-Pagan Community. But as I matured and grew in the Goddess, I longed for more structure on my religious path. I desperately yearned for ancient rituals, teachers, temples, scripture, and organization. I began to seriously consider what one religious studies professor once asked me, "Why do you look to the West when the Goddess has been worshiped since the dawn of time in the East?" About the same time, my brother returned from a year abroad where he lived with a Hindu family. His firsthand account of miracles, rituals, temples, and deities fascinated me. I began to recall my childhood fascination with Indian culture. So, I tentatively began to explore Hindu Goddesses and started taking yoga classes. It was as if floodgates had opened. I felt most drawn to the Goddess Durga and made every attempt to learn all I could about Her. I was overcome with tears when I read Hindu scripture. And within a month I had

received two dreams of Ganesh who encouraged me to continue down this particular path.

On the last night of July 1998 everything intensified. I had the most realistic, powerful, awe-inspiring dream of my entire life. As the dream began, I found myself in a deep, dark, pit. The pit was filled with flames of fire. Though I was completely naked and surrounded by the flames, I was not being burned. In fact, I wasn't even hot. Though I was not in physical pain, I felt a horrible internal burning—a horrible sense of anguish and despair. I felt as if my soul was on fire, and the pain of it was unbearable. I was completely and utterly helpless. There appeared to be no way to leave the pit and the flames were licking closer. Seeking relief, I turned my face up into the darkness above and cried out, "Ma!" The sound of it filled my body and conveyed my longing. Immediately Durga appeared riding up on Her lion. She was both unspeakably beautiful and utterly terrifying. Both She and Her lion were radiant and filled the darkness with their luminosity. Both had the appearance of liquid gold, as if you touched them your fingers would sink right in. It was if they were made of gold, including the lion's fur and Durga's hair, jewelry, and clothes. Both had tremendous energy pouring out of them and filled the void with rumblings of sound. Both had fierce looks on their faces and wild looks in their eyes, as if going into battle. Durga's eighteen arms wielded dangerous weapons and were flailing through the air. And yet, the beauty of the Mother shown forth equally.

As I looked into Her face, I was not afraid. Just then, Mother Durga made a frightening face, let out a loud war cry, and plunged Her spear into my chest. I was surprised but not scared. I felt no pain. When She withdrew the spear, a very small version of myself emerged out of my body, hanging on the tip of Her spear. This smaller me was also naked but was slimy wet as if newly born. She had waist-long brown hair and appeared fit and healthy. When I saw it, I knew immediately that this was the real me, my essence, my soul. Durga had claimed the authentic me for Her own by saving me from the flames of myself. She turned and rode off into the darkness with that part of me still dangling on Her spear tip. My body that was left behind crumpled like an empty shell and was consumed by the flames. As the body sunk into the flames I awoke.

Knowing that Durga came to me and claimed me as Her devotee has changed my life. I have devoted myself fully to Her. Through Durga, I am learning to cultivate the very best of myself as a spiritual being. Each day I strive to embody Her and to continue learning about and practicing Her ways.

> Since that first meeting with the Mother, She has visited me four other times in my dreams. I feel as if my walk with the Goddess is truly now just beginning. As Durga continues to reveal Herself through dreams, scripture, and the voices of others, I know I will continue to grow in many wonderful ways.[68]

These dreams of the goddess affected her strongly, to the point of now wearing saris, learning Sanskrit hymns and mantras, and performing daily rituals to Durga. Such calls are quite rare in the West.

The more traditional forms of goddess worship, such as goddess pujas, have never really been accepted in the West, even by New Age writers. Although there are a few goddess pujas performed by Western Hindu converts, most are performed by immigrant Indians in abbreviated fashion, often in rented halls with statues reused every year, and taped prayers and kirtans. I have attended Durga Pujas in the United States and Great Britain, in which the participants followed *bideshi niyam*, "foreigner's rules." This meant that variations in the traditional worship techniques were allowed. The rituals were abbreviated, with only the most necessary mantras used. Women listened in the front and men talked about business in the back, and children played outside. There was usually a small statue and a lot of food.

In his article "Durga Puja in South California," Pratapaditya Pal noted how Kali Puja tends to be left to the swamis of the Vedanta Center (with the Shiva below Kali's feet so covered up as to be invisible), while Durga Puja was a big community party with food and entertainment, a cultural program. He noted that the Western version of Bengali *barwari* or Durga worship was usually in a rented hall, and in both Europe and the United States it is not celebrated on the appropriate days from the almanac. This is because most businesses do not have five-day puja holidays, so the holiday is condensed into one weekend, which may or may not coincide with the correct days (sometimes different Bengali groups celebrate on different weekends).[69] There is Indian or semi-Indian dress (men wearing *kurta* and pants), and occasionally non-Indians attend. There is an emphasis on food and entertainment, especially fish or meat curry, rice pullao, and as close as anybody can get to Bengali desserts (*rasagullas* and sweet yogurt). Because it is difficult to get Durga statues in the West, they tend to be kept from year to year rather than immersed; thus there are no exciting farewell ceremonies in the Bengali style.[70] It may not have the grandeur of Durga Puja in Calcutta, but it is a way for immigrants in a new land to keep in touch with their traditions. People at the pujas in the United States speak of it as a locale for family solidarity (members of the extended family attend) and for supporting the Indian (or sometimes Indo-Pak) community, a place for young Indian men and women to meet, and occasionally a place to begin arrangements for marriages.

## Closing Notes

Whereas Hindu goddess pujas have changed little in the United States, and even encourage ties with orthodox Indian tradition, such practices as kundalini yoga and tantra have changed drastically. Why have such changes occurred?

There is greater freedom to change traditions in the United States than in India, perhaps related to the Protestant notion of the "priesthood of all believers." Everybody has his or her own access to the divine, and old traditions can be changed when necessary. We see a belief in essentialism, an ability to abstract what is important about a tradition and throw out the rest. This is not based on history or philosophy but rather on personal intuition. In a priesthood of all believers, a few images can be the basis of a new interpretation, and these are then mixed and matched in the cultural blender. Making up one's own religion gives the founder such Western virtues as freedom, power, and creativity, while its ties with older religions give authority. It is partly academic laziness, and partly the idea that religions are unfinished systems, and that continuing revelation allows the religion to stay alive. We have charismatic tantra and spontaneous kundalini yoga, revealed by religious leaders, inner Masters, visiting deities, aliens from UFOs, dolphins, and people claiming the right to forge their own interpretations of traditions—foreign or otherwise. Such interpretations are based on revelation, not on scholarly knowledge of the field. Traditional ritual worship is simply less interesting for these practitioners than spontaneous experience. Ancient knowledge is decorative, not authoritative. The goals of religion are this-worldly healing and bodily ecstasy.

As Rachel McDermott notes in her article on "The Western Kali," there are serious academic problems with New Age Western interpretations of the Kali tradition. The claims of ancient matriarchal societies have been discredited, the tendency to merge all goddesses into the same Great Goddess is problematic, Kali is not an ancient, primordial goddess (or the originator of the Sanskrit language, for she is first seen in the religious literature much later). The Western feminist claims of male "demonization" of Kali are not accurate to Kali's current, idealized bhakti image, and there are broader problems in transferring a deity out of context into a new cultural setting.[71] McDermott suggests that learning some history of the goddess might be an act of devotion.

Certainly this would be the case for people who respect traditional history. For people who reject academic history in favor of intuitive "spiritual history," however, historical facts do not matter. Much of New Age religion is ahistorical and charismatic, depending upon individual experience rather than past events. Disproving primordial matriarchy by historical method does not make it any less real to believers; it is emotionally real if it is not historically real. A goddess's old history is not really important—that was her old marriage, this is her new one, and the present is more important than the past. Living in the eternal present comes to represent a rejection of the past. With all of the controversy about whether there is such a thing as history at all, the field of history becomes subjective, open to competing claims. New histories are a means of empowerment, and old histories written by oppressors are not to be trusted. New understandings are driven by new revelations, and by "entrepreneurs of ecstasy," as David White phrases it.[72]

Thus, in the worship of Hindu goddesses, traditional worship can remain for those who wish to follow the traditional understandings of the goddesses. For those who wish to use the goddesses as parts of a political argument or a justification for a different social order, however, their origins fall away as do their sympathies with various oppressive patriarchal gods, and new histories and interpretations are written for them. And for many New Age participants, using pieces of a tradition is not a sign of disrespect. It is a sign of accepting the modern form of Shakta Vedanta, in which all roads, and all pieces of those roads, lead to a divine end.

In the West, it is Shakta Vedanta that has become most popular, a path that encompasses all deities and philosophies. As it has developed in the United States, it becomes the justification for following many paths at once and incorporating different theologies and ritual systems into a single unique collage, one's religious life as a personal combination of spiritualities and imagery. Originally spread by the various Vedanta Centers and Ramakrishna Missions, it has developed a life of its own, and become the theological justification for a wide variety of American new religions. Shaktism has changed in transit, remade in a new image.

# 6

# Conclusions

## The Goddess: One or Many?

In his book *All the Mothers Are One*, Stanley Kurtz looks at some of the arguments about Hindu goddesses, and whether they are separate deities or really only one goddess in many forms.[1] He mentions the venerable Great and Little Traditions, Lawrence Babb's opposition between married benevolent goddesses and unmarried malevolent ones,[2] Lynn Bennett's opposition between dangerous wives marrying into families from outside and sisters and daughters who give merit,[3] and Lynn Gatwood's unmarried Devis versus married Spouse Goddesses.[4] Following the title of his book, Kurtz has found that all goddesses are believed to be really one, and that these dichotomies and models are only partially accurate.

Kurtz's main bases for his understanding of goddesses are the statements of his informants, who equated the newly publicized goddess Santoshi Ma (his main area of interest) with a variety of other goddesses. Listening to informants is a very good way to find out about popular ideas, and he cites them well and clearly. Different groups of informants often have different perspectives, however.

Kurtz's informants told him that Santoshi Ma and Vaishno Devi, as well as other goddesses, were really the same being. I also had informants who would equate various goddesses. But I also had tribal and village informants in West Bengal tell me that not only were goddesses like Kali, Durga, and Lakshmi different beings but that the Kali of one village was not the same Kali that another village worshiped. They were in rivalry for who was the best and most powerful Kali.

There were also many villages who worshiped the goddess Chandi, and these were also in competition rather than being the same goddess. There were dramatized battles between the village goddesses, to show that they were opposed, and insults toward other goddesses, who were called ugly, weak, and beggars in village songs. Sometimes battles between villages reflected the battles between their deities. Goddesses who appeared in dream commands were often jealous, and forbade the worship of other gods and goddesses.[5] Unlike the goddesses in the famous Hindi film *Santoshi Ma*, however, these goddesses were never reconciled to each other, and remained permanently alienated.

This approach of deities in rivalry for status is not unique to Shaktism. I visited a rural village in West Bengal where each year there was a *thakur panchayat*, a meeting where the Krishna statues of the village would be carried in procession and feasted, after which the statues would get together to discuss the next year's budget and future festivals. There was much rivalry as to which Krishna would lead the procession and sit at the best seat at the table. The villagers each argued for the superiority of their own Krishna over the neighbors' Krishna, and the Krishnas were understood to be rivals, rather than identical. None of them was good or evil—the question was where they stood on the status continuum.

Whether the goddess is one or many is a conscious political decision, a statement of affiliation as well as faith. Does the person identify with a particular caste, family, or tribal group represented by a particular goddess? Or does he or she identify with a goddess representing a broader group—let us say that form of Kali who is universal consciousness, the basis of the modern Ramakrishnaite universalists, who can subsume even Western religions?

These perspectives are reflected in understandings of the goddesses, and each has its advantages. Identification with a particular group (as standing against other groups) and glorifying a particular goddess gives a sense of loyalty, tradition, lineage, reverence for ancestors, and the security of continuity with a particular situation from the past. Identification with the whole, and equating goddesses together, shows a broader perspective, often education and upper-caste status, and a more cosmopolitan outlook. Whereas particular and individual goddesses tend to be immanent, associated with a place or a group, universal goddesses tend to be transcendent, living in paradises and only visiting earth temporarily. In many folk stories, goddesses are bound in rocks and statues—and perhaps it is their bondage to matter that gives them their individuality.

Goddesses also have multiple identities because they have multiple origins. For example, Durga, as shown in chapter 4, incorporates a cannibalistic tree goddess, a vegetation goddess, a fierce warrior goddess, a black tribal goddess, a jackal goddess, an old tribal ancestress, a young bride, a baby-killing demoness, a burning ground goddess, a goddess of purity and courage, a virgin defending her honor, the power of good over evil, a personification of virtue, and the sustainer of the universe. Is she negative or positive, one or many?

No single answer can be given—as noted in the Introduction, Shaktism includes monism, monotheism, dualism, polytheism, henotheism, and animism. As Kurtz states of nurturing and destructive goddesses, "Thus we are faced not with a simple duality but with a double poled malevolence and benevolence along which move a multiplicity of beings whose identities constantly split and merge."[6] Whether the goddess is one or many is certainly influenced by early childhood experience, as Kurtz suggests. It is also influenced by schooling, theological perspective, political philosophy, group identity, and concepts of community, as well as the individual's religious experiences.

The use of typology in this book allows for some of this complexity to be examined, though the weaving together of the folk, tantric, and bhakti strands of Shaktism.

## On Postcolonialism, Postmodernism, and Those Who Can Say What the Natives Think Better than the Natives Themselves

Another relevant issue that has involved Indologists recently, both in terms of ideas and emotions, is the topic of colonialism. It has become linked with postmodern thought, and questions how much outsiders can know about religious traditions of oppressed people. The colonialism being challenged is Western, primarily the domination of British concepts ("intellectual hegemony") and economic and political organization over native Indian concerns. Such dominance is thought to have warped both Indians' views of themselves, and the Western religionists' understanding of India as a culture.

Postcolonial and postmodern writers write about various sorts of oppression among diverse populations. In India and other countries, they look at situations (according to Homi Bhabha) "where populations are culturally diverse, racially and ethnically divided—the objects of social, racial, and sexual discrimination."[7] He speaks of the "articulation of Language" as central to an understanding of identity, especially for those "on the lookout for marginalization" in the "politics of difference." Language is the major way to redefine identity and think "outside the certainty of the sententious," which is necessary to eventually redefine social structure and "conceive of a political strategy of empowerment and articulation" by the "disjunctive, fragmented, displaced agency of those who have suffered the sentence of history."[8]

Generally, such theorizing is quite alien to the actual oppressed groups. At least in West Bengal, many of the most oppressed groups (and here I mean low-caste and tribal groups) are not literate, and would not be terribly concerned about "Language" and the new redefined terminology and abstract empowerment strategies of the postcolonial writers. As Lata Mani writes,

> Curiously, despite disavowal of theorizing as disembodied activity, the history of cultural analysis in the past forty years can often sound like a bloodless tale of theoretical innovation and reformulation. This effectively banishes to the margins people whose collective hopes and struggles have ruptured hitherto dominant fictions. They are refigured as "evidence" in a story that is partly of their own making; their practices serving to corroborate, or refine, not produce theory. As such they come to represent the "nature" (raw material) out of which (Western) "cultural analysis" is produced.[9]

Most tribal people or Adivasis with whom I have spoken are not interested in being redefined or serving as "evidence"—they want to keep their land because it is sacred, or they want to get it back from industrialists and developers and they want people to respect their beliefs and customs, and their deities. If postcolonial writers are truly interested in defending the oppressed, they should be interested in the response of the oppressed to their theories—and they should try to learn about and respect the religions and customs of the people.

Besides the fact of widespread illiteracy, postcolonial writing and critiques of the British are not influential among low-caste and tribal groups (and high castes are a small minority in West Bengal) because they had little encounter with the British in the first place. Mani notes that the colonial state "achieved not hegemony but dominance" as it affected Indian society very unevenly.[10] Western intellectual categories may have had a noteworthy effect upon the upper castes (popularly known in West Bengal as the "chattering classes"), but its effect on the more seriously oppressed was much more minor—they had other concerns.

Much modern colonialist writing deals with damage to Indian self-esteem as a result of British education. This is a problem, but mostly for those who have an education. For those without education, or only a few years' worth, oppression is often more than a problem of self esteem, for the rural poor there are problems of survival, of both the individual and the culture. India has been independent for over fifty years, and many rural people have little idea who the British were or what they did.

I discussed the topic of colonialism and the effects of outside domination in India in passing with Shaktas of various types in different areas of West Bengal. Although there is no colloquial Bengali term for "colonialism," everybody understood the concept of outsiders coming in and telling people what to do and how to think, and there is a term for colony.

Among tribals and many low-caste Shaktas, the true colonialists were not the British (with whom they had very little communication or concern), but rather the high-caste Hindus and government representatives who burn their houses and force them off their land because that land is wanted for building projects, dams, factories, or mining. Because tribal and low-caste villagers tend to own their land as an inheritance from their ancestors, as opposed to having a basis in written forms and deeds, they can be understood by bureaucrats as not owning or having any right to the land upon which their families have lived for generations, even centuries. They are told that they are ignorant, and being moved off their land for their own good or for the good of more important others, and they should accept it without protest. Often these are sacred lands, with places blessed by deities and holding the spirits of their ancestors. This has been a major problem in recent years with the building of dams and roads through tribal areas, and with developers building on cheap rural land. Sometimes the inhabitants are expelled from their lands without compensation or other lands given in exchange.

This is the reason why many tribal and low-caste people banded together for the creation of the Jharkhand state—to gain freedom from the people who look down at their religion and culture as "primitive," and tell them that they cannot make legitimate decisions about their land unless they are educated "correctly." These aggressors and colonialists, however, are not Western—they are brahmanical Hindu. I spoke with Jharkhand activists who told me that their children were not allowed to speak their traditional languages in the schools, that their local customs (such as tree marriage) were forbidden, and that their voices were not heard.

As Roma Chatterji describes a protest in Purulia:

> the people of the forests, of the mountains and bushes, had come out of their isolation, out of their silence—the men with their falchions and axes and the women (the mothers and sisters) with kitchen knives and brooms in their hands. They were prepared to challenge the usurpers—the rich men, the *mahajans, thikedars* and *purohits* who were trembling in fear because the earth (i.e. the people of this land) was slowly beginning to slide from under their feet. The usurpers, they said, sometimes in the name of Marx and sometimes in the name of Gandhi, had taken Jharkhand away from the people and had exploited them.[11]

Although currently the term *Hindu* (or *Indian*) *diaspora* is often used to refer to Hindus in other countries for jobs or education, the term *diaspora* refers to people who have been forced out of their land, not those who left to gain wealth. It seems that the real diaspora is not outside of India but within India—the rural poor who have left their lands involuntarily and under threat of force.

Among Shakta tantrikas, both urban and rural, I also encountered great anger and fear toward the powerful group that was persecuting them. This group told them that they were primitive and superstitious, and that their ideas were wrong and not in accord with history and science. It was not British colonialist influence determining this attitude, however—it was the Communist leaders in West Bengal and the criminals (*goondas*) hired by them (as well as the public school children sent out by the communist "clubs" to harass tantrikas). Sadhus and tantrikas were being blamed for West Bengal's lack of wealth and backwardness, and the state wanted to be rid of them—partly because their religious ideology was in competition with communist ideology. Tantrikas were called parasites, freeloaders, and dangers to the state; they were accused of being loafers if they meditated, and black magicians if they acted. Bengali communists wished to reeducate them, telling them how to think, what to value, and how to act. Tantrikas interviewed feared these quasi-colonialist aggressors (they recognized that the ideas came from Russia and China, not India or the United States), but there was little that they could do, having little social organization and political power themselves.

Shakta bhaktas had mixed views of colonialism, the strongest opinions coming from the Shakta nationalists and Shakta universalists. I encountered very few Shakta nationalists, and their views were a conglomeration of perspectives. There was pro-Marxist, anti-Western-imperialist feeling, for those who saw Marxism as the goddess's blessing of future wealth. This was a small group, however, most Marxists (and there are many in West Bengal) are not Shakta, but rather atheist. For others, there was disillusion with communism (the Soviet Union had fallen, and its promises of wealth and power based on following Marxist ideology were shown to be empty). There was a sort of malaise, and for some a return to nationalism and patriotism. Some had joined the BJP political party and focused on Rama as the fighter for Bharat Mata (or they said that Durga supported him and gave him his strength). Yet others said that both Muslim and British colonialists were past threats, ancient history, and one needed to pay attention to the current threats—radical Islam and the "Muslim Crescent" over India, and China's aggressive action in taking Indian border land. Weapons were the goddess's gift, and that was what India really needed. The Shakta nationalists did not understand their views to be shaped by the distant West—they were shaped by real and present political and economic threats.

Shakta universalists on the whole were extremely positive about Western influence; it brought greater literacy, science, humanitarianism, and incidentally greater status for their own perspective. Since a universalist perspective can incorporate other traditions and belief systems fairly easily, the West was not a religious or intellectual threat. All of the West's ideas came ultimately from *brahman*, so no Western idea was unique or original. British philosophy came originally from *brahman*, so there was no threat to Indian ideas or self-esteem. The British political rule was a difficult period, but like Muslim rule, that is ancient history. The great challenge is for India to organize itself politically and economically today.

The concerns about Western colonialism and intellectual hegemony heard so frequently among Western-trained Indologists were notably absent among my Bengali informants, especially the rural ones. There was anger about specific events. At that time, many Bengalis were very much against the GATT treaty and its effects (especially on the patenting of seeds), and a few of the Marxists in street protests called this "colonialism" and "imperialism" (they spoke English). But the Marxists had strikes (*bandhas*) over all sorts of things, not just actions by the United States—and people obeyed them not because they agreed with the strikes but rather because they feared being harassed or beaten if they went outside (or thought that joining them would lead to increased political power, or possibly a job). Alternatively, some older people whispered that they wished the British would come back, as one older informant phrased it, "When the British were here, the trains ran on time and the streets were cleaned every day. Look at the mess things are in now."[12]

It is important to remember that insider and outsider are relative terms, and colonialism can only come from outsiders (otherwise, no matter how aggressive and domineering a group may be, it is still "us" and not a foreign power). For the tribals and low-caste Hindus, it is the high-caste Hindus and Bengali Marxists who are the colonial power, taking their land and resources and justifying it by the primitive and inferior mental state of the villagers. For the tantrikas, it is primarily the communists with their Russian and Chinese ideologies who are the colonialists, chasing them out of jobs (if they are discovered to be tantrikas) and ashrams, and justifying it by denigrating the tantrika's superstitious and ignorant nature. For the Shakta nationalists, colonialists could be Pakistani, British, or Chinese—whoever was understood to be a threat to the country. They were most concerned about China and Pakistan having usurped parts of Kashmir; this was the biggest outside threat. All of these "outsiders" had their own way of thinking, and their own desire for land, wealth, and power, which they tried to impose on others.

In the area of Shakta religion, early British scholarship has had relatively little influence upon most serious study of the field. This is because Shaktism was initially ignored—most early British scholars focused upon sacred Sanskrit texts (primarily the Vedas, Upanishads, and epics), and the highest castes. The people who paid most attention to Shaktas were not scholars but rather Christian missionaries and travelers who fulminated about Shaktism as demon-worship, perversion, and licentious sinfulness. Most serious scholars have seen this sort of denigration of other cultures and religions before, and recognize the biases it contains. The first real scholar of Shaktism, Sir John Woodroffe, was a sympathizer who wrote of ways in which the East was advanced and the West was primitive.

Colonialism is not a product of only one set of villains. It is multidimensional, with all sorts of groups trying to dominate one another. Its great current danger, to my view, is the way it motivates scholars to substitute politics or moral judgments for scholarship. It is easier to be an armchair hero and ethicist and talk about the evils of other people than it is to travel through rural India and learn firsthand the cultures and values of village people. I was struck by the number of urban, educated Calcutta Marxists with whom I spoke who would talk about their solidarity with the villagers against the imperialists, yet who had never even visited a village (they gave various excuses, the most popular being "They speak a different dialect—we wouldn't even understand each other"). These were not Western writers who had never visited villages. These were Indian, who had spent their lives in India, but they were more interested in speaking about the oppressed than with the oppressed.

Anticolonialist writing often claims that outside observers can never really know a culture, and therefore the only role left to observers and scholars is to focus upon the uses of language about the culture, or to defend the culture against various abstract threats by outsiders. This theorizing and alienated approach leaves people ignorant about cultures and religions that are worthy of our attention and respect.

## Shaktism and the Future

One of the reasons why the explosion of nuclear weapons appeals to India (besides the fear of dangerous neighbors), I believe, is because it unites the opposite sides of the modern and ancient traditions—the scientific knowledge and technology of modern India with the traditional folk commitment to the sanctity and defense of the land. By uniting these extremes of ancient and modern, it came to be a uniting force in India, until its negative international and economic implications began to appear. But concern for weapons cannot be entirely rejected, because of the dangers at India's borders.

One can only hope that in the future there will be healthier mixtures of ancient and modern. Certainly the emergence of another great Shakta poet like Ramprasad (who was both a bhakta and a tantrika), or a teacher and sage who can incorporate diverse elements of local traditions with other global traditions like Ramakrishna, would bring together many aspects of the tradition, or even India as a nation. Bengali Shaktism is a charismatic tradition, continually changing with new revelations. Goddesses can unite castes and act as an opposing force for India's tendency to differentiate and create hierarchies, and they can give a sense of religious optimism, countering the tendency toward secular and poetic pessimism about corrupt Bengali or Indian society. Although the fall of the Soviet Union still casts a malaise over much of urban West Bengal (many people hoped for a secular salvation through political change), Shaktas talk enthusiastically about Ramakrishna, Anandamayi Ma, Vamakshepa, and other religious role models. Such figures seemed immune to the temporal changes in India, especially in political and economic circumstances. Despite the political focus of the urban culture, many Bengali Shakta informants who were professional people maintained a traditionally religious approach to life and planned on having retirements in which they would perform religious ritual and meditation.

There are many ways that newer ideas may appear in older idioms, and thus be able to appeal to a wider range of people. I would suggest dream commands, especially as found in some types of folk Shaktism and Shakta bhakti, as the perfect modern symbol. What might some of the goddesses say to modern Bengalis?

*Lakshmi*, goddess of wealth and fortune, might give a dream command that her temples be purged of black money (untaxed money gained and stored illegally), that black marketeers and tax evaders actually be prosecuted, and unnecessary government bureaucracy and resistance to innovation be trimmed as a special blessing to devout businessmen.

*Durga*, goddess of morality and martial victory, might give a dream command that triumph should be understood as successfully gaining peace as well as successfully waging war. She might bless victory in diplomacy and statesmanship, and international agreements that are honored. Her manifestation as *Vana Durga*, goddess of the woods, might call for reforestation and ecological concern.

*Sarasvati*, goddess of literature and the arts, might give a dream command that all village children, male and female, must learn to read, and that some of the many unemployed PhDs from the cities should do volunteer work in the villages. They could teach reading, and the arts as well. She might also demand that schools and universities hire trained teachers instead of politically connected people with little qualification for the job. *Shitala*, the disease goddess (traditionally of smallpox, and today the AIDS goddess) could send a command about care in disease transmission and research on cures and vaccinations, while *Shashthi*, protector of children, might demand the adoption of street children and war orphans, or the creation of crisis centers for abused women and children.

And of course poor *Ma Ganga*, the eternally pure and vastly polluted river Ganges, might command her devotees to save their mother and cleanse her waters. While they are at it, they could also do some work on air and noise pollution, and *Kali* could dance in the burning grounds upon the corpses of old rusted cars and three-wheelers devoid of pollution equipment.

One can only dream. . . . The future uses of the goddesses remains to be seen.

# Notes

## INTRODUCTION

1. Birendramohan Dasgupta, ed., *Saṃsad Bengali-English Dictionary*, 2nd ed. (Calcutta: Sahitya Samsad, 1983), p. 818.

2. Pupul Jayakar, *The Earth Mother: Legends, Goddesses, and Ritual Arts of India* (San Francisco: Harper and Row, [1980] 1990), pp. 178–179.

3. June McDaniel, *The Madness of the Saints: Ecstatic Religion in Bengal* (Chicago: University of Chicago Press, 1989).

4. Milton Singer, ed., *When A Great Tradition Modernizes: An Anthropological Approach to India Civilization* (New York: Praeger Publishers, 1972, p. 56

5. Mircea Eliade, *Shamanism: Archaic Techniques of Ecstasy* (Princeton: Princeton University Press, 1974), p. 5.

6. I chose the term "emotional Shakta bhakti" mindful of Friedhelm Hardy's *Viraha-bhakti: The Early History of Krsna Devotion in South India* (Delhi: Oxford University Press, 1983). In this book, he distinguishes between intellectual bhakti, which involves loyalty and yogic concentration, and emotional bhakti, which involves passionate love. These are important distinctions that clarify styles of bhakti, though they work out slightly differently in Vaishnavism than in Shaktism.

7. J. Hastings, ed., *The Encyclopedia of Religion and Ethics* (New York: Charles Scribner's Sons, 1928), vol. 6, pp. 705–706.

8. Ramaprasad Chanda, *The Indo-Aryan Races* (New Delhi: Indological Book Corp., 1976), p. 148.

9. Informal interviews, 1983–1984, 1993–1994, of about forty informants in various professions.

10. Subalcandra Mitra, *Saral bangala abhidhān* (Calcutta: New Bengal

Press, 1991), p. 1, 210; Jnanendramohan Das, *Bangala bhāsar abhidhān* (Calcutta: Sahitya Samsad, 1991), vol. 2, p. 1934.

11. *Vyāvahārika śabdakośa* (Calcutta: Presidency Library, 1958), p. 897.

12. Haricarana Bandyopadhyaya, *Bangiya śabdakośa* (Calcutta: Sahitya Akademi, 1988), vol. 2, p. 2,004.

13. Asutosa Dev, *Śabdabodh abhidhān* (Calcutta: A. Dev, 1949), p. 1,147.

14. Baridbaran Ghosh, ed. *Bhāratvārśīya upāsaka-saṁpradāya* (Calcutta: Karuna Prakasani, 1397/1990), p. 108.

15. Joseph Wilkins, *Modern Hinduism, an Account of the Religious Life of the Hindus in Northern India* (London: Curzon Press, 1901/1975) p. 340–41.

16. John Campbell Oman, *The Brahmans, Theists and Muslims of India: Studies of Goddess Worship in Bengal, Caste, Brahmaism, and Social Reform, with Descriptive Sketches of Curious Festivals, Ceremonies and Faquirs* (London: T. Fisher Unwin, 1907), p. 24.

17. Interview, Satyakam Sengupta, Calcutta, 1984.

18. Interview, Narendranath Bhattacaryya, Calcutta, 1984.

19. Sankar Sen Gupta, *Folklore of Bengal—A Projected Study* (Calcutta: Indian Publications, 1976), p. 6.

20. Shashibhusan Dasgupta, *Obscure Religious Cults* (Calcutta: Firma KLM, 1976) p. xxxiii.

21. From news note in *Christian Science Monitor*, August 17, 1999, citing *1999 World Almanac and Book of Facts.*

22. Sukumar Sen, *A History of Bengali Literature* (New Delhi: Sahitya Akademi, [1960] 1979), p. 4.

23. Ibid., p. 35.

24. Dasgupta, *Obscure Religious Cults*, p. xliii.

25. Sen Gupta, *Folklore of Bengal*, p. 14.

26. Narendranath Bhattacharyya, *History of the Śakta Religion* (New Delhi: Munshiram Mahoharlal, 1974); and Bhattacharyya, *Indian Mother Goddess* (Calcutta: Indian Studies Past and Present, 1971); Sukumar Sen, *The Great Goddesses in Indic Tradition* (Calcutta: Papyrus, 1983); Vijaya Lakshmi Chaudhuri, *The Development of Mother Goddess Worship* (Shantiniketan: Visva-Bharati Research Publications, 1987).

27. Jayakar, *The Earth Mother*; Ernest A. Payne, *The Saktas: An Introductory and Comparative Study* (Calcutta: Y.M.C.A. Press/Oxford University Press, 1933).

28. Kathleen Erndl, *Victory to the Mother: The Hindu Goddess of Northwest India in Myth, Ritual, and Symbol* (New York: Oxford University Press, 1993); William S. Sax, *Mountain Goddess: Gender and Politics in a Himalayan Pilgrimage* (New York: Oxford University Press, 1991).

29. Jeffrey J. Kripal, *Kālī's Child: The Mystical and the Erotic in the Life and Teachings of Ramakrishna* (Chicago: University of Chicago Press, 1995); Stanley N. Kurtz, *All the Mothers Are One: Hindu India and the Cultural Reshaping of Psychoanalysis* (New York: Columbia University Press, 1992).

30. David Kinsley, *Hindu Goddesses: Visions of the Divine Feminine in the Hindu Religious Tradition* (Berkeley: University of California Press, 1988); John Stratton Hawley and Donna Marie Wulff, eds. *Devī: Goddesses of India* (Berkeley: University of

California Press, 1996); Tracy Pintchman, ed. *Seeing Mahādevī: Constructing the Identities of the Hindu Great Goddess* (Albany: State University of New York Press, 2001).

31. Subrata Kumar Mukhopadhyay, *Cult of the Goddess Sitala in Bengal: An Enquiry into Folk Culture* (Calcutta: Firma KLM, 1994); P. K. Maity, *Historical Studies in the Cult of the Goddess Manasā* (Calcutta: Punthi Pustak, 1966).

32. C. Mackenzie Brown, *The Triumph of the Goddess: The Canonical Models and Theological Visions of the Devī-Bhāgavata Purāna* (Albany: State University of New York Press, 1990); Thomas B. Coburn, *Encountering the Goddess: A Translation of the Devī-Māhātmya and a Study of Its Interpretation* (Albany: State University of New York Press, 1991); and Coburn, *Devī-Māhātmya: The Crystallization of the Goddess Tradition* (Delhi: Motilal Banarsidass, 1988).

33. Rachel Fell McDermott, *Mother of My Heart, Daughter of My Dreams: Kālī and Umā in the Devotional Poetry of Bengal* (New York: Oxford University Press, 2001); Leonard Nathan and Clinton Seely, trans. *Grace and Mercy in Her Wild Hair: Selected Poems to the Mother Goddess* (Prescott, Ariz.: Hohm, 1999).

34. Tracy Pintchman, *The Rise of the Goddess in Hindu Tradition* (Albany: State University of New York Press, 1994); Usha Dev, *The Concept of Śakti in the Purānas* (Delhi: Nag Publishers, 1987); Pushpendra Kumar, *Śakti and Her Episodes: On the Basis of Ancient Indian Traditions and Mythology* (Delhi: Eastern Book Linkers, 1981),

35. Teun Goudriaan and Sanjukta Gupta, *Hindu Tantric and Śākta Literature* (Wiesbaden: Otto Harrasowitz, 1981); David R. Kinsley, *Tantric Visions of the Divine Feminine: The Ten Mahāvidyās* (Berkeley: University of California Press, 1997); Narendranath Bhattacharyya, *History of the Tantric Religion* (New Delhi: Manohar, 1982).

36. Arthur Avalon (Sir John Woodroffe), *Shakti and Shakta* (New York: Dover, [1918] 1978); Sir John Woodroffe (Arthur Avalon), ed. *Principles of Tantra* (Madras: Ganesh, [1918] 1986); Douglas Renfrew Brooks, *The Secret of the Three Cities: An Introduction to Hindu Śākta Tantrism* (Chicago: University of Chicago Press, 1990).

37. Edward C. Dimock, Jr., *The Place of the Hidden Moon: Erotic Mysticism in the Vaisnava-Sahajiyā Cult of Bengal* (Chicago: University of Chicago Press, [1960] 1989); Hugh Urban, *The Economics of Ecstasy: Tantra, Secrecy and Power in Colonial Bengal* (New York: Oxford University Press, 2001).

## 1. FOLK SHAKTISM

1. W. L. Smith, *The One-Eyed Goddess: A Study of the Manasā Mangal* (Stockholm: Almqvist and Wiksell, 1980), p. 74.

2. *Adhyatma Ramayana: The Spiritual Version of the Rama Saga*, translated by Swami Tapasyananda (Madras: Sri Ramakrishna Matha, 1985), vv.27–32, pp. 26–27.

3. We see this is the story of Tarakhya Devi, in Asok Mitra, ed., *Paścimbangera pūjā-parban o melā* (Delhi: Controller of Publications, 1992), vol. 4, p. 49.

4. Having people receive commands to unearth statues of deities is not unique to India. For instance, in their book *Image and Pilgrimage in Christian Culture: Anthropological Perspectives* (New York: Columbia University Press, 1978), Victor and Edith Turner describe the "shepherds' cycle" of the Spanish cult of Virgin Mary. This was a collection of legends, current between the ninth and thirteenth centuries, describing

the miraculous discovery of Virgin Mary statues by shepherds, cowherds, and farmers. The discoverer is led to the image by various supernatural events: visions of Mary or angels, acts of devotion by animals, mysterious lights, and sounds. Often a church is built on the site of the statue's discovery, after the statue is taken away to another locale but then is reported to have returned on its own to the place where it was found. Silver statues were sometimes hidden to protect them; when they were unearthed, the silver had often tarnished, thus creating the "black Virgins" found in many European shrines. See Turner and Turner, *Image and Pilgrimage*, pp. 41–42.

5. See the story of Adya Shakti and Annada Thakur in chapter 4 below.

6. Bholanath Bhattacharya, "The Spring Time Fair of Makar Chandi of Makardah," *Modern Review* (Calcutta), September 1971, p. 174.

7. R. M. Sarkar, *Regional Cults and Rural Traditions* (New Delhi: Inter-India Publications, 1986), p. 134.

8. Interview, elementary school teacher, Bolpur, 1994.

9. Sarkar, *Regional Cult*, p. 139.

10. Gopendra Krsna Basu, *Baṅglar laukika debatā* (Calcutta: Ananda, 1969), p. 104.

11. Tushar K. Niyogi, *Aspects of Folk Cults in South Bengal* (Calcutta: Anthropological Survey of India, 1987), p. 6.

12. Ibid., p. 38.

13. Nanimadhab Chaudhuri, "The Cult of the Old Lady," *Journal of the Royal Asiatic Society of Bengal*, Letters, Vol. 5, 1939, pp. 417–18.

14. Ibid., p. 419.

15. Interview, Pashupati Mahato, Purulia, 1994.

16. Chaudhuri, "Cult of the Old Lady," p. 419.

17. Mitra, *Paścimbangera pūjā-parban o melā*, vol. 4, pp. 271–72.

18. Sibendu Manna, *Mother Goddess Candi* (Calcutta: Punthi Pustak, 1993), p. 90.

19. Interview, Deyashi (nonbrahmin priest), Purulia, 1994.

20. Manna, *Mother Goddess Candi*, p. 199.

21. The anthropologist describing this ritual does not discuss its meaning, but one might speculate that thread linking people with a sacred tree could be appropriate for weavers.

22. Manna, *Mother Goddess Candi*, pp. 157–60.

23. Ibid., pp. 140–147.

24. Ibid., p. 108.

25. Himangsu Mohan Ray, *Savara, the Snake Charmer* (Calcutta: ISRAA, 1986), p. 135. Chandi is here called the Hadi's daughter, or the daughter of a low-caste person. It is sometimes said that Chandi once took on human form as a member of the Hadi caste, thus blessing all members of that caste. This chant is retranslated here, in order to represent the original rhythm and imagery (the book translated it into a prose paragraph).

26. Ibid., p. 138.

27. *Kālikā Purāna*, 14.14–21.

28. Ibid., 14.54.

29. Ibid., 43.1–10.

30. Ibid., 43.15–24.

31. Ibid., 43.26–49. Kali/Parvati/Uma performing austerities to gain the god's love became a sort of model for other humans and goddesses. For instance, the *Brahmavaivarta Purana* has stories of Tulsi performing austerities "for a celestial lakh of years" to win Krishna's love.

32. From this event came the Bengali expression that it as difficult for a new wife to be accepted into her husband's household as it is to cook iron beans. It takes a woman of great skill to make iron beans edible, and to please her in-laws.

33. Since this story, the phrase "crossing the ocean on a banana raft" has come mean in Bengal accomplishing a difficult or impossible feat due to one's bravery or faith. See Chitrita Banerji, *Life and Food in Bengal* (New Delhi: Rupa and Co, 1991), p. 8.

34. Pradyot Kumar Maity, *Historical Studies in the Cult of the Goddess Manasā* (Calcutta: Punthi Pustak, 1966), chapter 3.

35. Other writers also say that Aniruddha and Usha were exiled from heaven and cast into human form because Usha had married secretly and become pregnant, and that Lakhindar was married to Behula because he had forcibly embraced and kissed his aunt, which made his parents think that it was time for him to marry.

36. R. S. Dineschandra Sen, *The Folk Literature of Bengal* (Calcutta: University of Calcutta, 1920), p. 266.

37. Ibid.

38. Interviews, members of Charak Gajan procession and observers, Calcutta, 1983.

39. See the biographies of several such holy women in my *The Madness of the Saints: Ecstatic Religion in Bengal* (Chicago: University of Chicago Press, 1989), chapter 5.

40. For details of her life, see Yogesvari Devi in chapter 5 of my *The Madness of the Saints.*

41. Interview, Jayashri Ma, Birbhum, 1994.

42. Ibid.

43. Interviews, Archanapuri Ma, Calcutta, 1994; Jayashri Ma, Birbhum, 1994.

44. See the story of Lakshmi Ma in my book *The Madness of the Saints*, pp. 215–20.

45. L. P. Varma, D. K. Srivastava, and R. N. Sahay, "Possession Syndrome," *Indian Journal of Psychiatry* 12 nos. 1 and 2 (January–April, 1970).

46. Pramanatha Bose, *A History of Hindu Civilization during British Rule.* Volume 1, *Religious Condition* (New Delhi: Asian Publishing Services, [1894] 1978), p. 74.

47. Interview, Moyda, milkseller, 1993.

48. Interview, Moyda, temple priest or *sevait*, 1993.

49. Parvati lives in a Santal village, where the huts are made of mud and thatch. A layer of liquified cow dung is placed on the dirt floor in order to purify the environment.

50. Interviews, Birbhum, 1994.

51. Pranab, *Thakur as Revealed to Pranab* (Howrah: A. K. Sanyal, 1963), pp. 1–3.

52. Predicting the future is often associated with *vak siddhi*, in which whatever a

person says becomes true. To my knowledge, no statistics were kept of the truth of these predictions.

53. A violation of their ritual practice in giving offerings.

54. Pranab, *Thakur*, pp. 40–44.

55. Story translated by Bengali devotees, Brooklyn, 1976.

56. Story translated by Bengali devotees, Brooklyn, 1976.

57. Informal interview, devotee, Brooklyn, 1976.

58. Informal interview, devotee, Brooklyn, 1976.

59. Informal interview, devotee, Brooklyn, 1976.

60. Informal interview, *patua* artists, Calcutta, 1984.

## 2. TANTRIC AND YOGIC SHAKTISM

1. Satindramohan Chattopadhyaya, *Tantrer kathā* (Calcutta: Sahitya Samsad 1983), p. 99.

2. Interview, elementary school principal, Bakreshwar, 1993.

3. These issues have been much discussed by the Society for Tantric Studies, and came to mind most recently after a discussion with Charlie Orzech.

4. Cited in Sriyukta Siva Candra Vidyarnava Bhattacarya Mahodaya, *Tantra Tattva*, translated by Sir John Woodroffe as *Principles of Tantra* (Madras: Ganesh, 1986), Part I, p. 70. Cited hereafter as Bhattacarya, *Principles of Tantra.*

5. Chattopadhyaya, *Tantrer kathā*, p. 38.

6. Robert Levy, *Mesocosm* (Berkeley: University of California Press, 1990), p. 294.

7. Interview, Kali priest, Birbhum, 1994.

8. Chattopadhyaya, *Tantrer kathā*, p. 1.

9. Interview, faculty member, Vishvabharati University, Shantiniketan, 1993.

10. Bhattacarya, *Principles of Tantra* vol. 1, p. 202.

11. From pamphlet, "Bangiya Tantrik Samaj," society registered under West Bengal Act XXVI of 1961.

12. Gour Chandra Bagchi, "Village Survey Monograph on Bhumij Dhan Sol," *Census of India 1961, West Bengal and Sikkim*, vol. 16, part 6(5) (Calcutta: Government of India Publications, 1967), pp. 186–88. Blowing various substances may transmit power, and it may also allow deities to enter and influence the objects blown upon.

13. W. J. Culshaw, *Tribal Heritage—A Study of the Santals.* (London: Lutterworth, 1949), pp. 94–97.

14. Tantrik Acharya Shri Bhairava Shastri, Siddha Bhairava, *Dākinī Tantra* (Calcutta: Rajendra Library, n.d.).

15. The verb used here, *ayatta kara*, means to subjugate, dominate, seize, and control the knowledge. Book knowledge is conquered as an animal might be tamed. See *Dākinī Tantra*, p. 85. It evokes irresistably the classical teacher's response: for all the time that they spent doing ten thousand mantras, they could have been studying. . . .

16. The term used for dancing girl is *nati* rather than *apsaras*, which is unusually Sanskritic for folk tantra. However, the role is similar—this is a heavenly dancing girl.

17. A. N. Moberly, "The Use of Amulets as Agents in the Prevention of Disease in Bengal," *Memoirs of the Asiatic Society of Bengal*, Vol. 1 no.11 (Calcutta: Baptist Mission Press, 1906), p. 231.

18. Ibid.

19. Tamonash Chandra Das Gupta, *Aspects of Bengal Society from Old Bengali Literature* (Calcutta: University of Calcutta Press, 1935), p. 2.

20. Upendrakumar Das, *Bhāratīya śakti-sādhana* (Shantiniketan: Vishvabharati Publications, 1373) BS), vol. 1, pp. 522–23.

21. Vidya Dehejia, *Yoginī Cult and Temples: A Tantric Tradition* (New Delhi: National Museum, 1986), p. 2.

22. *Kaulajñananirnaya*, patala 23, cited in Dehejia, *Yoginī Cult*, p. 24.

23. *Skanda Purāna*, Kashikhanda, cited in Dehejia, *Yoginī Cult*, p. 24.

24. For instance, the *Kulārṇava Tantra*, 8.76. For this chapter, the version of the text that I shall be using is the Sanskrit text with Bengali translation, *Kulārṇava Tantram*, edited by Upendrakumar Das (Calcutta: Nababharat Publishers, 1363) [1976]). This version of the text was the most popular one with practitioners interviewed, and is cited hereafter as KT.

25. See KT, 8.103.

26. See KT 10.107. The one who does not practice becomes an animal (*pashu*) of the yoginis.

27. *Skanda Purāṇa*, Kashikhanda, puvardha 45.34–41, cited in Itamsanarayna Bhattacarya, *Hinduder debadebī*, (Calcutta: Firma KLM, 1986), p. 346.

28. Chattopadhyaya, *Tantrer kathā*, p. 109.

29. S. C. Banerji, *Tantra in Bengal* (Calcutta: Naya Prokash, 1978), p. 154.

30. Narendranath Bhattacharya, *History of the Tantric Religion* (New Delhi: Manohar, 1982), pp. 354–55.

31. Banerji, *Tantra in Bengal*, p. 155.

32. Bholanath Bhattacharya, "Some Aspects of the Esoteric Cults of Consort Worship in Bengal: A Field Survey Report." *Folklore* 214 (November 1977), part 2, pp. 364–65.

33. Dehejia, *Yoginī Cult*, p. 36.

34. Ibid., p. 221.

35. Cited in Chanda, *The Indo-Aryan Races*, p. 135.

36. KT 11. 66–67.

37. William Ward, *History, Literature, and Mythology of the Hindoos* (reprint by B.R. Publishing Corp, New Delhi, n.d.), vol. 4, p. 91.

38. C. H. Tawney, *The Katha Sarit Sagara* (1880), vol. 1. pp. 154–58, cited in Dehejia, *Yoginī Cult*, p. 16.

39. Narendranath Bhattacharyya, *History of the Śakta Religion* (New Delhi: Munshiram Manoharlal, 1974), p. 104.

40. Alexis Sanderson, "Śaivism and the Tantric Traditions" in *The World's Religions*, edited by Stewart Sutherland et al. (London: Routledge, 1988), p. 680.

41. H. C. Das, *Tāntricism: A Study of the Yogini Cult* (New Delhi: Sterling, 1981), p. 41.

42. Dehejia, *Yoginī Cult*, p. 79.

43. Chattopadhyaya, *Tantrer Kathā*, p. 29.

44. Sohaila Kapur, *Witchcraft in Western India* (Bombay: Orient Longman, 1983), p. 67.

45. Cited in S. C. Banerji, *A Brief History of Tantra Literature* (Calcutta: Naya Prokash, 1988), p. 364.

46. Bhattacharyya, *History of the Tantric Religion*, p. 264.

47. Cited in Jadunath Sinha, *The Cult of Divine Power: Saktisadhana* (Calcutta: Sinha Publishing House, 1977), p. 16.

48. Pushpendra Kumar, *Śakti Cult in Ancient India, With special Reference to the Purānic Literature* (Varanas: Bharatiya Publishing House, 1974), p. 21.

49. A. G. Krishna Warrier, trans., *Śākta Upanisad-s* (Adyar:Adyar Library and Research Center, 1967), p. 77.

50. Sanderson, "Śaivism and the Tantric Traditions," p. 679.

51. Interview, Shakta priest, Calcutta, 1984.

52. Teun Goudriaan and Sanjukta Gupta, *Hindu Tantric and Śākta Literature* (Wiesbaden: Otto Harrassowitz, 1981), p. 75.

53. Cited in Bhattacharyya, *History of the Tantric Religion*, p. 345.

54. KT 14.25.

55. KT 13.3–22.

56. KT 7.46–51.

57. KT 3.40,43.

58. *Śāradātilaka* 2.57.59. Cited in Banerji, *A Brief History of Tantra Literature*, p. 22.

59. KT 15. 63–64.

60. KT 15. 20–21.

61. KT 14. 3.

62. KT 14. 4–7.

63. KT 14. 30–39.

64. Banerji, *A Brief History of Tantra Literature*, pp. 248–49.

65. Gopinath Kaviraj, *Pūjā-tattva*, translated by Swami Premananda Tirtha (Varanasi: Sri Krishna Sangha, 1976), p. 87

66. Ibid., p. 87.

67. *Kāmakalā-vilāsa*, v. 21. Cited in Madhu Khanna, *Yantra: The Tantric Symbol of Cosmic Unity* (London: Thames and Hudson, 1979), p. 30.

68. Khanna, *Yantra*, pp. 98–99.

69. There is a partial translation of the *Kulārnava Tantra* by Woodroffe, to which I shall occasionally refer, *Kulārnava Tantra*, edited by John Woodroffe (Madras: Ganesh, 1965). It is difficult to get an exact correspondence, as he leaves out a great deal, and does not use line numbers. As in the *Good News Bible*, the translator adds his own commentary, and does not distinguish between the the actual words of the text and his own additions and interpretations. For this quote, see p. 3.

70. Chattopadhyaya, *Tantrer kathā*, p. 39.

71. See note 24, this chapter.

72. Avalon translates this as "caught up in the subtleties of the Śastras."

73. KT 1.101.

74. Oddly enough, Avalon translates this as: "Even if you lack the full knowledge

of this doctrine, faith and dedication to it is enough to deliver." This is why I work from the original text, and not Avalon's translation.

75. KT 2.78, 79.

76. These definitions come from Birendramohan Dasgupta, ed., *Samsad Bengali-English Dictionary*, 2nd. ed (Calcutta: Sahitya Samsad, 1983), p. 214.

77. KT 2.60. These are the five *bhutas*, who in this case enforce proper religious etiquette.

78. In traditional Indian thought, there is an intermediate gender between male and female. This "third gender" includes hermaphrodites and others who do not fall easily into either of the other categories.

79. Not all of it comes from Indian tradition, however. The issue of the Theosophical and later New Age adoption of kundalini yoga and its chakras will be discussed in chapter 5.

80. Sri Swami Sivananda, *Kundalini Yoga* (Sivanandanagar: Divine Life Society, 1971), p. xiii.

81. Ibid., p. xxix.

82. Swami Vishnu Tirtha Maharaj, *Devatma Shakti (Kundalini) = Divine Power*, (Rishikesh: Yoga Shri Peeth, [1962] 1980), p. 38.

83. Ibid., p. 72.

84. Ibid., p. 78.

85. Ibid., pp. 102–105.

86. KT 7.47–49.

87. KT 7.49–51.

88. *Kālī Tantram*, edited by Pandit Srinityananda Smrititirtha (Calcutta: Nababharat Publishers, 1388 [1981]), 8. 5–10. Sanskrit text with Bengali translation.

89. Banerji, *A Brief History of Tantra Literature*, pp. 222–23.

90. Ibid., p. 183.

91. *The Kulacūdāmani Tantra and the Vāmakeśvaratantra, with the Jayaratha Commentary*, translated by Louise M. Finn (Wiesbaden: Otto Harrassowitz, 1986), pp. 95–96.

92. Ibid., p. 98.

93. Banerji, *A Brief History of Tantra Literature*, p. 261.

94. Ibid., pp. 262–63.

95. Literally *navapushpa*, or new flower.

96. *Māyā Tantram*, edited by Jyotirlal Das (Calcutta: Nababharat Publishers, 1385 [1978]), 12.1–8. Sanskrit text with Bengali translation.

97. *Kāmākhya Tantram*, edited by Jyotirlal Das (Calcutta: Nababharat Publishers, 1385 [1978]), 4. 35–37. Sanskrit text with Bengali translation and commentary.

98. KT, 8.67–75.

99. Banerji, *A Brief History of Tantra Literature*, p. 184.

100. The reasons for my informants' refusal to help me get in touch with this type of tantric female practitioner are varied. Some said that they didn't know any; some said that if I wrote about them it would give West Bengal a bad reputation; quite a few said that I would be corrupted by them (and it was their duty to protect me); and some said that it was not a suitable topic for research. Even those who de-

fended them, largely by the argument from pity, said that it would be unsuitable for me to interview them.

101. Interview, *sadhika* and head of ashram, Bakreshwar, 1994.

102. Interview, *brahmacharini* and head of ashram, Suri, 1994.

103. Swami Saradananda, *Sri Ramakrishna the Great Master*, translated by Swami Jagadananda (Mylapore: Sri Ramakrishna Math, 1984), II.2.8.

104. For further details of her life, see my *The Madness of the Saints: Ecstatic Religion in Bengal* (Chicago: University of Chicago Press, 1989), pp. 215–20.

105. Interview, Sahajiya practitioners, Birbhum, 1983.

106. Interview, ashram head, Calcutta, 1994.

107. Interview, Sahajiya couple, Birbhum, 1983.

108. Bholanath Bhattacharjee, "Some Aspects of the Esoteric Cults of Consort Worship in Bengal: A Field Survey Report," *Folklore* (Calcutta) 18 no. 10 (October 1977); no. 11 (November 1977); and no. 12 (December 1977). The first two parts of this series of articles dealt with yakshinis, and the third article (pp. 385–97), which was used in this chapter, had interviews with female practitioners.

109. I should note that I have only seen this attitude of scorn toward widows among Vaishnava groups. The Shakta widows I have seen were strong women, and respected. They did not shave their heads, and often lived householder lives that resembled the situation of women with their husbands alive.

110. KT 8.102. This tantra also states that all of the people in the chakra should be worshiped as Shiva and Shakti (8.105). It also says, however, that "Whether female or male . . . everyone is understood as Shiva" (8.97).

111. Interview, *sadhika* and ashram head, Bakreshwar, 1994.

112. As an example, the sacrificial Meriah rites in Orissa are well documented.

113. See David N. Lorenzen, *The Kapalikas and Kalamukhas* (New Delhi: Thomson, 1972), p. 13.

114. Cited ibid., p. 62.

115. Cited ibid., p. 64.

116. Bhattacarya, *History of the Tantric Religion*, p. 139.

117. Benoy Kumar Sarkar, *The Folk Element in Hindu Culture* (New Delhi: Cosmo Publishing, 1972), pp. 89–90.

118. André Padoux, "Hindu Tantrism" in Mircea Eliade, ed., *The Encyclopedia of Religion* (New York: Macmillan, 1987), vol. 14, p. 279.

119. Shaikh Chilli, *Folk-tales of Hindustan* (Bahadurganj: Bhuwaneswari Asrama, 1920), p. 126.

120. Jonathan Parry, "Sacrificial Death and the Necrophagous Ascetic" in Maurice Bloch and Jonathan Parry, eds., *Death and the Regeneration of Life* (New York: Cambridge University Press, 1982), p. 78.

121. Ibid., pp. 104–105.

122. Aghori practice in the cremation ground is said to grant many *siddhis* or powers, including curing the sick, raising the dead, flying in the air, and entering other bodies, as well as control of spirits.

123. West Bengal, too, has its share of Shaivite Aghoris. The Bakreshwar Temple is a gathering place for many of them, and informants warned me not to visit an Aghori living nearby, as he tended to throw excrement and parts of corpses at visitors.

Buddhadeb Chaudhuri describes a Bakreshwar sadhu known as Aghoribaba or Jatababa, who lived in a hut near the burning ground and Shiva temple. It was said that he would construct a sitting platform made of corpses, and cook his meals with the fat of dead bodies. The local villagers respected him, and believed that he had protected them through his divine powers. When an epidemic broke out, it was believed that he had stopped it by absorbing its evil, from which he died. See Buddhadeb Chaudhuri, *The Bakreshwar Temple* (Delhi: Inter-India Publishing, 1981).

124. David Kinsley, "The Death That Conquers Death," in *Religious Encounters with Death*, edited by F. Reynolds and E. H. Waugh (University Park: Pennsylvania State University Press, 1977), p. 100.

125. From the Devi Gita, cited in Sinha, *The Cult of Divine Power*, p. 87. Similar descriptions are found in the *Tantrasara* of Krishnananda Agambagish and in the *Kali Tantra*.

126. Chintaharan Chakravarti, *Tantras* (Calcutta: Punthi Pustak, 1965), p. 88.

127. Arthur Avalon (Sir John Woodroffe), *The Serpent Power: Being the Sat-cakra nirupana and Paduka-pañcaka: Two Works on Laya Yoga* (New York: Dover Publishing, 1974), p. 204, n. 1.

128. Bhattacarya, *Tantra-Tattva*, translated by Woodruffe as *Principles of Tantra*, 1986, vol. 2, p. 318.

129. Ibid., vol. 1, p. 140. Slightly rephrased.

130. Ibid., vol. 2, p. 298.

131. Ibid., vol. 2, p. 296.

132. Ibid., vol. 1, pp. 256–57.

133. This is a conglomerate story from both informants and literature. For a good middle-ground version, see Swami Tattwananda, *The Saints of India* (Calcutta: Nirmalendu Bikash Sen, n.d.), pp. 87–91.

134. *Kālī Tantram*, edited by Smrititirtha, 6.12.

135. Bhattacarya, *Principles of Tantra*, p. 360.

136. These points have been well argued by Jonathan Parry in his article "Sacrificial Death and the Necrophagous Ascetic."

137. This story is the result of several visits to the temple and his house, and was told in response to general questions: "Tell me about your life," "Tell me about the temple," "Tell me about tantric sadhana."

138. Interview, Kali priest, Bolpur, 1994.

139. This interview was more fortuitous than usual—I encountered Jayashri Ma by the accident of walking up to the wrong house in Shantiniketan. Its occupant (an academic at Vishvabharati University) asked me about my research and invited me in for tea. He told me that he had searched for gurus all his life, and only one woman seemed to him to be a true guru. This was Jayashri Ma.

## 3. SHAKTA BHAKTI

1. Interview, Kali devotee, Calcutta, 1993.

2. In many cultures, we see the transformative power of ritual in relation to angry ghosts and ancestors; such a ghost may be evil and demonic, but he or she may be transformed by worship and ritual action into a benevolent ancestor who helps the

community and watches over it. Among the Bengali goddesses, this transformation seems to focus on two requirements: food and respect. In more literal interpretations of these stories, the goddess is actually hungry—she has been "eating wind," starving for offerings. Such goddesses are often on restricted diets and must eat only food offered by others; they are bound by the natural locale in which they dwell, and cannot move freely. They cannot gather and eat their own food, because their bodies are made of rock or metal, and they cannot pursue or collect dinner. Food must be dedicated and offered for them to eat. Sometimes they are restricted to eating "essences," and as such require ritual to make that food essence available to them.

3. Asutosh Bhattacharyya, *An Introduction to the Study of the Medieval Bengali Epics* (Calcutta: Calcutta Book House, 1943), p. 19.

4. P. K. Maity, *Historical Studies in the Cult of the Goddess Manasā* (Calcutta: Punthi Pustaka, 1966), p. 80.

5. Ibid., pp. 80–81.

6. Ibid., p. 85.

7. Ibid., p. 87.

8. Ibid., pp. 102–103.

9. A short version of this story is found in R. M. Sarkar, *Regional Cults and Rural Traditions* (New Delhi: Inter-India Publications, 1986), pp. 88–93.

10. Chintaharan Cakravarti, *Tantras* (Calcutta: Punthi Pustak, 1965), p. 45.

11. This story is compressed from the *Brahmavaivarta Purana*, Prakriti khanda, 45. 1–118.

12. Bholanath Bhattacharya, *The Deified Saints of Bengal* (Calcutta: Indian Publications, 1972), p. 22–24.

13. Maity states that the word "Domni" means a Dom woman and could over time have been changed to Dumni, but the word is also related to the term Dombi, a name of the Tantric Buddhist Niratma (Nairatmya) Devi. He suggests that Ma Dumni is actually the Niratma Devi of the Sahajayana Buddhists, whose four-armed statue with the iconography of the Buddhist goddess Tara is still worshiped. She had been worshiped between the eighth and eleventh centuries as a Buddhist goddess, and when Buddhism was chased from Bengal the statue remained and was transformed into a folk goddess. See P. K. Maity, *Human Fertility Cults and Rituals of Bengal: A Comparative Study* (New Delhi: Abhinav, 1989), pp. 153–55.

14. Bhattacharya, *Deified Saints*, p. 25.

15. Interview, Puruliya, 1994.

16. In the *manjari sadhana*, the devotee in his *siddha rupa* or spiritual body assists in the eternal love-play between Radha and Krishna, which occurs in the paradise of the eternal Vrindavana.

17. Jahnavikumar Cakravarti, *Śaktapadābalī o śaktisādhana* (Calcutta: D. M. Library, 1367 [1960], pp. 228–29.

18. Nigamananda Sarasvati, *Mayer krpā* (Halisahar: Swami Atmananda/Saraswati Math, 1382 [1975], pp. 3–13.

19. Sriyuhta Siva Candra Vidyarnava Bhattacarya Mahodaya, *Tantra Tattva*, translated by Sir John Woodroffe as *Principles of Tantra* (Madras: Ganesh, 1986), vol. 2, pp. 450–51. Cited hereafter as Bhattacarya, *Principles of Tantra*.

20. *Śrîmad Devî Bhâgawatam*, translated by Swami Vijnanananda (New Delhi: Munshiram Manoharlal, 1977 7.37.4–9.

21. Ibid., 7.37.11–24.

22. Ibid., 40.7.23–24.

23. Ibid., 7.37.24–25. Karma that is *prarabdha* comes from one's last life, and must be experienced in this life to avoid future births.

24. *Māhābhāgavata Purāṇa*, edited by Pushpendra Kumar (Delhi: Eastern Book Linkers, 1983), chapters 17–19. See pages 35–36.

25. Gopinath Kaviraj, *Pūjā Tattva*, translated by Swami Premananda Tirtha (Varanasi: Sri Krishna Sangha, 1976), p. 10.

26. Bhattacarya, *Principles of Tantra*, vol. 1, pp. 385–86.

27. ibid., p. 411.

28. Dušan Zbavitel, *Bengali Literature* (Wiesbaden: Otto Harrassowitz, 1976), p. 203.

29. Ibid., p. 204.

30. This biography comes primarily from the chapter "Matṛ Sādhaka Rāmprasād" in Gangescandra Cakravarti, *Baṅglar sādhaka* (Calcutta: Nabendu Cakravarti, 1379 [1972]), vol. 1, pp. 173–94.

31. Ramprasad Sen, *Rāmprasādī Saṅgīt* (Calcutta: Rajendra Library, n.d.), p. 47. Kali is traditionally believed to have red feet, though her body may be black, blue, or even white. Such red feet are considered to be very beautiful by her devotees.

32. Ibid., p. 46.

33. These chakras are at the top and bottom of the *sushumna*, the channel of energy that runs along the spine.

34. Sen, *Rāmprasādi Saṅgīt*, p. 24.

35. Ibid., p. 48.

36. Jadunath Sinha, *Ramaprosada's Devotional Songs* (Calcutta: Sinha Publishing House, 1966) p. 86, #160. Rephrased.

37. Leonard Nathan and Clinton Seely, trans., *Grace and Mercy in Her Wild Hair: Selected Poems to the Mother Goddess* (Boulder: Great Eastern, 1982), p. 35.

38. Amarendranath Raya, ed., *Śākta padābalī* (Calcutta: Kālikata Viśvavidyālaya, 1963), p. 187, no. 281.

39. Ibid., no. 280.

40. Ibid., p. 144, no. 211.

41. Ibid., p. 194, no. 294.

42. Edwin Thompson and Arthur Spenser, eds. and trans., *Bengali Religious Lyrics* (Calcutta: Association Press, 1923), poem no. 76.

43. An excellent source on these traditions is Sasibhusan Dasgupta, *Bhāratera śakti-śādhana o śākta śāhitya* (Calcutta: Sāhitya Saṁsad, 1393 [1985]).

44. The *Kālikāpurāṇa*, translated by B. N. Shastri (Delhi: Nag Publishers, 1991–1992), chapter 41.

45. Radhaprasad Gupta, "Gobindarāmer Durgā Pūjā" in *Deś*, September 26, 1987, p. 54.

46. These songs are rarely sung today, except by professional singers and on the radio.

47. Gupta, "Gobindarāmer Durgā Pūjā," p. 55.

48. Ibid.

49. Panchkuri Bandhopadhyaya, cited ibid., p. 54.

50. Bandhopadhyaya, cited ibid., p. 55.

51. Kali Mirja (Kalidas Chattopadyaya), in Dasgupta, *Bhāratera śākti-sādhana*, p. 87.

52. Narada is the troublemaker of the gods, a sage known for spreading gossip and mischief from Indra's heaven down to earth.

53. Jayanarayana Bandyopadhyaya, in Dasgupta, *Bhāratera śākti-sādhana*, p. 88. There is a pun here, for to be without shakti or power is to be unable to move—here Menaka refers to the lack of her daughter as a lack of shakti.

54. Gupta, "Gobindarāmer Durgā Pūjā," p. 55.

55. Hariscandra Mitra, in Dasgupta, *Bhāratera śākti-sādhana*, p. 238.

56. Ishvara Gupta, ibid.

57. Mahendranath Bhattacarya, ibid.

58. Sinha, *Ramaprosada's Devotional Songs*, pp. 143–44. Rephrased.

59. Pyarimohan Kaviratna, in Dasgupta, *Bhāratera śākti-sādhana*, p. 239.

60. Gadadhara Mukhopadyaya, ibid., p. 240.

61. Sinha, *Ramaprosada's Devotional Songs*, pp. 144–45. Rephrased.

62. Rupacand Paksi, in Dasgupta, *Bhāratera śākti-sādhana*, p. 241.

63. Raghunatha Dasa, ibid., p. 242.

64. Anonymous, ibid., p. 244.

65. Kamalakanta Bhattacarya, ibid.

66. Rama Basu, ibid., p. 245.

67. Bhattacarya, *Principles of Tantra*, pp. 321–23. It may well be this song, or one like it, that inspired the movie *Devi*. In this movie, a householder determines that his son's wife is really the goddess, as in this poem Himalaya discovers that his daughter is really the goddess. However, the movie is a tragedy, for such a revelation may require more than an ordinary person can give.

68. Sung by Purnima Sinha, interview, 1994.

69. Asok Mitra, ed., *Paścimbangera pūjā-parban o melā* (Delhi: Controller of Publications, 1992), p. 20.

70. Thakur, Shree Shree Annada, *Autobiographical Scenes from a Life of Visions* (Dakshineswar: Adyapeath Press. [1928] 1968), p. 83.

71. K. C. Shasmal, *The Bauris of West Bengal*, (Calcutta: Indian Publications, 1972), p. 198.

72. Sukumar Ray, *Folk Music of Eastern India (with Special Reference to Bengal)* (Calcutta: Naya Prokash, 1988), p. 68.

73. Cited, ibid., p. 134.

74. Ibid., p. 90, rephrased. Such songs are obviously of universal appropriateness in new meetings.

75. Ibid.

76. Ibid., p. 98.

77. Ibid., p. 104, rephrased.

78. Anil Ranjan Biswas, *A Book of Bengali Verse* (Calcutta: Writer's Workshop, 1990), p. 239, no.167.

79. Niels Nielsen, Jr., et al., *Religions of the World*, 2nd ed. (New York: St. Martin's, 1988), p. 192.

80. Peter Heehs, *The Bomb in Bengal: The Rise of Revolutionary Terrorism in India (1900–1910)* (Delhi: Oxford University Press, 1993), pp. 16–17. The song *Bande Mataram* has since become very popular in India, and in recent years it has been associated with the BJP political party.

81. Biswas, *A Book of Bengali Verse*, pp. 237–38, no. 166. Slightly rephrased.

82. Bhavani was the form of the goddess Durga worshiped by the famous Maratha general Shivaji, and invoking her also invoked Shivaji's heroism and military success.

83. Heehs, *Bomb in Bengal*, pp. 65–66.

84. Ibid., p. 192. It could be argued that this glorification of terrorism paved the way for communist terrorism to enter Bengal in the form of the Naxalite movement, a violent political movement which is periodically active in India, and is still a problem for the Indian government.

85. Rezaul Karim Talukdar, *Nazrul—The Gift of the Century* (Dhaka: Manan, 1994), pp. 46–47. Rephrased.

86. Raya, ed., *Śākta padābalī* (Calcutta: Calcutta University Press, [1963] 1989), p. 191.

87. Rafiqul Islam, ed., *Kazi Nazrul Islam: A New Anthology* (Dhaka: Bangla Academy, 1990), pp. 18–19.

88. *The Fiery Lyre of Nazrul Islam*, translated by Abdul Hakim (Dhaka: Bangla Academy, 1974), pp. 110–16. Slightly rephrased.

89. Mahendranath Gupta, *Rāmakṛṣṇa Kathāmṛta*, translated by Swami Nikhilananda as *The Gospel of Sri Ramakrishna* (Mylapore: Sri Ramakrsna Math, 1980), vol. 1, p. 14.

90. Ibid., vol. 1, pp. 31–32.

91. I was told of these views by several urban disciples, as well as by members of the Ramakrishna Math.

92. The understanding of freedom of divine image can take a variety of unusual forms. I spoke with a communist engineer in Calcutta who had performed worship during his college days. He and his friends worshiped the Holy Trinity of Marx, Lenin, and Stalin by means of puja, offering incense, red jaba flowers (sacred to Kali), and food to an altar with three red light bulbs symbolizing the trinity. Later Mao's Little Red Book was added as an offering.

93. Swami Vivekananda, "My Life and Mission," in his *Complete Works*, vol. 8, p. 73, cited in M. D. McLean, "Are Ramakrishnaites Hindus? Some Implications of Recent Litigation on the Question," *South Asia* 14, no. 2 (1991): 99–117.

94. Swami Gambhirananda, *History of Ramakrishna Math and Ramakrishna Mission* (Calcutta: Advaita Ashrama, [1957] 1983), p. 7.

95. C. Rajagopalachari, *Sri Ramakrishna Upanishad* (Mylapore: Sri Ramakrishna Math, 1953), p. 57.

96. Ibid., pp. 75–76.

97. Ibid., pp. 72–73.

98. Swami Lokeswarananda, *Practical Spirituality* (Calcutta: Ramakrishna Mission Institute of Culture, 1989), pp. 87–88.

99. Ibid., p. 29.

100. Jeffrey J. Kripal, *Kālī's Child: The Mystical and the Erotic in the Life and Teachings of Ramakrishna* (Chicago: University of Chicago Press, 1995), p. 4.

101. Ibid., pp. 24–25.

102. *Kathāmṛta* 3.253, cited, ibid., p. 26.

103. *Kathāmṛta* 3.173, cited ibid., p. 159.

104. M. D. McLean, "Ramakrishna: The Greatest of the Śaktas of Bengal?" in *Religions and Comparative Thought*, edited by Purusottama Bilimoria and Peter Fenner (Delhi: Sri Satguru Publications, 1988), p. 170. The author decided that Ramakrishna was not the greatest of Bengali Shaktas, for that title went to Ramprasad. However, Ramakrishna may eventually capture the title.

105. Walter J. Neevel, Jr. "The Transformation of Sri Ramakrishna" in *Hinduism: New Essays in the History of Religion*, edited by Bardwell Smith (Leiden: E. J. Brill, 1976), p. 76.

106. Ibid., p. 84. This is in the biographies by both Nikhilananda and Mahendranath Gupta.

107. *Andul Kālī kīrtan o baul gitāvalī* (Andul: Andul Kālī Kīrtan Samiti, 1987).

108. This is their preferred spelling of Adyapitha, or place sacred to the goddess Adya.

109. Thakur, *Autobiographical Scenes*, pp. 25–27.

110. Ibid., p. 57.

111. Ibid., p. 58.

112. Ibid.

113. Ibid., p. 69.

114. Ibid., p. 83.

115. Ibid., p. 110.

116. Ibid., p. 111.

117. Ibid., pp. 371–73.

118. Ibid., p. 376.

119. *Jugala murti*, which means the joint image or the statue of the two, usually refers to Radha and Krishna. This may be its referent here, or it may refer to the joint image in the Adyapeath temple.

120. *Guruguṇa Gan* (Adyapeath: Dakshineswar Ramakrishna Sangha, 1397 [1990], p. 29.

121. The song does not specify which mother is intended here: Annada's physical mother? His wife, who is also called mother? His divine mother Adya Shakti?

122. Mount Kailash is the home of Shiva and Shakti/Parvati. This line asks if Manikuntala is an incarnation of Shakti, who incarnated on earth out of compassion.

123. *Guruguṇa Gan*, pp. 35–36. Thakur is lord, and Thakurani is lady or goddess. This poem mourns her death.

124. Sometimes lesser gods and goddesses are punished by their devotees and priests if they do not take care of situations for which they are responsible, but this is rarely seen with very powerful deities. The most frequent type of punishment is refusing to feed them, though the deities may also be verbally insulted by their priests and worshippers.

## 4. THE GREAT BHAKTI GODDESSES OF WEST BENGAL

1. Santosh Kumar Mukherji, *Psychology of Image Worship of the Hindus* (Calcutta: Oriental Agency, n.d.), p. 102.

2. Cited in P. V. Kane, *History of Dharmasastra* (Poona: Bhandarkar Oriental Research Institute, [1958] 1975), vol. 5, p. 157.

3. *Harivamsa*, v. 3274. Cited in Sibendu Manna, *Mother Goddess Candi* (Calcutta: Punthi Pustak, 1993), p. 40.

4. Satindramohan Chattopadhyaya, *Tantrer Kathā* (Calcutta: Sahitya Samsad, 1983), p. 94.

5. N. M. Chaudhuri, "The Cult of Vana-Durga, a Tree Deity" *Journal of the Royal Asiatic Society of Bengal*, Letters, vol. 8, 1945, p. 75.

6. Ibid., p. 76.

7. Ibid.

8. Ibid., pp. 76–77.

9. Ibid., pp. 78–79. He does not give the dynamics or the reason for this change.

10. Pupul Jayakar, *The Earth Mother: Legends, Goddesses, and Ritual Arts of India* (San Francisco: Harper and Row, [1980] 1990), p. 186.

11. *Mahābhārata* 3.220.16. Cited in J. N. Tiwari, *Goddess Cults in Ancient India, With Special Reference to the First Seven Centuries AD* (Delhi: Sundeep Prakashan, 1985), p. 21.

12. B. C. Mazumdar, "Durga: Her Origin and History" *Journal of the Royal Asiatic Society of Great Britain and Ireland* (1906), p. 361.

13. Aśok Mitra, ed., *Pascimbangera pūjā parban o melā* (Delhi: Controller of Publications, 1992) p. 37.

14. Several Bengali writers from the nineteenth century mention the use of sticks (*lathi*) to beat members of the in-laws' party during wedding disagreements.

15. Mitra, *Paścimbangera pūjā-parban o melā*, pp. 39–40. Mitra suggests that the statue may have come originally from Agra, as a group of Rajbangshi kshatriyas migrated from Agra to Edua several centuries ago, to work for the kings of Burdwan and Bengal. Shakambhari had been worshiped as a rain goddess in dry Agra, with devotees asking her to save them as she had saved her children ages ago during a hundred-year drought. Certainly her martial style of ritual is unusual for Bengal, even for Durga.

16. Carmel Berkson, *The Divine and the Demoniac: Mahisa's Heroic Struggle with Durga* (Delhi: Oxford University Press, 1995), p. 216.

17. William Ward, *History, Literature and Mythology of the Hindoos including a minute Description of Their Manners and Customs* (Delhi: BR Publishing, n.d.), vol. 3, p. 122.

18. P. W. Jacob, trans. *Hindoo Tales (or, the Adventures of Ten Princes)* (London: Strahan and Company, 1873), p. 16.

19. Ibid., p. 225.

20. Ramaprasada Chanda, *The Indo-Aryan Races* (New Delhi: Indological Book, [1916] 1976), p. 148.

21. See the chapter on Durga in David Kinsley, *Hindu Goddesses: Visions of the*

*Divine Feminine in the Hindu Religious Tradition* (Berkeley: University of California Press, 1988) for references to various puranic texts.

22. *Devi Mahatmyam (Glory of the Divine Mother)* translated by Swami Jagadiswarananda (Mylapore: Sri Ramakrishna Math, 1953), 1. 54–58.

23. Ibid., 12.24–28.

24. Ibid., 13.11–15.

25. Ibid., 12.40.

26. Basanta Coomar Bose, *Hindu Customs in Bengal* (Calcutta: Book Company, 1875), p. 48. Similar comments were made by modern informants, along the lines of Karttikeya not wanting to marry so as to avoid creating dissension in the family.

27. Paul Thomas, *Hindu Religion, Customs and Manners: Describing the Customs and Manners, Religious, Social and Domentic Life, Arts and Sciences of the Hindus* (Bombay: D. B. Taraporevala Sons, 1960), p. 124.

28. Cited in Berkson, *The Divine and Demoniac*, p. 36.

29. Ibid., p. 37.

30. Swami Jyotirmayananda, "Attain Victory over the Mind," *International Yoga Guide*, 31 no. 1 (September, 1993): 5.

31. Ibid.

32. Ibid., p. 6.

33. Berkson, *The Divine and Demoniac*, pp. 8–9.

34. Ibid., p. 10.

35. *Devi Mahatmyam*, translated by Swami Jagadiswarananda, 11.38

36. For a discussion of the time of origin of Jagaddhatri puja and the debates in the literature, see Hamsanarayana Bhattacarya, *Hinduder debadebī* (Calcutta: Firma KLM, [1982] 1995), vol. 3, p. 308–309.

37. Narendranath Bhattacharyya, *History of the Śakta Religion* (New Delhi: Munshiram Manoharlal, 1974), p. 135.

38. Krishnananda Agambagish, *Tantrasāra*, pp. 409–410, cited in Bhattacarya, *Hinduder debadebī*, vol 3 p. 309.

39. Pratapachandra Ghosh, *Durga Puja* (Calcutta: Hindoo Patriot, 1871).

40. Rajendra Kumar Bhattacharyya and Sarat Chandra Mitra, "A Note on the 'Dhatree Puja' as Performed by the Hindusthanis Resident in Calcutta" *Journal of the Anthropological Society of Bombay* 13 (1924–1927): 320–22.

41. *Brahmavaivarta Purāna*, translated by Rajendranath Sen (Bahadurganj: Bhuvaneshwari Ashram, 1920), Prakriti khanda, 1.16–21, pp. 83–84.

42. Ibid., 57. 12–20, p. 243.

43. *Mahābhāgavata Purāṇa*, edited by Puspendra Kumar (Delhi: Eastern Book Linkers, 1983), chapters 36–48.

44. Kane, *History of Dharmasastra*, vol. 5, p. 155.

45. Progya Paramita Pine, "Festival Architecture," *Statesman*, Miscellany, October 17, 1993, p. 2.

46. *Kālikā Purāṇa* 63. 12–13. Cited in P. V. Kane, *History of Dharmasastra*, p. 156.

47. P. Thomas, *Festivals and Holidays of India* (Bombay: D. B. Taraporevala and Sons, 1971), p. 5.

48. Pranab Bandyopadhyay, *Mother Goddess Durga* (Calcutta: Image India, 1987), p. 15.

49. Ashokanath Shastri, "Durga Puja," *Bharatiya Vidya* 10 (1949): 255–256.

50. *Sholapith* (Solapith) is a white plant fiber taken from water plants, used for elaborate decorations on statues and for the groom's traditional wedding hat. It is also the material from which pith helmets are made.

51. Bandyopadhyay, *Mother Goddess Durga*, pp. 68–70.

52. "Devi in a 'Copter, Asura in a Submarine" from *Ājkal*, October 21, 1993, p. 6.

53. Ibid, p. 6.

54. Dipak Rudra, "A Goddess in Our Hearts," *Statesman*, Festival '91 Durga Puja Special, 1991.

55. Shastri, "Durga Puja," pp. 256–58.

56. This Hinduized ritual still associates Durga with trees, but feels it necessary to make the tree attractive for her. The folk Durga lived in trees naturally, and required no such scruples.

57. These rituals are given in much greater detail in Kane, *History of Dharmasastra*, vol. 5, Part 1, chapter 9.

58. Manna, *Mother Goddess Candi*, p. 47.

59. Pratapachandra Ghosh, *Durga Puja* (Calcutta: Hindoo Patriot, 1871), pp. 67–68. The sixty-four yoginis are also worshiped, and each is invoked by name and established separately.

60. Some people say that Ganesha has one wife, some say two wives, and others say he is unmarried. Durga's other son, Karttika, is a lifelong bachelor. Bose, *Hindu Customs in Bengal*, p. 48.

61. Manna, *Mother Goddess Candi*, p. 49.

62. S. R. Das, cited in Sankar Sen Gupta, ed., *Rain in Indian Life and Lore* (Calcutta: Indian Publications, 1963), p. 15.

63. He believes that the singing of Dalkhai songs or Navamir Kheiid (obscene songs of Navami day) is a low-caste shudra ritual, borrowed from non-Aryan tribes of Bengal. See Mazumder, "Durga: Her Origin and History," pp. 360–61.

64. S. C. Banerji, *A Brief History of Tantra Literature* (Calcutta: Naya Prokash, 1988), p. 477.

65. Reverend Eyre Chatterton, B.D. *The Story of Fifty Years [of] Mission Work in Chhota Nagpur* (London: Society for Promoting Christian Knowledge, 1901), p. 146.

66. Amal Kumar Das and Manis Kumar Raha, *The Oraons of Sunderban* (Calcutta: Tribal Welfare Dept., Government of West Bengal, 1963), p. 298.

67. Sarat Chandra Roy, *Oraon Religion and Customs* (Ranchi: Industry Press, 1928), pp. 266–67.

68. K. C. Shasmal, *The Bauris of West Bengal* (Calcutta: Indian Publications, 1972), p. 186.

69. Mitra, *Paścimbanger pūjā-parban o melā*, vol. 4, p. 121.

70. P. K. Maity, *Human Fertility Cults and Rituals of Bengal* (Delhi: Abhinav, 1989), p. 106.

71. Ibid., p. 106.

72. Indra Deva, *Folk Culture and Peasant Society in India* (Jaipur: Rawat Publishers, 1989), p. 203.

73. Narendranath Bhattacharyya, *Indian Mother Goddess* (Calcutta: Indian Studies Past and Present, 1971), p. 48.

74. This name is actually an alias for the village in which anthropological research was done. It is a small village in Midnapore.

75. Gouranga Chattopadyaya, *Ranjana: A Village in West Bengal* (Calcutta: Bookland, 1963), pp. 203–204.

76. Pranavesa Cakravarti, *Ei Baṅglai* (Calcutta: Dev Sahitya Kutir, 1992), pp. 56–57.

77. Ibid., pp. 56–58.

78. Sasibhusan Dasgupta, *Bhārater śakti-sādhana o śākta sāhitya* (Calcutta: Sāhitya Saṁsad, 1392 [1985]), p. 63.

79. Ibid., p. 64.

80. Ibid.

81. E. B. Cowell and F. W. Thomas, trans., *The Harsa-carita of Bana* (Delhi: Motilal Banarsidass, 1961), p. 256.

82. Dasgupta, *Bharater śakti-sādhana*, p. 66. Kali is here also called Chamunda, in the Devi Mahatmya she is the killer of the demons Chanda and Munda.

83. *Devī Mahatmyam*, 7.5–9.

84. *Liṅga Purāṇa* 1.106, 1.72,66–68. Cited in Kinsley, *Hindu Goddesses*, p. 118.

85. *Vāmana Purāṇa* 25–29. Cited in Kinsley, *Hindu Goddesses*, p. 119.

86. Interview, hotel waiter, Kalimpong, 1994.

87. Interview, physician, Calcutta, 1994.

88. Details described in Dineshchandra Sen, *The Bengali Ramayanas* (Calcutta: University of Calcutta, 1920), pp. 227–28. According to some informants who discussed this story, Sita did not really go back to Ayodhya with Rama, but maintained her form as Kali and came to live in Calcutta. In the *Adbhuta Rāmayāna*, Sita was the daughter of Mandodari, Ravana's queen. See Sen, p. 35.

89. *Adbhuta Rāmayāṇa*, 25.30–31. Cited in Bhattacarya, *Hinduder debadebī*, p. 268.

90. Shankarnath Ray, *Bhārater sādhaka* (Calcutta: Karuna Prakasani, 1993), vol. 3, pp. 161–62.

91. *Mahābhāgavata Purāṇa*, chapters 49–54. See pages 31–32.

92. In this song, Radha's husband had heard that Radha was with Krishna, and he came running over to find them together. However, Krishna changed his form, turning into a statue of the goddess Kali. He found Radha worshiping the image, and he also bowed down to worship it. Radha's reputation was safe.

93. Interview, hotel manager, 1994, Calcutta (the informant was born in south India, and there may be some south Indian perspective in this view).

94. Interview, Shakta priest, Kankalitala, 1994. This story also appears in a longer form in the local booklet *Satītīrtha Kankālī* by Basudeb Chaudhuri, pp. 6–12.

95. *Tantrasāra*, Bangabasi edition, p. 479, cited ibid., p. 267.

96. *Tantrasāra*, pp. 480–81, cited ibid., p. 267.

97. Ibid., p. 267.

98. Ibid., p. 268.

99. *Kūrmapurāṇa*, Purvabhaga, 12.198, cited in Bhattacarya, *Hinduder debadebī*, p. 125.

100. *Devi Mahatmyam* 2.38–39.

101. *Skandapurāṇa*, Reva khanda, 14.33–34, cited in Bhattacarya, *Hinduder debadebī*, p. 277.

102. Devi Gita, cited ibid., p. 295.

103. *Śrimad Devī Bhāgawatam Purāṇa*, translated by Swami Vijnanananda (Allahabad: Bhuvaneswari Ashram, n.d.), 3.3.48.

104. Sankarnath Ray, "Kṛṣṇananda Agamvagisa" in *Bhārater sādhaka* (Calcutta: Karuna Prakasani, 1993), vol. 3, p. 95.

105. Upendrakumar Das, *Bhāratīya śakti-sādhana* (Shantiniketan: Vishvabharati Publications, 1373 BS [1966], vol. 1, p. 493.

106. Shiva Chandra Vidyarnava Bhattacarya, *Principles of Tantra* (Madras: Ganesh, Co., 1986), pp. 318–19.

107. Many scholars believe that the *Mahanirvana Tantra* was influenced by or entirely written by Rammohan Raya of the Brahmo Samaj, or possibly by his guru. This is partly because the tantric rituals in it tend to be described as symbolic rather than literal events, and because such Brahmo Samaj ideas as education for women and remarriage of widows are included in the text. There is also internal inconsistency, such as one section of the tantra that speaks in favor of alcohol, and another that speaks against its use. Despite the many claims that this tantra is a spurious text, it is still used by many practicing tantrikas. Considering the wealth of classical tantric ritual and traditional use of mantra in the text, and the internal inconsistencies, it seems most likely that the Brahmo sections were added later to an already existing text.

108. *Mahānirvāṇa Tantra*, translated as *The Great Liberation (Mahānirvāṇa Tantra)* by Arthur Avalon, (New York: Dover [1913] 1972), chapter 4, pp. 10–15. The language in the quotations to be used here is a bit updated from Woodroffe's archaic English, but the meaning is unchanged. Hereafter abbreviated MT.

109. MT 4.156. Slightly rephrased.

110. MT 7.12–30.

111. *Mahābhāgavata Purāṇa*, chapter 59. See pages 33–34.

112. *Śrīmad Devī Bhāgawatam Purāṇa*, 7.40.26, 31.

113. Ibid., 3.3 and 3.4.13–15.

114. Sudhakar Chattopadhyaya, *Ethnic Elements in Ancient Hinduism* (Calcutta: Principal Sanskrit College, 1979), p. 74.

115. Asutosh Bhattacarya, *Folklore of Bengal* (New Delhi: National Book Trust, [1978] 1983), pp. 17–19.

116. Benoy Kumar Sarkar, *The Folk Element in Hindu Culture* (New Delhi: Cosmo Publishing, 1981), pp. 198–99. Sarkar dates the *Shunya Purana* from the twelfth or thirteenth century. Other texts are more direct about Dharma's relations with Adya; according to the *Chandi* of Manik Datta and the works of Brahma Haridasa, "Dharma embraced Adya and made her sit on his knees." See Sarkar, *The Folk Element*, p. 199.

117. Sarkar, *The Folk Element*, p. 222–23.

118. Ibid., pp. 200–201.

119. Ibid., pp. 230–31.

120. MT 4.32–34.

121. MT 7. 37–46.

122. Interview, sari merchant, Suri, 1994.

123. Interview, Shakta priest, Calcutta, 1993.

124. R. K. Dasgupta, "The Inescapable Mother" in the Autumn 1991 "Durga Puja Special" edition of the *Statesman* newspaper, Festival '91 magazine.

125. India has problems with affirmative action and prejudice, as does the West. In the case of the Kali with non-Aryan features, the statue shows respect for the Adivasi or tribal people who wish representation and concern for their cultures.

126. None of the devotees standing at the shrine could determine the gender of her attendants, or explain why Kali was white in color.

127. John Campbell Oman, *The Brahmans, Theists and Muslims of India* (London: T. Fisher Unwin, 1907), p. 16.

128. *Curiosities and Remarkable Customs in Pagan and Mohammedan Countries* (Troy: Caleb Wright, 1848), pp. 30–31.

129. W. Crooke, "The Divali, the Lamp Festival of the Hindus" *Folk-lore* (London) 34 no. 4 (1923): 277.

130. Ibid., p. 281.

131. Ibid., p. 285.

132. "Two Cheers—So Far" in *Statesman*, November 10, 1993. The newspaper also had large, forceful announcements over the course of the month: "Government of West Bengal; Warning against Forcible Collection of Kali Puja Subscriptions It Is a Punishable Offence (which detailed the definition and punishments for extortion, and told people where to submit complaints, emphasizing that such complaints may be anonymous).

133. Tanmay Chatterjee, "Community Puja That Is the Preserve of the Dons," *Statesman*, November 12, 1993.

134. Story cited in Bhattacarya, *Hinduder Debadebī*, vol. 3, p. 265.

135. Bhattacarya, *Principles of Tantra*, vol. 1, p. 266.

136. Bhattacarya, Ibid., pp. 259–61.

137. The *Shaktisangama Tantra* lists ten: Kali, Tara, Chinna, Sundari, Lakshmi, Bagalamukhi, Matangi, Shamala, Bhairavi, and Dhumavati. The *Niruttara Tantra* lists eighteen Mahavidya goddesses: Kali, Tara, Chinna-matangini, Bhuvanesvari, Annapurna, Nitya, Durga, Tvarita, Tripura, Puta, Bhairavi, Bagala, Kamala, Dhumavati, Sarasvati, Jayadurga, and Tripurasundari. They are often portrayed together, along a wheel known as the circle of Mahavidya goddesses (*mahavidya shakti chakra*). The most frequently seen list of ten goddesses is found in both the *Chamunda Tantra* and the *Mundamala Tantra*.

138. Banerji, *A Brief History of Tantra Literature*, p. 30.

139. Das, *Bharatiya śakti-sādhana*, vol. 1, pp. 472–73.

140. Ibid., p. 480.

141. Interview, Shakta priest, Calcutta, 1984.

142. Narendranath Bhattacharyya, *History of the Tantric Religion* (New Delhi: Manohar, 1982), p. 351, and Sarbeswar Satpathy, *Dasa Mahavidya and Tantra Sastra* (Calcutta: Punthi Pustak, 1992), p. 59. The rest of these descriptions come from Bhattacharyya and Satpathy. There is also information added from the *Tantrer kathā*.

143. Chattopadhyaya, *Tantrer Kathā*, p. 89.

144. Interview, Shakta priest, Tarapith, 1983.

145. Alain Daniélou, *The Myths and Gods of India* (Rochester, N.Y.: Inner Traditions, 1991), p. 281.

146. Madhu Khanna, *Yantra: The Tantric Symbol of Cosmic Unity* (London: Thames and Hudson, 1979), p. 58.

147. For instance, some further categorizations are described by Shivachandra Vidyarnava Bhattacharya: "Kali and Tara are Mahavidyas; Sodasi, Bhuvanesvari, Bhairavi, Chhinnamsta, and Dhumavati are Vidyas; Bagala, Matangi and Kamala are Siddhavidyas. These ten Mahasaktis are Mahavidyas, Vidyas, and Siddhavidyas in order. . . . In the Syama-Rahasya, however, all the ten Saktis have been called Mahavidyas. Kali, Tara, Sodasi, Bhuvanesvari, Bhairavi, Chhinnamasta, Matangi, Kamala, Dhumavati, and Bagala are called Mahavidyas. . . . according to the Visvasara Tantra, Kali and Tara are Mahamahasiddhavidyas, Sodasi, Bhuvanesvari, Bhairavi, Chhinnamasta, and Dhumavati are Mahasiddhavidyas, and Bagala, Matangi, and Kamala are Siddhamahasiddhavidyas." See Bhattacarya, *Principles of Tantra*, vol. 1, p. 345.

148. Interview, retired professor, Navadvipa, 1994.

149. Interview, Shakta priest, Calcutta, 1984.

## 5. SHAKTISM AND THE MODERN WEST

1. It may be noted that going through a period of apparent insanity is common for gurus and holy people. See my book, *The Madness of the Saints: Ecstatic Religion in Bengal* (Chicago: University of Chicago Press, 1989), for numerous examples.

2. James S. Gordon, *The Golden Guru: The Strange Journey of Bhagwan Shree Rajneesh* (Lexington, Ky.: Stiphen Greene, 1987), p. 48.

3. Osho, *Tantric Transformation: Discourses on the Royal Song of Saraha* (Shaftesbary: Element, 1978), p. 4.

4. Ibid., p. 277.

5. Ibid., p. 114.

6. Ibid., p. 184.

7. Charles Muir and Caroline Muir, *Tantra* (San Francisco: Mercury House, 1989), p. ix.

8. Ibid., p. 49.

9. Ibid.

10. Ibid., p. 55.

11. Ibid., p. 62.

12. Ibid., p. 74.

13. Advertising pamphlet, Hawaiian Goddess Source School. The advertisements were mailed to me from Maui, along with price lists.

14. Some writers claim that whales' songs are monotonous because they are chanting mantras, thus showing their advanced spirituality.

15. Advertising pamphlet, Kahua Hawaiian Institute.

16. Advertising pamphlet for fall equinox weekend, run in California by Stephanie Rainbow Lightning Elk and Guy Lone Eagle, September 1996.

17. A most problematic definition. From the pamphlet "Sacred Spiritual Sexuality," 1996.

18. Pamphlet on Ipsalu Tantra from Tantrika International in Taos, New Mexico.

19. From an advertisement for Ipsalu Tantra Level I Workshop, with Bodhi Avinasha, founder of Ipsalu Tantra "in her soulful, down-to-earth style."

20. Pamphlet from Ipsalu Tantra, "Beyond Beyond," April 1995.

21. From the 1995 brochure, "SkyDancing Institute USA: Tantra Love and Ecstasy Trainings with Margo Anand."

22. Margo Anand, "The Training for Ecstasy and Love," *Tantra: The Magazine,* Al'lat issue, 1992, p. 23.

23. Ibid.

24. Pamphlet, "Celebrations of Love" at the Sunrise Center, Corte Madera, Spring/Summer 1996 Calendar.

25. Its full address is http://www.tantra.com, for those interested.

26. Ashley Thirleby, *Tantra: The Key to Sexual Power and Pleasure* (New York: Dell, 1978), p. 9.

27. Ibid., p. 15.

28. Howard John Zitko, *New Age Tantra Yoga: The Cybernetics of Sex and Love* (Tucson: World University Press, 1975), pp. 7–8.

29. Ibid., p. 63.

30. Ibid., p. 67.

31. Andre van Lysebeth, *Tantra, the Cult of the Feminine* (York Beach: Samuel Weiser, 1995), p. 31.

32. Ibid., p. 85.

33. Ibid.

34. Ibid., p. 225.

35. Maryse Cote with Dove Sterling, "Tantra and Sexual Healing for Women," *Tantra: The Magazine,* Kali Issue, no. 9, 1994, p. 62.

36. Ibid., pp. 62–63.

37. G. S. Arundale, *Kundalini: An Occult Experience* (Adyar: Theosophical Publishing House, [1938] 1988), pp. 10–11.

38. Ibid., p. 35.

39. Ibid., pp. 93–94.

40. Kenneth Grant, "Cults of the Shadow" in John White, ed., *Kundalini, Evolution and Enlightenment* (Garden City: Anchor Books, 1979), pp. 396–98.

41. Interview, ex-member of 3HO, New York, 1996.

42. Pandit Gopi Krishna, *Kundalini: Path to Higher Consciousness* (New Delhi: Orient Paperbacks, [1976] 1992), p. 8.

43. John Selby, *Kundalini Awakening: A Gentle Guide to Chakra Activation and Spiritual Growth* (New York: Bantam Books, 1992), p. 7.

44. Barbara Condron, *Kundalini Rising: Mastering Creative Energies* (Windyville: SOM Publishing, 1992), p. 46. The notion of root races was most developed by the Theosophists. According to this theory, throughout history, various races have emerged, lived, and died in cataclysms, and each race differed from the previous ones. The lost civilizations of Atlantis and Lemuria, whose inhabitants were said to have advanced psychic abilities, involved earlier root-races.

45. Ibid., p. 144.

46. Vicki Noble, *Shakti Woman* (San Francisco: Harper and Row, 1991), p. 76.

47. Ibid., pp. 27–28.

48. Ibid., p. 7.

49. Ibid., p. 201.

50. Ibid.

51. Diane Stein, *The Women's Book of Healing* (St. Paul: Llewellyn Publishers, 1987), p. xvii.

52. Ibid., p. xix.

53. Ibid., p. 12.

54. Ibid., p. 33.

55. Ibid., p. 83.

56. Monica Sjoo and Barbara Mor, *The Great Cosmic Goddess* (San Francisco: Harper and Row, 1987), pp. 182–83.

57. Bhagavan Das, "Mashani," *Tantra: The Magazine*, Kali issue, no. 9, 1994, p. 21.

58. Lex Hixon, "Tantric Hymns of Enlightenment," ibid., p. 36.

59. Lex Hixon, "Pilgrimage to India," ibid., p. 33.

60. Hixon, "Tantric Hymns of Enlightenment," p. 37.

61. David Alan Ramsdale, "Kali Ma—A Personal Encounter" *Tantra: the Magazine*, ibid., p. 57.

62. Ibid.

63. Le'ema Kathleen Graham, "Kali's Dance" *Tantra: The Magazine*, Kali issue, no. 9, 1994, p. 56.

64. Ibid.

65. Ibid.

66. Cassia Berman, "Dancing with Mother Kali," *Tantra: The Magazine*, Kali issue, no. 9, 1994, p. 52.

67. Ibid., p. 53.

68. Informant, Charleston, S.C., 1998.

69. It is a legitimate question in such circumstances to ask: is the ritual valid if performed on inappropriate days? For many orthodox Hindus, a ritual performed at the wrong time is no ritual at all.

70. Pratapaditya Pal, "Durga Puja in South California," *Statesman*, Festival '91 magazine, Durga Puja special, Autumn 1991.

71. Rachel Fell McDermott, "The Western Kālī," in John Stratton Hawley and Donna Marie Wulff, eds., *Devī: Goddesses of India* (Berkeley: University of California Press, 1996), pp. 296–298.

72. David Gordon White, *Kiss of the Yogini* (Chicago: University of Chicago Press, 2003), p. 272. He notes how understandings of tantric sexuality have changed over time.

## CONCLUSIONS

1. Stanley N. Kurtz, *All the Mothers Are One: Hindu India and the Cultural Reshaping of Psychanalysis* (New York: Columbia University Press, 1992).

2. Lawrence Babb, *The Divine Hierarchy: Popular Hinduism in Central India* (New York: Columbia University Press, [1970] 1975).

3. Lynn Bennett, *Dangerous Wives and Sacred Sisters: Social and Symbolic Roles of High-Caste Women in Nepal* (New York: Columbia University Press, 1983).

4. Lynn Gatwood, *Devi and the Spouse Goddess: Women, Sexuality and Marriage in India* (Riverdale: Riverdale Company, 1985).

5. For instance, see the biography of Parvati Soren, in which the goddess Manasa forbade her to worship Santal deities.

6. Kurtz, *All the Mothers Are One*, p. 98.

7. Homi Bhabha, "Postcolonial Authority and Postmodern Guilt," in *Cultural Studies*, edited by Lawrence Grossberg, Cary Nelson, and Paula Treichler (New York: Routledge, 1992), p. 57.

8. Ibid., p. 56.

9. Lata Mani, "Cultural Theory, Colonial Texts: Reading Eyewitness Accounts of Widow Burning," ibid., p. 393.

10. Ibid., p. 394, citing the arguments of Ranajit Guha in his article "Dominance without Hegemony and Its Historiography." In R. Guha, ed, *Subaltern Studies*, edited by R. Guha (Delhi: Oxford University Press, 1989), volume 6, pp. 210–309.

11. Roma Chatterji, *Folklore and the Formation of Popular Consciousness in a Village in the Purulia District of West Bengal*, Ph.D. dissertation, University of Delhi, 1985, p. 244. The author later notes that Marx was called a "fool" by Jharkhandis for his statement that religion was the opium of the people (p. 246).

12. Interview, taxi driver, Calcutta, 1994. It may be noted that the hydrants throughout Calcutta were built by the British and used to clean the streets. They are no longer used for this purpose.

# Diacritical List

This list does not include historical individuals, place names, months, or plants.

*Adbhuta Rāmāyaṇa*
*adhikāra*
*Ādhyātma Rāmāyaṇa*
Ādi Śakti (Adi Shakti)
Ādivāsī
Advaita
Adya Bhubaneśvarī (Adya Bhubaneshvari)
Adya Śakti (Adya Shakti)
Adya Sundarī
Adya Tāriṇi
āgama
*āgāmanī*
Aghori
*Agni Purāṇa*
Ahalyā
*Aitareya Brāhmaṇa*
*akāla pūjā*
Alakṣmi (Alakshmi)
*alaṃkāra*
*alpana*
*amarta*
*amār ṭhakur*
*-ambā*
Ambikā
Ambuvacī
*aṃśa* (*amsha*
*-ānanda*
Ānanda Maṭh
Ānandamayī
Ānandamayir āgamanī
Aniruddha
Annada Ṭhakur
Annapūrṇā
Anuraginī
*apsaras*
*āratī*
Aruṇa
*āsana*
*aśāstrīya* (*ashastriya*)
*asītā* (white)
Aṣṭamī (Ashtami)
*aṣṭapārīkṣa* (*ashtapariksha*)
āstika
*asura*
Aśvatthāmā (Ashvatthama)
*atimārga*
*ātmā*
Avadhūta, *avadhūta*
*avāraṇa devatā*

*āuś* (*aush*)
āyanā
*āyatta karā*

Bābā
Baḍa Kālimā
Bagalā
Bagalāmukhī
Banbībī
*bandha*
*baṅgalitvā*
Bankālī
*bao*
*barwāri*
Bāul
Bhadrākālī
Bhadu
Bhadurānī
*bhagat*
*Bhagavad Gītā*
Bhagavān
*Bhāgavata Purāṇa*
*Bhāgavatī Gītā*
*bhāginībhāva*
*bhāī*
Bhairava, *bhairava*
Bhairavī, *bhairavī*
*bhajan*
bhakta
bhakti
bhāṅg
*bhaoa*
*bhaoaiā*
*bhar, bhor*
Bhārat
*bhārater sādhaka*
*bharjabhāva*
*bhar*-lady
*bhāva*
*bhāvamukha*
*Bhavānī Mandir*
Bhavatāriṇī
*bhāvāveśa* (*bhavavesha*)
*Bhaviśya Purāṇa* (*Bhavishya Purana*)
*Bhavṛcopaniṣad* (*Bhavrichopanishad*)
*bhoga*
*bhukti*
Bhurloka
*bhūta*
*Bhūtadamara Tantra*
*bhūtaśuddhi* (*bhutashuddhi*)
Bhūtinī, *bhūtinī*
Bhuvaneśī (Bhuvaneshi)
Bhuvaneśvarī (Bhuvaneshvari)
Bhuvarloka
Bidhātā
*bidéśī niyam*
*bīja*
*bindu*
*bodhana*
*bon*
*boṅga*
Brahmā
*brahmacāriṇi* (*brahmacharini*)
*brahmajñāna*
Brahmamāyī
*brahman*
Brahmanī
Brahmamāyī
*Brahmavaivarta Purāṇa*
Brahmavidyā
*brata*
*Bṛhaddharma Purāṇa* (*Brihaddharma Purana*)
Bṛhaspati (Brihaspati)
Būḍa Śiva (Buda Shiva)
*buddhi*
*būḍī*
Būḍī Mā, Būrī Mā
Būḍir Pūjā
Būra-Būrī
Būrhi Māī
Būrhia Mātā
Būri Thakurānī
*burir jāṭ*

Caitanya (Chaitanya)
*caitanya-śakti* (*chaitanya-shakti*)
cakra (chakra)
*cakrapūjā* (*chakrapuja*)
Camār (Chamar)
Cāmuṇḍā (Chamunda)

Caṇḍa (Chanda)
Caṇḍāla (Chandala)
Caṇḍī (Chandi)
Caṇḍidāsa (Chandidasa)
Caṇḍikā (Chandika)
*Caṇḍī Maṅgal Kāvya* (*Chandi Mangal Kavya*)
Caṇḍī Saptasatī (Chandi Saptasati)
Candramaṇik (Chandramanik)
Candrāvalī (Chandravali)
Carak gājan (Charak Gajan)
*caryāpada* (*charyapada*)
*catka* (*chatka*)
*cetika sādhana* (*chetika sadhana*)
Cānda Sāgar (Sadagar)
Cāndo
Chinnamastā
*Cinācara Tantra* (*Chinchara Tantra*)

*dādā*
dainir dṛṣṭi (*dainir drishti*)
Daitya
Ḍākinī, *ḍākinī*
*Ḍākinī Tantra*
Dakṣa (Daksha)
*dakṣinācāra* (*dakshinachara*)
Dakṣinakālī (Dakshinakali)
Dakṣsineśwar Śiva (Dakshineshwar Shiva)
Dakṣin Ray (Dakshin Ray)
*dānava*
*ḍaṇḍavat*
*ḍaṇḍi khātā*
darśan (darshan)
Dāruka
*daśa mahāvidyā* (*dasha mahavidya*)
*Daśakumāracaritam* (*Dashakumaracharitam*)
*daśvandh*
*dasyu*
*deśi*(*deshi*)
Deuleśvar Śiva (Deuleshvar Shiva)
*deva*
*devabhāva*
Devakī
*devatā*
Devātma Śakti (Devatma Shakti)
Devī
*Devī Bhāgavata Purāṇa*
Devī Gītā
*Devī Māhātmya*
*Devī Purāṇa*
*Devī Sūkta*
*Devī Upaniṣad* (*Devi Upanishad*)
*deyāsī* (*deyashi*)
*deyāsinī* (*deyashini*)
Dhakeśvarī (Dhakeshvari)
Dharā
Dharma, dharma
dharmaśāstra (dharmashastra)
*Dharma-pūjā-paddhati*
Dharma Ṭhakur
Dhelai Caṇḍī (Dhelai Chandi)
*dhātṛ* (*dhatri*)
*dhulopara*
Dhūmāvatī
*dhunapore*
*dhūnī*
*dhyāna*
*dīdī*
*dīkṣā* (*diksha*)
*divya bhāva*
*divyācāra*
Ḍom
Draupadī
Durgā
Durgāgītā
Durgā Pūjā
Durgā Saptasatī
Duryodhana
Dvapara yuga

Ekajaṭā
*ekātmika bhāva*
*ektārā*

*gachbera*
Gajalakṣmī (Gajalakshmi)
*gambhira*
*gandharva*
Gaṇeśa (Ganesha)
Gaṇga

*gāñja*
Garuḍa
*Garuḍa Purāṇa*
Gauḍīya Vaiṣṇavism (Gaudiya Vaishnavism)
Gaurī
Gayādham
Ghaghrabūḍī
Girija
Girinandinī
Girirāja
Girirānī
*Gītā Govinda*
*gopī*
Govindadāsa
*graha*
*grāmadevatā*
*gṛhi sādhika* (*grihi sadhika*)
*Guhyakalupaniṣad* (*Guhyakalupanishad*)
*guṇa*
Gundi Ṭhakurānī
*guṇin*
*gupta dhāna*
Gupta Durgā
*Guptasādhana Tantra*
*gutika*

Hāḍī
Hanumān
Harapriya
*Hariṣ Maṅgal Caṇḍī* (*Harish Mangal Chandi*)
*Harivaṃśa* (*Harivamsha*)
Harṣa-carita (*Harsha-charita*)
Hathi-Dhara-Būrī
*hatyā deyā*
Himālaya
Himavat
*homa*
*-huṃ*
*huruṅg caṇḍiko* (*hurung chandiko*)

*icchāmṛtyu* (*icchamrityu*)
*īḍā*
Indra
Indranī

Īśa (Isha)
*iṣṭa-devatā* (*ishta-devata*)
*iṣṭa-devī* (*ishta-devi*)
Īśvara (Ishvara)

jaba
Jagadambā
Jagaddhatri
*jagarāṇa*
Jagatgaurī
*jagat mūrti*
*Jagatām dhātrī*
*jaher thān*
Janaloka
japa
Jaratkaru
*jaṭā*(matted hair)
Jatapaharinī
Jayadeva
Jayadurgā
*jhumur*
*jīva*
*jñāna*
*Jñānodāyinī*
Joṭe Mā
*jugala mūrti*

Kailāsa (Kailash)
Kaiṭabha
Kaivalyadāyinī, *kaivalyadayini*
Kalābau
*kāla kuṇḍa*
Kāla Mukha
Kālarātṛ (Kalaratri)
*kalā*
Kālī
Kālī Bhāvatarinī
Kālikā
*Kālikā Purāṇa*
*Kālī-kīrtan*
Kālī-kula
Kālī Māī
Kālīsthān
*Kālivilāsa Tantra*
Kali yuga
*kāma*

Kāmadeva
*Kāmakalā-vilāsa*
Kāmākhyā Mā
*Kāmākhyā Tantra*
Kamalā
Kāmapāla
*Kāma Sūtra*
Kāmeśvarī (Kameshvari)
Kaṁsa
Kanaka Durgā
Kanakavatī
Kanakeśvarī (Kanakeshvari)
Kankālidevī
Kanyā-Kumārī
*kapāla*
*kapāla kriyā*
Kapālikā
*kapalīn*
Karnapiśācī (Karnapishachi)
Karnapūrnā
Kārttikeya
Kāruṇamāyī
Kāśi (Kashi)
Kaśyapa (Kashyapa)
Kathāmṛta (Kathamrita)
Kathāsaritsāgara
Katṛka-nyāsa (Katrika-nyasa)
Kātyāyanī
*kaulajñāna-nirnaya*
*kaula mārga*
*Kaumudimitrānanda*
Kaurava
Kauśikī (Kaushiki)
*kavaca* (*kavacha*)
*khatvaṅga*
*Khila Harivaṁśa* (*Khila Harivamsha*)
*kinnari*
*kīrtan*
*koṭwal*
*kriyā*
*kriyā-śakti* (*kriya-shakti*)
*kriyāvatī*
Kṛṣṇa (Krishna)
*kṛṣṇa ṣaṭkarma* (*krishna shatkarma*)
kṣatriya (kshatriya)
*Kubjikā Tantra*
Kubera, Kuvera
kula
*kula cakra* (*kula chakra*)
*kulācāra* (*kulachara*)
*Kulacūḍāmaṇi Tantra* (*Kulachudamani Tantra*)
*kulajñāna*
*kula kuṇḍa*
*kula mārga*
*Kulārṇava Tantra*
*kula sādhaka*
*kumārasambhava*
Kumārī, *kumārī*
*kuṁkuṁ*
*kuṇḍala*
Kuṇḍalinī, kuṇḍalinī
*Kūrma Purāṇa*
*kurtā*
Kuvalayavatī

Lakhindar
Lakṣmī (Lakshmi)
Lalitā
Lambodarī
*latā sādhana*
*lāṭhī*
*laukika*
laya yoga
*līlā*
*liṅga*
*Liṅga Purāṇa*
*loka*

Mā
Mabarag Mālika
Madhu
Mā Dumni
Mā Gaṅgā
*Mahābhāgavata Purāṇa*
*Mahābhārata*
*mahābhāva*
Mahācīna (Mahachina)
Mahādeva
Mahādevī
Mahāgra
Mahākālī

*mahājan*
*mahājñāna*
*mahājyoti*
Mahākāla
Mahākālasaṁhita
Mahākālī
*mahā-kuṇḍa*
Mahālaksmi (Mahalakshmi)
Mahāmāyā
*mahāmudrā samādhi*
*mahānanda*
Mahānatī
*mahānavamī pūjā*
*Mahānirvāṇa Tantra*
Maharloka
*mahārthamañjari*
Mahāśakti (Mahashakti)
Mahāvidyā, *mahāvidyā*
Mahāyanā
Mahaśī (Maheshi)
Maheśvarī (Maheshvari)
Mahiṣamardinī (Mahishamardini)
Mahiṣāsura (Mahishasura)
Mahiṣāsuramardinī (Mahishasuramardini)
Makar Caṇḍi (Makar Chandi)
*mālā*
Malancamālā (Malanchamala)
*Mālatīmādhava*
Manasā
*Manasā Maṅgal Kāvya*
*Manasā-Vijayā*
*mānasika*
*manat*
*maṇḍala*
Maṇidvīpa
Maṅgal Caṇḍī (Mangal Chandi)
*maṅgal-kāvya*
Maṇidvīpa
*mañjarī sādhana*
Manohara
mantra
*mantrajapa*
mantra-śakti (mantra-shakti)
*mantrasiddhi*
*mantrasuddhi*
*māraṇa*
*Mārkaṇḍeya Purāṇa*
Maśān Cāmuṇḍa Kālī (Mashan Chamunda Kali)
Mātā
Mātaṅga
Mātaṅgī
*mati*
*mātṛbhāva* (*matribhava*)
*mātṛka* (*matrika*)
*mātṛka-nyāsa* (*matrika-nyasa*)
Mātṛ-pūjā (Matri-puja)
*Matsya Purāṇa*
*māyā*
*māyā-cāyā* (*maya-chaya*)
*Māyā Tantra*
*mela*
Menakā
*māyer kṛpa* (*mayer kripa*)
*mokṣa* (*moksha*)
Mṛtunjaya (Mritunjaya)
mudra
mukta nārī
mukta puruṣa
*mūla*
*mūlādhāra*
Muṇḍa
*Muṇḍaka Upaniṣad* (*Mundaka Upanishad*)
*muṇḍake khāo nāo*
*Muṇḍamālā Tantra*
*mūrti*
Musā (Musha)

*nādī*
Nāga
*nāginī*
*nāgkanyā*
Nakuleśwar (Nakuleshwar)
*-namas*
Nanda
Nārada
Narasiṃha
Nārāyaṇa
Nārāyaṇi
*nārī*

Natanī
Nāth
*naṭī*
Nava-Durgā, *navadurgā*
*navakanyā*
Navapattrikā
*navapuṣpa* (*navapushpa*)
Navarātra
*nava vidhā*
*nigama*
Nīlamaṇi
*nīlasādhana*
Nīlasarasvatī
*Nīla Tantra*
Niranjan
*nirguṇa*
Nirṛtidevī (Nirritidevi)
*Niruttara Tantra*
Niśumbha (Nishumba)
Nityā
*nyāsa*
Nyāya

*ojhā*
Ola Bībī
Olāi Caṇḍī (Olai Chandi)
*oṁkār*
*Oṁ hrīṃ śrīṃ klīṃ Manasā Devyai svāhā*
*Oṁ namaḥ Śivāyaḥ* (*Om namah Shivaya*)

Pada Durgā
*paddhati*
*Padmā Purāṇa*
Padminī
Palli Jānānī
*pañcamakara* (*panchamakara*)
*pañcamuṇḍa āsana*
*pañcākāśa* (*panchakasha*)
Pañcānanda (Panchananda)
*pañcatattva* (*panchatattva*)
Pañcāvati (Panchavati)
*pāṇḍal*
Pāṇḍava
*paṇḍit*
*panjikā*
*parabdha*
*parabhakti*
parabrahman
Parabrahmansvarūpinī
*parakīya*
Parama Śakti (Parama Shakti)
Paramaśiva (Paramashiva)
Pārvatī
*paśu* (*pashu*)
*paśubhāva* (*pashu bhava*)
*paśu cakra* (*pashu chakra*)
*paśucāra* (*pashuchara*)
*paśu-veśya* (*pashu-veshya*)
*pāta*
*patramūrti*
*patuā*
*-phaṭ*
*piṅgalā*
*piśāca* (*pishacha*)
Piśacī (Pishachi)
*pīṭha*
*pīṭha pūjā*
Prakṛti, prakṛti (prakriti)
*prāṇa*
*prāṇa-pratiṣṭha* (*prana-pratishtha*)
*Prāṇatoṣiṇī* (*Pranatoshini*)
*prārabdha*
*prasād*
*prati-vātsalya*
*pratyakṣa* (*pratyaksha*)
*prema*
*preta*
pūjā
*pūjā maṇḍapa*
*pujāri*
*pujāriṇī*
*punjika*
purāṇa
*puraścarana* (*purashcharana*)
Puruṣa, puruṣa (purusha)
*Puruṣa Sūkta* (*Purusha Sukta*)
Puṣkara (Pushkara)

Rādhā
Rājarājeśvarī (Rajarajeshvari)
*rajas*
*Ṛg Veda* (*Rig Veda*)

Rājballabhī
*rāj-beś*
Rakṣa Kālī (Raksha Kali)
Raktabīja
Raktadantī
Rāma
Rāmacandra (Ramachandra)
*Rāmāyaṇa*
Rambha
Ramaṇa-Kālī
Rāna Caṇḍī (Rana Chandi)
Rasa
*rāsa*
*rasagullā*
Rati
Ratipriyā
Ratisundarī
Ratṛ (Ratri)
Ratṛ Sūkta (Ratri Sukta)
Rāvaṇa
*ṛṣī* (*rishi*)
Rudrakaṇṭha
rudrākṣa (rudrakshn)
*Rudrayāmala*
Rukminī
*rūpa*
Rūpasī
Rūpeśvari (Rupeshvari)

*śabdabrahman* (*shabdabrahman*)
Sadāśiva (Sadashiva)
Sadgopa
*sādhana*
*Sādhanamala*
*sādhaka*
*sādhika*
sādhu
*saguṇa*
Sahajiyā
*sahasrāra cakra* (*sahasrara chakra*)
Śakambharī (Shakambhari)
*sakhī*
Śākta (Shakta)
*Śāktānandatarangini* (*Shaktanandatarangini*)
*Śākta padābalī* (*Shakta padabali*)
*śākta pīṭha* (*shakta pitha*)
*śāktādvaitavāda* (*shaktadvaitavada*)
Śakti, śakti (shakti)
*śakti lābh kāra* (*shakti labh kara*)
*śaktipāt* (*shaktipat*)
*śakti pīṭha* (*shakti pitha*)
*samādhi*
*samāj*
*samanvayi*
*samāveśa* (*samavesha*)
Sāṃkhya
*saṁpradāya*
saṁsāra
Sanaka
*saṅgha*
Saṅkhacūṛā (Shankachura)
Śaṅkara (Shankara)
*sannyāsa*
sannyāsi
sannyāsinī
*śānta bhāva* (*shanta bhava*)
*santan*
Santoṣī Mā (Santoshi Ma)
*Śāradatilaka* (*Sharadatilaka*)
*śāradīya pūjā* (*sharadiya puja*)
Sarasvatī
Sarvamanoharī
Ṣaṣṭhī (Shashthi)
*śāstra* (*shastra*)
*śāstrīya* (*shastriya*)
*Śatapatha Brāhmaṇa* (*Shatapatha Brahmana*)
*ṣaṭ-cakra-bheda* (*shat-chakra-bheda*)
*satcidānanda*
Satī
*satī piṭha*
*ṣaṭkarma* (*shatkarma*) or ṣaṭkarmāṇi
*sattva*
Satyaloka
Satya yuga
*śava* (*shava*)
*śava sādhana* (*shava sadhana*)
Śavaśiva (Shavashiva)
*śavavāda* (*shavavada*)

Sāvitrī
*sevāit*
*siddha*
*siddhi*
*siddhi lābh kāra*
*sindūr*
Sītā, *sītā*
Śītalā (Shitala)
Śiva (m), Śiva (f) (Shiva)
Śivagāma (Shivagama)
Śiva Mahākāla (Shiva Mahakala)
*Śiva Purāṇa* (*Shiva Purana*)
*śivatva* (*shivatva*)
*Skanda Purāṇa*
Śmaśāna Kālī
Ṣoḍaśi (Shodashi)
Śokarahita
*solāpīṭh*
*sphoṭa*
*śraddhā* (*shraddha*)
Śrī (Shri)
Śri-kula (Shri-kula)
*Śrī Rāmakṛṣṇa Upaniṣad* (*Shri Ramakrishna Upanishad*)
Śrī Vidyā (Shri Vidya)
*stambhana*
*strī*
*strī-ādhāra*
*strīmāyā*
Subhāga
śūdra (shudra)
Śūlapāni (Shulapani)
Śūlinī Durgā (Shulini Durga)
Śumbha (Shumbha)
Sundarī
*Śunya Purāṇa* (*Shunya Purana*)
Surasundarī
*suṣumnā* (*sushumna*)
sūtra
*śyāma-saṅgīt* (*shyama-sangit*)
*svapnadeśa* (*svapnadesha*)
Svarūpa
Svarloka
*svastayana*
*svayambhu*
Śyāma (m), Śyāmā (f) (Shyama)
*Śyāma saṅgit* (*Shyama sangit*)

*tamas*
*Tantrasāra*
*Tantra Tattva*
tantrika
*tantrikācārya* (*tantrikacharya*)
*tapas*
Tapoloka
Tārā
*tārā-guru*
*Tārārahasyam*
Tārinī Śakti (Tarini Shakti)
*tattva*
*tattvajñāna*
*-tha*
*ṭhākur*
Ṭhākurānī
*ṭhākur ghar*
*Ṭhākurdādār Jhuli*
*ṭhākur pañcāyat* (*thakur panchayat*)
*thān*
*tomār jaya hok*
Tretya yuga
Tripurā Bhairavī
Tripurā Sundarī
*Tripurā-tāpini Upaniṣad* (*Tripura-tapini Upanishad*)
Tulsī, tulsī
Tuṣu (Tushu)

*ucchāṭaṇa*
Ucchiṣṭacaṇḍalinī (Ucchishtachandalini)
*Uddisa Tantra*
*ugra*
Ugracaṇḍā Durgā (Ugrachanda Durga)
Ugrātārā
*ullāsa*
Uluicaṇḍī (Uluichandi)
Umā
Unani
*upalabdhi*
Upaniṣad (Upanishad)

Uṣa (Usha)
*Utpatti Tantra* (?)
*uttara sādhika*

Vaiṣṇava (Vaishnava)
Vaiṣṇavī (Vaishnavi)
vaiśya (vaishya)
Vaiṣṇo Devī
*vajra*
Vajratārā
Vajrayāna
*vāk*
*vāmācāra* (*vamachara*)
Vāmācāri Śakta (Vamachari Shakta)
Vāma Kālī
Vāmākṣepā
*Vāmana Purāṇa*
Vana Durgā
Vanaprastha
*Varāhi Tantra*
varṇa
*varṇadharma*
Varninī
Vāsantī Pūjā
*vāsikaraṇa*
Vasiṣṭha (Vasishtha)
Vasudeva
Vāsuki
*vaṭa*
*vātsalya*
Vāyu
*Vāyu Purāṇa*
Vedānta
*vedha dīkṣā* (*vedha diksha*)
*veśya* (*veshya*)
*vibhūti*
*vidveṣana* (*vidveshana*)
*vidyā*
*Vidyāpati*
*vidyā-sundar*
*vijayā*
Vijayā Daśami (Vijaya Dashami)
*vikṣepa* (*vikshepa*)
*vīṇā*
Vindhyādevī
*viparita*
*vīra*
*vīrācāra* (*virachara*)
*viraha*
Vīralakṣmī (Viralakshmi)
*virat rūpa*
Viṣṇu (Vishnu)
*viśvarūpa* (*vishvarupa*)
*viveka*
Vṛddheśvarī (Vriddheshvari)
*vṛddhika* (*vriddhika*)
*Vṛkṣa mātri* (*Vriksha matri*)

*yajña*
*Yajñavalkya-smṛti* (*Yajnavalkya-smriti*)
*yakṣa* (*yaksha*)
*yakṣiṇī* (*yakshini*)
Yama
yantra
yoga, yogi
Yoganidrā
yoginī
*yoginīcakra* (*yoginichakra*)
*Yoginī Sādhana Prayoga*
*Yoginītantra*
*yoni*
yuga devī

zamindār

# Bibliography

BENGALI SOURCES

*Andul Kālī kīrtan o baul gitāvalī.* Andul: Andul Kālī Kīrtan Samiti, 1987.

Bandyopadhyaya, Haricarana. *Baṅgiya śabdakośa.* Calcutta: Sahitya Akademi, 1988.

*Baṅgala bhasar abhidhān.* Calcutta: Sāhitya Saṁsad, 1991.

"Baṅgiya Tantrik Samāj." Pamphlet for Bengali Tantric Society, registered under West Bengal Act XXVI of 1961.

Basu, Gopendra Krsna. *Baṅglar laukika debatā.* Calcutta: Ananda Publishers, 1969.

Bhattacarya, Asutosa. *Baṅglar loka-sāhitya.* Calcutta: Calcutta Book House, 1985.

Bhattacarya, Gopalcandra, and Rama Debi. *(Baromaser) Meyeder bratakathā.* Calcutta: Nirmal Book Agency, n.d.

Bhattacarya, Hamsanarayana. *Hinduder debadebī: Udbhaba o korambikāśa.* Calcutta: Firma KLM, 1986.

*Bṛhat Tantrasāra.* Edited by Mahamahopadhyaya Shrimat Krsnacandra Bhattacarya and Shrimat Prasanakumar Sastri Bhattacarya, Calcutta: Prasannakumar Shastri, 1303 BS [1896].

Cakravarti, Amitabha. "Durgotsab—kālikata o kalkatar." In *Biśeṣa pratibedana,* 1398 BS [1991] (special Śaradīya issue).

Cakravarti, Gangescandra. *Baṅglar sādhaka.* Calcutta: Nabendu Cakravarti, 1379 BS [1972].

Cakravarti, Jahnavikumar. *Śaktapadābalī o śaktisādhana.* Calcutta: D. M. Library, 1367 BS [1960].

Cakravarti, Pranavesa. *Ei baṅglai.* Calcutta: Dev Sahitya Kutir, 1992.

Chattopadhyaya, Satindramohan. *Tantrer kathā.* Calcutta: Sāhitya Saṁsad, 1983.

Chaudhuri, Yajnisvara. *Bardhaman: Itihāsa o saṁskrti*. Vol. 2. Calcutta: Ānandamāyī Chaudhuri, 1991.
Das, Jnanendramohan. *Baṅgala bhāsar abhidhān*. Calcutta: Sāhitya Saṁsad, 1991.
Das, Upendrakumar. *Bhāratīya śakti-sādhana*. Shantiniketan: Vishvabharati Publications, 1373 BS [1966].
Dasgupta, Sasibhusan. *Bhāratera śakti-sādhana o śākta sāhitya*. Calcutta: Sahitya Samsad, 1393 BS [1985].
Dev, Asutosa. *Śabdabodh abhidhān*. Calcutta: A. Dev, 1949.
*Devī Purāṇa*. Edited by Pancanan Tarkaratna and Shrijiva Nyayatirtha. Calcutta: Nababharat Publishers, 1400 BS [1993].
Ghosh, Baridbaran, ed. *Bhāratvārśīya upāsaka-saṁpradaya*. Calcutta: Karuna Prakasani, 1397 BS [1990].
Gupta, Radhaprasad. "Gobindaramer Durgā Pūja." *Deś*, September 26, 1987.
*Guruguṇa gan*. Adyapitha: Dakṣineśwar Rāmakṛṣṇa Saṅgha, 1397 BS [1990].
*Kāmākhya Tantra*. Edited by Jyotirlal Das. Calcutta: Nababharat Publishers, 1385 BS [1978].
Karan, Sudhir. *Sīmānta bāṅglār lokjān*. Calcutta: E. Mukherji, 1965.
Kaviraja, Gopinath. *Tantrik sādhana o siddhānta*. Barddhaman: Barddhaman University, 1376 BS [1969].
*Kālī Tantram*. Edited by Pandit Nityananda Smrititirtha. Calcutta: Nababharat Publishers, 1388 BS [1981].
*Kulārṇava Tantra (Mūla, Tīkā o Baṅganubadsaha)*. Edited by Upendrakumar Das. Calcutta: Nababharat Publishers, 1363 BS [1976].
*Mahābhāgavata Purāṇa*. Edited by Puspendra Kumar. Delhi: Eastern Book Linkers, 1983.
Mitra, Asok, ed. *Pściṁbangera pūjā-parban o melā, Bardhaman District*. Delhi: Controller of Publications, 1992.
Mitra, Subalcandra. *Saral baṅgala abhidhān*. Calcutta: New Bengal Press, 1991.
*Nīla Tantra*. Edited by Jyotirlal Das. Calcutta: Nababharat Publishers, 1399 BS [1992].
Raya, Amarendarnath, ed. *Śākta padābalī*. Calcutta: Kālikata Viśvavidyālaya, 1963; reprint. Calcutta: Calcutta University Press, 1989.
Sarasvati, Nigamananda. *Mayer kṛpā*. Halisahar: Swami Atmananda/Sarasvati Math, 1382 BS [1975].
Sarvanandanath, *Sarvollāsatantram*. Edited by and translated into Bengali by Gopala Siddhantavagisa. Calcutta: Bireśhacandra Raya Chaudhuri, 1989.
Sastri, Bahubidh Tantra-Grantha Praneta Tantrikacarya Sribhairab. *Dākiṇī tantra*. Calcutta: Rajendra Library, n.d.
Sen, Ramprasad. *Rāmprasādī saṅgīt*. Calcutta: Rajendra Library, n.d.
Sengupta, Pallab. *Pūjā parban utsakathā*. Calcutta: Anup Kumar Mahinda, 1990.
Sengupta, Utpal. *Chotadera batrisa siṁhasana*. Calcutta: Mahesa Publication, n.d.
Siddha Bhairava, Tantrik Acarya Sri Bhairava Sastri. *Dākiṇī tantra*. Calcutta: Rajendra Library, n.d.
Sinha, Kali Prasanna. *Hutam pañcar nakṣa*. Calcutta: Natun Sahitya Bhavan, 1868.
*Vyāvahārika śabdakośa*. Calcutta: Presidency Library, 1958.

## ENGLISH SOURCES

*Adhyatma Ramayana.* The Spiritual Version of the Rama Saga. Translated by Swami Tapasyananda. Madras: Sri Ramakrishna Math, 1985.

Aiyer, V.A.K. *Stories of Vikramaditya (Simhasana Dwatrimsika).* Bombay: Bharatiya Vidya Bhava, 1988.

Archer, W. G. *The Hill of Flutes: Life, Love and Poetry in Tribal India, A Portrait of the Santals.* Pittsburgh: University of Pittsburgh Press, 1974.

Arundale, G. S. *Kundalini: An Occult Experience.* Adyar: Theosophical Publishing House, (1938) 1988.

Avalon, Arthur (Sir John Woodroffe). *Shakti and Shakta.* New York: Dover, (1918) 1978.

Babb, Lawrence. *The Divine Hierarchy: Popular Hinduism in Central India.* New York: Columbia University Press, (1970) 1975.

Bagchi, Gour Chandra. "Village Survey Monograph on Bhumij Dhan Sol." In *Census of India 1961, West Bengal and Sikkim,* edited by Sukumar Sinha. Vol. 16, part 6 (5). Calcutta: Government of India Publication, 1967.

Bagchi, P. C. *Studies in the Tantras.* Calcutta: University of Calcutta, 1939.

Bandyopadhyaya, Pranab. *Mother Goddess Durga,* Calcutta: Image India, 1987.

Banerji, Amiya Kumar, ed. *West Bengal District Gazetteer—Hooghly.* Calcutta: State Editor, West Bengal District Gazetteer, 1972.

Banerji, Chitrita. *Life and Food in Bengal.* New Delhi: Rupa, 1991.

Banerji, S. C. *A Brief History of Tantra Literature.* Calcutta: Naya Prokash, 1988.

———. *Tantra in Bengal: A Study on Its Origin, Development and Influence.* Calcutta: Naya Prokash, 1978.

Basu, Manoranjan. *Fundamentals of the Philosophy of Tantras.* Calcutta: Mira Basu, 1986.

Bennett, Lynn. *Dangerous Wives and Sacred Sisters: Social and Symbolic Roles of High-Caste Women in Nepal.* New York: Columbia University Press, 1983.

Berkson, Carmel. *The Divine and Demoniac: Mahisa's Heroic Struggle with Durga.* Delhi: Oxford University Press, 1995.

Bhabha, Homi. "Postcolonial Authority and Postmodern Guilt." In *Cultural Studies,* edited by Lawrence Grossberg et al. New York: Routledge, 1992.

Bhattacarya, Arapana. *Religious Movements of Bengal and Their Socio-Economic Ideas (1800–1850).* Patna: A. Bhattacarya, 1981.

Bhattacarya, Asutosh. *Folklore of Bengal.* New Delhi: National Book Trust, [1978] 1983.

Bhattacharya, Bholanath. *The Deified Saints of Bengal: A Profile.* Calcutta: Indian Publications, 1972.

———. "Some Aspects of the Esoteric Cults of Consort Worship in Bengal: A Field Survey Report" *Folklore* (Calcutta) numbers 10–12 (October–December 1977).

———. "The Spring Time Fair of Makar Chandi of Makardah," *Modern Review,* (Calcutta), September 1971.

Bhattacarya, Sriyukta Siva Candra Vidyarnava. *Tantra-Tattva.* Edited by Sir John Woodroffe as *Principles of Tantra.* Madras: Ganesh, 1978.

Bhattacharyya, Asutosh. *An Introduction to the Study of the Medieval Bengali Epics.* Calcutta: Calcutta Book House, 1943.

Bhattacharyya, Narendranath. *History of the Śākta Religion*. New Delhi: Munshiram Manoharlal, 1974.

———. *History of the Tantric Religion: A Historical, Ritualistic and Philosophical Study*. New Delhi: Manohar, 1982.

———. *Indian Mother Goddess*. Calcutta: Indian Studies, Past and Present 1971.

Bhattacharyya, Rajendra Kumar, and Sarat Chandra Mitra. "A Note on the 'Dhatree Puja' as Performed by the Hindusthanis Resident in Calcutta." *Journal of the Anthropologocial Society of Bombay* 13 (1924–1927).

Bhowmik, P. K. *Socio-Cultural Profile of Frontier Bengal*. Calcutta: Punthi Pustak, 1976.

Bhowmik, Suhrid, and James D. Robinson. *Tushu Songs*. Mecheda: Marang Buru, 1990.

Biswas, Anil Ranjan. *A Book of Bengali Verse*. Calcutta: Writers Workshop, 1990.

Bose, Basanta Coomar. *Hindu Customs in Bengal*. Calcutta: Book Company, 1875.

Bose, Pramanatha. *A History of Hindu Civilization During British Rule*. Vol. 1: Religious Condition. New Delhi: Asian Publishing Services, (1894) 1978.

Bose, Shib Chunder. *The Hindoos as They Are: A Description of the Manners, Customs and Inner Life of Hindoo Society in Bengal*. Calcutta: W. Newman, 1881.

Boss, Medard. *A Psychiatrist Discovers India*. London: Oswald Wolff, 1965.

*Brahmavaivarta Purāṇa*, translated by Rajendranath Sen. Bahadurganj: Bhuvaneshwari Ashram, 1920.

Brooks, Douglas Renfrew. *The Secret of the Three Cities: An Introduction to Hindu Śākta Tantrism*. Chicago: University of Chicago Press, 1990.

Brown, C. Mackenzie. *The Triumph of the Goddess: The Canonical Models and Theological Visions of the Devī-Bhāgavata Purāṇa*. Albany: State University of New York Press, 1990.

Chakravarti, Chintaharan. *Tantras: Studies on Their Religion and Literature*. Calcutta: Punthi Pustak, 1963.

Chanda, Ramaprasad. *The Indo-Aryan Races: A Study of the Origin of Indo-Aryan People and Institutions*. New Delhi: Indological Book, [1916] 1976.

Chatterjee, Tanmay. "Community Puja That Is the Preserve of the Dons." *Statesman*, November 12, 1993.

Chatterji, Roma. *Folklore and the Formation of Popular Consciousness in a Village in the Purulia District of West Bengal*. PhD dissertation, University of Delhi, 1985.

Chatterji, Suniti Kumar. "Buddhist Survivals in Bengal." In *B. C. Law Volume*. Edited by D. R. Bhandarkar et al. Calcutta: Indian Research Institute, 1945.

Chatterton, Reverend Eyre, B. D. *The Story of Fifty Years [of] Mission Work in Chhota Nagpur*. London: Society for Promoting Christian Knowledge, 1901.

Chattopadhyaya, Gouranga. *Ranjana: A Village in West Bengal*. Calcutta: Bookland, 1963.

Chattopadhyaya, Sudhakar. *Ethnic Elements in Ancient Hinduism*. Calcutta. Principal Sanskrit College, 1979.

Chaudhuri, Buddhadeb. *The Bakreshwar Temple*. Delhi: Inter-India Publishing, 1981.

Chaudhuri, N. M. "The Cult of Vana-Durga, a Tree Deity." *Journal of the Royal Asiatic Society of Bengal*, Letters. Vol. 8, 1945.

Chaudhuri, Nanimadhabh. "The Cult of the Old Lady." *Journal of the Royal Asiatic Society of Bengal*, Letters. Vol. 5, 1939.

Chaudhuri, Vijaya Lakshmi. *The Development of Mother Goddess Worship*. Shantiniketan: Visva-Bharati Research Publications, 1987.

Chilli, Shaikh, *Folk-tales of Hindustan*. Bahadurganj: Bhuwaneswari Asrama, 1920.

Coburn, Thomas. *Devī-Māhātmya: The Crystallization of the Goddess Tradition*. Delhi: Motilal Banarsidass, 1988.

———. *Encountering the Goddess: A Translation of the Devī-Māhātmya and Study of Its Interpretation*. Albany: State University of New York Press, 1991.

Colman, Charles. *The Mythology of the Hindus, with Notices of Various Mountain and Island Tribes, Inhabiting the Two Peninsulas of India and the Neighboring Islands*. London: Parbury, Allen, 1832.

Condron, Barbara. *Kundalini Rising: Mastering Creative Energies*. Windyville: SOM Publishing, 1992.

Crooke, W. "The Divali, the Lamp Festival of the Hindus," *Folk-lore*. London: Folk-lore Society, 34, no. 4, 1923.

Culshaw, W. J.. *Tribal Heritage- A Study of the Santals*. London: Lutterworth, 1949.

*Curiosities and Remarkable Customs in Pagan and Mohammedan Countries*. Troy: Caleb Wright, 1848.

Daniélou, Alain. *The Myths and Gods of India*. Rochester, N.Y.: Inner Traditions, 1991.

Das, Amal Kumar, and Manis Kumar Raha. *The Oraons of Sunderban*. Calcutta: Bulletin of the Cultural Research Institute, Tribal Welfare Dept., Government of West Bengal, Special Series no. 3, 1963.

Das, H. C.. *Tantricism: A Study of the Yogini Cult*. New Delhi: Sterling, 1981.

Das Gupta, and Tamonash Chandra. *Aspects of Bengal Society from Old Bengali Literature*. Calcutta: University of Calcutta Press, 1935.

Dasgupta, Shashibhusan. *Obscure Religious Cults*. Calcutta: Firma KLM, 1976.

Dehejia, Vidya. *Yogini Cult and Temples: A Tantric Tradition*. New Delhi: National Museum, 1986.

Demetrius, J. G. *Tales of Wonder and Mystery—Strange Yet True—That Occurred in the Annals of a Landowner of Dacca (Bengal) from AC 1780 Onwards*. Calcutta: J. G. Demetrius, n.d.

Dev, Usha. *The Concept of Śakti in the Purānas*. Delhi: Nag Publishers, 1987.

Deva, Indra. *Folk Culture and Peasant Society in India*. Jaipur: Rawat Publishers, 1989.

*Devi-Mahatmyam (Glory of the Divine Mother), Seven Hundred Mantras on Sri Durga*. Translated by Swami Jagadiswarananda. Mylapore: Sri Ramakrishna Math, 1953.

Dimock, Edward C., Jr. *The Place of the Hidden Moon: Erotic Mysticism in the Vaiṣṇava-Sahajiyā Cult of Bengal*. Chicago: University of Chicago Press, (1960) 1989.

Edgerton, Franklin. *Vikrama's Adventures, or the Thirty-two Tales of the Throne: A Collection of Stories about King Vikrama, as Told by the Thirty-two Statutuettes That Supported His Throne*. Harvard Oriental Series, Vol. 26. Cambridge: Harvard University Press, 1926.

Eliade, Mircea. *Shamanism: Archaic Techniques of Ecstasy*. Princeton: Princeton University Press, 1974.

———. *Yoga: Immortality and Freedom*. Princeton: Princeton University Press, 1969.

Erndl, Kathleen. *Victory to the Mother: The Hindu Goddess of Northwest India in Myth, Ritual and Symbol*. New York: Oxford University Press, 1993.

———. *The Fiery Lyre of Nazrul Islam*. Translated by Abdul Hakim. Chaka: Bangla Academy, 1974.
Finn, Louise M., trans. *The Kulacūḍāmaṇi Tantra and the Vāmakeśvara Tantra*. Wiesbaden: Otto Harrassowitz, 1986.
Frawley, David. *Tantric Yoga and the Wisdom Goddesses: Spiritual Secrets of Ayurveda*. Salt Lake City: Passage Press, 1994.
Gambhirananda, Swami. *History of the Ramakrishna Math and Mission*. Calcutta: Advaita Ashrama, (1957) 1983.
Ganguli, T. N.. *Svarnalata, or Scenes from Hindu Village Life in Bengal*. Translated by D. C. Roy. Calcutta: Sannyal, 1906.
Gatwood, Lynn. *Devi and the Spouse Goddess: Women, Sexuality and Marriage in India*. Riverdale: Riverdale Company, 1985.
Ghosh, Pratapachandra. *Durga Puja: With Notes and Illustrations*. Calcutta: Hindoo Patriot, 1871.
Gordon, James S. *The Golden Guru: The Strange Journey of Bhagwan Shree Rajneesh*. Lexington: Stephen Green, 1987.
Goudriaan, Teun, and Sanjukta Gupta. *Hindu Tantric and Śākta Literature*. Wiesbaden: Otto Harrassowitz, 1981.
*Grace and Mercy in Her Wild Hair: Selected Poems to the Mother Goddess*, Translated by Leonard Nathan and Clinton Seely. Prescott, Ariz: Hohm Press, 1999.
Grant, Kenneth. "Cults of the Shadow." In *Kundalini, Evolution and Enlightenment*, edited by John White. Garden City: Anchor Books, 1979.
Guha, Ranajit, ed. *Subaltern Studies*. Delhi: Oxford University Press, 1989.
Gupta, Mahendranath. *Rāmakṛṣṇa Kathāmṛta*. Translated by Swami Nikhilananda as *The Gospel of Sri Ramakrishna*. Mylapore: Sri Ramakrishna Math, 1980.
Gupta, Shakti M. *From Daityas to Devatas in Hindu Mythology*. Bombay: Samaiya, 1973.
Hardy, Friedhelm. *Viraha-bhakti: The Early History of Kṛṣṇa Devotion in South India*. Delhi: Oxford University Press, 1983.
*The Harsa-carita of Bana*. Translated by E. B. Cowell and F. W. Thomas. Delhi: Motilal Banarsidass, 1961.
Hastings, J. ed. *The Encyclopedia of Religion and Ethics*. New York: Charles Scribner's Sons, 1928.
Hawley, John Stratton, and Donna Marie Wulff, eds. *Devī: Goddesses of India*. Berkeley: University of California Press, 1996.
Heehs, Peter. *The Bomb in Bengal: The Rise of Revolutionary Terrorism in India (1900–1910)*. Delhi: Oxford University Press, 1993.
*Hindoo Tales (or, the Adventures of Ten Princes, a Translation of the Dasakumaracharitam)*. Translated by P. W. Jacob. London: Strahan, 1873.
Hunter, W. W.. *The Annals of Rural Bengal*. Delhi: Cosmo, 1975 (1868).
———. *Imperial Gazetteer of India*. Vol. 6. London: Trubner, 1886.
———. *The Imperial Gazetteer of India: The Indian Empire*. Vol. 1, *Descriptive*. Oxford: Clarendon Press, 1909.
Hutton, J. H., ed. *Census of India, 1931, with a Complete Survey of Tribal Life and System*. Delhi: Gian Publications House, 1989 (1931).

Islam, Rafiqul, ed. *Kazi Nazrul Islam: A New Anthology*. Dhaka: Bangla Academy, 1974.

Jayakar, Pupul. *The Earth Mother: Legends, Ritual Arts and Goddesses of India*. San Francisco: Harper and Row, (1980) 1990.

Jyotirmayananda, Swami. "Attain Victory Over the Mind." *International Yoga Guide*, 31 no. 1 (September 1993).

Kane, P. V. *History of Dharmasastra: Ancient and Medieval Religious and Civil Law in India*. Poona: Bhandarkar Oriental Research institute, [1958] 1975. Vol. 5.

Kapur, Sohaila. *Witchcraft in Western India*. Bombay: Orient Longman, 1983.

Kaviraj, Gopinath. *Pūjā Tattva*. Translated by Swami Premananda Tirtha. Varanasi: Sri Krishna Sangha, 1976.

Khanna, Madhu. *Yantra: The Tantric Symbol of Cosmic Unity*. London: Thames and Hudson, 1979.

Kinsley, David. "The Death That Conquers Death: Dying to the World in Medieval Hinduism." In *Religious Encounters with Death: Insights from the History and Anthropology of Religions*. Edited by F. Reynolds and E. H. Waugh. University Park: Pennsylvania State University Press, 1977.

———. *Hindu Goddesses: Visions of the Divine Feminine in the Hindu Religious Tradition*. Berkeley: University of California Press, 1988.

———. *Tantric Visions of the Divine Feminine: The Ten Mahāvidyās*. Berkeley: University of California Press, 1997.

Kripal, Jeffrey J. *Kālī's Child: The Mystical and the Erotic in the Life and Teachings of Ramakrishna*. Chicago: University of Chicago Press, 1995.

Krishna, Pandit Gopi. *Kundalini, Path to Higher Consciousness*. New Delhi: Orient Paperbacks, (1976) 1992.

*Kulārṇava Tantra*, edited by Sir John Woodroffe. Madras: Ganesh, 1965.

Kumar, Pushpendra. *Śakti and Her Episodes: On the Basis of Ancient Indian Traditions and Mythology*. Delhi: Eastern Book Linkers, 1981.

———. *Śakti Cult in Ancient India, with Special Reference to the Puranic Literature*. Varanasi: Bharatiya Publishing House, 1974.

Kurtz, Stanley N. *All the Mothers Are One: Hindu India and the Cultural Reshaping of Psychoanalysis*. New York: Columbia University Press, 1988.

Levy, Robert. *Mesocosm*. Berkeley: University of California Press, 1990.

Lokeswarananda, Swami. *Practical Spirituality*. Calcutta: Ramakrishna Mission Institute of Culture, 1989.

Lorenzen, *The Kapalikas and Kalamukhas: Two Lost Saivite Sects*. New Delhi: Thomson, 1972.

Lysebeth, André van. *Tantra: The Cult of the Feminine*. York Beach: Samuel Weiser, 1995 (1992).

*Māhābhāgavata Purāṇa*. Edited by Pushpendra Kumar. Delhi: Eastern Book Linkers, 1983.

*Māhānirvāṇa Tantra*. Translated by Arthur Avalon as *The Tantra of Great Liberation*. New York: Dover, (1913) 1972.

Maharaj, Swami Vishnu Tirtha. *Devatma Shakti (Kundalini)*. Rishikesh: Yoga Shree Peeth Trust, 1980.

Maity, P. K. *Folk-Rituals of Eastern India*. New Delhi: Abhinav, 1988.
———. *Human Fertility Cults and Rituals of Bengal*. Delhi: Abhinav, 1989.
———. *Historical Studies in the Cult of the Goddess Manasā, A Socio-Cultural Study*. Calcutta: Punthi Pustak, 1966.
Majumdar, R. C., ed. *The History of Bengal*. Vol. 1, *Hindu Period*. Dacca: University of Dacca, 1943.
Mani, Lata. "Cultural Theory, Colonial Texts: Reading Eyewitness Accounts of Widow Burning." In *Cultural Studies*, edited by Lawrence Grossberg et al. New York: Routledge, 1992.
Manna, Sibendu. *Mother Goddess Candi: Its Socio-Ritual Impact on the Folk Life*. Calcutta: Punthi Pustak, 1993.
Mazumdar, B. C. "Durga: Her Origin and History." *Journal of the Royal Asiatic Society of Great Britiain and Ireland*, 1906.
Mazumdar, Shudha. *Memoirs of an Indian Woman*. Edited by Geraldine Forbes. London: M. E. Sharpe, 1989.
McDaniel, June. *The Madness of the Saints: Ecstatic Religion in Bengal*. Chicago: University of Chicago Press, 1989.
———. *Making Virtuous Daughters and Wives: An Introduction to Women's Brata Rituals in Bengali Folk Religion*. Albany: State University of New York Press, 2003.
McDermott, Rachel Fell. *Mother of My Heart, Daughter of My Dreams: Kālī and Umā in the Devotional Poetry of Bengal*. New York: Oxford University Press, 2001.
———. "The Western Kālī" in *Devī: Goddesses of India*. Edited by John Stratton Hawley and Donna Marie Wulff. Berkeley: University of California Press, 1996.
McLean, M. D. "Are Ramakrishnaites Hindus? Some Implications of Recent Litigation on the Question." *South Asia* 14 no. 2 (1991): pp. 99–117.
———. "Ramakrishna: The Greatest of the Saktas of Bengal?" In *Religions and Comparative Thought*. Edited by Purusottama Bilimoria and Peter Fenner. Delhi: Sri Satguru Publications, 1988.
Moberly, A. N. "The Use of Amulets as Agents in the Prevention of Disease in Bengal." Memoirs of the Asiatic Society of Bengal 1 no. 11. Calcutta: Baptist Mission Press, 1906.
Muir, Charles, and Caroline Muir. *Tantra: The Art of Conscious Loving*. San Francisco: Mercury House, 1989.
Mukerji, Abhay Charan. *Hindu Fasts and Feasts*. Allahabad: Indian Press, 1916.
Mukherjee, Govinda Gopal. "The Tantras in Bengal." *Bulletin of the Ramakrishna Mission Institute of Culture*. 23, no. 10, (October 1972).
Mukherjee, K. L. "The Birth of a Cult: Chandi in Barbandha." *Man in India* 52 (January–March 1972).
Mukherji, Santosh Kumar. *Psychology of Image Worship of the Hindus*. Calcutta: Oriental Agency, n.d.
Mukhopadhyay, Subrata Kumar. *Cult of the Goddess Sitala in Bengal: An Enquiry into Folk Culture*. Calcutta: Firma KLM, 1994.
Muller-Ortega, Paul E. "The Kashmiri Roots of the Tantra: Some Preliminary Observations Towards a Definition of Tantra." Unpublished paper.
Neevel, Walter J. Jr.. "The Transformation of Sri Ramakrishna." In *Hinduism: New Essays in the History of Religion*. Edited by Bardwell Smith. Leiden: E. J. Brill, 1976.

Niyogi, Puspa. *Brahmanic Settlements in Different Subdivisions of Ancient Bengal.* Calcutta: Indian Studies Past and Present, 1967.

Niyogi, Tushar K. *Aspects of Folk Cults in South Bengal.* Calcutta: Anthropological Survey of India, 1987.

Noble, Vicki. *Shakti Woman: Healing Our World, The New Female Shamanism.* San Francisco: Harper and Row, 1991.

O'Malley, L.S.S., ed. *Bengal District Gazetteer, Rajshahi.* Calcutta: Bengal Secretariat Book Depot, 1916.

O'Malley, L.S.S., and Monmohan Chakravarti, eds. *Bengal District Gazetteer, Hooghly District.* Vol. 29. Calcutta: Bengal Secretariat Book Depot, 1912.

Oman, John Campbell. *The Brahmans, Theists and Muslims of India: Studies of Goddess Worship in Bengal, Caste, Brahmaism and Social Reform, with Descriptive Sketches of Curious Festivals, Ceremonies and Faquirs.* London: T. Fisher Unwin, 1907.

On, Rev. P. Dehon. "Religion and Customs of the Uraons." *Memoirs of the Asiatic Society of Bengal,* 1no. 9, 1906.

Osho, *Tantric Transformation: Discourses on the Royal Song of Saraha.* Shaftesbury: Element, 1978.

Padoux, André. "Hindu Tantrism." In *The Encycolpedia of Religion.* Edited by Mircea Eliade. New York: Macmillan, 1987. Vol. 14, p. 279.

Pandey, Rajbali. *Vikramaditya of Ujjayini.* Varanasi: Vishwavidyalaya Prakashan, 1951.

Parry, Jonathan. "Sacrificial Death and the Necrophagous Ascetic." In *Death and the Regeneration of Life.* Edited by Maurice Bloch and Jonathan Parry. New York: Cambridge University Press, 1982.

Paterson, J.C.K., ed. *Bengal District Gazetteer: Burdwan.* Calcutta: Bengal Secretariat Book Depot, 1985 (1910).

Payne, Ernest. *The Śāktas: An Introduction and Comparative Study.* Calcutta: YMCA Press, 1933.

Pine, Progya Paramita. "Festival Architecture." *Statesman,* Miscellany, October 17, 1993.

Pintchman, Tracy. *The Rise of the Goddess in Hindu Tradition.* Albany: State University of New York Press, 1994.

———, ed. *Seeing Mahādevī: Constructing the Identities of the Hindu Great Goddess.* Albany: State University of New York Press, 2001.

Porter, A. E., ed. *Census of India, 1931,* Vol. 5. *Bengal and Sikkim.* Calcutta: Central Publication Branch, 1933.

Pott, P. H. *Yoga and Yantra: Their Interrelation and Their Significance for Indian Archaeology.* Translated by Rodney Needham. The Hague: Martinus Nijhoff, 1966.

Pranab. *Thakur as Revealed to Pranab.* Howrah: A. K. Sanyal, 1963.

Priestley, Joseph. *A Comparison of the Institutions of Moses with Those of the Hindoos and Other Ancient Nations, with Remarks on Mr. Dupuis' Origin of All Religions, The Laws and Institutions of Moses Methodized, and An Address to the Jews on the Present State of the World and the Prophecies Relating to It.* Northumberland: A. Kennedy, 1799.

Rajagopalachari, C. *Sri Ramakrishna Upanishad.* Mylapore: Sri Ramakrishna Math, 1953.

Ray, Himangsu Mohan. *Savara, the Snake Charmer.* Calcutta: ISRAA, 1986.

Ray, Sukumar. *Folk Music of Eastern India (with Special Reference to Bengal)*. Calcutta: Naya Prokash, 1988.

Roy, Indrani Basu. *Kalighat: Its Impact on Socio-Cultural Life of Hindus*. New Delhi: Gyan, 1993.

Roy, Samaren. *The Roots of Bengali Culture*. Calcutta: Firma KLM, 1981.

Roy, Sarat Chandra. *Oraon Religion and Customs*. Ranchi: Industry Press, 1928.

Rudra, Dipak. "A Goddess in Our Hearts." *Statesman*, Festival '91 Durga Puja Special, 1991.

*The Sakta Upanisad-s*. Translated by A. G. Warrier. Madras: Adyar Library and Research Centre, 1975.

Sanderson, Alexis. "Saivism and the Tantric Traditions." In *The World's Religions*. Edited by Stewart Sutherland et al. London: Routledge, 1988.

Saradananda, Swami. *Sri Ramakrishna the Great Master*. Translated by Swami Jagadananda. Mylapore: Sri Ramakrishna Math, 1984.

Sarkar, Benoy Kumar. *The Folk Element in Hindu Culture: A Contribution to Socio-Religious Studies in Hindu Folk Institutions*. New Delhi: Cosmo Publishing, 1972.

Sarkar, R. M. *Regional Cults and Rural Traditions: An Interacting Pattern of Divinity and Humanity in Rural Bengal*. New Delhi: Inter-India, Publications, 1986.

Sarma, Nabin Chandra. *Essays on the Folklore of North-Eastern India*. Guwahati: Bani Prokash, 1988.

Satpathy, Sarbeswar. *Dasa Mahavidya and Tantra Sastra*. 2nd ed. Calcutta: Punthi Pustak, 1992.

———. *Sakti Iconography in Tantric Mahavidyas*. Calcutta: Punthi Pustak, 1991.

Sax, William S. *Mountain Goddess: Gender and Politics in a Himalayan Pilgrimage*. New York: Oxford University Press, 1991.

Selby, John. *Kundalini Awakening: A Gentle Guide to Chakra Activation and Spiritual Growth*. New York: Bantam, 1992.

Sen, Dineshchandra. *The Bengali Ramayanas*. Calcutta: University of Calcutta, 1920.

Sen, Sukumar. *A History of Bengali Literature*. New Delhi: Sahitya Akademi, 1979 (1960).

———. *The Great Goddesses in Indic Tradition*. Calcutta: Papyrus, 1983.

Sengupta, Jatindra Chandra. *West Bengal District Gazetteer, Malda*. Calcutta: State Editor, West Bengal District Gazetteer, 1969.

Sen Gupta, Sankar. *Folklore of Bengal-A Projected Study*. Calcutta: Indian Publications, 1976.

———, ed. *Rain in Indian Life and Lore*. Calcutta: Indian Publications, 1963.

Shasmal, K. C. *The Bauris of West Bengal: A Socio-Economic Study*. Calcutta: Indian Publications, 1972.

Shastri, Ashokanath. "Durga Puja." *Bharatiya Vidya* 10, (1949).

Singer, Milton. *When a Great Tradition Modernizes: An Anthropological Approach to Indian Civilization*. New York: Praeger Publishers, 1972.

———, ed. *Traditional India: Structure and Change*. Philadelphia: American Folklore Society, 1959.

Singh, Khushwant. *Kalighat to Calcutta: 1690–1990*. New Delhi: Lustre, 1993.

Sinha, Jadunath. *The Cult of Divine Power: Saktisadhana*. Calcutta: Sinha Publishing House, 1977.

———. *Ramaprosada's Devotional Songs: The Cult of Shakti*. Calcutta: Sinha Publishing House, 1966.

Sinha, Surajit. "Kali Temple at Kalighat and the City of Calcutta." In *Cultural Profile of Calcutta*. Edited by Surajit Sinha. Calcutta: Indian Anthropological Society, 1970.

Sinha, Surajit, Biman Kumar Dasgupta, and Hemendra Nath Banerjee. "Rituals in Agriculture, Chapter Five." *Bulletin of the Anthropological Survey of India* 10 no. 1, (January 1961).

Sircar, D. C. "The Śākta Pīṭhas." *Journal of the Royal Asiatic Society of Bengal*. 14 no. 1, (1948).

Sircar, Mahendranath. *Eastern Lights: A Brief Account of Some Phases of Life, Thought and Mysticism in India*. Calcutta: Arya, 1935.

Sivananda, Sri Swami. *Kundalini Yoga*. Sivanandanagar: Divine Life Society, 1971.

Sjoo, Monica, and Barbara Mor. *The Great Cosmic Goddess: Rediscovering the Religion of the Earth*. San Francisco: Harper and Row, 1987.

Smith, W. L. *The One-Eyed Goddess: A Study of the Manasā Mangal*. Stockholm: Almqvist and Wiksell, 1980.

*The Srimad Devi Bhagawatam*. Translated by Swami Vijnanananda. New Delhi: Munshiram Manoharlal, 1977.

Srivastava, M.C.P. *Mother Goddess in Indian Art, Archaeology and Literature*. Delhi: Agam Kala Prakashan, 1979.

Stein, Diane. *The Woman's Book of Healing*. St. Paul: Llewellyn Publishers, 1987.

Talukdar, Rezaul Karim. *Nazrul—the Gift of the Century*. Dhaka: Manan, 1994.

*Tantra of the Great Liberation (Mahanirvana Tantra)*. Translated by Arthur Avalon. New York: Dover, 1972.

Tattwananda, Swami. *The Saints of India*. Calcutta: Nirmalendu Bikash Sen, n.d.

Thakur, Shree Shree Annada. *Autobiographical Scenes from a Life of Visions* (from the Bengali *Svapna Jiban*). Dakshineswar: Adyapeath Press, [1928] 1968.

Thirleby, Ashley. *Tantra: The Key to Sexual Power and Pleasure*. New York: Dell, 1978.

Thomas, P. *Festivals and Holidays of India*. Bombay: D. B. Taraporevala and Sons, 1971.

Thompson, Edwin, and Arthur Spenser, eds. *Bengali Religious Lyrics. Śākta*. Calcutta: Association Press, 1923.

Tiwari, J. N.. *Goddess Cults in Ancient India, with Special Reference to the First Seven Centuries AD*. Delhi: Sundeep Prakashan, 1985.

Turner, Victor, and Edith Turner. *Image and Pilgrimage in Christian Culture: Anthropological Perspectives*. New York: Columbia University Press, 1978.

Urban, Hugh. "The Cult of Ecstasy: Tantrism, the New Age, and the Spiritual Logic of Late Capitalism." *History of Religions*. 40 no. 2 (November 2000).

Urban, Hugh. *The Economics of Ecstasy: Tantra, Secrecy and Power in Colonial Bengal*. New York: Oxford University Press, 2001.

Varma, L. P., D. K. Srivastava, and R. N. Sahav. "Possession Syndrome." *Indian Journal of Psychiatry*. 12 numbers 1 and 2 (January–April 1970).

Ward, William. *History, Literature and Mythology of the Hindus: Including a Minute description of their Manners and Customs, and Translations from Their Principal Works*. London, 1817, reprinted by B. R. Publishing Corp of New Delhi, n.d.

White, David Gordon. *Kiss of the Yogini: 'Tantric Sex' in Its South Asian Contexts*. Chicago: University of Chicago Press, 2003.

Wilkins, Joseph. *Modern Hinduism: An Account of The Religion and Life of the Hindus in Northern India*. London: Curzon Press, (1887) 1975.

Woodroffe, John. *Serpent Power: Being the Ṣat-cakranirūpana and Pādukā-pañcaka: Two works on Laya Yoga*. New York: Dover Publishing, 1971.

Zbavitel, Dušan. *Bengali Literature*. Vol. 9 of *A History of Indian Literature*. Edited by Jan Gonda. Wiesbaden: Otto Harrassowitz, 1976.

Zitko, Howard John. *New Age Tantra Yoga: The Cybernetics of Sex and Love*. Tucson: World University Press, 1975.

# Index

Printed in Great Britain
by Amazon.co.uk, Ltd.,
Marston Gate.